The Legal Philosophy of H. L. A. Hart

The Legal Philosophy of H. L. A. Hart

A Critical Appraisal

Michael Martin

Temple University Press
Philadelphia

Temple University Press, Philadelphia 19122

Published 1987
Printed in the United States of America

The paper used in this publication meets the minimum requirements of American National Standard for Information Sciences—Permanence of Paper for Printed Library Materials, ANSI Z39.48-1984

Library of Congress Cataloging-in-Publication Data

Martin, Michael, 1932 Feb. 3–
The legal philosophy of H.L.A. Hart.

Includes index.
1. Law—Philosophy. 2. Hart, H. L. A. (Herbert Lionel Adolphus), 1907–
I. Title.
K230.H3652M37 1987 340′.1 86-23095
ISBN 0-87722-471-4 (alk. paper)

To Tim and Tom

Contents

Preface

The initial research for this book was done when I was a Liberal Arts Fellow in Law and Philosophy at the Harvard Law School during the academic year 1979–1980. I am grateful to the Harvard Law School for providing me with the opportunity and facilities for doing this research. I would like especially to thank Professor Louis Sargentich of the Harvard Law School, the Chairman of the Liberal Arts Fellowships in Law during that year, for his help and encouragement.

Two Janes have played an important role getting this book into print. Without the help of my wife, Jane Roland Martin, this book would never have been completed. In addition to providing warm support she read the entire manuscript carefully several times and made detailed suggestions that greatly improved both its style and substance. I owe her more than I can say. Jane Cullen, my editor, has been everything an editor should be. She gave me not only her encouragement but her wise counsel.

I am also grateful to two anonymous readers for Temple University Press whose suggestions have improved the book.

Finally, I would like to thank the editor of *Archives for Philosophy of Law and Social Philosophy* for permission to adapt material from my article "A Critique of Hart's Theory of Natural Law," *Archives for Philosophy of Law and Social Philosophy* 68 (1982): 388–399, in Chapter 6.

Introduction

IN THIS BOOK I critically evaluate the work of one of the most important, if not *the* most important, legal philosophers in the English-speaking world today: H. L. A. Hart. Herbert Lionel Adolphus Hart[1] was born in 1907 and educated at Cheltenham College, Bradford Grammar School, and New College, Oxford. After taking a first in Greats at Oxford in 1929, he read for the bar examination and was called to the bar in 1932. He practiced as a Chancery barrister for eight years and, then, during World War II, worked as a civil servant in military intelligence.

After the war Hart became a Fellow and Tutor in philosophy at Oxford, and in 1952, upon the resignation of A. L. Goodhart, he was elected to the Chair of Jurisprudence. In 1968 Hart resigned from the Chair and spent the next four years as Senior Research Fellow at University College. In 1972 he was elected Principal of Brasenose College, Oxford, and he held this position until he retired in 1978.

Hart is an Honorary Fellow of New College, Brasenose College, and University College, Oxford, and has been awarded honorary doctorates from the universities of Stockholm, Glasgow, Chicago, Kent, Edinburgh, Mexico, Hull, and Cambridge and from Harvard University. He is the author of *The Concept of Law* (1961), *Law, Liberty, and Morality* (1968), *Punishment and Responsibility* (1968), *Causation in the Law* (with A. M. Honoré, 1953), *Essays on Bentham* (1982), and *Essays in Jurisprudence and Philosophy* (1983), as well as numerous articles and reviews.

The importance of Hart's work for contemporary philosophy of law can hardly be exaggerated.[2] Carrying on the tradition of John Austin, Jeremy Bentham, and Hans Kelsen in defending the clear separation of the questions "What is law?" and "What is good law?," he is the most widely cited and articulate defender of legal positivism in contemporary thought. In 1958 the *Harvard Law Review* published an exchange between Hart and Lon Fuller, Professor of Law at the Harvard Law School and a modern-day advocate of a version of natural law theory. In that debate Hart defended the legal positivist position according to which law and morality are logically distinct while Fuller criticized Hart's position. This exchange of ideas was continued in other writings for another decade and became the most widely cited debate on the connection between morality and law in modern times.

He is also the most important contemporary advocate of analytic jurisprudence. Again carrying on the tradition of Austin, Bentham, and Kelsen, as well as that of Wesley Hohfeld, Hart has consistently stressed the value of analytic investigations of legal concepts.

Furthermore, Hart is renowned for his application to the law of modern techniques of philosophical analysis, in particular the techniques of British ordinary language analysis practiced by Ludwig Wittgenstein and by Hart's Oxford colleague, J. L. Austin. In 1953 Hart pointed out[3] that it was not until 1945 that Glanville Williams introduced modern ordinary language analytic techniques into the study of law.[4] Hart suggested at that time that "the auspices are very favorable for a rapprochement between jurisprudence and philosophy."[5] He thought that contemporary philosophers' concern with ordinary language—not metaphysical jargon—and its concentration on topics that are of special interest to lawyers, for example, on rules and intentions, were an indication of this possible rapprochement. Indeed, in the years that followed, Hart himself led the way in bringing Oxford ordinary language analysis to the discipline of law. Although Glanville Williams may have been the first to introduce Oxford analytic techniques into jurisprudence, it was certainly Hart who made this rapprochement work and provided the prime examples of how it was to be done. As William Twining has noted:

> Hart's main achievement, it is generally agreed, has been to re-establish a sustained and particularly fruitful link between academic law and English analytic philosophy. He has done this more by applying techniques of philosophical analysis to a range of jurisprudential concepts and issues than by sustained theorising about the nature of the relationship.[6]

Hart is also one of the leading proponents of English liberalism in contemporary jurisprudence. His position on the death penalty and abortion, his enlightened views on punishment, all indicate a deep liberal commitment. Unlike many other liberal thinkers, however, Hart's liberalism is based on sophisticated arguments, conceptual distinctions, and an overall clarity of thought.

Hart's liberalism is perhaps most clearly seen in his debate with Lord Patrick Devlin, a distinguished judge and a modern advocate of the position that the positive morality of a society should be enforced. In that debate Hart defended the position that there should be no laws against private homosexual behavior while Devlin argued that society, in order to preserve itself, should outlaw such behavior. The Hart-Devlin confrontation on the enforcement of morality is as widely cited in contemporary jurisprudence as the Hart-Fuller exchange.

To characterize Hart as a legal positivist, an analytic jurist, an ordinary language analyst,[7] and a liberal moral philosopher is, however, to ignore the complexity of his thought. Part of Hart's importance lies in the fact that he has constructed new arguments for old ideas, thereby transcending old distinctions, and that he has attempted to tread a middle ground between philosophical extremes. Thus, although Hart defends legal positivism, he also defends a minimum natural law theory, a position that is novel as well as difficult to maintain. Again, although he defends Mill's views on liberty up to a point, he also defends paternalism and other stances that Mill would surely reject. Furthermore, in his discussion of punishment he attempts to transcend the traditional debate between retributivists and utilitarians just as in his theory of legal interpretation he attempts to take a middle position between legal formalism and rule skepticism. Thus, on many issues Hart cannot be classified in any simple way: sophisticated, subtle, and novel, his positions challenge our traditional ways of viewing the issues and our either-or type of thinking.

Summary of Hart's Legal Philosophy

Hart is a legal philosopher in the tradition of legal positivism. The classical legal positivists such as Austin and Bentham advocated three major theses. The first is that what the law is and what the law should be are distinct questions. Thus, from the fact that some rule is a valid rule of law in a legal system, nothing follows about whether the rule is moral or immoral. They believed that many laws were evil and should be changed, but they thought that nothing but confusion could result from supposing that if a rule is immoral it is not a law. They also argued that it is important to analyze legal concepts such as a legal system, rules, and rights. (Theorists who hold this second thesis—the importance of the analysis of legal concepts—are said to be advocating the position of analytic jurisprudence.) And finally they maintained that laws are commands of a sovereign whom the populace habitually obeys.

Traditionally, legal positivism has been pitted against natural law theory. Natural law theorists reject the positivist view that what the law is and what the law ought to be are separate questions. They maintain instead that the validity of the law and the morality of a law are connected. Indeed, on some interpretations of natural law they believed that an evil rule cannot be a law. Consequently, on these interpretations they maintain that iniquitous governments have no rule of law.

Hart accepts two of the three tenets of classical legal positivism. He certainly believes that the questions of what the law is and what the law ought to be must be separated, and he maintains that iniquitous regimes can still be governments of laws. Not only has Hart defended the position of analytic jurisprudence, he himself has provided analyses of key legal concepts. However, Hart rejects the command theory of law adopted by Austin and Bentham and presents in his best-known work, *The Concept of Law*, an analysis of law in which the commands of a sovereign play no role.

Hart's analysis of the concept of law is based on several interrelated ideas. He maintains that a legal system—in contrast to a set of unrelated laws—consists of a union of primary rules of obligation and secondary rules. The most important secondary rule is the rule of recognition, which specifies the criteria for identifying a law within the system. Other secondary rules specify how primary rules are changed or modified and when primary rules have been violated.

Furthermore, in distinguishing primary rules of obligation from secondary rules, Hart takes the position that there is at least one type of law that imposes an obligation. This type tells citizens that they must not do this or must do that. Raising the crucial question of what an obligation with respect to legal rules means, Hart rejects the idea that to say that law imposes an obligation is merely to assert a prediction. Nor does he accept the view that laws imposing an obligation are simply coercive orders. Hart attempts to provide a general analysis of obligation in terms of certain kinds of social rules. He sees this analysis as clearly distinguishing his view from that of American legal realists, who analyze laws in terms of predictions of the court, but also from that of Austin, who considered laws as coercive commands of the sovereign.

Finally, in order to understand secondary and primary rules and the obligation the law imposes, Hart insists that the point of view of people who follow and apply the law must be considered. In particular, he emphasizes the importance of an internal point of view of the law—that is, the point of view of those who operate within the law rather than of external observers of the law. So, according to Hart, a legal theorist who wishes to understand a legal system must view the legal system from the point of view of the actor in the system.

The internal point of view enters into Hart's theory in a second way, for he insists that the officials of a legal system must themselves look at the law from the standpoint of an actor in the system. Social actors can view their own behavior in different ways: they can accept the rules of a system and use them to guide their actions and to evaluate the actions of others or they can follow the rules without accepting them. Hart maintains that to have a legal system at least the officials of the system must take the internal point of view: they must accept the rules of the system and evaluate others' actions in terms of them. Hart thus excludes as *legal* systems ones in which the officials are simply following the rules. He also stresses that in order for a system to be a legal system the laws governing the behavior of some group of people in the system must have a minimum natural law content.

If a legal system is a union of primary and secondary rules, as Hart maintains, some officials of the system—the judges—must apply its secondary rules. But this application of the secondary rules to concrete cases involves interpretation of key words, of phrases, and even of entire passages that appear in statute books, previous legal decisions, legislative preambles, and various other documents.

Hart has provided a theory of judicial interpretation. Although it has changed over the years, Hart's position has consistently been based on a particular view of language. Language, he maintains, is open-textured and, thus, in its application, there is always inherent vagueness. Hart's theory of interpretation has also consistently taken into account the social purposes of the law. He believes that there are social advantages in having some legal flexibility and discretion. Given this view of language and social purpose, he has attempted throughout his work to tread a moderate position between two extreme positions on judicial interpretation.

From even this brief characterization of Hart's position it should be clear that he has rejected legal formalism, the view that legal interpretation is always simply the straightforward application of a legal rule to a case. Hart does believe that legal interpretation is sometimes like this, but he denies that it always is. Sometimes the judge must exercise discretion and a mechanical application of rule to case is impossible.

On the other hand, Hart rejects the extreme position of rule skepticism—a view often associated with legal realism—that judges always have wide discretion and that the application of rules to cases plays no significant role in judicial decision. Maintaining that rule skepticism as a general account of judicial interpretation is in error, Hart holds that rules sometimes are applied in a straightforward way and that no judicial discretion is needed.

Despite certain continuities in Hart's views of interpretation, it has changed in at least two significant respects. In his debate with Fuller he maintained that in those cases in which judges exercise discretion, there are no guiding legal standards and that judicial decisions in unclear cases are based on extra-legal considerations. In his more mature thought, however, he has maintained that judges' decisions, even in unclear cases, are made against a background of *legal* standards that include both principles and policies. Although Hart now believes that these legal standards constrain a judge's decisions in unclear cases, he maintains that there may be alternative decisions in such cases that are equally justified in terms of these standards. Moreover, whereas in his earlier thought Hart maintained that it is rare that a judge's decisions are guided by a sense of what is a natural continuation of a line of decisions, in his more mature thought he has come to believe that a judge's decisions are often so guided.

The most famous critic of Hart's theory of judicial interpretation is Ronald Dworkin, Hart's successor to the Chair of Jurisprudence at Oxford University. Against Hart, Dworkin maintains that even in unclear cases there is always one correct decision although what this decision might be is unknown. In addition, Dworkin argues that a judge's decisions in unclear cases is characteristically determined, and should be, entirely by principles specifying rights and entitlements. Policy specifying what is in the public interest and general welfare should be used, not by judges, but by legislators. Hart has answered Dworkin in his later writings, arguing that Dworkin's view of the law is not an accurate account of the way the law operates.

As we have seen, Hart maintains that, although legal language is indeterminate, it is not completely so, and he holds that the interpretation of legal language is guided by certain standards. In *Causation in the Law* Hart and A. M. Honoré argue that legal interpretation is and should be guided not only by considerations of legal standards but by ideas of common sense causality embodied in the law. Hart and Honoré maintain not only that the ordinary notion of cause is helpful in understanding legal causality because the courts use the ordinary concept of cause but that there is good reason to use this notion.

In studying the concept of causality in ordinary language and legal thought, Hart and Honoré argue that traditional philosophical approaches to causation have been of little help. Hart and Honoré believe that when a person picks out *the* cause among many causal factors in ordinary life and the law the person's choice is not arbitrary. They maintain that the philosophical analysis they provide should determine the principles that guide our causal choices. Just as Hart and Honoré reject traditional philosophical accounts of causality because these do not reflect common sense causal notions found in ordinary language, they reject prevailing accounts of legal causality because these do not reflect the common sense causal notions found in legal language.

Hart and Honoré criticize two prevailing views of legal causality. The most common view of legal causality held today—Hart and Honoré call it the modern view—maintains that there are only two basic questions in making judgments of legal causality. In deciding whether an agent A's action is the legal cause of some harm one must first decide whether A's action is a proximate cause. This is a purely factual question: Would B have occurred but for A's action? The second question, according to the modern theory, is basically a policy, not a factual, one. Hart and Honoré reject the modern theory because it does not provide an accurate account of how legal language actually operates in the law or the way it should operate.

The other theory of legal causality rejected by Hart and Honoré is the traditional theory. On this theory questions of legal causality are purely factual. But Hart and Honoré say that this theory often appeals to rules of causation that are couched in unclear metaphors. Hart and Honoré reject this appeal to unclear metaphors in the traditional view and attempt to provide an analysis of legal causality in terms of the relatively clear ideas of ordinary language and common sense.

As an analytic jurist, Hart not only uses analytic techniques in his work but has developed theories on the nature of legal definition and analysis. His views of legal definition have changed over the years and have been influenced by the prevailing ideas of analytic philosophy to which he was exposed. In a very early essay, "The Ascription of Responsibility and Rights" (1948–1949), Hart argued that legal definitions could not provide a sufficient condition for the application of legal concepts and that legal language was ascriptive rather than descriptive. These ideas he has subsequently given up. For example, in his Inaugural Lecture to the Chair of Jurisprudence at Oxford, "Definition and Theory in Jurisprudence" (1953), Hart argues that legal terms cannot be defined in isolation, but must be defined in the sentences in which they appear. In giving a contextual theory of definition, Hart not only specifies truth conditions for the application of the sentence but also gives an account of the function of legal sentences, thus rejecting some of the main theses about legal definition that he had held earlier.

In *The Concept of Law*, Hart puts forth a theory of definition that contrasts in relevant ways with his earlier ones. Here Hart's thesis is that all definitions are inadequate—presumably even the one expounded in "Definition and Theory in Jurisprudence"—to clarify the concept of law and to dispel the philosophical puzzlement connected with legal concepts. The concept of law, Hart says, must be elucidated, not defined. For the first time, Hart explicitly introduces theoretical and practical criteria for evaluating conflicting conceptions of the law.

Since Hart is a moral philosopher as well as an analyst of legal concepts, his moral views are often an integral part of his analysis of some legal concept or position. However, it would be a mistake to separate sharply his moral philosophy and his analysis of legal concepts, for in his moral arguments Hart draws distinctions, analyzes arguments, and clarifies ideas. Thus, Hart's use of analytic techniques is closely connected with his doing moral philosophy and, conversely, his philosophical analysis has moral implications.

In particular, Hart has developed a complex theory of punishment, one that combines retributive and utilitarian elements. In this theory, formulated in *Punishment and Responsibility*, one sees Hart the philosophical analyst at work distinguishing different questions about punishment and relating these to traditional theories. According to Hart, advocates of retributivist and utilitarian theories of punishment are usually attempting to answer very different questions. They fail to see that their own theory provides at best an appropriate answer to one question and not another; they fail to see that an adequate account of punishment must combine retributive and utilitarian elements. Hart gives a utilitarian answer to the question of why there should be an institution of punishment—such an institution brings about certain desirable social goals—and a retributive answer to the question of who should be punished—only those who are guilty should, in all fairness, be punished. This complex mix of utilitarian and retributive elements is also found in his theory of legal excuses and his justification of the punishment of criminal negligence.

An essential part of Hart's theory of punishment is his account of the place of *mens rea* and of mental abnormality in the criminal law. Hart has criticized Lady Barbara Wootton's radical proposal to eliminate all considerations of *mens rea* from the law. Wootton argued that crimes should be defined purely in terms of people's overt behavior and that considerations of people's mental states should only enter into a court's deliberations in determining what to do with the criminal, for example, whether to put the criminal in prison or give the criminal therapy. Although Hart rejects Wootton's proposal in this radical form, he accepts a more modest version of it. He maintains that consideration of mental abnormality should play no role in deciding whether someone committed a crime, but he allows it to enter in the court's deliberations about what to do with the criminal.

Hart the analytic-cum-moral philosopher is also clearly seen in his theories of natural rights and natural law as well as his theory of punishment. In an early essay, "Are There Any Natural Rights?" (1955), Hart maintained that, if there are any moral rights, there is at least one natural right. Although Hart's argument was in large part an analytic exercise of spelling out what, on his view, the concept of moral right entailed, it was also an exercise in the tradition of liberal social theory. Hart's thesis was more modest than traditional liberal views in that it proposed a hypothetical and non-absolute theory of natural rights yet it acknowledged that human beings have a natural right to wide freedom if they have any moral rights at all. In his evaluation of the rights-based theory of Ronald Dworkin and Robert Nozick in *Essays in Jurisprudence and Philosophy*, Hart has shown great skepticism about rights. Although he now believes that a viable theory of rights is needed, he does not seem to believe that at present such a theory exists. Thus in his mature work, although he remains sympathetic to a natural rights position, he does not expound even a hypothetical one.

In *The Concept of Law*, Hart maintains that, given certain general and obvious features of human nature and the world, the legal system of every society must have a certain minimum content. Hart believes that his minimum content natural law theory captures some virtues of traditional natural law theories without their problems. His theory of natural law can thus be seen as part of his elucidation of the concept of law as well as a result of his work as a philosophical analyst of the law.

One final evidence of Hart's interest in moral philosophy can be found in *Law, Liberty, and Morality*. Arguing in this work against the legal enforcement of morality, a view proposed by his contemporary Patrick Devlin and by J. S. Mill's contemporary J. F. Stephen, Hart defended a modified version of the liberal position of Mill. This book constituted one stage in an ongoing controversy with Devlin that continued for several more years. Although Hart was concerned throughout the controversy with a very live issue of his day, namely, whether private homosexual behavior should be made illegal, in the course of his discussion he not only dissected Devlin's arguments but distinguished various general positions that have become standard points of departure in contemporary discussions of the law. Going beyond Mill's harm principle, Hart advocated the principle of legal paternalism and the public offense principle and argued that none of these principles justifies laws against private homosexual behavior.

The Present Study

There has been only one systematic critical study of Hart's major doctrines—Neil MacCormick's *H. L. A. Hart*—which constitutes a fine introduction to Hart's thought. The present work goes beyond his in presenting a relatively more comprehensive and systematic critique of Hart's philosophical achievements up to the present time. It evaluates critically the major doctrines and arguments developed by Hart over a long and distinguished career. There are, however, some omissions. Confining my attention to those doctrines, arguments, and debates that are directly related to Hart's legal philosophy, I disregard his views on the philosophy of mind and action except as they relate to legal questions. I also consider Hart's scholarly writings on Bentham only as they throw light on his own philosophy of law.

In the chapters to follow I evaluate Hart's major work as an analytic jurist and moral philosopher and will also discuss the important debates he has engaged in. In the case of a philosopher such as Hart, whose complex philosophical work covers many topics and who has no systematic world view or grand theory, there are many lines of criticism to pursue that do not all lead in the same direction and whose importance to his overall thought it is difficult to assess. Some themes that emerge in the course of this investigation I critically pursue here. But although they are important to a critical appraisal of Hart, they do not begin to exhaust his philosophy and its problems. Some of the problems Hart's theories face are problems particular in nature; they are problems not found in other aspects of his thought. Hence, it would be a serious mistake in an evaluation of Hart to concentrate solely on the central themes in his work. Whatever gain there might be in unification, the loss in understanding of what is correct and incorrect in his philosophy would be greater.

Although my critique of Hart does not revolve around a central theme or insight, I will be pursuing certain questions that are crucial to an evaluation of his theory. Some of these are internal questions about the coherence of various aspects of Hart's position; others are external questions about whether certain assumptions or claims that Hart makes are justified or supported. Some of the questions I raise are methodological in that they have to do with the way Hart seems to arrive at his conclusions; others are clearly substantive in that they are about his legal and moral philosophies. Some typical questions that will guide the discussion are: Could the critical points Hart raises against the position of others be used against his own position? Are there unreconciled tensions in Hart's legal philosophy? Are the specific definitions that Hart gives successful? Independent of his particular definitions of legal terms, is Hart's theory of legal definition adequate? What is the methodological basis of Hart's claims about language? Could the controversies between Hart and his critics be reconciled in principle by empirical evidence?

This book is divided into two parts. Although in Hart's own writing there is no clear and sharp separation between his analysis of concepts and his writings as a moral philosopher and critic, it is still useful to separate his work along these lines. Consequently, in Part I I will critically consider some of Hart's major analyses. Chapter 1 examines Hart's analysis of the concept of law; Chapter 2 examines his analysis of judicial interpretation, along with Dworkin's critique of Hart's position; Chapter 3 examines his analysis of legal causality;[8] and Chapter 4 examines his theory of legal definition and elucidation, which might alternatively be called his theory of legal analysis.

In the second section of the book I evaluate Hart's moral philosophy insofar as it relates to the law. Chapter 5 presents and criticizes his complex views on punishment. Chapter 6 evaluates his novel doctrines of natural rights and natural law. The "great debates" are considered next: Hart's debate with Fuller on the separation of law and morality is analyzed in Chapter 7 and Hart's debate with Devlin on whether morality as such should be enforced in Chapter 8. Finally, in the Conclusion I will consider whether, in his most recent reflections, Hart has modified his theories or raised considerations that answer any of the criticisms made about his work in the preceding chapters.

PART I

The Analysis of Concepts

Chapter

1

The Concept of Law

Hart's Views in Brief

HART'S MOST SYSTEMATIC analysis of the concept of law is to be found in his most widely cited work, *The Concept of Law*.[1] That analysis reflects the influence of two historically significant analytic jurists: the nineteenth-century British jurist John Austin and Hans Kelsen, a contemporary German-American legal philosopher. Indeed, three of the early chapters of *The Concept of Law* are devoted to a detailed critique of a simple model of a legal system based on Austin's theory, a critique that Hart later uses in forming his own theory.

On the Austinian model of a legal system, one that has, according to Hart, "perennial attractions whatever its defects may be,"[2] laws are commands of the sovereign that are backed by threats of punishments; the sovereign is habitually obeyed by the bulk of the population and does not habitually obey anyone. Arguing that this analysis has a number of problems, Hart maintains that it is nevertheless instructive in developing an adequate analysis of law. He argues that it cannot be maintained that all laws are commands. For example, rules that enable people to get married, make wills, and form contracts as well as rules that enable officials of the government or the legal system to change laws, to create laws, and to enforce laws cannot be understood without serious distortion as commands backed by threats of punishment. As we shall see, the type of rules distorted by the Austinian command theory—Hart calls these "secondary rules"—plays an important role in his development of his own analysis.

In addition to the distortion caused by considering all laws commands backed by threats of punishment Hart points out that the Austinian model gives an inaccurate account of modern legal systems. For instance, in the Austinian system, the sovereign is portrayed as above the law since the sovereign habitually obeys no one. Although Hart admits that this may be an accurate picture of some simple legal systems, he maintains it is not an accurate account of modern constitutional monarchies, where the sovereign's powers are restricted by law. Furthermore, the Austinian model cannot give an adequate account of the transition from one sovereign to another even in a simple legal system. For, if we interpret the Austinian picture quite literally, immediately after the death of the reigning sovereign—following Hart let us call him Rex I—the bulk of the population cannot habitually have been obeying his eldest son and successor, Rex II.[3] Consequently, according to the Austinian model, at that moment there would be no laws in the system since there would be no sovereign who has been habitually obeyed. But this is absurd. In fact one would normally expect that there would be a smooth legal transition in this situation and that there would still be laws even though no habitual obedience could have yet been paid to Rex II.

For these and other reasons Hart argues that what is needed is a different account of the foundations of a legal system, one that is not based on habitual obedience to a unlimited sovereign but on the acceptance of a fundamental rule. The transition from Rex I to Rex II presumably involves the acceptance of a rule that specifies what is the law in the country even during periods of transition. This rule—Hart calls it the rule of recognition—would provide authoritative criteria for the recognition of laws within the system.

Years before Hart's attack on the Austinian theory Kelsen raised objections against this analysis of law and also stressed the fundamental importance of a basic rule (the Basic Norm) for understanding a legal system.[4] Hart sees his rule of recognition as capturing the insights of Kelsen's Basic Norm but avoiding its *a priori* character and unclarity. While Kelsen's Basic Norm is a non-empirical postulate of legal science needed to give unity and coherence to the various laws that constitute a legal system, for Hart the existence of a rule of recognition in any legal system is a complex sociological fact, not an *a priori* postulate.

In addition, Hart argues that Kelsen did not go far enough in rejecting the Austinian command theory of law. Although Kelsen rejected the Austinian theory that laws are commands of a sovereign, he still maintained that laws are a type of impersonal command. For, according to Kelsen, laws are legal norms that legal scientists should represent as hypothetical statements stipulating that a sanction should be applied by the officials of the system under certain conditions. Hart argues that Kelsen's impersonal command theory distorts the function of secondary rules in a way similar to that in which Austin's analysis does.[5] Thus Hart sees his own theory as incorporating Kelsen's correct rejection of an unacceptable personal command theory of law without embracing Kelsen's equally unacceptable impersonal command theory.[6]

Several interrelated ideas provide the foundation of Hart's analysis of the concept of law. Hart argues that, in contrast to a set of unrelated laws, a legal system consists of a union of primary rules of obligation and secondary rules. The rule of recognition is the most important secondary rule since it specifies the criteria for identifying a law within the system. For example, a rule of recognition of a simple legal system might be:

> Any rule is a valid rule of the system if and only if this rule either was enacted by the legislature or was derived from a rule enacted by the legislature.

The other secondary rules of the system specify when primary rules have been violated or how primary rules are modified or changed. Hart's distinction between these two kinds of rules is widely recognized to be his most important contribution to the analysis of legal systems. He stresses its importance in his own work and, indeed, claims that the introduction of secondary rules is a step from what he calls the pre-legal to the legal world.

Second, Hart argues that primary rules impose an obligation on citizens, telling them what they must or must not do. For example, a primary rule of a typical system might be:

> All citizens must pay their taxes by April 16.

But what does it mean to say that a legal rule imposes an obligation? Hart rejects the idea that to say a law imposes an obligation is merely to assert a prediction of what the court will do along with the view that a law imposing an obligation is simply a coercive order. Hart believes that his general analysis of obligation in terms of certain kinds of social rules distinguishes his view from that of John Austin, who considered laws as coercive commands of the sovereign, as well as from that of American legal realists, who analyze laws in terms of predictions of the court. On the former view laws imposing an obligation are simply coercive orders like "Pay your tax or you will be punished!"

Third, Hart maintains that in order to understand secondary and primary rules and the obligation imposed by the law the point of view of people who follow and apply the law must be considered. He stresses the importance of an internal point of view of the law, that is, the point of view of those who operate from within the legal system rather than that of external observers of the law. A legal theorist, then, who desires to understand a legal system must view the legal system from the internal point of view.

There is a second way that the internal point of view is important to Hart's theory. He argues that the officials of a legal system must view the law from the standpoint of an actor in the system. Although social actors can view their own behavior in different ways—for example, they can accept the rules of a system and use them to guide their actions and to evaluate the actions of others or they can follow the rules without accepting them—according to Hart, at least the officials of the system must accept the rules of the system and evaluate others' actions in terms of them to have a legal system. On Hart's view, then, if the officials are simply following the rules, there would be no *legal* system.

Finally, Hart maintains that if there is no group in a system that is governed by laws with a minimum natural law content, then it is not a legal system.

In sum, a legal system is a system of primary and secondary rules where the secondary rules specify how the primary rules are ascertained, changed, and adjudicated. Further, in order to be a legal system this system must have a minimum natural law content; the officials of the system must accept the secondary rules of the system; the general populace must in general follow these rules but their obedience cannot be analyzed either in terms of predictions or in terms of coercive orders; and the legal theorist in order to understand a legal system must at least in part view the system from the point of view of the legal actors.

Elements of the Elucidation

Obligation in General

Hart approaches the analysis of legal obligation by giving analyses of obligation in general. He begins by distinguishing between being obliged to do something and having an obligation to do something. Being obliged to do something is often expressed as a statement about the belief and motive with which the action is done. Thus to say that a person is obliged to hand over his money to a gunman may just be to say that the person believes that he would be harmed if he did not hand over the money. But to say that someone has an obligation is, according to Hart, not to refer to the person's belief or motive. A statement that someone has an obligation may be true without the person's having any particular beliefs or motive.

Nor, according to Hart, can having an obligation be explicated in terms of the likelihood of someone's being punished. On this view statements about obligations are merely predictions of the chance of getting punished. There is nothing contradictory, however, in saying that Jones has an obligation to pay a fine but he will never be punished if he fails to do so (since, for example, the legal officials are corrupt).

So Hart urges us to understand legal obligation not in terms of the gunman model of being obliged nor in terms of the prediction model of the likelihood of punishment. Rather, one must understand legal obligation in terms of the existence of social rules. Social rules provide norms of behavior and deviations from these norms are subject to criticism. This is not to say that whenever social rules exist the norms involved are conceived of in terms of obligation. One does not speak of having an obligation to follow rules of etiquette although rules of etiquette are social rules.

There are, according to Hart, three characteristics of a social rule that impose obligation:

(a) The general demand for conformity to the rule is consistent, and social pressure brought to bear upon those who deviate or threaten to deviate is great.
(b) The rule is thought important because it is believed to be necessary to the maintenance of social life or some highly prized feature of it.
(c) The conduct required by the rule may conflict with what the person who owes the duty may wish.[7]

Hart's words suggest a definition of having an obligation along the following lines:[8]

Definition (I): P has an obligation to do A (or to refrain from doing A) IFF (1) there is a social rule (R) in P's society that says, in effect, that anyone in circumstances C must do (or not do) A and (2) P is in circumstances C and (3) (R) has the three characteristics (a), (b), and (c).

As I understand Hart, he is attempting to give a descriptive account of obligation, not a normative one. By "a descriptive account of obligation" I mean the sort of account that social or cultural anthropologists might give when they investigate an alien society or culture; the anthropologists are not interested in whether the natives *really* have an obligation but only in whether they have one according to the mores of the society under investigation.[9] Thus it is possible for P to have an obligation (in this descriptive anthropological sense) to do A and yet have no real normative obligation to do A. Indeed P may have a normative obligation not to do A. Suppose (R) is a rule saying that fathers must sacrifice their first-born sons to the gods and this rule has characteristics (a), (b), and (c). In such a case, fathers would have a descriptive obligation to do so but presumably no moral one.

But this definition of descriptive obligation seems to be mistaken. On the one hand, the conditions specified in Definition (I) do not provide a sufficient condition for an obligation. Bernstein[10] in criticizing Hart points out how in certain social orders there may be rules of etiquette that have characteristics (a), (b), and (c), yet by Hart's own admission rules of etiquette impose no obligation. Bernstein argues as follows:

> If I associate with certain elements of a social elite, I may discover that a great stress is placed on dressing correctly for various occasions. To appear at a formal dinner or the races in my business or working clothes may be taken as a severe breach of etiquette, so severe that I may be prevented from desirable opportunities for marriage or employment. Judged in terms of attitudes or con-

> sequences the social pressure may be extremely serious, and yet it is highly dubious whether one would say that I had an obligation to dress correctly.[11]

Does Definition (I) at least provide a necessary condition of obligation? I think not. However, in critically evaluating Hart on this point we should not confuse descriptive and normative obligation. Bernstein, for example, argues that there may be no great social pressure not to commit adultery in a society[12] but one may still correctly claim that there is an obligation not to do so. What is not clear in Bernstein's example is whether the obligation not to commit adultery is a normative obligation or a descriptive one. If it is a normative obligation, his purported counterexample to Definition (I) would not be a legitimate one. Bernstein's example will work only if it is clear that the obligation not to commit adultery is a descriptive obligation.

Can there be a descriptive obligation to obey a rule when there is no great social pressure to conform to the rule? Can there not be great psychological pressure in terms of pangs of conscience and feelings of guilt if the rule is not followed? The pressure can be internalized and this can provide the basis for the descriptive obligation. Thus in order to constitute a necessary condition, characteristic (a) (the general demand for conformity to the rule is consistent, and the social pressure brought to bear upon those who deviate or threaten to deviate is great) should be replaced by:

> (a′) Either the general demand for conformity to the rule is consistent, and the social pressure brought to bear upon those who deviate or threaten to deviate is great or the psychological pressure in terms of the guilt feelings of the doer to conform to the rule is strong.

A group in a society might well experience psychological pressure to conform to the rule that one should not commit adultery without there being any social pressure to do so. I conclude, therefore, that as it stands Definition (I) provides neither a necessary nor a sufficient condition for obligation.

The Internal and External Aspects of Rules

The relation between Definition (I) and Hart's notion of legal obligation will be discussed later, but first some other ideas that play a large role in Hart's thought must be considered. Hart, as we have seen, attempts to explain what it means to say that someone has an obligation in terms of social pressure to conform to social rules. However, Hart stresses that it is possible to conceive of social rules in two different ways. From the external point of view one looks at the rules as an outsider, as a visiting anthropologist. But from an internal point of view one sees the rules as someone *within* the society, not as an anthropologist but as a native. He argues that the officials of the legal system at least (in contrast to the ordinary citizen) must view the secondary rules of the system from an internal point of view.

Hart's stress on the internal point of view indirectly connects Hart's theory with the Verstehen tradition in the social sciences.[13] Although Hart does not acknowledge his debt to this older perspective, he explicitly refers[14] to Peter Winch's influential *The Idea of a Social Science*,[15] a book published in 1958 that attempted to combine the insights of this earlier tradition with the later philosophy of Wittgenstein.

Although the notions of an internal and an external point of view play a crucial role in Hart's thought, it is not completely clear what he means by these ideas.[16] In one sense, to say that someone takes the internal point of view with respect to some set of rules and some actor who accepts these rules is to say that, although he or she does not accept the rules him or herself, the person understands the actor's behavior in terms of *the actor's* acceptance of these rules. With respect to a legal system this would mean that a person who takes the internal point of view would explain why a motorist waits at a red light in terms of the motorist's acceptance of certain traffic laws. Let us call this the *cognitive internal point of view*. Although the term "Verstehen" has been understood in several ways, in one important sense a Verstehen approach to the social sciences is the attempt to understand social phenomena from the point of view of the social actor. Thus, to take a Verstehen perspective is in this sense to take the cognitive internal point of view.

There is another sense of internal point of view, however. To say that someone takes the internal point of view with respect to some rules and some actor may be to say that the person accepts the rules and evaluates the actor's behavior in terms of them. With respect to the law this would mean that someone who takes the internal point of view accepts, for example, traffic laws about stopping at red lights and uses these laws to guide his or her own behavior and criticize that of others. Such a person would believe that people have a legal obligation to obey the traffic laws where "obligation" is understood in a normative sense. Let us call this the *standard evaluative internal point of view*.

The standard evaluative internal point of view should be distinguished from still another type of internal point of view. A person who takes the internal point of view may not accept the rules but may nevertheless act as if he or she does. With respect to the law such a person does not believe that there is an obligation to obey the law yet "plays along." Out of fear, expediency, or habit the person acts exactly as one who believes that he or she does have an obligation to obey. The person evaluates people in terms of such standards and uses them as a guide of his or her own behavior in the sense that the person would say "Jones had an obligation to obey . . . ," "I have an obligation to obey. . . ." But the person does not believe that he or she and others have obligations. The person's verbal behavior is for appearances only without reflecting his or her actual beliefs. Let us call this sort of evaluative internal point of view the *as if evaluative internal point of view*.

There is a variant of the standard internal point of view that should be mentioned. Suppose someone believes that he or she has an obligation to obey the law but does not obey for this reason; the person in fact obeys the rule out of fear or social pressure. In such a case there is a lack of connection between the person's cognitive and volitional life. This variant of the standard evaluative internal point of view is to be contrasted with the as if evaluative internal point of view. In the as if evaluative internal point of view the motivation for obeying the law may be the same as in this variant, but unlike this variant there is no belief that there is an obligation to obey the law. Let us call this variant the *impure standard evaluative internal point of view*.[17] Before we consider which of these various positions Hart seems to hold several things should be noted: First, someone with a cognitive internal point of view may feel no pressure (social or psychological) to conform to the rule. Second, someone who takes the standard evaluative internal point of view may feel no social pressure to conform but may obey the rule simply because of the belief that it is the right thing to do. He or she would feel guilty not doing so. This would not be true with the as if evaluative internal point of view or the impure evaluative internal point of view. Third, from the internal point of view someone who says "Jones has an obligation to obey . . ." is not using "obligation" in the descriptive sense, but in a normative sense. Consequently Hart's analysis is irrelevant in elucidating this sense of obligation. This is certainly clear in relation to the standard evaluative internal point of view (both pure and impure). But it is also true in relation to the as if evaluative internal point of view. Although someone speaking from the as if evaluative internal point of view says in public, "Jones has an obligation to obey . . . ," he or she is using obligation in the normative sense and saying something believed to be false. Fourth, in supposing that someone takes the as if evaluative internal point of view one is not attributing to the person some subjective state. This point of view could be defined in terms of the person's disposition to behave in certain ways, for example, to express criticism when the rules of the system are not followed. Whether the standard evaluative internal point of view could be so defined is another question. Clearly it could not be defined in terms of *public* behavior.[18]

What exactly is Hart's position in terms of the distinctions specified above? Some of the things he says indicate that what we have called the cognitive internal point of view is not in fact part of what he means by the internal point of view.

What Hart says indicates that for him the cognitive internal point of view is simply a less extreme external point of view. For the cognitive internal point of view is compatible with the cognizer's not accepting the standards that govern the actor's behavior. Acceptance, then, seems to be essential for Hart's internal point of view.

Now although Hart does not distinguish between the as if evaluative internal point of view and the standard evaluative point of view, some things he says suggest that by the internal point of view he means what I have called the standard evaluative internal point of view. Thus, according to Hart, people who reject the rules of a legal system may still conform to the law in their behavior. They might obey the law because they were likely to suffer if they did not. According to Hart such people would not be viewing the law from the internal point of view. In my terms these people would not have taken a standard evaluative point of view, but it would not obviously follow that such people did not have an as if standard evaluative point of view. For Hart says that such people would have no need of an expression such as "I had an obligation to obey . . ." but only for expressions such as "I was likely to suffer if I had not obeyed. . . ." However, from an as if evaluative internal point of view a person may use both kinds of expressions: a person may need one type of expression to express his or her private thoughts, for example, "I would suffer pain if I did not obey . . . ," and another kind of expression to express his public persona, for example, "I have an obligation to obey. . . ." In some societies the need for the two types of expression may be very important since a person who did not act as if he or she had an obligation to obey the law might not be able to survive. Part of acting as if one has an obligation to obey may be saying, "I have an obligation to obey. . . ."

Perhaps Hart, if pressed, would admit this and would consequently drop as necessary for holding an external point of view the condition that people who have an external point of view have no need for the language of obligation. So construed, then, on Hart's view the external point of view would include not only viewing the legal system simply in terms of regularities (without any conception of rules or norms) but also what I called above the cognitive internal point of view and the as if evaluative internal point of view. Essential for the internal point of view in Hart's terms, on this interpretation, would be, not the use of the language of obligation, but the belief that one has an obligation to obey.

But, in any case, is pure motivation necessary? Would Hart count someone as taking the internal point of view if he or she believed the person had an obligation to obey yet obeyed out of fear or social pressure and not because he or she had an obligation; that is, would Hart count someone as taking the external point of view if the person took what I called above the impure standard evaluative internal point of view? It is unclear what Hart's position is on this question, but I believe that the most plausible interpretation is that Hart would still consider someone with an impure standard internal point of view as having an internal point of view.

With the help of this explication, one can now state two of Hart's theses. The first thesis is stated explicitly by Hart as follows:

> (A) The officials of a legal system must view the rule of recognition from the standard evaluative internal point of view.

The other thesis is never really explicitly stated by Hart but seems to be assumed in his own philosophical work:

> (B) Philosophers of law must view a legal system both from an external point of view and from the cognitive internal point of view.

Closely connected with Hart's distinction between an internal and an external point of view is his distinction between an internal statement and an external statement. Hart introduces the distinction in this way:

> The natural expression of this external point of view is not 'it is the law that . . .' but 'In England they recognize as law . . . whatever the Queen in Parliament enacts. . . .' The first of these forms of expression we shall call an *internal statement* because it manifests the internal point of view and is naturally used by one who, accepting the rule of recognition and without stating the fact that it is accepted, applies the rule in recognizing some particular rule of the system as valid. The second form of expression we shall call an *external statement* because it is the natural language of an external observer of the system who, without himself accepting its rule of recognition, states the fact that others accept it.[19]

Hart's distinction between an internal statement and an external statement has all the unclarities of his distinction between the internal and external points of view and more problems besides. When someone makes what Hart calls an internal statement, for example, when someone says, "it is the law that . . . ," which type of internal point of view is being manifested in such a statement? The cognitive internal point of view? The as if evaluative point of view? The standard evaluative point of view?

Furthermore, it is certainly not obvious that the natural expressions of the internal and external points of view (in whatever sense of these expressions we are talking about) are what Hart claims they are.[20] Might not an *external* observer say, "In England it is the law that . . . ," and a loyal Englishman living in the United States say, "In England we recognize as law . . . whatever the Queen enacts and Parliament enacts. . . ." These seem natural expressions of the external point of view and internal point of view respectively and yet they do not fit easily into what Hart claims are the natural expressions of these points of view.

Moreover, Hart seems to link making an external statement to making an explicit statement about the rule of recognition, and making an internal statement to the implicit assumption of the rule of recognition that specifies what counts as a law in a legal system. But it is unclear why there needs to be this explicit linkage. A person who is an outsider to a legal system, for example, a visiting anthropologist, may well make a statement such as, "In this society they recognize as law that there can be no marriages between first cousins." Why not call this an external statement? The fact that it is not explicitly about the rule of recognition of this system seems irrelevant. On the other hand, a member of a society who accepts the laws of the society may say, "What the chief says while seated on this throne is the ultimate standard of what is law." This, although made from the internal point of view, explicitly states the rule of recognition and does not merely tacitly assume this rule.

Hart is surely correct that there is an important distinction to be made between explicitly stating that a rule of recognition is accepted and tacitly assuming this rule while making a statement about a law that tacitly assumes a rule of recognition. But this distinction seems to have no relevance to the external and internal points of view, and consequently no relevance to external statements and internal statements.

Beyond the Internal and External Points of View

Besides the problems concerning Hart's distinction between the internal and external points of view and statements, there is a larger issue that Hart never really faces. In order for a legal theorist to have a deep understanding of a legal system it might be necessary to transcend both the internal and external points of view. If we take science as our guide, we recognize that in order to understand some social institution it is often necessary to ascend to a level of abstract theory that leaves behind both the point of view of the committed parties to an institution and that of an external observer who utilizes the categories of the participants or who merely describes the behavior of the participants in common sense terms. There is no reason to suppose that the ascension to abstract theory may not be necessary in order to understand a legal system.[21] A legal system can be analyzed in terms of economic, sociological, or psychological theory having little or no connection with the point of view of the legal actors and the results may be a deep theoretical understanding connecting legal phenomena to other social phenomena.

For example, in the theory of law developed by Donald Black in *The Behavior of Law*[22] the point of view of the legal actor plays no role. Black says that the sort of theory that he advocates "predicts and explains social life without regard to the individual as such. . . . It neither assumes nor implies that he is, for instance, rational, goal directed, pleasure seeking, or pain avoiding. It has no concept of human nature. It has nothing to do with how an individual experiences reality."[23] The explanatory categories that Black uses in his theory of law, for example, stratification, morphology, marginality, relational distance, are unlikely to be categories that legal actors would use, let alone understand.

Further, scientific categories of analysis may have little to do with what Hart seems to mean by the external point of view. Hart seems to identify the external point of view either with the cognitive internal point of view (that is, the point of view of someone who, although not accepting the legal rules accepted by the legal actor, understands the actor's behavior in these terms) or with the view that simply describes behavioral regularities of the legal actor. Although Hart does not say so explicitly, this latter, more extreme, external viewpoint seems to describe legal behavior in rather straightforward empirical terms, utilizing the categories of common sense. Such descriptions would result in what might be called low-level empirical generalizations (for example, "People who drive through a red light when policemen are watching are usually stopped and arrested"). From the external point of view there would be no attempt to go beyond these low-level generalizations.

It apparently did not occur to Hart to consider another possibility, namely that the low-level generalizations could be understood in terms of the categories of theoretical social and behavioral science. For example, Black uses an abstract nomological statement, "An increase in social stratification brings an increase in legal control," to explain a wide variety of low-level generalizations of legal behavior taken from anthropology and history.[24] One may still call this kind of perspective the external point of view if one wishes, but it is significantly different from the one Hart seems to have in mind.

Now it may be argued that, although the objections raised above might be relevant if Hart intended his work to be a sociological study, in fact, Hart's work is intended as a study in analytic jurisprudence. To criticize it from the point of view of scientific theory construction is thus to apply inappropriate standards. But Hart says that *The Concept of Law* may be regarded, not just as an essay in analytic jurisprudence, but as an essay in "descriptive sociology."[25] So the above criticisms are quite appropriate. Furthermore, the restrictions Hart places on philosophical theory construction are unwarranted. In the Preface to *The Concept of Law* Hart mentions J. L. Austin's view that the examination of standard usage may sharpen "our awareness of the phenomena."[26] But Austin also pointed out that "superstition and error and fantasy of all kinds" may become incorporated in ordinary language.[27] The implication that Hart neglects to draw from Austin's warning is that the point of view of the social actor who uses this ordinary language may need to be transcended in philosophical theories about the law in order to eliminate superstition and error.

In his book on Hart, Neil MacCormick says that there are other "dimensions of understanding than the hermeneutic"[28] (that is, what I have called the cognitive internal point of view). He goes on to say, however, that "the method of observation of conduct [from the external point of view], however useful it might be for certain scientific purposes including at least some varieties of sociological inquiry, is inadequate to capture these concepts of lawyers and of laymen which are bound up with rules and standards of conduct."[29]

But MacCormick's defense of the necessity of the cognitive internal point of view will not do. First, it may be questioned whether an elucidation of a legal system that is adequate from a theoretical point of view needs to be concerned with the concepts of lawyers and lay people, for example, rules or standards of conduct. Such concepts may be adequate for practical purposes but may have no relevance for theoretical purposes. Second, even if the concepts of a rule or a standard of conduct are utilized in an elucidation of a legal system, one may question whether they must be understood in terms of the categories of lawyers and lay people. After all, rules and standards can be understood from various theoretical points of view. Philosophers of law may deem that the categories of the actor are inadequate to their purposes.

A weaker position is, of course, possible. Someone might argue that, although philosophers of law may go beyond the point of view of the actor in a legal system, the philosopher of law must take this point of view into account. However, this more moderate position does not seem to be MacCormick's and one infers it is not Hart's since MacCormick seems to be defending Hart on this point.[30] But even if the more moderate position were accepted by Hart, it is not obviously correct. If "take into account" means utilize or rely upon, then the philosopher of law may not need to take the point of view of the actor into account: the actor's point of view may be so inadequate and confused that the theorist may be well advised to by-pass it completely.

The Concept of Law as Sociology

As I have pointed out Hart believes that *The Concept of Law* is an essay in "descriptive sociology." I have been arguing that despite Hart's commitment to the internal point of view, social theorists as well as philosophers of law may have to ascend to abstract theory in order to gain a theoretical understanding of a legal phenomenon. However, independent of the point that Hart's theoretical perspective is too limited for social science, one may wonder how adequate Hart's theory is from a social scientific point of view.

The first thing to notice is that, although Hart maintains that his essay is in descriptive sociology, it contains very little sociology as that discipline is normally understood. Indeed, Hart develops his insights about the law in virtual isolation from social theory and social science. This attitude is typical of the followers of analytical jurisprudence, who, as one commentator says, "have frequently remained rather innocent of social theory and empirical social research, and have at times manifested an attitude of haughty, and not always benign, neglect towards work in these fields."[31] Although Hart certainly believes that social scientists who study legal phenomena have a great deal to learn from the analysis of legal concepts that analytic jurisprudence provides, it is unclear just what he believes analytic jurisprudence can learn from social science. Hart's neglect of social science is difficult to understand since, unlike Kelsen, Hart believes that many of his claims are empirical claims, including the central one that a rule of recognition is found in every legal system.

Despite Hart's apparent avoidance of sociological theory and evidence he does make certain sociological assumptions in his theory. For example, Hart maintains that the principle functions of the law are "a means of social control."[32] However, as Martin Krygier has pointed out, "social control" has a variety of different theoretical meanings and what Hart means by it is not clear.[33] Further, the hypothesis that the law has social control as its principal function is one that been criticized by some social scientists as naive on the ground that the law has many functions.

Fortunately, although Hart does maintain that the principal function of the law is social control, in the actual working out of his theory he assumes that the law has many functions. Indeed, one of his major criticisms of the Austinian model of law is that it neglects the major function of secondary rules, that is, to enable people to create duties. However, as Krygier argues, it is at this point in his discussion that Hart needs to pay more attention to social theory and evidence. Since "similar institutions can perform different functions in different societies, and in the same societies at different times, and in developed Western societies law is continually called upon to perform different functions" it is extremely difficult to determine the social functions of law.[34] Unfortunately, Hart attempts to determine the functions of different kinds of rules in the law using the armchair methods of Oxford analytic philosophy.

Primary and Secondary Rules

After introducing the distinction between the internal and external aspects of rules, Hart introduces another distinction that plays a crucial role in his analysis, namely that between primary and secondary rules. Primary rules are initially described by Hart as ones that require human beings to do or abstain from certain actions. Secondary rules are characterized as rules that enable human beings to introduce new primary rules or to eliminate or modify primary rules.

Primary rules impose duties; secondary rules provide power to change or modify the primary rules. Primary rules impose duties; secondary rules enable people to create duties.[35] On this characterization primary rules would include laws, for example, prohibiting speeding and requiring the payment of income tax while secondary rules would presumably include marriage laws, laws governing the creation of wills, and laws governing the creation of contracts.

Later in his book Hart seems to conceive of the distinction between primary and secondary rules in a different way. Primary rules impose obligations, he says. But a society with only primary rules would have to be a small, closely knit primitive community. A more complex society would need and develop other types of rules. With only primary rules there would be no authoritative way of telling what was a primary rule of society; there would be no way of changing any rule and no authoritative way of telling whether any primary rule had been broken. The remedy for these defects is the introduction of secondary rules, and Hart considers the introduction of such rules as a step from the pre-legal to the legal world. Secondary rules on this view are about primary rules themselves: "They specify the ways in which the primary rules may be conclusively ascertained, introduced, eliminated, varied, and the fact of their violation conclusively determined."[36]

The difference can be specified in this way:

First Account
- Primary rules: duty-imposing rules
- Secondary rules: duty-creating rules

Second Account
- Primary rules: duty-imposing rules
- Secondary rules: rules that enable primary rules to be introduced, changed, identified, and so on

The second account of secondary rules is, of course, different from the first account. Some secondary rules on Hart's second account would not be secondary rules on his first account. One important secondary rule on his second account is what Hart calls the rule of recognition, specifying how one tells which is a valid law in a legal system. Such a rule does not create duties. Indeed, the rule of recognition specifies an obligation of the officials of the legal system to judge certain rules as part of the legally valid rules of the system and certain rules as not part of the system.[37] In fact the rule of recognition is a duty-imposing rule, not a duty-creating rule and, according to Hart's first account of the distinction between secondary and primary rules, should be classified as a primary rule.

One curious feature of Hart's second construal of the distinction between primary and secondary rules is that it seems to give no account of how rules that create obligations (what were called secondary rules in Hart's first construal) are recognized, changed, or adjudicated. Consider, for example, the following rule:

(R_1) In order to create a contractual obligation one must do X, Y, Z.

This would be a secondary rule under Hart's first construal. Now consider a rule that specifies the way to change R_1:

(R_2) In order to change (R_1) do A, B, C.

Clearly (R_2) is not a primary rule of obligation; nor is it a secondary rule in Hart's first construal since secondary rules are meant to enable humans to introduce new primary rules or to modify primary rules. Further, (R_2) is not a secondary rule in Hart's second construal since (R_2) does not specify the ways in which primary rules are ascertained, introduced, eliminated, or varied or in which violations are determined. In short, Hart's scheme seems to give no account of rules like (R_2).

This problem can be generalized: Given any rule (R) that is a secondary rule, Hart's theory provides no account of a rule (R′) that would specify how (R) is to be changed, modified, eliminated, and so on. This may merely be an oversight on Hart's part. Nevertheless, the distinction between primary and secondary rules does not seem adequate to handle rules like (R′), let alone higher-level rules that specify how (R′) itself is to be changed, modified, eliminated, and so on.

Is Hart correct in supposing that the introduction of secondary rules marks a shift from a pre-legal system to a legal system? Perhaps the idea is this: Primitive societies have a pre-legal system and civilized societies have a legal system; the essential difference between these two types of systems is that in a pre-legal system there are no secondary rules and in a legal system there are. If we interpret secondary rules as rules that create obligation this thesis becomes:

(P_1) No primitive societies have rules that create obligations.

However, this bit of armchair anthropology seems mistaken. For many primitive societies have marriage laws and such laws are rules creating laws. So (P_1) is false.

But Hart's position is not (P_1). He does not argue that in the introduction of secondary rules there is the step from a pre-legal society to a legal one (at least if one interprets secondary rules as rules that create obligations). What he does say at one point is that the introduction into society of rules enabling legislatures to change and add to the rules of duty and enabling judges to determine when the rules of duty have been broken is "a step from the pre-legal into the legal world."[38]

This makes it sound as if what makes the crucial distinction between pre-legal and legal systems is the introduction of rules of change, rules of adjudication, and a rule of recognition. Interpreted in this way Hart is saying:

(P_2) No primitive societies have rules of change, rules of adjudication, or rules of recognition.

However, in a footnote Hart maintains that few societies have existed in "which legislative and adjudicative organs and centrally organized sanctions were entirely lacking."[39]

It is far from clear if all primitive societies are included in the few societies Hart refers to. Hart goes on in the footnote to refer the reader to works on primitive law that deal with the "nearest approximation" to the state where there is no legislative or adjudicative organs and centrally organized sanctions. This suggests that even some primitive societies have these legal organs at least in a rudimentary form. Further, even if no primitive society had such organs, this would be compatible with the society's having rules of adjudication, change, and recognition. It is one thing for a society to have some organ that administers or enforces the laws; it is quite another thing for the society to have rules of adjudication, change, and so on that may be administered informally. An organ of adjudication presupposes a rule of adjudication; a rule of adjudication does not presume an organ of adjudication.

At other points Hart only makes the claim that one can imagine a society without a legislature, courts, or officials of any kind and that there exist many studies of primitive societies that claim that this possibility is realized. Here Hart seems only to say:

(P_3) There are primitive societies without legislatures and courts.

As I have already argued, it is possible that there could be secondary rules of change, adjudication, and recognition without legislatures and courts. Hart admits in another footnote that in some primitive societies provisions are made for dispute settlement by rudimentary forms of adjudication although there are no centrally organized sanctions.[40] Thus even if one admits the truth of (P_3) this is compatible with the falsehood of:

(P_4) There are primitive societies without any rules of change, adjudication, and recognition.

So (P_4) is not well supported by the evidence cited by Hart. In fact, as far as I can determine, Hart does not even cite evidence for the existence of societies that are the "nearest approximations" to societies without rules of change, adjudication, and recognition.

We can conclude, I believe, that Hart has not shown that the step from the pre-legal to the legal system is to be understood in terms of the introduction of secondary rules in either sense of that phrase.[41]

Rule of Recognition

Hart's theory of the rule of recognition is relatively independent of his armchair speculations on the step from pre-legal to legal system. Although, according to Hart, the existence of a rule of recognition in any given legal system is not something that can be established *a priori*, once it is established, it provides a powerful analytic tool and explanatory device. In particular, it enables us to analyze and understand legal validity.

According to Hart a rule of recognition of a legal system specifies some feature or features such that if a rule has this feature or features it is a rule of this legal system. A rule of recognition can take a wide variety of forms. In simple societies the rule of recognition may merely be an authoritative list of rules found in some written document. In more complex and highly developed legal systems it may specify that a rule is part of a legal system if it has been enacted by some specific body or is a long customary practice or stands in some relation to judicial decision.

Hart maintains that in general the rule of recognition of a legal system is not stated explicitly. Its existence is *shown* in the way the particular rules are identified by either courts, other officials, or private persons. As we have seen, this use of an unstated rule of recognition by the courts and others in identifying particular rules of the system is, according to Hart, characteristic of the internal point of view.

Given Hart's analysis of the rule of recognition, legal validity can be characterized. One can simply say that a rule is valid if it passes all the tests specified by the rule of recognition if one remembers that this is an internal statement, a statement made from the internal point of view. However, the question of whether a rule of a legal system is legally valid, according to Hart, is not to be confused with the question of whether the rule is generally obeyed, that is, with the question of the efficacy of the rule. Hart argues that a law may be valid even if it is not generally obeyed. Thus there is no necessary connection between the legal validity of a particular rule and the efficacy of this rule.

But consider a situation in which rules of a legal system are generally disregarded. Here Hart says that it would be "pointless"[42] except in certain special circumstances to say that certain rules were valid in terms of a rule of recognition. Someone who makes an internal statement concerning the validity of a particular rule of a system "may be said to *presuppose* the truth of the external statement of fact that the system is generally efficacious."[43] However, suppose one were teaching Roman law. It might be a useful pedagogical device to speak *as if* the Roman legal system were efficacious and to consider the validity of certain rules in this system. This would be a special circumstance where talking of the validity of a rule of a legal system that is generally inefficacious was not pointless.

The rule of recognition is, according to Hart, an *ultimate* rule and, where there are several criteria specified by the rule of recognition that are ranked in order of importance, there is a criterion that is *supreme*. For example, although a rule of recognition may specify criteria of legal validity in terms of legislative enactment, judicial decision, and custom, legislative enactment may be ranked more important than the other two criteria; that is, legislative enactment would be the supreme criterion. Hart says that one criterion of legal validity is supreme if "rules identified by reference to it are still recognized as rules of the system, even if they conflict with rules identified by reference to the other criteria, whereas rules identified by reference to the latter are not so recognized if they conflict with the rules identified by reference to the supreme criterion."[44] The notion of a supreme legal criterion refers to the relative place on a scale of importance; it does not imply any legally unlimited legislative power. Thus the legislative power of a body may be limited by the constitution. Nevertheless, there may still be a rule of recognition in this system and in the clauses of its constitution a supreme criterion of validity.

In what sense is the rule of recognition the ultimate rule of the system? If we ask if some rule of a local ordinance is valid, we answer this question in terms of some further rule, perhaps some rule that grants power to the city to pass ordinances. If we press for a justification of this rule, our question may be answered in terms of some state rule permitting cities to have laws that enable them to pass ordinances. If we press our questions and ask about the validity of the state law, we may be referred to certain sections of the Constitution and perhaps some Supreme Court cases in which these sections are given a particular gloss. The rule of recognition in our system is specified at least in part by reference to what is said in the Constitution. Here, as Hart puts it, "we are brought to a stop in inquiries concerning validity."[45] Unlike the local and state rules, there is no further rule specifying the criteria for the validity of the rule of recognition.

Although it makes no sense to ask questions about the legal validity of the rule of recognition of a system since it is the test of legal validity in that system, one can ask other questions. One can ask whether officials and private citizens actually do use it as a rule of recognition. One can also ask if the legal system with this rule of recognition is a just and moral system of law.

According to Hart the existence of the rule of recognition is a matter of fact. This matter of fact is established by the practice of the courts, officials, and private citizens of a system. Since the rule of recognition is unstated, its existence is inferred on the basis of actual practice. Unlike other rules of a mature system that can be said to be valid even if they are disregarded, the rule of recognition exists only if it is accepted by the officials and courts of the system. Because of this, Hart suggests that there are two senses of "exist" operating in legal discourse, one appropriate in speaking about subordinate rules and one appropriate in speaking about the rule of recognition. In speaking of a subordinate rule, to say it exists in a legal system is just to say that it is valid according to a rule of recognition. Whether anyone accepts it is irrelevant. To say that a particular rule of recognition exists in a legal system is just to say it is accepted by the courts and officials.[46]

Hart argues that the rule of recognition is difficult to classify and that this creates puzzles. Since it cannot be classified with other rules of law, some people say it is not a rule of law; others say it is a meta-legal or pre-legal rule. Hart argues that one cannot do justice to its unique and complex nature by classifying it as either a sociological fact or a law, that is, a normative claim. The rule of recognition can be looked at from both the internal and external points of view and in order to understand it both points of view are necessary.

This double perspective is also helpful in understanding what it means to say that a legal system exists in a given society. In order for a legal system to exist the officials of the system must accept the system's criteria of validity. This does not mean that the officials of the system obey the rule of recognition in the way that private citizens obey the primary rules. To speak of obedience here would be not only linguistically inappropriate but misleading. Ordinary citizens may obey the rules of the system for a variety of reasons, for example, because of considerations of prudence, from habit, out of fear; in particular they may not accept the rules of the system as imposing any obligations, and, consequently, they would not take the standard evaluative internal point of view. This, according to Hart, cannot be the attitude of the officials of the system.[47] Courts must be critically concerned with deviations and lapses and appraise their actions in terms of the rule of recognition.

Thus Hart says that "the assertion that a legal system exists is therefore a Janus-faced statement looking both towards obedience by ordinary citizens and to the acceptance by officials of secondary rules as critical common standards of official behavior."[48] However, in primitive legal systems that consist only of primary rules the rules are widely accepted as critical standards for the behavior of the group. As we have seen, Hart maintains Thesis (A):

> (A) The officials of a legal system must view the rule of recognition from the standard evaluative internal point of view.

But is it the case that the officials of the system must view the rule of recognition from the standard evaluative point of view? Must the officials of the system believe that they have an obligation to use the rule of recognition to decide which rules are rules of the system in order to have a legal system?

It would seem not. It is enough that officials act *as if* they believed it. They might apply the rule of recognition but not believe they have any obligation to do so. They might apply it because they are afraid that if they do not they will lose their jobs or worse. Now in order to apply this rule they would, of course, have to use the language of obligation at least as far as their public personas are concerned. They might say in public, "I have an obligation to declare this rule as legally binding." In fact, they do not believe they have such an obligation. Or they might say in public, "It is the law that . . ." but not in fact believe that anyone has an obligation to obey the law or that they, as officials, have the obligation to declare this rule as the law. (This might be true despite the fact that people hearing them might be justified in supposing that they did have such beliefs.)

Hart at times seems to deny that the existence of a legal system is incompatible with judges' believing that they have no obligation to apply the rule of recognition. His reason seems to be that, if judges applied the rule of recognition only on the basis of expediency or fear, they would make no criticisms of those who did not respect the rule of recognition. Consequently the unity and continuity of the legal system would disappear. But judges might be motivated by fear or expediency to criticize people who did not apply the rule of recognition as well as motivated by fear or expediency to use the rule themselves. Criticism of deviation from a rule is quite compatible with skepticism about the obligatory nature of the rule. In the light of this objection perhaps the best way to handle the problem is to interpret Hart's concept of the internal point of view as involving both what we have called the standard evaluative internal point of view or the as if evaluative internal point of view.

Circularity and the Rule of Recognition

As we have seen, the rule of recognition is not a power-conferring rule. It is most plausibly interpreted as a rule imposing an obligation on the officials of the system to decide whether a rule is legally valid in terms of certain specific criteria. But it would seem that such a characterization of the rule of recognition poses a problem of circularity. MacCormick puts the problem in this way:

> The rule of recognition presupposes the existence of 'judges' whose official duties are regulated by the rule of recognition. And these are, *per* Hart, 'judges' only if there are people empowered by a rule (or rules) of adjudication to make authoritative determinations of legal disputes. Are we to say that the rule of adjudication is a 'valid' rule or not? It can be so only if it satisfies some criterion set in the rule of recognition. But the rule of recognition presupposes 'judges' and 'judges' presupposes a rule of adjudication.[49]

MacCormick's solution to the problem, as I understand it, is to try to show that judicial duty does not depend on the existence of a power-conferring rule of adjudication. He does this by defining a judicial role. Someone has a judicial role in a society if he or she has a duty to pass judgment in disputed complaints by reference to independent standards and has a monopoly over the use of justified force.

MacCormick uses this notion of a judicial role in a hypothetical example of a primitive society. In this society the elders have a judicial role. Since being an elder is defined by the physical properties of age and sex and not by what procedures one follows, there is no power-conferring rule of adjudication. (In a power-conferring rule one must go through certain procedures in order to settle disputes. The elders need not go through any procedures.) MacCormick thinks that this example shows that circularity can be avoided.

But the problem of circularity does not depend on there being power-conferring rules of adjudication. A problem of circularity can be generated even from MacCormick's example. MacCormick admits that there is a rudimentary rule of adjudication (that is not power-conferring) and a rule of recognition in his example. Roughly speaking the rule of adjudication is this:

(1) Elders of the society have a duty to make judgments upon disputed cases.

and the rule of recognition is this:

(2) All disputes must be settled by making reference to customary standards.

The crucial question is whether (1) is a valid rule according to (2). Suppose Mr. Smith says that (1) is a valid rule. He argues that since he is an elder he has the duty to decide and that, using customary standards as per (2), (1) is valid. But how can we legally establish that Smith is an elder? Although age and sex are supposed to be the sole criteria of an elder, must not the question of whether Smith is of the right sex and age be determined by some person who is an elder? But if so, how is the question of whether this person is an elder to be decided?

If, on the other hand, being an elder need not be established by some elder, why is there any problem of circularity about a power-conferring rule of adjudication? Suppose instead of (1) we had the following power-conferring rule of adjudication:

(1′) Only if a person follows procedures $P_1, P_2, \ldots P_n$ in disputed cases is his decision law.

If one can legally determine whether a person follows procedures $P_1, P_2, \ldots P_n$ and yet not oneself follow procedures $P_1, P_2, \ldots P_n$ in doing so, the problem of circularity would seem to disappear. However, it would seem to be impossible on

Hart's scheme either to decide whether someone was an elder without having already decided that someone was an elder or to decide whether someone had followed procedures P_1, P_2, . . . P_n without having already done so. Thus, MacCormick's proposed solution to the circularity problem generated by Hart's theory does not work.

MacCormick also suggests what might be another approach to the circularity problem. He argues that legal history "shows that rules of recognition, changes and adjudication are indeed necessarily interlocking and interacting, so that change in or redefinition of one must be mirrored by change in or redefinition of another. But since the process of development and redefinition is an historical one, it does not involve a vicious circularity after all."[50]

However, it is not clear that this historical perspective can help matters. I take it that MacCormick's historical perspective might work something like this:

At (t_1) there is a legal system consisting in part of judges who decide disputes using a rule of recognition.

At (t_2) the legislature enacts a rule of adjudication (R_1) specifying how procedures are to be used after (t_3) to decide disputes.

At (t_3) judges decide that (R_1) is valid for they decide that (R_1) is in accord with the rule of recognition that they accept.

At (t_4) judges start to use the procedures specified in (R_1) to decide disputes.

There is no circularity because there were judges prior to the creation of the rule adjudicating (R_1) and prior to the judges' decision that (R_1) was valid. However, this suggestion seems only to push the question back. On what legal basis are there judges at (t_1)? Was there an earlier rule of adjudication, say (R_0), that specified how legal decisions were to be made? If so, how is the validity of this rule to be judged? Either prior to the creation of (R_0) there was a legal institution with judges or there was not. If there was not, the problem remains. If there was, the question seems to be pushed back again. On what basis at that still earlier time did judges decide disputes? Thus history does not really seem to solve the problem.

Is there any way out of the problem of circularity? I think there is but it has nothing to do with taking a historical perspective *per se* or with invoking a distinction between different kinds of rules of adjudication. Suppose that somewhere along the way—either now or in the past—there is or was an accepted legal practice of how to decide who the judges of the system are. This practice is not specified by some rule of adjudication. For if we start thinking of this practice as codified in some rule, then the question of who decides the validity of this rule arises and circularity threatens. The existence of such a practice at some point in the development of a legal system seems essential to get the system off the ground. Once this practice is in place, rules of adjudication may be introduced that codify or modify the future practice.

How does this affect Hart's thesis? As we have seen, Hart argues that the emergence of secondary rules marks the difference between a pre-legal system and a legal system. Although we have found reason to question some aspects of Hart's account, his theory seems compatible with the solution to the problem of circularity proposed here. Before the emergence of one type of secondary rule—a rule of adjudication—it is necessary for there to be an accepted social practice of deciding who the judges of the system are. To put the point in MacCormick's terms: in order for there to be a rule of adjudication specifying the judicial role of people in the society, it is necessary to have an accepted social practice for deciding who has a judicial role. Although it is true that Hart does not mention the problem of circularity, there seems to be nothing in his theory that would exclude this solution.

Legal Obligation

At the beginning of this chapter we discussed Hart's general theory of obligation. At that point it would have been impossible to understand his theory of legal obligation since it is based on concepts, for example, the rule of recognition, that had not yet been explained. Now, however, we can return to it.

Given the above account of the rule of recognition one might define Hart's account of legal obligation in the following way:

> Definition (II): P has a legal obligation to do A (or to refrain from doing A) in legal system S IFF (1) P is subject to legal system S and (2) there is a legal rule (R) in S that specifies in effect that if anyone is in circumstance C, then they must do A (or not do A) and (3) (R) is valid according to the rule of recognition of S and (4) P is in circumstance C.

On this account there is very little relation at all between Hart's general theory of obligation and his theory of legal obligation. For in his general theory obligation was a function of whether the social rule meets characteristics (a), (b), and (c).[51] These characteristics, it will be recalled, were specified in terms of certain sociological factors. But according to Definition (II), having a legal obligation to obey a law is a purely formal property of the law, namely whether the law meets the criteria specified by the rule of recognition. There need be no social pressure, for example, to obey the law and the law need not be thought to be necessary to the maintenance of social life or to some highly prized feature of it.

I believe that Definition (II) does indeed capture one important aspect of Hart's theory of legal obligation. However, since (II) is formulated in terms of legal rules, if one also allows legal standards that are not legal rules to operate in a legal system, then (II) cannot be an adequate account of legal obligation. One's legal obligation may well be based on such standards. Furthermore, (II) gives no account of the obligation of the officials of the system to apply secondary rules.

Clearly Definition (II) cannot be an adequate account of the officials' obligations to apply the rule of recognition since, as we have seen, the rule of recognition is not valid in terms of its own criteria. In short, (II) defines only one sense of legal obligation that is assumed by Hart. Perhaps, then, a different descriptive notion of legal obligation that would apply to the officials of the system could be specified as follows:

> Definition (III): P has a legal obligation to do A (or to refrain from doing A) in legal system S IFF (1) P is an official of the system S and (2) A is some official legal act in administering the law in S and (3) there is a secondary rule (R) in S which says, in effect, in circumstances C do (or not do) A and (4) P is in circumstances C and (5) (R) has characteristics (a), (b), and (c).

For example, Judge Jones has a legal obligation to judge law L as invalid IFF there is a rule of recognition with properties (a), (b), and (c) that says, in effect, if any law L has property P, then L is invalid, and L has property P.

This definition has a problem similar to the one we found in Hart's general theory. A rule of recognition may not meet conditions (a), (b), and (c) and yet it would be correct to say in a descriptive sense of obligation that a judge has a legal obligation to judge a law unconstitutional. Suppose that the judges and other officials of the system never bring social pressure to bear on their colleagues to apply rules of the system. Then there is no social pressure from the officials of the system to apply the rule of recognition. Nevertheless a judge may believe, for example, that there is a duty to apply the rule of recognition and feel guilty if he or she does not. In this case, I suggest, it would be correct to say in a descriptive sense that the judge has a legal obligation to declare the law unconstitutional. It should be noted that if an official does experience psychological pressure to apply the rule of recognition, he or she is viewing the law from the standard evaluative internal point of view. The as if standard evaluative internal point of view would normally apply when there is social pressure. In order to avoid criticism and rebuke, the official may apply the rule although he or she would experience no guilt feelings if the rule were not applied. Thus the present criticisms of Definition (III) are perfectly compatible with my criticism of Thesis (A) above.

A Definition of a Legal System

I have explicated and critically evaluated some of the major elements in Hart's elucidation of a legal system. It should be noted that he denies that he is attempting to give a definition of the concept of law and speaks instead of giving an elucidation. In Chapter 4 I examine his reasons for this stance and show that they are neither clear nor persuasive. Here let us take a more direct approach. One might wonder if, despite Hart's protestations, a definition of law can be found in *The Concept of Law*. Once the answer to this question is determined it will be possible to specify the relation between Hart's theory of legal obligation and his account of the existence of a legal system.

The Analysis

In *The Concept of Law* Hart says:

> There are therefore two minimum conditions necessary and sufficient for the existence of a legal system. On the one hand those rules of behaviour which are valid according to the system's ultimate criteria of validity must be generally obeyed, and, on the other hand, its rules of recognition specifying the criteria of legal validity and its rules of change and adjudication must be effectively accepted as common public standards of official behaviour by its officials.[52]

It might be thought from this passage that, although Hart does not define law, he has defined a legal system. Indeed, it might be thought that he has defined a legal system in the way he recommended in his Inaugural Lecture.[53] There he recommends that in defining a term such as "legal system" one should not specify some synonym for "legal system" but specify under what conditions the sentence "A legal system exists" is true. Thus one might interpret Hart as giving the following definition:

> Definition (1): A legal system S exists if and only if the primary rules of S are generally obeyed and the secondary rules are accepted by the officials of S.

However, as Rolf Sartorius has pointed out,[54] Definition (1) has serious problems, for this statement provides at most purely formal criteria for the existence of a legal system. These criteria could be satisfied by many rule-governed social organizations that would not be considered legal systems.

One counterexample suggested by Sartorius is the National Football League. Some of the rules that are followed by the officials and players of the League specify how football is to be played. These are the primary rules of the system. The League also has rules that specify how these primary rules may be changed and who has the authority to interpret and apply ambiguous rules. These are the secondary rules of the system. They are accepted by the officials. One suggestion Sartorius makes to overcome this problem would be to combine what Hart says about primary and secondary rules and what he says about the minimum content of natural law, a topic we shall discuss in detail in Chapter 6. This gives us a second definition:

Definition (2): A legal system S exists if and only if (1) the primary rules in S are generally obeyed and the secondary rules are accepted by the officials of S and (2) the rules that apply to some group in S have the minimum content of natural law.

Now it may be objected that condition (2) is not part of Hart's definition of a legal system. A critic might argue that rather than supposing that this condition is part of a definition of a legal system Hart assumes that unless a legal system meets condition (2) it is unlikely that it would long endure. However, there is good reason to interpret Hart's theory as including condition (2) as part of his definition of a legal system. To be sure, if one only considers *The Concept of Law*, it may not be clear that my interpretation is correct. If, however, one takes into account what Hart says in his earlier work, my interpretation gains support. There is in fact a historical continuity between Hart's earlier attempt to define a legal system and his later attempts that suggest that he believed and continued to believe that a certain minimum moral content is part of the definition of a legal system.[55]

As Sartorius points out, Definition (2) is inadequate since some purely moral systems could meet conditions (1) and (2). He argues that what is needed is an additional condition distinguishing moral rules from law. Indeed Hart suggests four conditions that distinguish law from morals: (1) immunity from deliberate change; (2) importance; (3) voluntary character of moral offenses; (4) forms of moral pressure. Let us call these conditions C. Then one might suggest:

Definition (3): A legal system S exists IFF (1) the primary rules are generally obeyed and the secondary rules are accepted by the officials of S, and (2) the rules that apply to some group in S have the minimum content of natural law, and (3) the rules of S meet C.

But it is doubtful that C is adequate to the task of distinguishing between law and morality.[56] According to Hart, legal rules can be deliberately changed, whereas moral rules cannot be; moral rules are not repealed or corrected. But one can certainly imagine a society in which the morals of some particular group are dictated by a religious leader. This moral leader can change moral rules as easily as legislatures can change legal rules. Hart is misled perhaps by thinking that all moral rules are like traditions. But they are not.

Moreover, according to Hart, legal rules unlike moral rules may be unimportant. An unimportant law remains law until it is repealed. But rules that cease to be considered important are no longer considered moral rules. However, this distinction does not always hold. One can imagine a group of people whose moral system is based on the dictates of a religious leader whose pronouncements define what is morally obligatory for the members of this group. Suppose the leader specifies at one time that going to church on Sunday is a moral obligation of the faithful. At the beginning people follow this command, and so doing is considered essential to Life Eternal. But after many years fewer and fewer people follow the command and many people in this group regard this moral command as unimportant in their total scheme of values. People high in the Church hierarchy now fail to insist that this rule be followed and the Leader is too old to know or care. This would not mean that this rule is no longer a moral rule in this system, but rather that this rule is no longer considered important.

Further, one can also imagine a legal system that contained a rule of recognition that was based in part on the criterion of importance. In terms of this rule of recognition a rule would not be considered a legal rule of the system if it was no longer considered to be important.

Moreover, according to Hart it is always an excuse for someone's breaking a moral rule that the person could not keep it. But this is not the case in the law. Some laws are based on the notion of strict liability and no excuse is possible. So in moral responsibility "ought" always implies "can," but in legal responsibility this implication does not always hold. However, if we understand someone's legal responsibility as including all and only those things that the law requires the person to do or refrain from doing, then "ought" does imply "can" even in the usual cases of strict liability. Even in strict liability the law requires that when some event E occurs, a person P_1 must do something, for example, pay damages to another person P_2, although E's occurrence was not the fault of P_1. It is a presupposition of the law that P_1 is able to pay P_2. Of course, this presupposition is not always true; P_1 may have no money and depending on the circumstances P_1 may be excused by the court. So, if interpreted in this way, even in strict liability "ought" implies "can."

There is, indeed, a moral analogue to legal responsibility interpreted in this way. Sometimes people have a moral responsibility to do something about events whose occurrence was not their fault. For example, one has a moral responsibility to save a drowning child (if this can be done without danger to oneself) despite the fact that the child's desperate situation is not your fault. However, legal responsibility may be construed not in terms of what one must do, for example, pay damages, but in terms of some sanction that is imposed. On this construal someone's legal responsibility includes all and only those acts that are subject to legal sanction. Thus there may be a law making possession of a firearm punishable by a year in jail (such a law may be interpreted in terms of strict liability where no excuses are permitted). However, whether the imposition of sanctions on people without their being at fault distinguishes laws from morality remains to be seen.

This brings us to Hart's last criterion for distinguishing morals from laws. According to Hart, legal pressure is characteristically exerted by fear of punishment, while moral pressure is characteristically exerted not in this way but rather by a "remainder of the moral character of the action and the demand of morality." However, the distinction between law and morality in terms of sanctions cannot be drawn as sharply as Hart supposes. First, one can imagine a moral system that imposes physical sanctions for breaking moral rules. Indeed, there could be a moral system that would impose physical sanctions on people for acts or omissions that they could not help. Thus some religious sect may impose sanctions on its members who no longer believe in God although the non-believers may not be able to help their non-belief. Furthermore, although I have spoken of moral systems that impose physical sanctions in *this* world, some moral systems threaten sanctions after death, for example, in hell. Indeed, if one considers these systems, then it is plausible to suppose that the pressure many moral systems characteristically exert is the fear of punishment. In holding the opposite Hart must be talking about secular moral systems, not religious moral systems, at least not those in the Christian tradition. In addition, many people in modern society follow the law because they believe they have a moral duty to do so; the fear of punishment does not enter into their motivation.

There is perhaps another way of characterizing the difference between law and morality in terms of sanctions that is more plausible. This way is hinted at by some of Hart's remarks in *The Concept of Law*.[57] Although both types of systems might impose sanctions, there is still this difference. A legal system has a monopoly over physical sanctions for enforcement. A moral system may impose physical sanctions but has no monopoly on the use of physical sanctions. If a moral system in society uses physical sanctions, it is authorized—either explicitly or tacitly—by legal systems in this society; the legal system has the ultimate power, not the moral system.

Consider a system of rules existing in a given society and enforced by physical sanctions. Now within this larger society there exists a religious sect that wishes to enforce its rules by physical sanctions. There are in this situation several possible scenarios. First, the larger system may explicitly authorize the religious sect's sanctions. In this case the sect becomes an official organ of the legal system. Second, the legal system may not explicitly authorize the sanctions. In this case the sect becomes an unofficial arm of the legal system. Third, the sect may be stopped from using physical sanctions and in this case it remains a moral system.

Of course, a leader of a particular religious sect that wishes to impose physical sanctions for breaking the rules of the sect may believe that this sect should have a monopoly to impose sanctions. But so long as the sect does not have an actual monopoly, that is, so long as the larger system can effectively prevent the sect from imposing its rules by physical sanctions, the sect remains a moral system.

Given this distinguishing feature one might interpret Hart's definition of a legal system in the following way:

Definition (4): A legal system S exists if and only if (1) the primary rules are generally obeyed and the secondary rules are accepted by the officials of S, (2) the laws that apply to some group in S contain the minimum content of natural law, and (3) S has an effective monopoly over physical sanctions.

However, Sartorius disagrees that Hart can be interpreted in this way.[58] According to Sartorius, Hart is not giving a definition in terms of necessary and sufficient conditions. He argues that Hart's concept of a legal system is a cluster concept in the sense explicated by Hilary Putnam. According to Putnam's explication a cluster concept consists in a set of properties P_1, P_2, . . . P_n that are neither individually necessary nor jointly sufficient for the application of the concept. However, if most of the properties in the set are present, then the concept applies. Sartorius maintains that Hart advocated the idea that a legal system is a cluster concept in his 1955 paper "Theory and Definition in Jurisprudence," although he did not use this term. According to Sartorius, Hart has not abandoned this idea and, indeed, has carried it out in *The Concept of Law*.

Sartorius' evidence is not persuasive. He argues that Hart does not claim that a rule of recognition is necessary for a legal system. His evidence of this is to cite passages in which Hart argues that one can imagine a society without a legislature, courts, and officials that only has primary rules of obligation. This is supposed to show that there can be rules of obligation without a rule of recognition and other secondary rules. But these passages do not show that Hart believes that a legal *system* can exist without a rule of recognition. They simply show that Hart believes that there can be sets of laws without a rule of recognition. Indeed, Hart is at great pains in *The Concept of Law* to make a distinction between a legal system and a set of laws.[59]

The other reason Sartorius gives for not supposing that Definition (4) is adequate is Hart's characterization of the minimum content of natural law. As we will see in Chapter 6, Hart maintains that, given some truisms and people's desire to survive, it is a *natural necessity* that any viable legal system must provide some minimum protection, for example, minimum restrictions on the free exercise of violence, for some group of persons in the legal system through a system of mutual forbearance enforced by a sanction.[60] But Hart is careful *not* to claim that this is logically necessary. Consequently, Sartorius argues that condition (2) in Definition (4) is not a necessary condition for the application of a "legal system."

But this is a *non sequitur*. Sartorius' argument would hold only if Definition (4) were meant to specify logically necessary conditions. But there is no reason to construe Hart in this way. As we will see in Chapter 4, in his Inaugural Lecture Hart talks about giving a definition of terms by specifying the conditions under which a sentence containing this term is true. Hart does not say that statements specifying these truth conditions must be necessary truths, and there is no good reason to suppose he intends these conditions to be logically necessary conditions. The idea that minimum natural law content is a necessary condition (although not a logically necessary condition) for saying that a legal system exists seems perfectly compatible with his views in his Inaugural Lecture. Thus, just because the necessity involved in Hart's natural law theory is not logical necessity is no reason to suppose that Hart's definition of a legal system could not contain condition (2) above. To put it in a slightly different way: although Hart's minimum content natural law thesis is a contingent thesis concerning the conditions under which human beings survive, it does not follow that Hart does not assume that a minimum content of natural law is part of a definition of a legal system. This is because Hart does not assume that a definition specifies logically necessary conditions.

There is still Sartorius' point that Hart in his 1955 reply to Cohen construes legal system as a cluster concept. But there is a difference between what Hart said in 1955 and Sartorius' construal of a cluster concept. As explicated by Putnam and accepted by Sartorius, in a cluster concept there is a set of properties none of which taken individually must be present for a term to apply; in normal circumstances the term applies when most of the properties in the set are present. However, according to Hart's idea, there is a set of properties a few of which may be necessary for the application of the term "legal system." All the properties of the remaining sub-set are present only in standard cases; only some of the sub-set is present in non-standard cases.[61]

It would seem that Definition (4) is compatible with Hart's 1953 thesis in his Inaugural Lecture as well as with his 1955 commentary on this lecture. However, the cluster concept idea of Putnam and Sartorius would seem to entail that the three conditions in Definition (4) would not need to be present in all standard cases where a legal system is said to exist. This, I suggest, was not Hart's view in 1961. According to my interpretation of Hart, the three conditions of Definition (4) are present in all standard cases of a legal system and, if all these conditions are present, then there is a standard case of a legal system. If this interpretation is correct, this means that in all standard cases of a legal system, the system has minimum natural law content. This is compatible with Hart's view that the minimum natural law content of a legal system is a matter of natural, and not logical, necessity.

Critique of the Definition

I have argued that Definition (4) is a plausible interpretation of Hart's definition of a legal system. The question can now be raised whether this definition is correct. It is important to note that any counterexamples showing that Definition (4) does not specify necessary conditions for a legal system must be standard cases of a legal system. Similarly, to show that Definition (4) does not provide a sufficient condition for legal systems we would need to show that these conditions could be met and yet there would not be a standard case of a legal system.

But what is a standard case? I assume that a standard case of a legal system is a non-controversial case: a system that does exist or has existed or could exist that has been or would be generally considered to be a legal system. The determination of what is standard usage is an empirical problem, not something that philosophers are particularly competent to answer. Thus the following remarks should be considered hypotheses that must be empirically confirmed; as they stand they only have some intuitive plausibility.

First, conditions (1), (2), and (3) of Definition (4) may not provide a sufficient condition of a standard case of a legal system. The system of rules in Nazi Germany seems to meet conditions (1), (2), and (3). (For example, there was some group in Nazi Germany—the Nazis themselves—for whom minimum natural law standards seem to apply.) Yet whether Nazi Germany had a legal system is controversial.

Second, condition (1) may not be a necessary condition. As I have already argued, in one sense of internal point of view, the judges of a legal system have an internal point of view if they act as if they have an obligation to apply the secondary rules of the system: they need not accept these rules. Indeed, for all we know the majority of judges in many existing legal systems have an as if evaluative internal point of view. Yet some of these systems are surely uncontroversial cases of a legal system.

Third, it seems to me that there could be a system that would not meet condition (2), the minimum natural law requirement, and yet would be considered a non-controversial case of a legal system. In Chapter 6 I criticize Hart's argument for a minimum natural law theory and some of the examples I use there also work in showing that condition (3) is not a necessary condition for a standard case of legal system. Consider, for example, a system like our own except that people are not punished. In order to control their behavior so that they conform to the law they are given positive reinforcement rather than punishment. As we shall see, such a system would not meet the conditions of Hart's natural law theory. According to Hart, given people's desire to survive and people's limited strength of will, sanctions are a natural necessity for some groups in any legal system. However, it is certainly not obvious that a system that used positive reinforcement would not because of that be considered a standard case of a legal system.[62]

Fourth, if valid, the argument given above to show that condition (2) is not a necessary condition casts doubt on Definition (4). There could be a legal system that did not have a monopoly over physical sanctions if positive reinforcement rather than physical sanctions were used to have people conform their behavior to the law.

One must admit, of course, that points three and four are harder to establish than points one and two since these latter are based on hypothetical systems. In order to establish them with any certainty it would be necessary to describe the hypothetical system to sophisticated English speakers and see if they would call them legal systems. In short, these criticisms involve hypotheses not about people's actual linguistic usage but about their hypothetical usage and thus are much more speculative.

I have argued that a definition can be extracted from Hart's work, but that this definition may be inadequate if it is meant to capture standard legal usage. Whether this definition is inadequate with respect to standard usage I leave ultimately as a hypothesis to be confirmed by science although I have given some intuitive considerations that suggested this definition may be inadequate.

But perhaps Hart's definition should not be evaluated in terms of standard usage but rather on theoretical and practical grounds. If so, the task would not be to capture the standard concept of a legal system but to develop a concept of a legal system that would be useful. There is surely no particular reason to suppose that Definition (4) would be justified on these grounds. For example, there is no attempt in Definition (4) to transcend the standard categories used by the legal actor and to understand a legal system in terms of theoretical social science. As I argued above with respect to the internal and external points of view, a deep understanding may involve abstract theory that goes beyond these points of view. Definition (4) is in large measure directly committed to the internal-external point of view distinction. In particular, the acceptance of secondary rules in condition (1) of the definition is directly tied to the internal point of view idea. A theoretically fruitful elucidation may well be couched in rather different terms.

Further, as I argue in Chapter 4, Hart's theory of definition is compatible with the reduction of legal concepts and statements to non-legal concepts and statements especially if one accepts a broad notion of reduction. Although Definition (4) is not reductionistic since legal notions are used in the definition of a legal system, Hart has not shown that a reductionistic definition is impossible.

One way of showing the theoretical connections between a legal system and social science would be to construct a definition of a legal system in non-legal terms, in particular in the theoretical terms of social science. It is important again to stress that such a definition would not be judged entirely in terms of whether it captures standard usage but whether it fulfills certain, for example, theoretical goals. Standard usage might have to be sacrificed.

It would be inappropriate for me to speculate here about what such a definition would look like. But it should be noted that Hart does not even consider the possibility of such a definition let alone its advantages or disadvantages.

The Existence of a Legal System and Legal Obligation

I have attempted to explicate Hart's views on legal obligation as well as his definition of a legal system. Although neither of these was stated explicitly by Hart, I have extracted them from his writing in order to make sense of what he says.

The following question now arises: What is the relation between the existence of a legal system and legal obligation? For example, could a legal system exist and yet there be no obligation for people to follow the primary rules of the system where obligation is understood in the descriptive sense of Definition (II) above? The answer is yes.

Given Definition (4) of a legal system, ordinary citizens may have no legal obligation under Definition (II) to obey the primary rules of the legal system. Thus, although the primary rules of the system may be generally obeyed, these rules may be invalid in terms of the rule of recognition of the system. Consequently, according to Definition (II) there is no obligation to obey the law. (The general populace may not know this or, if they know it, they may not care.) Further, the officials of the system may accept the secondary rules of the system yet out of fear or ignorance not apply them correctly; thus the primary rules followed by the populace would not be valid.

This implication of my explication of Hart's analyses is not surprising although it may seem so initially. One certainly wants to allow for the possibility of people's obeying laws that are not valid and consequently for the possibility that, although they obey the law, they have no legal obligation to obey.

Could a legal system exist where the officials of the system have no obligation to follow the secondary rules of the system in the sense of a descriptive obligation specified in Definition (III) above? Again the answer is yes. The officials of a system could accept the secondary rules of the system without there being any social pressure on them to do so. But since social pressure, as we have seen, seems to be a necessary ingredient of Definition (III) above, there could exist a legal system without the officials' having a descriptive obligation to obey. If, on the other hand, we expanded the notion of pressure to include psychological pressure, then it is difficult to see how a legal system could exist without its officials' having a descriptive obligation.

Chapter

2

Theory of Judicial Interpretation: The Hart-Dworkin Controversy

WE HAVE SEEN that Hart conceives of a legal system as a union of primary and secondary rules and that in order for a legal system to exist the officials of the system must accept these secondary rules. But this leaves us with a problem. Some officials of the system—the judges—must apply these secondary rules; for example, they must determine whether a particular rule is a legally valid rule of the system, and they must determine when a particular rule has been broken. In order to apply the secondary rules to concrete cases the judges must make interpretations of important terms, phrases, and even entire passages that appear in legal documents including previous legal decisions, statute books, and legislative preambles.

But what is involved in giving a legal interpretation? Hart supplies an answer in his theory of judicial interpretation. The first statement of his theory appeared in his debate with Fuller, "Positivism and the Separation of Law and Morals" (1958). In *The Concept of Law* (1961) his view had become more complex and had changed slightly. By the time he had written "Problems of the Philosophy of Law" for P. Edwards' *Encyclopedia of Philosophy* (1967), it had changed even more. Although his views have changed over the years, Hart has attempted in all his work to avoid the pitfalls of two extreme positions on judicial interpretation.

Hart rejects legal formalism, the view that legal interpretation is always the mechanical application of a legal rule to a concrete case. According to this extreme view, a judge simply takes a legal rule (R_1), combines it with a statement S of the facts of the case, and from (R_1) and S deduces a legal conclusion. As we shall see, Hart thinks that legal interpretation is sometimes like this, but not always. Sometimes the judge must exercise discretion and the straightforward application of rule to case is out of the question. Hart also rejects the position of rule skepticism, a view of legal rules that is associated with American legal realism. On this view judges have wide discretion; consequently, the mechanical application of legal rules to cases plays no important role in judicial decision making. Rejecting rule skepticism as a general account of judicial interpretation, Hart maintains that rules are sometimes applied in a straightforward way and that there are cases where judicial discretion is not needed.

In this chapter I will explicate and critically evaluate Hart's theory of judicial interpretation. In the process I will consider objections to Hart's theory raised by Ronald Dworkin. Part of my own criticism of Hart will be to show that he has given neither legal formalism nor rule skepticism their just due. I will attempt, therefore, to reformulate these positions in ways that are not only more plausible than Hart's construal of them, but might even meet with his approval.

Hart's Developing Theory

Hart's theory has developed from a view in which judicial discretion in unclear cases is not based on any legal restraints to a view in which it is, from a position in which it is rare that a judge is guided by what is a natural continuation of a line of cases or the spirit of a rule to a position in which a judge is very often so guided.

The 1958 Position

As we will see in our discussion of the Hart-Fuller debate in Chapter 7, in 1958 Hart took a moderate position between legal formalism on the one hand and the rule skepticism of legal realism on the other.[1] According to Hart, the legal formalists were correct in holding that legal decisions are sometimes straightforward applications of rule to case, that is, logical deductions of legal conclusions from a rule and a statement of fact. On the other hand, the legal formalists were wrong to suppose that this is always so. Consider Hart's example, "No vehicles are allowed in the park." For the purposes of this rule, autos, buses, and trucks are clear cases of vehicles. In these clear cases the rule applies in a straightforward way. Here the legal formalists are right. But what about a toy truck? This is not a standard instance of the concept of a vehicle for the purpose of the rule, so it is unclear whether the rule applies to a child's taking his toy truck into the park. Hart calls such non-standard cases penumbra cases. Here the rule skeptic is correct. But the rule skeptic is only right here. Where there is a standard instance of the concept, the rule applies and the rule skeptic is mistaken.

What about the penumbra cases? What is a judicial decision based on in such cases? Hart's answer is that it is based on some notion of what the law ought to be, on some social policy or purpose. But Hart seems to reject the idea that these social policies or purposes are *part* of the law. Insofar as the judge appeals to such policies or purposes, he or she is exercising a creative choice and is not discovering the law or "drawing out" the implication of the rules. The law, in other words, is essentially incomplete. Hart does not deny that judicial decisions in the penumbra can be rational. But if rationality does not exist in a penumbra decision, it is not because the judge has failed to apply or misapply legal standards. There are no *legal* standards in such cases although there could be moral ones.

In one point in his debate with Fuller, Hart seems to modify slightly the extreme position that he takes in the rest of the debate. He admits that in some cases Fuller is correct to insist that a judge's interpretation is merely an elaboration of a rule or an argument found in previous judicial decisions. He says that "there are some cases which we find after reflection to be so natural an elaboration or articulation of the rule that to think of and refer to this as 'legislation', 'making law', or a 'fiat' on our part would be misleading."[2] It is much more natural to speak of elaborating a rule or drawing out its implications. But, Hart argues, "After all is said and done we must remember how rare in the law is the phenomenon held to justify this way of talking, how exceptional is this feeling that one way of deciding a case is imposed upon us as the only natural or rational elaboration of some rule. Surely it cannot be doubted that, for most cases of interpretation, the language of choice between alternatives, 'judicial legislation' or even 'fiat' (though not arbitrary fiat), better conveys the realities of the situation."[3]

What is not completely clear is whether Hart can afford to grant Fuller's point even in rare cases and keep the integrity of his view. Consider the rare sort of case in which Hart admits Fuller is correct, a case decided by what may be described as a natural elaboration of an existing rule that is applied to the case. Precisely how are such cases decided? Presumably not merely by the clear application of the rule to the case for, by hypothesis, the existing rule does not apply without elaboration. Is there some social policy or purpose that is part of the law that accounts for this phenomenon, this feeling that the rule is naturally elaborated in a certain way? If so, what is the social policy and purpose and how does one tell which social purposes are and which ones are not part of the law? Or is Hart's position that this phenomenon, the feeling that a decision is based on a natural elaboration of a rule, is an illusion or misleading and that in fact judicial legislation is operating *sub rosa*, that there are no social policies or purposes that are part of the law? If so how is this illusion explained?

One would have thought that Hart's position in 1958 was that laws were a type of rule and rather particular and specific rules at that. (The only example he gives is "No vehicles are allowed in the park.") But his acknowledgment that Fuller may be correct in rare instances indicates that he thought then that the law also consisted of more abstractly stated social policies and purposes. In any case, this possibly latent idea of a more inclusive view of what the law is becomes manifest in his later work.

Hart's 1961 Position

In *The Concept of Law*[4] Hart elaborates his 1958 position and in so doing seems to modify it. He discusses three areas of indeterminacy in judicial decisions. One with which we are familiar from his 1958 paper is that a statute ("No vehicles are allowed in the park") has unclear instances that must be decided by the choice of the judge. This choice need not be arbitrary or irrational. Suppose the purpose of the statute is to maintain peace and quiet in the park. This purpose is achieved at the cost of excluding motor cars, buses, and motorcycles (clear cases of the statute for this purpose). But now consider a penumbra case, for example, a toy motor car electrically propelled. Is this sufficiently close to the clear cases to be considered within the scope of the law? Hart argues that the criteria of relevance and closeness of resemblance between a clear instance of the law (a motor car) and a penumbra case (a toy motor car) will depend "on many complex factors running through the legal system and on the aims or purposes which may be attributed to the rule. To characterize these would be to characterize whatever is specific and peculiar in to legal reasoning."[5]

Hart does not attempt to characterize legal reasoning in any detail except to say that it involves the balancing of competing interests. In the case of toy motor cars the legal decision would involve weighing the general aim or purpose of maintaining quiet in the park against the pleasure and interest of children who use toy motor cars. In making this decision the judge gives the law a more determinate aim and for the purpose of the rule gives a general word ("vehicle") a more determinate meaning.

Another area of legal indeterminacy discussed in *The Concept of Law* is that of decisions based on precedent. Hart mentions three aspects of this area. First, there is no single method of determining the rule for which a given authoritative precedent is an authority although there is little doubt in a vast majority of cases. Second, there is no singularly correct formulation of any rule to be extracted from cases although, again, there is often wide agreement on the correct formulation. Third, an authoritative rule extracted from precedent is compatible with two kinds of legislative activities of the judge: courts may narrow the scope of a rule in applying the rule to a case before the bar or they may expand a rule, excluding certain restrictions, in applying the rule to the case. Thus, if a court chooses to add a new case to a line of old cases—presumably by limiting or expanding a rule from precedent—this is because the resemblance between the case and past cases can be reasonably defended as "legally relevant."[6] Courts make their choices in reasoning from precedent, as they do in reasoning from statutes in penumbra cases, by striking a balance between competing interests that vary in weight from case to case.

Still another area of indeterminacy in the law mentioned in *The Concept of Law* is the use of very general standards. Hart cites as one example the standard of due care in negligence. In civil and criminal law sanctions may be applied to people who fail to exercise reasonable care to avoid injury to others. There are clear cases where this standard applies and clear cases where it does not, but in large measure precisely which cases are covered by the standards cannot be known prior to determination by the court. Courts are left to determine whether the burden of proper precaution does or does not involve too great a sacrifice of others' interests in order to avoid substantial harm.

It is important to see that although Hart speaks of judicial legislation in these three areas of indeterminacy, he seems to believe that judges use legal reasoning to come to their decisions. In the application of statutes in penumbra cases the judge takes into account the purpose of the statute as well as interests that may conflict with this purpose; he or she balances such conflicting factors in coming to a decision. Hart's words certainly encourage the view that judges have an obligation *qua* judges to take these factors into account in their balancing act. In the indeterminacy involved in legal decisions involving precedent Hart's words also suggest that legal reasoning is involved in coming to a judicial decision. The resemblance between a new case and an old precedent, he says, can be defended as "legally relevant." In the indeterminacy involving general standards the same thing may be said. In deciding whether due care has been exercised judicial deliberation involves judges in determining whether the value of the expected harm outweighs the burden imposed in exercising due care. This determination by a judge is, so Hart implies, part of legal reasoning and not extra-legal.

So, although Hart does not completely specify what legal considerations a judge applies to making decisions in hard cases, his 1961 position seems very different from his 1958 position. It is plain that whatever the exact specifications of these factors are Hart considers them to be *legal* considerations and the reasoning that utilizes these factors to be legal reasoning. Further, whereas Hart's 1958 definition encouraged the view that the law consisted of a body of rules of a rather specific nature, his 1961 view indicates that the law consists of rules as well as general standards, such as the standard of due care, purposes such as the promotion of peace and quiet in parks, and general policies such as the balancing of interests.

Hart's 1967 Position

Hart's position in his encyclopedia article[7] departs still further from his 1958 position. He again distinguishes between cases that can be clearly subsumed under a rule and cases that cannot be, and he shows that judges' decisions about unclear cases need not be arbitrary. Judicial decisions in such cases

> do not arise in a vacuum but in the course of the operation of a working body of rules, an operation in which a multiplicity of divers considerations are continuously recognized as good reasons for a decision. These include a wide variety of individual and social interests, social and political aims, and standards of morality and justice; and they may be formulated in general terms as principles, policies, and standards. In some cases only one such consideration

> may be relevant, and it may determine decisions as unambiguously as a determinate legal rule. But in many cases this is not so, and judges marshal in support of their decisions a plurality of such considerations which they regard as jointly sufficient to support their decisions, although each separately would not be. Frequently these considerations conflict, and courts are forced to balance or weigh them and to determine priorities among them. These same considerations (and the same need for weighing them when they conflict) enter into the use of precedents when courts must choose between alternative rules which can be extracted from them, or when courts consider whether a present case sufficiently resembles a past case in relevant respects.[8]

Hart notes that some legal theories claim that, whether or not legal rules are indeterminable, it is still meaningful to speak of the uniquely correct decision. Other theories would deny this, however, and would claim that all judges can do is coolly and impartially consider the relevant considerations in making their decisions and that in some cases, at least, there is not one uniquely correct decision. Hart quite clearly counts himself among the latter theorists.

However, Hart admits that "very often the decision to include a new case in the scope of a rule or to exclude it is guided by the sense that this is the 'natural' continuation of a line of decisions or carries out the 'spirit' of a rule."[9] This last statement that "very often" the decision to include or exclude a new case in the scope of a rule is guided by the sense of the natural continuation of a line of decisions and carries the spirit of the rule should be contrasted with his 1958 paper, in which he maintained "how rare" in the law are phenomena that justify speaking of elaboration or articulation of a rule.

Hart's Mature Position

Combining what Hart said in *The Concept of Law* and the 1967 encyclopedia article, one can characterize Hart's mature thought on judicial interpretation in terms of several theses.

The Thesis of Naturalness: In many cases a decision is guided by the judge's sense of naturalness; the decision to include or exclude a case in the scope of a rule seems within the spirit of the rule or the natural elaboration of a line of legal argument.

The Thesis of Freedom: In certain cases judges have freedom to decide. In such cases legal rules do not apply in any straightforward mechanical way and even legal policies and principles, although they may restrain judicial decisions, have no mechanical application. In these cases legal formalism is in error.

The Thesis of Legal Non-arbitrariness: Despite this freedom the decisions of judges are not legally arbitrary. Legal decisions are restrained by a wide variety of legal standards—policies, principles—even when the straightforward application of rules to cases is not applicable. In such cases rule skepticism is at least misleading. Moreover, in some cases, at least, decisions are based on the straightforward application of a legal rule or legal standard to a case. In such cases rule skepticism is clearly incorrect.

The Thesis of Balancing: In some cases legal standards may be in conflict. In these cases the judge must balance the conflicting standards and come to a decision. In general this cannot be done in a mechanical way.

The Thesis of No Unique Answer: In some cases where the judge must balance conflicting standards, this balancing may not yield a unique answer.

Naturalness and Justification

In 1958 Hart seemed to believe that the sense of naturalness in judicial decisions was rare; in his most mature thought he seems to think that this sense is common. Hart supplies no evidence to support his change of mind. Without such evidence, however, we have no idea whether his early view or his mature view is correct, that is, whether the thesis of naturalness is correct.

Further, even if the thesis of naturalness is correct, this by itself would only be an interesting psychological fact that showed nothing about whether judges' sense of naturalness was justified. The extension of a line of argument or an inclusion of a case under a rule may seem natural and yet the extension of the line of argument could be fallacious and the inclusion of the case could be completely unjustified. This sense of naturalness could, of course, be a sign or symptom that the legal decision was legally justified. But the reliability of this sign would have to be established on independent grounds. Thus one might construct the following argument:

(1) Most of the time when a judge has a sense of naturalness about a decision, it can be justified by a good legal argument.
(2) Judge Smith has a sense of naturalness about this decision.

---

(3) (Probably) This decision can be justified by good legal arguments.

Premise (1) of the argument would be a factual statement linking a psychological feeling or impression to the existence of good legal argument. (1) and (2) together would provide a good inductive argument that Judge Smith's decision could be justified by good legal arguments. This sense of naturalness would be a reliable sign that legal justification of the decision was possible. The argument would not show this conclusively, nor would it show that Judge Smith would be able to construct a good legal justification. A legal justification may be available, but for various reasons Judge Smith might not be able to think of it.

However, although this sort of inductive reasoning is possible, its plausibility depends on the confirmation of premise (1). Hart does not establish anything even close to (1) and thus inductive arguments like the one above are not available to him. Moreover, it is not clear if Hart's remarks are meant as mere psychological observations or if he intends the sense of naturalness of a legal decision to be relevant to the justification of the decision.[10]

A Unique Answer as a Heuristic Device

As we have seen, Hart is skeptical that there is always a uniquely correct legal decision. He says, "In the law it seems difficult to substantiate the claim that a judge confronted with a set of conflicting considerations must always assume that there is a single uniquely correct resolution of the conflict and attempt to demonstrate that he has discovered it."[11]

Let us suppose that Hart is correct. One might raise another issue. Would it be a good practical idea for judges to act *as if* there were a unique answer? Would the presumption of a unique answer be a useful fiction? Hart does not really answer this question directly, but there is some reason to suppose that he would reject the idea. Hart refers to Bentham's critique of Blackstone's theory of the common law, "according to which judges' decisions do not make the law but are merely evidence of what law is." Bentham argued that Blackstone's theory was "a fiction which would enable the judge, in the misleading guise of finding what the law behind the positive law really is, to invest his own personal, moral or political views with a spurious objectivity as already law."[12] Bentham might well raise a similar objection to the proposal to treat the idea of a uniquely correct decision as a fiction. He would probably say that this fiction is not useful, that it would be used as a cover-up allowing a judge's personal views to become part of the law. Hart seems sympathetic with Bentham's position.

The dangers Bentham mentions are no doubt real. On the other hand, it is possible that great benefits would result from operating with a presumption of a unique answer. Such a presumption might stimulate judges to seek common ground in the case of a disagreement and it might encourage more diligent legal scholarship and research to find legal standards that could serve as a basis of agreement. Furthermore, there might be great disadvantages in supposing that there is no one correct right answer. If judges made the law in hard cases, it might erode people's confidence in the objectivity of the judicial process. Indeed, it has been argued[13] that, if the view that there is judicial discretion was widely held, it would be dangerous since it would undermine some of the most important practices of our legal system.

Whether the dangers mentioned by Bentham or the possible advantages I have listed are the more likely outcome of acting as if there is a unique answer is impossible to tell *a priori*. This is a matter for empirical research to determine. For now at least, although Hart's skepticism may be justified, that the practical disadvantages of the presumption of a unique answer outweigh the practical advantages has not been shown. Future legal research may give philosophers of law reasons to advocate that judges act as if there is always a unique legal answer even as the philosophers remain skeptical that there is one.

Freedom and Rationality

Throughout, Hart has maintained that judges have freedom to make certain decisions in cases in which it is unclear if the rules apply or not. But, even in his debate with Fuller, Hart has stressed that a judge's choice is not irrational or arbitrary. The difference between his earlier position and his later thought on the subject is that, in his later thought, Hart allows that legal considerations—standards, policies, principles—should enter into a judge's decision in cases where legal rules are indeterminate.

Put in a different way, in his earlier thought Hart seemed to believe that legal decisions in penumbra cases were arbitrary from a *legal* point of view, since there were no legal considerations that could justify a judge's choice. However, such choices were not necessarily arbitrary from some other standpoint—ethical, political, social. In his later work he allowed that such decisions were not even arbitrary from a legal viewpoint since legal standards that restrained a judge's choice were available even in penumbra cases.

Ronald Dworkin has introduced the notions of weak and strong discretion to clarify the above point. In Dworkin's weak sense of discretion, an official has discretion when the standards relevant to a decision cannot be applied mechanically but demand the use of judgment. In another weak sense of discretion distinguished by Dworkin, an official has discretion when the official has the final authority to make a decision. In Dworkin's strong sense of discretion, an official has discretion when he or she is not bound by any standard set by the authority. But, as Dworkin stresses, even in the strong sense of discretion the official is still subject to criticism in terms of, for example, rationality, fairness, and effectiveness; what the official is *not* subject to is criticism by standards "furnished by the particular authority we have in mind when we raise the question of discretion." [14] Interpreted in this way, in Hart's earlier view judges have discretion in the strong sense; in his later view judges have discretion only in the weak senses.

One difficulty in interpreting Hart's thought is that of reconciling his emphasis on freedom with the lack of irrationality in penumbra cases. For if a decision is not irrational, then presumably it is guided by reason. On the other hand, if it is guided by reason it may be asked in what sense the judge's decision is free.[15]

Let me return to the example of a rule used by Hart, "No vehicles are allowed in the park." Suppose little Johnny Jones is caught using an electrically propelled toy motor car in the park and is brought before Judge Brown. Does the rule apply to Jones? According to Hart, the electrically propelled toy motor car is a penumbra case and the judge has freedom to decide. But, as I have stressed, Hart argues that the judge's decision is not arbitrary; rather it is based on interest balancing.

Suppose Judge Brown has at her disposal the following two legal policies and one legal principle:

Policy (P_1) Parks are to be used for recreational purposes and should be free of the noise and bustle of the city.
Policy (P_2) Children's health and safety is an important consideration in adjudication.
Principle (PR_1) Children have the right to a place to play.

Suppose also that the following relevant facts are brought out:

Fact (F_1) Jones' toy motor car makes about as much noise as an electric mixer.
Fact (F_2) No one has complained about Jones' toy motor car.
Fact (F_3) Very few children use electrical toys in the park.
Fact (F_4) Children in this neighborhood have no other equivalent place to play.

The judge notes that Policy (P_1) and Fact (F_1) weigh in the direction of sanctioning that the rule applies. On the other hand, Facts (F_2) and (F_3) to some extent counter the implication of this policy. (Although such toys could be banned on principle, they are not noisy enough or widely used enough and apparently do not cause enough complaints to warrant this.) Furthermore, (P_2) and (PR_1), combined with (F_3), push in the other direction. The judge thus decides that the rule does not apply.

Is Judge Brown's decision free but rational? Although I have presented her reasoning in an informal way, it is possible to present it in a more formal way that tends to eliminate the appearance of freedom in the judge's decision. Indeed, it begins to look as if the judge who is rational has no choice.

(1) If the application of rule (R) to case X in terms of the usual meaning of the key terms in (R) is unclear, then (R) should apply IFF all the relevant facts, policies, and principles that argue for the application of (R) to X outweigh the relevant facts, policies, and principles that argue for its non-application.
(2) The application of the rule "No vehicles are allowed in the park" to the case of Jones' toy motor car is unclear because of the standard meaning of "vehicle."

(3) Policies (P_1) and (P_2), Principle (PR_1), Facts (F_1), (F_2), (F_3), and (F_4) are all the relevant policies, principles, and facts.
(4) Policy (P_2), Principle (PR_1), Facts (F_2), (F_3), and (F_4) argue for non-application.
(5) Policy (P_1), Fact (F_1) argue for application.
(6) Policy (P_2), Principle (PR_1), Facts (F_2), (F_3), and (F_4) outweigh Policy (P_1) and Fact (F_1).

---

(7) (Therefore) The rule "No vehicles are allowed in the park" should not apply to Jones' toy motor car.

Although it is possible to construe the judge's reasoning in this way, it should be pointed out that premise (6) seems arbitrary unless arguments are mustered to support it. There is also the problem of premise (3). What reason is there to suppose that the above-mentioned premises and principles and facts are all the relevant considerations? So even if (6) is granted, the conclusion (7) seems unsupported without arguments to support (3). However, if these arguments are filled in, how can the judge's decision be free? The rational judge seems to have no choice. On the other hand, if they cannot be filled in, then in what sense is the decision—at least in part—not arbitrary?

It is important to stress that Hart provides no analysis of legal reasoning that shows that such reasoning is non-arbitrary. Although, as we have seen, he stresses the complex factors involved in legal reasoning, as one commentator has put it, he "can thus be seen to leave out what may be considered the main purpose of the analysis of legal reasoning, viz., the elucidation of the relation between the 'many complex factors', whatever their particular nature, and the final conclusion."[16]

Despite Hart's unclarity about the nature of legal reasoning, at least two interpretations of what he means by a non-arbitrary but free judicial decision come to mind. One is that Hart means by "free," non-mechanical. On this interpretation judicial decisions are free in penumbra cases since they are non-mechanical applications of rule to case, but they are not arbitrary since they are guided by reason. In this sense of freedom, to say that a judge has freedom merely means that the judge has discretion in some sense of this ambiguous term.

On another interpretation, to say that judicial decisions are free but non-arbitrary is to say that although they are guided by reason—that is, standards, policy, principles—there may be occasions in which two conflicting decisions would be equally justified by the reasons—legal or otherwise. The trouble with this interpretation is that, if different interpretations are equally justified, how can one decision be preferred over the other except on an arbitrary basis?

One might say in response that Hart means something different by "arbitrary," namely that an arbitrary decision is one in which there are no limits or no constraints. However, in the case we are considering there are constraints, but they are not so strong as to rule out all alternatives; there is more than one rational decision. The reasons—judicial or otherwise—provide a framework in which judicial decisions operate. *Within* this framework legal decisions are, if you will, arbitrary; but most decisions are ruled out by the framework. So in a more inclusive sense the decision is not arbitrary.

Reducing Indeterminacy

As we have seen, the freedom of judges in legal decisions (whatever exactly that might mean) is closely related in Hart's thought to the indeterminacy of legal language. Because the language in the rule "No vehicles are allowed in the park" is indeterminate in the sense that it is in certain cases unclear whether this rule applies or not, judges must make decisions that are free yet not arbitrary.

Hart seems to hold two independent theses concerning the indeterminacy of legal concepts. First, he maintains that all natural language is indeterminate.[17] Since legal language is a species of natural language, it is indeterminate as well. Second, he maintains that even if legal language were not indeterminate "we would not cherish, even as an ideal, the conception of a rule so detailed that the question of whether it applied or not to a particular case was always settled in advance."[18]

Now it seems to me that Hart's first thesis is not nearly as important as his second. This is because the problem posed by the indeterminacy of natural language could at least in principle be solved or at least drastically reduced within the law.

Consider legal rules. According to Hart there are penumbra cases because cases arise that are not standard instances of a rule. Thus an electrically propelled toy motor car is not a standard instance of the rule "No vehicles are allowed in the park." The question then arises: Should such a case be covered by the rule? But surely the problem caused by such a case could be easily overcome. The legislature could amend the law with a rider that says the law applies *only* to standard instances of vehicles. Since a toy motor car is by hypothesis not a standard instance of the rule, the rule would not apply. Now such a rule may be undesirable from a social point of view since it may be too inflexible in its application. But it seems to solve the problem posed by Hart's example.

There is another problem that could arise. Could there not be disagreement over what is a standard instance of the rule? Suppose that Mr. Smith is arrested for bringing an ice cream truck into the park. Is an ice cream truck a standard instance of the rule? There may be disagreement even among the authors of the law.

But again such problems could seemingly be eliminated by legislative fiat. The legislature could stipulate that the rule applies only to agreed-upon standard instances. If there is disagreement over the ice cream truck, the rule does not apply. But the problem here is of which group must agree that X is a standard case where rule (R) applies. After all, there always is going to be some disagreement. For example, Mr. Smith's lawyer may well disagree that an ice cream truck is a standard instance of the rule. Still it seems possible in principle to specify some group whose agreement is decisive, for example, the jury. Again, whether this is the best way to decide cases is another issue.

The indeterminacy of general standards might be handled in a similar way. The legislature could give much more concrete guidance in determining what is, for example, a standard case of due care. This could be done by defining terms more explicitly and in greater detail. Whether such explicit legislative definition could eliminate all possible disagreement and uncertainty is doubtful. Presumably one could always imagine a case in which it would be unclear whether the legislature's definition of "due care" was applicable. Nevertheless, although it may be impossible to eliminate all possible unclear cases, it may be possible to eliminate all actual uncertainty. It may be true that given the way the term "due care" is defined there is universal agreement among, for example, judges or juries over actual cases. This is an issue that would have to be decided experimentally by proposing and testing various definitions.

Still, even if such indeterminacy is eliminated, Hart argues that this would be undesirable. He argues that to eliminate the indeterminacy

> is to secure a measure of certainty or predictability at the cost of blindly prejudging what is to be done in the range of future cases, about whose composition we are ignorant. We shall thus indeed succeed in settling in advance, but also in the dark, issues which can only reasonably be settled when they arise and are identified. We shall be forced by this technique to include in the scope of a rule cases which we would wish to exclude in order to give effect to reasonable social aims, and which the open textured terms of our language would have allowed us to exclude, had we left them less rigidly defined. The rigidity of our classification will thus war with our aims in having or maintaining the rule.[19]

Are there any conditions under which complete determinacy would be desirable? Hart argues that such a state would be desirable if we did not need to make a fresh choice and that we would not need to make a fresh choice if we were gods and did not suffer from two handicaps, namely that we are relatively ignorant of the facts and have relatively indeterminate aims. The second handicap, Hart seems to suggest, is contingent on the first. Because we lack the ability to anticipate what the future may hold this "brings with it a relative indeterminacy of aim."[20] Once we are confronted with a situation we could not have anticipated, for example, a toy motor car that is electrically propelled, our aim may have to change in the light of the new situation. Thus Hart seems to assume that if we could predict the future with complete accuracy, the determinacy of legal concepts would not be undesirable.

Our human inability to predict the future "varies in degree in different fields of conduct" and "legal systems cater for this inability by a corresponding variety of techniques."[21] Thus, a legislature may set up a very general standard and "then delegate to an administrative, rule-making body acquainted with the varying types of case, the task of fashioning rules adapted to their special needs."[22] In a similar way, "at the margin of rules and in the fields left open by the theory of precedents, the courts perform a rule-producing function which administrative bodies perform centrally in the elaboration of the variable standards."[23]

Given this construal one might suppose that Hart would suggest that judicial ability to predict the future should be increased by the use of social and behavioral science information combined with inductive inferences. If our lack of ability to predict the future is the basis of our indeterminacy of aim and if this indeterminacy in turn makes it desirable to have indeterminate rules and other legal standards that result in uncertainty and unpredictability in the legal system, one would suppose that we should attempt to overcome this inability as much as we can.

One way of understanding this idea would be in terms of certain methodological rules, rules that direct research relevant to legal decision making. Their utility would be determined in terms of whether following these rules would tend to solve the problem posed by Hart (the problem of judicial indeterminacy) without causing other problems. Two relevant rules would be:

(MR_1) Decrease judicial indeterminacy as much as possible so long as the decrease is based on reliable knowledge about the future.

(MR_2) Try to achieve reliable knowledge of the future that is relevant to the decrease in judicial indeterminacy.

(MR_1) urges decrease in judicial indeterminacy but only on grounds Hart would presumably not object to; (MR_2) urges increase in knowledge that makes decrease in judicial indeterminacy possible and unobjectionable. However, Hart does not advocate anything remotely resembling (MR_1) and (MR_2). One basic reason for this is that Hart is merely attempting to describe how judicial interpretation works; he does not seem interested in reforming or changing the procedures of judicial interpretation. Related to this is Hart's seeming lack of interest in the application of scientific theory and evidence to the law. These are tendencies in Hart's thought that we have already seen at work in his analysis of a legal system.

There may be reason, of course, why such application of scientific method to judicial interpretation is undesirable. For example, in judicial contexts the costs of the increase of knowledge about the future versus the benefits of decreased uncertainty concerning the law may not make the effort worthwhile. But this would have to be shown. It is doubtful, however, that any general economic argument of this kind could succeed since the costs and benefits of increased knowledge are likely to vary widely in different areas of the law and with respect to different types and amounts of uncertainty.

However, the point is that Hart gives no arguments—economic or otherwise—that (MR_1) or (MR_2) should not be followed. He simply ignores questions of this sort.

Legal Formalism Reconsidered

We are now in a position to evaluate Hart's critique of legal formalism. Legal formalism, he says, consists "in an attitude to verbally formulated rules which both seeks to disguise and to minimize the need for such choice, once the general rule has been laid down."[24] Presumably, by "need for such choice" Hart means need for interpretation or for discretion in the first of Dworkin's weak senses of the term. To put Hart's point in the opposite way, legal formalism attempts to maximize the mechanical application of rules and disguises the fact that a mechanical application of rules is not always possible. Although Hart does not state legal formalism in these terms, it may be useful to approach legal formalism as a program of legal interpretation. As such it can be usefully formulated as a set of maxims that guide action. Consider the following:

(LF_1) Maximize the mechanical application of legal rules.
(LF_2) Disguise the fact of the non-mechanical application of rules as much as possible.

(LF_1) is none other than a directive to eliminate as much legal indeterminacy as possible. As we have seen, this is a maxim Hart argues against on the grounds that such a directive would not be desirable unless we could predict the future in great detail. I have shown, however, that his view seems compatible with allowing for the maximization of the mechanical application of legal rules provided our scientific knowledge of the future is reliable. Thus the maxim (LF_1) can be reformulated in the light of (MR_1) (Decrease judicial indeterminacy as much as possible so long as the decrease is based on reliable knowledge about the future) as:

(LF_1') Maximize mechanical application of rules by basing them on available knowledge of the future.

As we have seen, Hart gives no argument to show the undesirability of (LF_1'); all his arguments seem to be directed to (LF_1). So a legal formalist who advocated (LF_1') would not be subject to Hart's critique.

What about (LF_2)? Hart gives no explicit arguments against the maxim. One might argue, however, that deception is wrong *per se* or else that there are utilitarian considerations against it. For example, if it were to become known, such deception would erode public confidence. On the other hand, it might be argued that if the public knew that judges had wide discretion this would cause great anxiety and worry and that on utilitarian grounds disguise is justified. In order to overcome this problem (LF_2) could be replaced by a more plausible maxim:

(LF_2') Disguise the fact of the non-mechanical application of rules as much as possible insofar as such disguise is justified on utilitarian grounds.

The only objection against (LF_2') would be the deontological one that deception is wrong in itself. It is unclear, however, whether Hart would voice such an objection. Thus, legal formalism, when formulated as a program characterized by the maxims (LF_1') and (LF_2'), may be a position that is acceptable to Hart.

But perhaps legal formalism could be further reformulated as a program of legal interpretation in terms of the insights Hart has provided. As we have seen, even in cases where policies come into play and discretion in the weak sense is used, a judge's reasoning can be reformulated in terms of formally stated arguments. The example of legal reasoning I used above concerning Johnny Jones and his toy motor car was a deductive argument, but there is no reason in principle why such reasoning could not be inductive with the conclusion probable but not necessary in the light of the premises. As we also have seen, the premises of these formally stated arguments need to be established by further arguments if the reasoning is to be sound. This suggests the following maxim:

(LF_3) Decide cases in such a way that the reasoning that yields the conclusion should be statable in terms of either a valid deductive argument with well-supported premises or a strong inductive argument with well-supported premises.

(LF_3) requires comment. In the first place it is an ideal, something that should be striven for. As such, however, it may be in conflict with other ideals implicit in legal systems. Yet, if legal formalism is to have any real meaning, this ideal is a very important one. Furthermore, (LF_3) does not entail that all judicial decisions must actually be stated in terms of deductive or inductive arguments. The way judicial decisions are to be written is a pragmatic decision determined by considerations of cost, audience, and other factors. Finally, (LF_3) may be advocated independently of either (LF_1') or (LF_2'). Clearly (LF_2') is independent of (LF_3). (LF_1') is tantamount to advocating a special case of (LF_3), namely that in which judicial reasons can be stated in terms of the straightforward application of legal rules to cases and in which such legal rules are based on reliable knowledge of the future. One could well advocate (LF_3), therefore, without maintaining that (LF_1') is advisable.

It is unclear whether Hart would acknowledge (LF_3) as expressing an ideal having great importance. Nothing I can find in Hart's writing suggests that he would reject it. On the other hand, nothing he says seems to suggest that he takes such an ideal to be part of a more sophisticated type of legal formalism. (LF_3), however, seems *prima facie* to be a reformulation of legal formalism as a program of legal interpretation that captures some of the spirit of the view Hart has criticized yet is free of its problems.

Rule Skepticism Reconsidered

As we have seen, Hart rejects both legal formalism and rule skepticism in their extreme forms and attempts to walk a middle path between them. According to Hart, legal formalism is a correct account of judicial interpretation in settled clear cases of the law. Rule skepticism is a correct judicial interpretation in non-settled areas. Together they correct each other's exaggerations.

I have just argued that legal formalism can be interpreted in a way that is free from Hart's criticisms and yet captures some of the spirit of the original. Perhaps this is possible with rule skepticism, too.

Hart distinguishes two types of skepticism: an extreme view and a more moderate one. On the extreme view, "talk of rules is a myth, cloaking the truth that law consists simply of the decisions of courts and the predictions of them"; on the less extreme view, "statutes are not law until they are applied by courts but only sources of law."[25] Hart shows that both views are incoherent, for both assume the existence of a court and a court is based on certain rules of adjudication.

Hart is surely correct that the way rule skepticism is usually interpreted makes very little sense. Yet, if one distinguishes between the theoretical meaning of a rule and its empirical meaning, there is another way to understand it.[26] The theoretical meaning of the rule "No vehicles are allowed in the park" may be based on legislative intent or perhaps on the standard legal meaning of the key phrases in the rule. But the empirical meaning of the rule is based on the actual application of the rule by the courts. The way the rule is actually applied may have little to do with the intent of the legislature or the standard legal meaning of the key phrases.

Rule skepticism, like legal formalism, can usefully be interpreted as a program. In the case of rule skepticism, however, it is one of legal research rather than legal interpretation in that it is meant to guide legal scholars rather than judges. This program may be formulated in terms of the following methodological rules:

(RS_1) Concentrate one's study on the empirical meaning of legal rules.
(RS_2) Assume that the empirical meaning of a rule diverges considerably from its theoretical meaning.

Another aspect of rule skepticism that concerns Hart is that it maintains that judges do not decide according to any rules. They may cite rules later to rationalize their decisions but they do not have any rules in mind when they make their decisions; they decide intuitively or by "hunches." Thus the rules they cite are just window dressing; indeed, they pretend the rules they cite resemble the case before the bench. Hart admits that such window dressing may sometimes occur but he maintains that even if most decisions are intuitively reached, the decisions "are justified by rules which the judge was antecedently disposed to observe and whose relevance to the case in hand would generally be acknowledged."[27]

Hart may be correct about this, but the question of exactly how much legal reasoning reduces to window dressing and after-the-fact rationalization is an empirical one that needs investigation. Be that as it may, rule skepticism understood as a program of legal research may be taken to be suggesting two approaches to the investigation of judicial decision making that can be stated as methodological rules. One such rule would be relevant in the "context of discovery," the context of how legal decisions are actually generated. This would be a rule about what factors to look for or not look for in a causal explanation of why judges come to particular decisions. The other methodological rule would be relevant in the "context of justification," the context of how legal decisions are justified. This would be a rule about what factors to look for or not look for in determining whether a decision was justified. Consider:

(RS_3) Proceed on the assumption that reason R given by the court for decision D is completely irrelevant to causally explaining why D was made by the court.

(RS_4) Proceed on the assumption that the biases, prejudices, and emotions of the court causally explain its decisions.

(RS_5) Proceed on the assumption that reason R given by the court in decision D is completely irrelevant in justifying D.

Now, the question of whether (RS_1)–(RS_5) are fruitful methodological rules can only be determined by actual practice. Such rules are directed at investigators of legal decision making. Their value, if any, would emerge if, for example, in following them, these investigators would make discoveries they might not have made, or at least not have made so easily, or if they would save time and energy, or if in general they would serve to further inquiry.

It should be noted that (RS_1)–(RS_5) do not conflict with (LF_1)–(LF_3). Whereas (RS_1)–(RS_5) are directed to investigators of legal decisions—social scientists, legal historians, and so on—(LF_1)–(LF_3) are directed to judges and legislators. For example, (LF_3) tells a judge how legal decisions should be justified, but (RS_5) gives the investigator of judges' decisions directions how to proceed. (LF_3) may be an excellent rule for judges to follow; (RS_5) may be an excellent rule for investigators of legal decisions to follow. They need not be in conflict.

There is, of course, this connection between (RS_5) and (LF_3). If all judges followed (LF_3), then (RS_5) would probably be a bad rule, for (RS_5) would direct investigators away from what was actually happening. That is to say, whether (RS_5) is a fruitful rule for investigators to follow will depend on certain contingent facts of the world, facts that may be affected if (LF_3) is followed.

In any case, this reformulation of rule skepticism seems to capture some of the insights of the position while avoiding its obvious absurdities. Whether these methodological rules provide fruitful guidelines for legal research remains to be seen.

Dworkin's Critique of Hart and Hart's Response

Ronald Dworkin, Hart's successor to the Chair of Jurisprudence at Oxford University, is the most important critic of Hart's theory of judicial interpretation. Indeed, Dworkin's legal theories are, next to Hart's, the most widely discussed in contemporary jurisprudence and in large measure have been constructed in response to Hart's theories. Although it is impossible here to do full justice to either the complexities of Dworkin's theories or the ongoing debate, a brief survey of his criticisms of Hart and of the responses by Hart and his defenders is essential for an understanding of Hart's position.

Dworkin argues against Hart that even in unclear cases where Hart's supposes that judicial discretion comes into play there is always one correct judicial decision, although what this decision is may not be known.[28] Although a case may not be settled by any existing legal rules, a judge can and should utilize legal principles that are implicit in legal thought to decide the case. Hart errs, according to Dworkin, in assuming that the law consists only in rules. It also consists in principles, he says. For example, Dworkin argues that in *Riggs v. Palmer*, a case in which the court had to decide whether a grandson named as heir in the grandfather's will could inherit under the will although he had murdered his grandfather, the court relied upon a fundamental maxim of the common law rather than merely on the rules of the law of wills. Thus, the maxim "No one shall be permitted to profit by his own fraud, or to take advantage of his own wrong, or to found any claim upon his own iniquity, or to acquire property by his own crime" is not a rule of law; it is a principle.[29] Principles differ from rules, according to Dworkin. A principle, unlike a rule, is not applicable in an all-or-nothing way; it merely states a reason that argues in one direction. Moreover, principles, unlike rules, have different weights or importance. Judges must take into account these different weights when two or more principles come into conflict. A principle exerts a gravitational pull on the judge and some principles exert a stronger pull than others.

According to Dworkin, when more than one principle is involved it is often difficult to decide which principle should be given more weight. In order to settle unclear cases—what Dworkin calls "hard cases"—it may be necessary for a judge to develop a comprehensive constitutional, political, and legal theory consisting of a complex set of principles that could justify his or her scheme of government. The judge "must develop that theory by referring alternately to political philosophy and institutional detail. He must generate possible theories justifying different aspects of the scheme and test the theories against the broader institution."[30] But the judge must also explicate and develop the fundamental concepts of the theory and decide what basic values are protected by the system. Since this judicial task would take incredible mental ability and effort, Dworkin calls the judge that he imagines would develop this theory "Hercules." Real life judges, of course, can only approximate what Hercules would accomplish and because of this may differ in their decisions. But Dworkin insists that, given the comprehensive and complex theory developed by Hercules, only one decision would be correct.[31]

There is one implication that Dworkin draws from his theory of law that, if correct, would affect Hart's theory profoundly: if principles are considered part of the law, then Hart's rule of recognition must be abandoned.[32] If Dworkin is correct, then Hart's mature position on judicial decision making is incompatible with his views on the rule of recognition and, consequently, with his concept of law.

Dworkin argues that, according to Hart, most rules are valid because a competent institution enacted them. For example, some rules are enacted by a legislature, while others are created by the courts and are used as precedents in future cases. But this "test of pedigree," Dworkin argues, will not work for principles. The origin of principles lies not in a particular decision of some legislature or court "but in a sense of appropriateness developed in the profession and the public over time."[33] In arguing that some principle is a principle of law, we cite that the principle has institutional support. For example, we show that it was mentioned in prior cases or was exemplified in statutes.

However, according to Dworkin, there is no formula for testing how much and what kind of institutional support is necessary to make a principle a legal principle. There are various shifting considerations; what must be brought in is everything from contemporary moral standards to various sorts of legal precedents. There is no way, according to Dworkin, that these considerations could be joined together in a rule, even a complex one. And if one could join them, Dworkin says, it would bear little relation to some fairly stable master rule specifying "some feature or features possession of which by a suggested rule is taken as a conclusive affirmative indication that it is a rule."[34]

Furthermore, says Dworkin, the rule of recognition could not simply list all principles since the question of which principles are legally recognized is a controversial matter and the set shifts and changes as the law develops. Nor could we simply cite the complete set of principles in force as a way of specifying the rule of recognition without trivializing the rule, for this, according to Dworkin, would be like uttering the tautology that law is law. Dworkin concludes that if one treats principles as part of law, one must reject Hart's view that legal systems must have a rule of recognition. But this is tantamount to rejecting Hart's analysis of the concept of law.

Dworkin also maintains that a judge's decisions in unclear cases characteristically are decided and should be decided entirely by legal principles. These principles specify rights and entitlements, and he contrasts them with legal policies. Legal policies, according to Dworkin, specify what is in the public interest and general welfare. These policies, he says, are typically used, and should be used, by a legislator and not by a judge. He does not deny that people in a community may believe that the reason certain principles are embodied in their legal system is because their collective welfare is furthered by them. But this does not show that judges make or should make their decisions in terms of what furthers the collective welfare. Nor does Dworkin deny that economic considerations have entered into the common law. He maintains, however, that such considerations do not refute his thesis. Thus, the thesis that rules developed by judges in various fields of law serve the collective goal of making resources more efficient does not refute Dworkin's claim that only considerations of rights serve as the basis of a judge's decisions. Just because some rules serve some goal in some particular practice, it does not mean that these rules are applied *because* they serve this goal. Furthermore, Dworkin does not think that the use of Learned Hand's economic test by judges in negligence cases undermines his thesis. According to Hand's test, a defendant's action is unreasonable if he or she could have avoided the accident at less cost than "the plaintiff was likely to suffer if the accident occurred, discounted by the improbability of the accident."[35] Dworkin argues that this test is merely a method of comparing competing rights of individuals; it is not a test based on the cost and benefits to the community at large. This latter type of test would be a counterexample to Dworkin's thesis but this is not what the court characteristically uses or should use.

Dworkin not only maintains that policy considerations do not characteristically figure in judicial decisions but that they should not. He gives two basic arguments to support this contention. First, he maintains that judges, unlike legislators, are not responsible to the electorate and, consequently, should not make new law. Judges are not as well equipped as legislators to take into account the different interests and demands that need to be considered in making policy decisions. Second, he argues that, since judicial decisions based on policy have a retrospective effect, they are unfair. But judicial decisions based on principles have no such disadvantages. Unlike decisions based on policy, they do not need to take different interests and demands into account. Further, in arguments from principle, since the rights assumed by the principle already exist, there can be no retrospective unfairness.

In sum, Dworkin's theory is based on four basic claims that either explicitly or implicitly challenge Hart's theory:

(1) Judicial decisions are based on rules *and* principles.
(2) There cannot be more than one correct judicial decision.
(3) Legal principles are incompatible with a rule of recognition.
(4) Judicial decisions are not and should not be based on policy.

(1) As a critique of Hart's mature work, Dworkin's first claim can be dismissed quickly. As we have seen, his later views on judicial decision making are not as far from Dworkin's as the latter thinks.[36] For reasons of his own, Hart does not attempt to defend his position against Dworkin's critique by pointing out that, despite what Dworkin claims, he does allow for legal principles in his mature work. Nor does Hart take the tack of some of his defenders, who have attempted to combat Dworkin's charge either by trying to undermine Dworkin's distinction between rules and principles or by claiming that what Hart means by rules includes what Dworkin means by principles.[37] Moreover, although Hart assumes in his mature work that principles and policies are part of the law, he does not attempt to argue that other legal standards besides rules can be incorporated into his system without problems.

Defenders of Hart such as MacCormick maintain that standards other than rules can be incorporated into Hart's analysis of a legal system and that Hart's omission of standards that are not rules does not seriously affect his fundamental insights. On the other hand, Dworkin seems to believe that the existence of standards that are not rules completely undermines Hart's theory since they cannot be assimilated into his system.

The unclarity of the concepts of rule and principle makes it difficult to know who is right in this controversy. As we have seen, Dworkin maintains that the difference between legal rules and legal principles is that, while rules apply in an all-or-nothing fashion, principles merely state reasons that argue in one direction. On the other hand, MacCormick explicates the difference between rules and principles in a different way.[38] He says that rules are "cut and dried" and have a conventional element, for example, "Keep on the left side of the road," while principles provide rational grounds for conduct and are more general in scope than rules.

These two accounts of the differences between rules and principles seem to have very little in common unless one interprets MacCormick's idea that rules are "cut and dried" as being identical with Dworkin's idea that rules either apply or do not apply. There is nothing necessarily conventional in Dworkin's notion of a rule and nothing necessarily general about his notion of principle. On the other hand, if principles supply rational grounds for conduct, as MacCormick says, these grounds could be decisive; thus principles need not (contra Dworkin) argue merely in one direction. Furthermore, what Hart understands as the difference between legal rules and legal standards that are not rules remains quite unclear.

Given the unclarity in the concepts central to the controversy over whether standards that are not rules can be incorporated into Hart's scheme, it is difficult to know what to say. Yet I suspect that Hart's scheme could be generalized to incorporate standards that are not rules without serious distortion regardless of whether we take Dworkin or MacCormick as our guide. For example, one might generalize a scheme of primary and secondary rules to a scheme of primary and secondary standards. Primary standards would either impose obligations or else provide considerations that argue in the direction of some course of action. They could be cut and dried with conventional elements but they would not have to be. Secondary standards would provide either explicit rules for changing or modifying primary standards or else considerations for guiding change or modification of the primary standards. Alternatively (mirroring the ambiguity in Hart's concept of secondary rule) secondary standards would either specify the way primary standards are ascertained and modified and violations of primary standards are decided or else provide considerations that would guide these.

(2) As we have seen, Hart is skeptical that there is always a uniquely correct legal decision. Moreover, he remains skeptical after Dworkin's arguments to the contrary.

Hart's skepticism is illustrated in his criticism of Dworkin's review of Cover's *Justice Accused: Anti-slavery and the Judicial Process*.[39] According to the thesis of this book, before the American Civil War some famous Massachusetts judges, although opposed to slavery, enforced the Fugitive Slave Act. They did this, Dworkin says, because they believed it was their judicial duty to follow the intentions of Congress and the Constitutional Convention. Dworkin argues that these judges were guilty of a "failure of jurisprudence" for, from the perspective of a comprehensive theory of law (the kind presumably developed by Hercules), they would see that the American Constitution presupposes values that are opposed to slavery: the idea of procedural justice conflicts with the Fugitive Slave Act and the concept of federalism allows state judges to prevent the capture of men and women in their state. These ideas, Dworkin maintains, are not based on the personal morality of the judges; on the contrary, they are more central to American law than "the particular and transitory policies of the slavery compromise."

In reply to Dworkin, Hart says:

> It is right and illuminating to speak of the existing law as exerting a gravitational pull over the judge, but that there will not quite often be equal gravitational pulls in different directions seems to me something still to be shown. It is plain from Professor Dworkin's exposition that the underlying justificatory theory of the existing law from which the judges are to extract rules of decision includes principles that are hugely general and abstract. I find it difficult to believe that among these, just one principle or set of principles can be shown to fit the existing settled law better than any other.

He goes on to argue that "Principles *supporting* the decisions against the slaves seem to fit the then existing law at least as well as those proffered by Professor Dworkin."[40] In a footnote,[41] Hart specifies what these principles might be.

One might wonder if the controversy between Hart and Dworkin is capable of rational adjudication. Could there be any possible evidence that would tend to support one theory and refute the other? Suppose we take the idea of Hercules seriously. Then we could rank different judges and the rationales for their decisions according to how close they approximate to Hercules and the theoretical rationale that he is supposed to construct. One would assume that on Dworkin's theory one could predict that, the closer actual judges and their rationales approximate to Hercules, the less their decisions would diverge. On Hart's theory no such prediction would be possible. One might even perform an experiment that brought together a group of philosophers with legal training and had them construct rationales for their decisions on actual or hypothetical legal cases where all the usual practical constraints were operative. Given these constraints, they would not be able to begin to approximate the decision procedure of Hercules. They would then be asked to construct for similar legal cases large-scale theoretical rationales for their decisions where there were no practical constraints and where their philosophical talents had ample room to operate. (One would assume that without these constraints their philosophical training and talents would cause them to approximate to the procedures of Hercules.) One presumably could predict that on Dworkin's theory there would be wider agreement in the second set of decisions than in the first. Hart's theory, however, would have no such implication. Even if it were available, such evidence would not, of course, conclusively establish Dworkin's theory. It is a large step from the fact—if it is one—that the closer judges approximate to Hercules, the more they agree in their decisions, to the conclusion that there is *only* one correct answer in every case. Still, evidence of this sort would be relevant and would supply some support for Dworkin's claim.

Unfortunately, at present no such tests are available and, consequently, relevant evidence is lacking. As a result, one does not know if Dworkin's bold claim is justified. However, one can say that, without such evidence, Hart's skepticism is surely justified.

(3) Dworkin's argument against the rule of recognition seems only to assume what Hart admits, namely that the law contains principles. Nevertheless, I believe that Hart can answer Dworkin. The first thing to notice in evaluating Dworkin's critique is his assumption that Hart's rule of recognition is a test of legal pedigree, that is, the rule of recognition specifies legal validity in terms of whether a rule or other standard has been enacted by some competent institution.[42] This assumption is false. A rule of recognition could specify that laws must have certain content. Indeed the criteria used to specify laws could be moral. This would not show that laws and morality were necessarily connected and consequently that legal positivism was an incorrect view. For even granted that some or all rules of recognition use moral criteria, it would not follow that there is a necessary relation between morality and law. Rules of recognition with specific moral content would be a contingent fact: there could be a legal system with a rule of recognition without moral content[43] for there would be no necessity that all legal systems have rules of recognition with moral content.[44] Moreover, even if moral content were necessarily involved in the criteria specified by the rule of recognition, this would not necessarily mean that rules, principles, and policies, the legality of which a judge decided by the rule of recognition, would be moral. Moral criteria might be only one type taken into account in judging the legal validity of rules or principles, and, hence, it would still be possible to have evil laws.[45]

Furthermore, one need not take very seriously Hart's statement, quoted by Dworkin, that the rule of recognition "specifies some feature or features possession of which by a suggested rule is taken as a conclusive affirmative indication that it is a rule."[46] After all, Hart allows that there are penumbra cases in the application of ordinary laws; it seems plausible that he would allow that there may be penumbra cases in the application of the rule of recognition. Why would all rules and principles be either clearly legal or clearly non-legal according to the rule of recognition, yet not all objects be either clearly a vehicle or clearly not a vehicle with respect to the statute "No vehicles are allowed in the park"?

Finally, on Hart's view a rule of recognition can be complex. It can contain various types of criteria from formal ones, based on legal pedigrees, to moral ones. In particular, Hart's concept of a rule of recognition seems to allow for a test of legal validity to be specified in terms of how judges, taking into account the institutional support specified by Dworkin, should arrive at their decisions. Consider Dworkin's description of how legal principles are justified. Legal principles are determined, he says, by whether they have institutional support, and this, in turn, is determined by shifting considerations including moral considerations. As Sartorius has argued,[47] principles could be "recursively characterized" as those standards that are established, exemplified, or implied either directly or indirectly by other standards. Thus, Sartorius suggests three stages in a rule of recognition: (1) the statutes enacted by a particular legislative body; (2) the principles and policies embodied in valid laws according to (1); (3) extra-legal principles and policies made relevant by laws made valid according to (1) and (2). This suggests that part of a complex rule of recognition would state:

(RR_1) If principle P has institutional support, for example, if P is embodied in the valid rules of the system, P is a legal principle.

An obvious objection to (RR_1) is that its use would beg the question. In order to determine if P has institutional support it is necessary to know if other principles are legal principles, since principles gain institutional support in part by their relation to other legal principles. But this problem can be handled in several ways. One way is to suppose that the rule of recognition contains a list of rather uncontroversial principles. Other principles are judged to have institutional support relative to these listed principles as well as perhaps to moral standards that would also be specified as part of the rule of recognition. As Dworkin points out, the rule of recognition may change since what principles are legal may change over time. But this is not surprising. The rule of recognition need not be completely stable. Thus, one might specify one part of the rule of recognition as follows:

(RR_2) If principle P_i at time t has institutional support relative to principles P_1 . . . P_5, then P_i is a legal principle at time t (where P_1 . . . P_5 are specific principles that may change over time).

Such a construal would seem to avoid the problem Dworkin outlines. The list of principles would not be endless; the principles would not be controversial, since only clear cases of legal principles would be listed. Nor would such a construal be trivial in the manner of the statement "law is law." For some principles would not be on the list and would be evaluated in terms of ones that were. Furthermore, (RR_2) would only be part of the complete, more complex rule of recognition. Other parts of the rule might specify, for example, when legislative enactment or a court-created rule would override principles.

Another approach to solving Dworkin's problem would be to specify part of the rule of recognition this way:

(RR_3) A principle P is a legal principle if a sufficient number of enacted statutes or particular court decisions embody P.

Dworkin might object to this formulation on the ground that there is no formula for how much institutional weight is necessary to make a principle a logical principle. However, the virtue of (RR_3) is that it leaves this question open and allows judges to decide what is a sufficient number; it allows them to exercise judgment in deciding whether a particular principle's institutional support is sufficient in the circumstances. There will, of course, be disagreement among judges, but this hardly makes the situation different from that of other cases in which judges must apply vague general standards.

As I argued above, there could be various ways of tightening up the rule of recognition so that judicial discretion would be cut down. For example, (RR_3) could be modified by replacing the vague "sufficient number" with some particular number of enacted statutes or particular court decisions. Whether this replacement would be desirable would depend on the value we place on flexibility in the light of knowledge about the future and whether knowledge about the future could be obtained. If accurate predictions about the future could be made, then the vague phrase "sufficient number" could be replaced without loss by a definite number.

In his reply to Sartorius, Dworkin claims that he has been misunderstood.[48] He did not mean to deny either that in every legal system there is some particular, perhaps complex, rule (he calls it a normative rule) that is the proper standard for judges to use in identifying more particular rules of the system or that every judge in such a system accepts some such rule or other. What he denies is that most judges in a legal system accept *one* such rule. If they did, then the rule of recognition would be a social rule. But, Dworkin argues, the question of which rule of recognition should guide judges' decisions is a matter of great controversy and debate; there is no rule accepted by all or even most judges. He denies, then, that the rule of recognition is a social rule while maintaining that Hart holds it to be such.

In part the controversy between Hart and Dworkin seems to be a factual one over whether most judges in a legal system agree on some particular rule of recognition. Dworkin is no doubt correct that they disagree over particular decisions. But the evidence is not yet available to allow us to decide if this disagreement is based on the acceptance of different rules of recognition by different judges or on differences among judges over how one rule of recognition applies in a particular case. Hart can admit that a rule of recognition, although widely agreed to in the abstract, may have controversial applications.

In part, however, the controversy between Hart and Dworkin seems to be based on unclarities in the notion of acceptance. Dworkin is perhaps assuming that "acceptance" for Hart entails verbal acknowledgment and that there is no one articulated rule of recognition that most judges in a legal system would so acknowledge. As we saw in Chapter 1, Hart maintains that the officials of a legal system must view the rule of recognition from the standard evaluative point of view. This means that in judging whether some rule, principle, or policy is part of the legal system the officials must believe that they have an obligation to apply the rule of recognition. But even given the fact of Hart's commitment to the standard evaluative point of view it is doubtful that he would need to maintain this view of acceptance. Hart might say that a partial test[49] of a judge's accepting a rule of recognition (R) would be that the hypothesis that the judge uses (R) explains his or her judicial behavior better than any other hypothesis. On this interpretation, the controversy between Dworkin and Hart comes down to which of two hypotheses better explains judicial behavior, the hypothesis that one rule of recognition is used by most judges in a particular legal system in their decisions or the hypothesis that there is not one rule of recognition that is used by most judges. (The truth of the first hypothesis is compatible with its not being the case that there is any one rule of recognition that most judges would verbally acknowledge.) Needless to say, which of these two hypotheses is better supported by the evidence is not yet determined.

(4) Hart does not supply any detailed argument against Dworkin's thesis that policy considerations are not and should not be used by judges in deciding unclear cases. Hart says, however: "This exclusion of 'policy considerations' will, I think, again run counter to the convictions of many lawyers that it is indeed perfectly proper and indeed at times necessary for judges to take account of the impact of their decisions on the general community welfare."[50] In a footnote[51] Hart cites "others" who have reached similar conclusions. However, in order to refute the descriptive part of Dworkin's thesis about policy Hart does not cite legal cases where judges have actually appealed in justifying their decisions to the costs and benefits to the community at large in contrast to the costs and benefits to the defendant and plaintiff. Hart goes on to remark that Dworkin's exclusion of policy considerations from judicial decision making "is part of the general hostility to utilitarianism that characterizes his work."[52] He finds such hostility typical of recent American social philosophy. Hart concedes that utilitarianism has penetrated, "though not very far," into American legal theory, and he cites Roscoe Pound and the Chicago school of economic analysis as examples of this penetration.

It is clear that Hart has not succeeded in refuting Dworkin's thesis and, in fact, has not really tried to do so. How could a refutation be accomplished? Since Dworkin's thesis is at least in part descriptive, the descriptive part of his claim could be undermined by finding typical legal decisions where judges appeal either explicitly or implicitly to the costs and benefits of the community at large in justifying their decisions and not to the duties or rights of the plaintiff and the defendant. I say "typical" legal decisions since Dworkin would certainly admit that there may be rare and anomalous ones in which only policy considerations were used by judges. Although to my knowledge no systematic legal study of this kind is presently available, Dworkin's critics cite what they take to be evidence that his descriptive thesis is mistaken. Dworkin, in turn, maintains that these critics have confused arguments from policy with arguments that appeal to consequences.[53]

Hart makes no effort at all to refute the normative part of Dworkin's thesis. To be sure, he has given powerful arguments against Dworkin's theory of rights[54] and may, therefore, believe that his critique indirectly undermines Dworkin's exclusion of policy considerations from judicial decisions. If Hart does believe this, he is mistaken. Even if Dworkin's theory of rights is refuted, the two arguments given above—the argument from democracy and the argument from retroactivity—might still provide good reasons for not allowing policy considerations to enter judicial decision making. Whether they do in fact do so is another matter. With respect to the argument from democracy it has been claimed that legislators may not have the time to develop policy in certain areas of law and that this development is left to the court. In addition, it has been maintained that it is dubious that the legislature is better able than the courts to take into account factors promoting general welfare. Second, with respect to the argument from retroactivity, critics have pointed out that not all decisions of policy have retrospective unfairness. Consider, for example, a policy prohibiting some *future* class of action. Moreover, even when there is retrospective unfairness it is sometimes worth the price. Further, critics maintain that people may be expected to understand that their uncertain claims of rights must be consistent with the general welfare; thus, to deny a claim to a right on policy grounds may be no more offensive than to deny such a claim on the grounds of some arguable principle. Dworkin continues to defend his position.[55]

Conclusion

I have shown here that both legal formalism and rule skepticism can be reformulated in a way that captures much of the spirit of Hart's positions and blocks his criticism of these views. Further, although there is a tension in Hart's analysis between freedom and rationality, this can be reconciled. Thus, although Hart does not provide a completely worked-out account of legal reasoning his views are suggestive and capable of further development including the utilization of scientific predictions. I have also briefly reviewed here Dworkin's critique of Hart and Hart's actual and possible response. Although it is too soon to tell whose position is correct in this complex and ongoing controversy, it seems clear that Hart's positions have not been clearly and definitely refuted.

Chapter

3

Theory of Legal Causation

Background Theories of Causation

IN CHAPTER 2 we found Hart stressing that legal language is not completely indeterminate and that the interpretation of legal language is guided by certain principles, policies, and standards. Hart and Honoré's book *Causation in the Law*[1] can be understood as an attempt to specify the framework within which interpretation of causal judgment in the law operates. The judge has discretion in the weak sense—he or she must use judgment—but this judgment must be guided not only by considerations of policy but by ideas of common sense causality that are contained in the law.

In *Causation in the Law* Hart and Honoré argue that the study of the ordinary notion of causation will throw light on the legal notion. As we saw in the last chapter, Hart in his theory of judicial interpretation seems to suppose something analogous. He argues that legal language, like ordinary language, is open-textured in the sense that there are cases in which the application of a term will be indeterminable in the light of legal rules and procedures. He certainly seems to suppose, moreover, that given the open texture of ordinary language, in important respects the study of ordinary language will throw light on the open texture of legal language. As we will see, Hart and Honoré argue that the ordinary concept of cause is useful in understanding causality in the law because the courts use it; they also maintain there is good reason to use this concept. This parallels Hart's claim in his theory of judicial interpretation that the open texture of the law can be understood in terms of that of ordinary language and that this open texture is desirable. As we have seen, Hart argues that we "should not cherish" rules where the application of every rule would be settled in advance.[2]

Hart and Honoré maintain that traditional philosophical theories of causation have not been useful in understanding the notion of causality in ordinary language and legal thought. In both ordinary life and the law one is presented with a number of causal conditions all of which are relevant for bringing about a particular event. One major philosophical problem is that of selecting one of these factors as the cause. For example, the lawyer and the plain man make a distinction between the cause of a particular event, for example, a fire (someone striking a match) and a mere causal condition of the event (the presence of oxygen). In certain contexts, of course, oxygen would be considered to be the cause of a fire in both the law and common sense. For example, suppose a factory manufactures a product that requires the exclusion of oxygen, but due to a leak oxygen is introduced and a fire starts. In this situation one might well consider oxygen the cause of the fire. However, Hart and Honoré ask: Why in the normal situation is oxygen considered to be a mere condition while in the unusual circumstance oxygen is considered the cause?

Traditional philosophical approaches to causality have not been helpful in answering this question. According to Hart and Honoré this is because philosophy since Hume has been dominated by the doctrine that generalization constitutes the very essence of the notion of causation. According to the Humean view, single causal statements that seem to state a connection between two particulars are "covertly general":[3] two events are causally connected only because these events are instances of general laws asserting that events of these kinds are invariably connected.

This Humean idea, say Hart and Honoré, does not answer the question of why in normal circumstances someone's striking a match is picked out as the cause while the presence of oxygen is considered a mere causal condition. Claiming only that covertly general laws are utilized in these two cases, the Humean view is not able to deal with this question. Hart and Honoré believe that the choice of the cause is not arbitrary and that philosophical analysis should attempt to determine "what sort of principles guide our thoughts."[4]

J. S. Mill modified Hume's theory in several ways and, according to Hart and Honoré, his theory improves our understanding of the common sense and legal notions of cause considerably. Hume seemed to restrict causes to events or objects, but Mill maintained that persistent states and also failures or omissions can be causes. He is certainly right that in ordinary life and the law we use the term "cause" to refer to persistent states (for example, Jones' chronic absenteeism was the cause of his dismissal) as well as to failures and omissions (for example, the signalman's failure to pull the lever was the cause of the accident).

Mill also stressed that a cause is complex. A causal relation, he insisted, is not a constant conjunction of a single antecedent invariably followed by the consequence, for the cause may be the sum of several antecedents. Once this point is made one is able to see how the causal problem specified above may arise. In both ordinary life and the law we often pick one antecedent out of a complex cause and designate it as *the* cause. Recognizing this Mill distinguished the *philosophical* notion of cause (the total antecedent from which the consequent invariably follows) from the *common sense* notion in which one of the antecedents is singled out.

Finally, Mill, unlike Hume, allowed for a plurality of causes. Arguing that a cause is a sufficient condition whereas Hume seemed to maintain that a cause was both a sufficient and a necessary condition, Mill permitted there to be several independent causes for a given event. Again, this idea accords with common sense, which certainly assumes that there can be several causes of, for example, a death or an accident.

Now, Hart and Honoré maintain that, although Mill's analysis is an improvement over Hume's, it is not completely adequate for capturing the common sense and legal notion of causality. For one thing, Mill was wrong to suppose that an unqualified definition of cause in terms of invariable sequences "corresponds to the way in which causal notions are in fact used."[5] To be sure, when particular causal statements are challenged, general statements are marshalled in their defense. But these generalizations are not statements of invariable sequences; they are broader and less specific and tend to be platitudinous. Thus, if one says that A's blow to B's nose caused B's nose to bleed, one does not defend this particular statement by providing a statement of invariable sequences. Rather, one defends one's claim by citing some broadly framed generalization that asserts that doing one thing (striking someone's nose a hard blow) will commonly bring about another thing (bleeding). Moreover, there are some contexts in which even this use of platitudinous generalizations is not required. For in ordinary life and the law one speaks of one person's causing another to do something by exercising coercion. More generally, one speaks of someone's action being a consequent of someone else's advice or promises or false statements. In these "interpersonal transaction" cases, even broadly framed generalizations need not hold.

Another problem with Mill's view, according to Hart and Honoré, is that he restricted his examination of causal notions to the context of explanation. In this context we are puzzled by why or how something happened and an explanation relieves our puzzlement. But a lawyer may understand why or how something happened and yet be puzzled about whether harm can be attributed to the defendant's action. Hart and Honoré call this the attributive context. The puzzle here, they say, is generated less by questions of fact than by the vagueness and indeterminacy of the causal notions that are used. What typically generates the attributive problem, according to Hart and Honoré, is that there is a factor in addition to the defendant's action that "has some of the characteristics by which common sense distinguishes causes from mere conditions; so that there seems as much reason to attribute the harm to this third factor as to the defendant's action."[6]

Finally, even if all these other problems are waived, Hart and Honoré believe that although Mill recognized a common sense notion of causality his analysis of that notion was oversimplified and a better one is needed.

We have seen that Hart and Honoré reject traditional philosophical theories of causality because they do not reflect common sense causal concepts that are found in ordinary language. They also reject well-known accounts of legal causality because of similar reasons. These accounts, they maintain, do not reflect the common sense causal concepts that are found in legal language. Two prevailing views of legal causality are criticized by Hart and Honoré.

What Hart and Honoré call the modern view, the most widely accepted view of legal causality today, holds that there are only two fundamental questions in making judgments of causality in the law. One must first decide whether A's action is a proximate cause. That is one answers the purely factual question: Would B have occurred but for A's action? According to the modern theory, the second question is basically a policy question, not a factual one.

Different modern theorists take different approaches to the policy question. On one widely held version of the modern theory—the foreseeability theory—questions concerning proximate cause in negligence law are decided by the general policy of foreseeability: the defendant is responsible for and only for such harm as he or she could have reasonably foreseen and prevented. On another version of the modern theory—Hart and Honoré call it the sense of judgment theory—decisions of the court on the extent of a defendant's liability "are not and should not be reached by the application of *any* general principles but by the exercise of the sense of judgment, unhampered by legal rules, on the facts of each case."[7]

The other theory of legal causality rejected by Hart and Honoré is the traditional theory. On this theory questions of law are purely factual. But Hart and Honoré say that traditional legal thought often appealed to rules of causation that were couched in unclear metaphors "for which no literal translation was provided."[8] Hart and Honoré reject this appeal to unclear metaphors in the traditional view and attempt to provide an analysis of legal causality in terms of the relatively clear ideas of ordinary language and common sense.

They reject the modern theory because, they maintain, it does not provide an accurate account of how legal language actually operates in the law or how it should operate. They argue that causal judgments in wide areas of the law are not just based on whether some action was a *sine qua non* and a policy consideration, nor should they be based on just these factors. They maintain that in wide areas of the law the courts appeal to common sense notions of causality. Hart and Honoré admit that the modern theory has a point. Some causal judgments in the law are based on policy considerations. The modern theory is wrong, however, in maintaining that all judgments of legal causality are based on policy considerations.

The contrast between the modern theory, the traditional theory, and Hart and Honoré's theory can be illustrated by these examples used by the authors:[9]

Case 1:

A negligently causes a fire that damages B's house; the fire in B's house in turn damages C's house. In New York it has been the law since 1866 that if a fire is negligently started and spreads to several buildings, damage may be recovered only in respect to the first of the buildings damaged by the fire. So if the fire in this case occurred in New York, B but not C would be able to recover from A.

Case 2:

A negligently causes a fire. The fire is about to go out, but B pours paraffin on the fire. The fire spreads to C's house causing damage. A is not held responsible for damage to C's house.

In the traditional approach the two cases are treated very differently. In Case 1 causality is not at issue because the court has made a ruling on policy grounds. In Case 2 the question of whether A is liable is not based on considerations of policy but on the causal judgment that the causal chain between A's action and the damage to C's house has been broken by the intervention of B.

The modern approach to causality insists that the two cases be decided on similar grounds. Both cases involve the application of the concept of proximate cause and both are based on considerations of policy. The only factual causal consideration in these cases is the initial determination of whether A's action was the cause in fact or *sine qua non*; that is, whether the damage to the house would have occurred but for the action of A. After this has been established, the judgment is made whether A's action is the proximate cause. But these judgments are based on considerations of policy.

Hart and Honoré attempt to take a middle path between the two extremes of the traditional theory and the modern theory. They maintain that in both cases causal judgments are involved, thus rejecting the traditional view. But they maintain that the causal judgment in each case is based on very different considerations, thus rejecting the modern view. In Case 1 the judgment is based on policy considerations; in Case 2 the causal judgment is based on common sense causal notions.

Hart and Honoré thus reject both traditional philosophical accounts of causality and prevailing accounts of causality in the law for basically the same reason: they have failed to capture common sense causal notions. In the case of traditional philosophical accounts of causality there is a failure to capture the common sense notion of causality found in ordinary language; in the case of legal theories there is a failure to capture the common sense causal notion embodied in legal language, a language in part derived from ordinary language.

Hart and Honoré's Theory of Causation

Given their complaint about traditional philosophy and prevailing legal theories of causality it behooves Hart and Honoré to provide their own account. This they attempt to do. However, they argue that there is no single concept of causation but rather a group or family of concepts. These are united not by common features but by points of resemblance, some of them tenuous. Hart and Honoré first analyze what they call the central notion of common sense causality and then show how analogies with it help characterize the non-central notions and help distinguish causes from mere conditions and circumstances.

On their view, the central notion of common sense causality is based on the bodily manipulation of an object that brings about certain changes in the object,[10] for example, a person pushing a stone. This bodily manipulation makes a difference to what happens. Common experience teaches us that things left to themselves would not change at all or would change in ways different from those due to manipulation. In simple cases of bodily manipulation and resulting change we do not select out, as Mill seemed to think, one aspect of the total antecedent cause and designate it as *the* cause. Our intervention is recognized as the cause—the thing that makes the difference—right from the start.

In common sense thought, say Hart and Honoré, this central notion of causation has been developed and extended in several ways. Natural events that make a difference, for example, storms or floods, are thought of on an analogy to those human interventions that make a difference. These natural events are thus considered causes of other natural events. Also, by using threats, inducements, bribes, and commands human beings make a difference to the behavior of other human beings. Thus by analogy the central notion is extended to the context of interpersonal transaction. Further, people have learned that sometimes unless one intervenes harm will result. Consequently they have set up certain routines and procedures to prevent harm and these have come to be considered as much a part of the causal background of events as natural events have. Hence, an omission in following these conventional routines and procedures makes a difference. By analogy, then, the notion of causality is extended not only to human actions but to omissions of action.

As we have seen, according to Hart and Honoré, one of the most important problems in the analysis of the family of concepts making up our ordinary causal notion is that of distinguishing the cause from a mere causal condition. On their view, common sense draws this distinction in subtle and complex ways. For this reason, Hart and Honoré maintain that only two general contrasts are useful in distinguishing cause from condition: the one between what is normal and what is abnormal, the other between deliberate human action and other conditions.

Hart and Honoré point out that in ordinary life we often make distinctions between cause and condition in terms of what is abnormal and what is normal. In most situations the lighted match held to combustible material would be the abnormal factor and the cause of the fire. The presence of oxygen and the combustible material would be the mere condition of the fire. However, what is normal and abnormal varies contextually in two different ways. As we have already seen, in some special contexts the presence of oxygen would be the abnormal factor. But there is also another type of contextual relativity. For example, the wife of a man who suffers from an ulcerated stomach might identify eating parsnips as the cause of his indigestion and the ulcerated stomach as mere condition. But a doctor might identify the ulcerated stomach as the cause and the eating of the parsnips as a mere condition. The wife, according to Hart and Honoré, is in fact asking, "What has given this man in his condition indigestion when usually he gets by without it?"; the doctor's question in contrast to the wife's is, "What gives *this* man indigestion when other men do not get it?" [11]

Although Hart and Honoré do not put it in these terms, the wife and the doctor use what may be called different "contrast classes." [12] The contrast class for the wife is all the times her husband has dined and not gotten indigestion. The contrast class for the doctor is all men who do not get indigestion. Clearly there could be many other contrast classes that would yield different judgments of what is the cause since these different contrast classes produce different appraisals of what is abnormal and normal.

There is no suggestion in Hart and Honoré's work that the doctor's judgment is any better than the wife's. They seem to be saying that what is abnormal is a function of the point of view in terms of which one sees the situation, the point of view that determines the contrast class one uses. The point of view one takes and consequently the contrast class one uses will be based on one's interest and purpose and is itself no better or worse than any other.

Hart and Honoré point out that, in their analysis, what is normal in a particular context need not be events or conditions unaffected by human intervention. It may be a function of human habit, custom, and convention. It may be normal in a given context, for example, for the gardener to water the flowers every day. They also argue that what is abnormal in some contexts may well be an omission. Thus the gardener's failure to water the plants may be an abnormal factor and hence the cause of the flower's dying. Furthermore, they maintain that causal conditions (the normal causal factors) of an effect need not exist contemporaneously with what is the cause (the abnormal causal factor) of the effect. After A lights the fire (the abnormal condition) a breeze (a normal condition) spreads the fire to B's property. The breeze is a mere condition of the effects, not the cause, despite the fact that it comes after A's action.

This last example of the intervention of a normal outside factor, a breeze causing a fire, suggests that if the intervention of an outside factor were not normal, if it were, for example, a hurricane, A's lighting the fire would not be considered the cause of B's property loss. This is indeed the position Hart and Honoré take.

Hart and Honoré use what they call "the law's favorite though perhaps most misleading metaphor," [13] breaking the chain of causation, to describe such a case.

In the example of the normal breeze, "the chain of causality" between the fire and the property damage is not "broken." Hart and Honoré typically speak of tracing the chain of causation "through" the normal event, in our example, the breeze, that is, the intermediate causal connection between the harmful action, the starting of the fire, and the subsequent harm, the destruction of the house. Such tracing through is possible since the normal factor, although subsequent to the action and independent of it, is a common recurrent feature of the environment. But with an abnormal factor, for example, a hurricane, they speak of the chain of causation as being broken. It is impossible to trace the causal connection through the intervening hurricane because hurricanes normally are not a recurrent feature of the environment; rather, they intervene in the natural course of events and "break the chain of causation." Hart and Honoré also typically refer to the causal chain that is broken by some intervening factor as being "negatived" by this factor. Thus the hurricane, but not the breeze, negatives the chain of causation between A's harmful action and B's property loss.

Some abnormal occurrences that negative a causal chain are called coincidences. However, Hart and Honoré define "coincidence" in such a way that not every abnormal state of event would be a coincidence and hence break the causal chain. In particular, they argue that "*a state of the person or thing affected* existing at the time of the wrongful act (a 'circumstance') however abnormal, does not negative causal connexion."[14] According to Hart and Honoré, common sense "regards a cause as 'intervening' in the course of events at a given time and the state of affairs then existing as the 'setting of the stage' before the actor comes upon the scene."[15] Joel Feinberg has called this principle that circumstances existing at the time of the wrongful act do not break the causal chain the *stage-setting exclusion principle*.

For example, if A is injured by B's carelessness and is hit by a falling tree on the way to the hospital and dies, the causal chain is broken; B did not cause A's death. But if a tree fell on A prior to the injury by B and A dies, the causal chain is not broken even though A would not have died but for the tree's falling on him. Hart and Honoré admit that this stage-setting exclusion principle "may be criticized as irrational,"[16] but they insist that it is in accord with common sense.

Furthermore, Hart and Honoré argue that not even all abnormal events that come after a wrongful action break a causal chain. Sometimes causality is traced through abnormal events, for instance, if the abnormal event is *the* result of a deliberate human action (in such a case the abnormal event would not be considered a coincidence). If A knocks B to the ground and a tree falls on B, killing him, A's action would not be considered the cause of B's death so long as the fall of the tree was independent of A's action and A did not know that the tree was going to fall. But if A's action caused B to fall against the tree, thus causing the tree to fall on B, A's action would be considered the cause of B's death. Or if A knew that the tree was going to fall at that time and place and knocked B down in order to have the tree fall on B, A's action would be considered the cause of B's death.

The other contrast that Hart and Honoré suggest for distinguishing cause from mere condition is that between voluntary human action and all other conditions. To be sure, an action that is not wholly voluntary may be treated as a cause because it is abnormal in the context. Thus a person may discharge a gun by an involuntary movement and kill a bystander. The person's action would be considered the cause of what happened because it is an abnormal event in the circumstances. But voluntary action intended to bring about what in fact happens in the manner in which it happens has, according to Hart and Honoré, a "special place" in causal inquiries.[17]

Such voluntary action provides a barrier and a goal in tracing back causes. Thus if arsenic is found in a dead man's body, the arsenic provides an explanation "up to a point" for the cause of death. But we usually press for a fuller explanation and may find that someone deliberately put arsenic in the man's food. When we reach this point, Hart and Honoré say, we have something that has a "special *finality*" on the level of common sense.[18] The causal explanation has been brought to a deliberate stop. We do not trace the cause through the deliberate act. However, in ordinary life we do trace the cause *through* other events to reach a deliberate act, even though these other events are abnormal in the context. Feinberg has called this the *voluntary intervention principle*: the free, deliberate, and informed act or omission of a human being, intended to produce the consequences that it in fact produced, negatives causal connection. Negligent action is not deliberate and informed and it is not included under this principle.

It must be understood that Hart and Honoré are not maintaining that the voluntary intervention principle holds in all contexts in ordinary life where causal language is used. In particular, they maintain that, in the context of interpersonal transactions when one person induces another to act or in some situations where one person provides or fails to provide another person with an opportunity for acting, the voluntary intervention principle does not hold.

Thus far in considering Hart and Honoré's views on causality in common sense thinking I have treated the case of some event that is not a human action but that is an effect or consequence of some other event or human action or omission. According to Hart and Honoré, however, in ordinary language there are two other situations where causal language is used.

In what they call "interpersonal transactions" one person causes another to act or else a human action is done as a consequence or the result of another human action. Hart and Honoré point out that sometimes it would be unnatural to say "he caused me to act," when a person induced someone to act by threats, coercion, or exercise of authority. It would be more natural to say "he made me do it." The expression "he caused me to act" would be positively misleading if one acted as a result of someone's advice or request.[19]

When someone causes someone to act or makes someone act, the first person intends the second person to do the act in question and the first person's use of persuasion or coercion makes the second person's act not wholly voluntary. But when one advises or requests someone to do something, neither of these conditions are fulfilled. Yet, despite these differences between, say, inducing and advising someone to act, there are important similarities: (a) the first actor's words or deeds are part of the second actor's reason for acting; (b) the second actor forms the intention to do the act in question only after the first actor's intervention.

Hart and Honoré point out that there are borderline and mixed cases possessing some of the features of interpersonal transactions and some of the features of the non-interpersonal transaction context. In hypnosis the hypnotist causes the subject to act, but he or she does not give reasons. In cases of provocation in the law, another person's deeds or words cause someone to lose normal self-control, but here again the actor does not act in accordance with reasons provided by the provoker.

Causal language is also appropriate where there are opportunities. Sometimes one person does not provide another person with a reason for action but rather with an opportunity for action. A person may carelessly leave open a door to a home entrusted to his or her care and this may provide an opportunity for a thief to enter the house and steal some valuable possessions. In such a case one might speak of the loss of the valuable possessions as a result or consequence of the failure to lock the door and the careless person would be held responsible. In other cases someone's failure to provide something may be said to have resulted in some harm. Thus, one person's failure to provide another with a certain kind of machinery to which he or she is entitled may result in an economic loss.

According to Hart and Honoré, when causal language is used in circumstances in which someone has provided or failed to provide someone else with an opportunity, it is implied that there is a deviation from standard practice or expected procedure; in short, it is implied that the provision of or failure to provide someone with an opportunity is abnormal. Thus, if a person stores wood in a basement and thereby gives a pyromaniac an opportunity to burn down the house, we would not say that the fire was the result of storing the wood in the basement since there was no deviation from the normal. But if someone who is entrusted to look after a house carelessly leaves the door open and the silver spoons are stolen, we would say that the loss of the spoons was the result of the person's leaving the door open since this was abnormal in the context.

Hart and Honoré believe that common sense ideas of causality are to a large degree embodied in legal thinking. In *Causation in the Law* they show in great detail how in various aspects of the law from torts to criminal law common sense ideas of causality structure legal thought. Consider just a few of the many cases Hart and Honoré use to support their theory.

As we have seen, Hart and Honoré argue that in common sense causal thinking the intervention of a voluntary human action negatives a causal connection. Following Feinberg we have called this the voluntary intervention principle. Hart and Honoré find the same principle at work in the law of torts. For example, in *Alexander v. The Town of New Castle*[20] the defendant, who negligently allowed a pit to remain in the road, was not liable to the plaintiff, a sheriff, when an escaping prisoner threw the sheriff into the pit. The escaping prisoner's voluntary action of throwing the sheriff into the pit negatives the causal connection between the negligent action of the plaintiff and the harm to the sheriff. In the case of *Cole v. German Savings and Loan Society*[21] the defendant negligently left open an unguarded elevator shaft. But he was not held liable because another person, impersonating the elevator operator and knowing the elevator was not there, invited the plaintiff to step into the elevator, which he did, suffering injuries. Again the intervention of the voluntary action of the person impersonating the elevator operator broke the causal chain between the negligent action of the defendant and the subsequent harm to the plaintiff.

Hart and Honoré attempt to show that the voluntary intervention principle is at work in the criminal law too. In *Smith v. State*[22] the accused wrongly wounded the victim. But a doctor in probing the wound killed him. The court held that the intervention of the doctor relieved the defendant of the responsibility for homicide. In *People v. Elder*[23] the accused knocked the victim down and a bystander then kicked the victim so that he died. The court held in view of the bystander's intervention that the defendant was not guilty. In both these cases the voluntary action of another person broke the causal connection between the defendant's action and the victim's death.

We have seen that Hart and Honoré argue that in common sense causal thinking an abnormal intervening factor breaks the causal chain between someone's harmful action and some subsequent harm, but that a normal factor does not. Hart and Honoré find the same principle operating in the law. Consider the following two cases from the law of torts. In *Toledo and Ohio Central Railroad Co. v. Kibler and Co.*[24] a railroad negligently delayed a shipment of goods, which, during the delay, was destroyed by an unprecedented flood. The court held that the railroad was relieved of liability. Hart and Honoré argue that the causal chain was broken because of the unprecedented nature of the flood; they imply that, in geographical areas known for floods, it would not have been considered abnormal and would not break the chain of causality.

In *Carslogie Steamship Co. v. Royal Norwegian Government*[25] a ship was damaged by the appellant's negligence. After temporary repairs had made the ship seaworthy, it was further damaged in a winter storm while crossing the Atlantic to have permanent repairs. The court held that the storm's damage was not a consequence of the original negligence. Hart and Honoré apparently believe that the court's decision was based on the idea that the winter storm was abnormal; consequently it negatived the causal connection between the appellant's negligence and the damage to the ship while crossing the Atlantic.

As I pointed out above, Hart and Honoré argue that in common sense causal thinking there exists a context of interpersonal transactions in which causal language is used. In this context by threats, coercion, exercise of authority, and the like one person induces another to act. In these cases, but not in cases of giving advice, one may speak of one person's causing or making the second person act in a certain way. Hart and Honoré distinguish inducing from advising on the basis of two criteria. First, the advisee, unlike the inducee, is acting in a wholly voluntary manner. Second, the adviser is indifferent to what the advisee does whereas the inducer is not indifferent to the action of the inducee.

In the law, Hart and Honoré show the operation of this causal idea. For example, in *Smith v. Kaye*,[26] a wife's sister and sister-in-law were found to have enticed the wife to leave her husband and the husband was awarded damages. Hart and Honoré say, "Defendant appealed to the wife's emotions and thereby showed that, even if what they tendered was advice, they were not indifferent whether it was accepted."[27] One might say in this case that the defendants' action made the wife leave her husband.

Hart and Honoré also point out that in ordinary life causal language is used where one person provides or fails to provide another person with an opportunity for action. In such cases there is the assumption that there is a deviation from standard practice. Hart and Honoré show that this causal notion is also found in the law. For example, in *Stansbie v. Troman*[28] the defendant, a painter, "was held liable for the loss of goods stolen by a thief who entered when, in breach of contract, defendant had left the house where he was employed without locking the front door."[29] There was a causal connection between defendant's act and the subsequent harm; this connection, Hart and Honoré say, may be succinctly described by saying that the defendant "occasioned" it.[30]

Although Hart and Honoré stress the influence of common sense ordinary notions of causality in the law, they do not overlook the fact that policy questions sometimes determine judgments of legal causality. As we have seen, in New York[31] if a fire is negligently started and spreads to several buildings, damage may be recovered only with respect to the first building damaged by the fire. The negligent act is not the legal cause of the damage to the other buildings. This limitation is not based on any common sense notion of causality but on policy considerations. Hart and Honoré illustrate similar policy considerations that have entered into the law. They insist, however, that these are only an important factor in some legal causal judgments.

Evaluation of the Theory

Common Sense Causal Notions and Policy

Hart and Honoré are critical of modern theories of legal causation in which judgments of proximate cause are based on considerations of policy on the grounds that in a wide area of the law causal judgments are in fact based on common sense causal notions. However, it can be argued that common sense causal notions are themselves based on considerations of policy. If they are, then the modern view and Hart and Honoré's are not essentially different.

P. H. Nowell-Smith argues this thesis[32] by attempting to show that various aspects of what Hart and Honoré believe are part of common sense causal thinking—the attributive use of causal language, the appeal to abnormality, and voluntary action to break the causal chain—are in fact based on policy considerations. Nowell-Smith's argument seems to be this:

(1) Legal causal notions are based upon or identical with common sense causal notions.
(2) Common sense causal notions are based upon policy considerations.

---

(3) Therefore, legal causal notions are based upon policy considerations.

Notice that his conclusion, (3), is identical to one version of the modern theory.

Since Hart and Honoré accept premise (1), the key premise in Nowell-Smith's argument is (2). How does he support (2)? According to Nowell-Smith, Hart and Honoré's notion of the attributive use of causal language commits them to the thesis that causal judgments are not factual. Nowell-Smith argues: "To attribute is neither to describe nor to explain; what, then, is it? It is tempting to answer that it is to fix on the agent the responsibility for the subsequent harm, and this comes perilously near to saying that the concept of cause . . . presupposes the concept of liability."[33] However, Nowell-Smith is mistaken. There is no reason to suppose that, when some person P says "Jones did X" in an attributive context, P is not describing what happened. P might well be ascribing the harm to Jones by describing what happened. Of course, in one sense such a statement does fix the responsibility for X on Jones. As Nowell-Smith points out, Hart and Honoré distinguish two senses of the expression "Y is responsible for X." In the first sense "Y is responsible for X" means "Y is liable for X." In the second sense "Y is responsible for X" means "Y did X (caused X)." They admit that, in the *second* sense, P is fixing the responsibility for X on Jones in saying that Jones did X. But this sense is perfectly innocuous; it does not damage their thesis that causal judgments are descriptive. Hart and Honoré go on to argue that a judgment of responsibility in the second sense (Jones did X) might be a non-tautological reason for a judgment of responsibility in the first sense (Jones is liable for X).

Nowell-Smith objects to this line of reasoning: "But to say . . . the connexion between these two [expressions] cannot be analytic since causality is here the *ground* of liability is too brisk. Causality is not as factual as it seems if the idea of imputing responsibility must be used for establishing it."[34] However, he has nowhere shown that in order to establish "Jones did X" one must use the idea of imputing responsibility in the first sense of responsible, that is, imputing the liability to Jones for X. Clearly this sense of responsible is the only relevant one. Nowell-Smith goes on to argue: "This consideration is re-inforced by the fact that in attributive contexts our decision as to whether something is or is not a cause depends on the *purpose* of the inquiry. Now since the purpose of legal inquiries is to assign liability, if this dependence is *logical*, considerations of legal policy are built into causal principles from the start."[35] However, this argument seems to beg the question whether legal causality is based on policy considerations in the relevant sense. Let us grant that attributive inquiry depends on the purpose of the inquiry. Let us also grant that the purpose of legal inquiry is to assign liability. All of this is compatible with Hart and Honoré's view that one assigns the liability to Y for harming X by first determining whether Y did X and that this initial judgment is purely factual.

Nowell-Smith also argues that both factors used by Hart and Honoré to "break the causal chain"—abnormality and voluntary interventions—"are not as purely factual as they seem." Since "nature knows nothing of abnormality"[36] we decide what is sufficiently abnormal and we do so if and only if it is sufficiently abnormal to cut off responsibility.

One supposes Nowell-Smith means by "being responsible" being liable. If so, his view could not be correct, since one makes causal judgments based on considerations of abnormality when the causal agent could not be responsible in this sense. For example, suppose lightning strikes the ground igniting some dry wood. Because of a gentle breeze a fire spreads that destroys the woods. Here there is no abnormality; the causal chain is not broken. Contrast this with a similar case in which a hurricane spreads the fire. Here an abnormal event breaks the causal chain. In this example the causal agent, the lightning, being an inanimate thing, could not be liable in the sense at issue.

Furthermore, Nowell-Smith is misleading when he says that we decide what is sufficiently abnormal. Quite often what is abnormal is clear from the context so that a decision is not at issue. Surely, Nowell-Smith has set up a false dichotomy: either an abnormality must be based on a natural distinction or it must be a human decision.

Nowell-Smith also argues that judgments about whether an action is fully voluntary are not purely factual since in making them one covertly introduces the idea of being responsible for the action. Again one assumes that Nowell-Smith means by being responsible for the action being liable. But, if so, there are many cases in which one determines whether someone's action is fully voluntary without determining whether someone is liable. After all, there are many cases of voluntary action where there is no question of any harm being done, and no question of moral or legal blame, where, in short, the question of liability does not even arise. My getting out of bed and mowing the lawn may well be a fully voluntary action, but there is nothing I am liable for.

Finally, Nowell-Smith argues that the "twin third factors"—abnormality or voluntary action—that cut off causality have a "suspicious correspondence to the twin policy-substitutes of the modernist, foreseeability and moral fault." Consider abnormality. Nowell-Smith argues that "consequences that are too remote for causal connexion on the grounds of the occurrence of an abnormal event will be just those that are not foreseeable by the agent or 'within the risk' that makes his act negligent."[37]

Now Hart and Honoré at one point do say: "For present purposes it does not matter if 'unforeseeable' is substituted for 'abnormal'. 'Unforeseeable' is the word more commonly used by lawyers."[38] However, when they come to evaluate the foreseeability doctrine, foreseeability and abnormality are distinguished. They argue that the foreseeability theory is not a correct account of how the law does operate, nor a correct account of how the law should operate. They cite cases in which the courts have held a defendant liable for harm that is not foreseeable although the defendant caused the harm in terms of common sense categories. For example, in the famous case of *Re Polemis* "defendants' servants negligently allowed a heavy plank to fall into the hold of a ship. There was, unknown to them, petrol vapour in the hold of the ship and the ship caught fire, apparently because the plank in falling ignited a spark and set fire to the vapour."[39] The court found the defendant liable on the ground that "it was immaterial that the defendant could not reasonably have foreseen the destruction of the ship at the time of their negligent act, since the loss was the 'direct' consequence of it."[40] Hart and Honoré go on to argue that the court's reference to "direct" is simply an obscure way of saying that no abnormal facts intervened between the dropping of the plank and the fire. So here is a case in which foreseeability is absent and also any abnormal intervening factor. Hart and Honoré refer to other cases of a similar kind. Thus the law does not always base liability on foreseeability.

Hart and Honoré also argue that the law should not only hold defendants liable for what they can foresee. Duties in torts, they say, are for the protection of persons and property generally, "not only of those members whose presence within range defendant had reason to suspect in advance."[41] So they might well wish to maintain that *Re Polemis* was a fair decision and they would also argue that Nowell-Smith's claim that abnormality has a suspicious correspondence to foreseeability does not seem to be true.

In all fairness to Nowell-Smith, he only maintains that this correspondence holds "by and large."[42] But even if this is so, it would not show what he wants. The foreseeability doctrine and the theory of Hart and Honoré could produce similar results in a wide range of cases without judgments of abnormality themselves being based on policy considerations.

Consider voluntary action. Nowell-Smith asserts, "the idea that the fully voluntary act of another breaks the causal chain looks as if it may depend on the idea that there is now another agent on whom liability should fall." He goes on to argue that we "should not, of course, want [liability] to fall on a wholly innocent plaintiff or third party,"[43] but he claims that this can be avoided by showing that the act of the third party was not wholly voluntary. Indeed, Nowell-Smith says that he can find "no case in which a wholly *innocent* voluntary action of plaintiff or a third party is allowed to negative causal connexion between defendant's negligent act and the subsequent harm." This shows, he says, that voluntary action does not break the causal chain. "It does so only when it can be used in an argument for shifting liability onto someone else."[44]

But there are cases in which the person whose voluntary action breaks the causal chain is innocent of any crime. In a jurisdiction where suicide is not a crime one finds the following case.[45] A accuses B of killing A's daughter. B does not deny the charge and promises to commit suicide. After eight days B has not committed suicide. A fixes a noose and tells B to hang herself, which she does. The court holds that A did not commit murder since A did not threaten or coerce B. Interpreted in Hart and Honoré's terms, B's action was fully voluntary and broke the causal chain between A's action and B's death. But B was innocent of any wrongdoing since suicide was not a crime in this jurisdiction. In this case there is no shift of responsibility (liability) to someone else. Outside the law there are many cases in which innocent third parties break the causal chain for the simple reason that there is no harm or crime that is at issue.

Is Hart and Honoré's theory saved from the charge that no policy questions are involved in making causal judgments in the law? Another consideration may indicate that they are not. As we have seen, what one picks out as the abnormal factor in a situation is relative to a point of view. Recall the doctor who picked out the ulcer as the cause of a man's indigestion, while the wife picked out the man's eating parsnips as the cause. It may be suggested that the point of view one takes is determined by values and policy considerations and that the same sort of thing could occur in the law. One judge picks out X as the abnormal factor and another judge picks out Y. Consequently, depending on the point of view and hence the value orientation of the judges that make up the court, the court may come to conflicting judgments as to what is the proximate cause of a harm. Thus it may be the case that what was suggested by Nowell-Smith is correct after all.

Although I can find no evidence that Hart and Honoré deal explicitly with this problem, their theory can be interpreted in a way that mitigates the influence of value considerations in judgments of legal causation. To begin with, in general the court is not being asked to judge whether X or Y is the cause of some harm in contexts where considerations of abnormality are at issue. According to Hart and Honoré, the typical case is one in which some person P performs some act or omission that is alleged to result in some harm. The typical causal question is whether some outside factor negatives the causal relation between P's act and the harm. Typically, if the court finds some abnormal third factor, P is not responsible. Presumably this is true even if the court disagrees about what the abnormal factor is. So long as some abnormal factor is found, P is not liable. So in the typical case in which abnormality enters the picture, the question of whether or not abnormality itself is determined by value judgments has little practical import.

Moreover, sometimes the court is guided by statistical considerations of what is abnormal.[46] For example, in some cases involving the intervention of animals in a causal chain, what is considered abnormal may be a function of what is typical for animals of that species. Furthermore, as I have argued elsewhere,[47] it is possible to explicate abnormality entirely in terms of statistical considerations and to eschew judgments of abnormality based on value considerations. Thus even if some value considerations do in fact enter into judgments of causality in the law *via* judgments of abnormality, Hart and Honoré's theory still differs considerably from the modern policy theory, for the latter maintains that value considerations are involved in *all* judgments of proximate cause and that this involvement is impossible to eliminate.

One other consideration concerning the relation between policy considerations and Hart and Honoré's theory of legal causation should be mentioned. As we will see later in this chapter, the stage-setting exclusion principle may have implications in application that are unfortunate from a policy point of view. This does not mean that their theory of legal causation presupposes policy considerations as Nowell-Smith believes, but it may mean that, if Hart and Honoré are correct about certain causal principles found in the law, these should be reshaped in terms of policy considerations. There is no reason why Hart and Honoré should be opposed to this suggestion. It is one thing to say, as the modern theorists of legal causation do, that all causal judgments are based on policy judgments and another thing to say that some causal principles found in the law should be changed in the light of policy considerations.

I have argued so far that Nowell-Smith is unsuccessful in showing that the common sense causal concepts assumed by Hart and Honoré are in fact based on policy considerations; that the choice of which factor is abnormal in a common sense causal judgment does not mean that policy considerations enter into legal causal judgments; and that the stage-setting exclusion principle does not necessarily mean that policy considerations in causal judgments in the law is inevitable. It should be emphasized, however, that this defense of Hart and Honoré is only partial. I have not shown that

(1) Policy considerations do not enter into many legal causal judgments.

They may in fact enter into legal judgments in more subtle and indirect ways than we have considered. Furthermore, I have not shown that the normative assumption of Hart and Honoré that common sense causal notions should be utilized in wide areas of the law is not based on policy considerations. Thus even if (1), a factual claim, is established, the following normative thesis may still be true:

(2) Policy considerations should determine either directly or indirectly whether any causal judgments should be made in the law and what kind of causal judgments should be made.

The above considerations suggest that perhaps the modern theory of legal causation with its emphasis on policy considerations could be rehabilitated. We will return to this possibility in the conclusion to this chapter.

Common Sense Causal Notions and Empirical Investigation

Hart and Honoré argue that common sense causal notions are embodied in legal causal thinking and, in order to illuminate the latter, they attempt to give an account of what these notions are. One question to be raised about Hart and Honoré's attempt to specify some of the major elements of the common sense notion of causality has to do with the verification of their claims concerning these elements. Hart and Honoré do not appeal to empirical studies of language nor even to the writings of famous authors or to the *Oxford English Dictionary*. Rather they seem to rely primarily on their own linguistic intuitions. They use causal language in their everyday speech in such and such a way, and they assume that this is how it is used in general.

The appeal to linguistic intuition to verify statements of ordinary language is risky, however. The way one thinks one uses language and the way one actually uses it may be very different. For example, the way Hart and Honoré actually use causal language may not be in keeping with what was referred to above as the voluntary intervention principle. Perhaps this principle is reflected in their ordinary use of causal language, but they give us no reason to suppose that it is.

Moreover, even if it does reflect their own use, their principles may not reflect people's use of causal language in general; in other words, Hart and Honoré may be an unrepresentative sample. One might suspect that different sub-groups in society have different causal language. For example, people with a classic liberal ideology might be kindly disposed toward the principle of voluntary intervention and this would be reflected in their causal language. On the other hand, the causal language of socialists might not reflect this principle. The truth of these two hypotheses would have to be determined by empirical research. Hart and Honoré's theory of ordinary causal language should be treated, then, as an hypothesis to be verified by reliable methods. Until such verification is done, a skeptical attitude toward their theory is justified.

This point affects their theory of legal causality. Unless we have reliable evidence about our ordinary causal notions we cannot reasonably assume that they are embodied in legal thinking. Moreover, although Hart and Honoré's account of legal causal language could be correct even if they are mistaken about the characteristics of ordinary causal language, one may well suspect that their hypotheses about ordinary causal language have affected their views on legal causal language. At the very least, their beliefs about ordinary causal language will have influenced not only which legal cases they selected to support their theory of legal causality but their interpretation of these cases. Legal cases are numerous and are subject to various interpretations. It is not implausible to suppose that, if Hart and Honoré had held a different view of common sense causal notions, by citing and interpreting other cases, they still could have found support for their thesis that common sense causal notions are embodied in legal causal thinking.

Granted that Hart and Honoré's views should be considered as hypotheses to be tested by reliable evidence and that such evidence is not yet available, one can still raise doubts about the particular hypotheses they assume concerning common sense causal thinking. Because these doubts may themselves be based on unreliable linguistic intuitions they should be considered merely as plausible alternative hypotheses requiring reliable methods of testing.

But which of their ideas about common sense legal causality would it be interesting to consider hypotheses subject to empirical test and how would the possible falsification of these hypotheses affect their overall scheme? It should be clear from our discussion that Hart and Honoré's theory of ordinary causal notions is complex. They argue that there is a difference in how the judgments of causality can be defended by general statements in interpersonal transactions context and in other contexts; they specify different criteria that are used to say that a causal chain is broken (voluntary human intervention and abnormality); they maintain that there is a central notion of causality on which other concepts are based; they distinguish different contexts (explanatory and attributive contexts) in the use of causal judgments. It is difficult to see how all of these ideas are connected—or indeed if they are—and, in particular, which of these ideas are central to their major concerns. Hart and Honoré say very little explicitly to help us decide.

One must at least initially distinguish between Hart and Honoré's theory of ordinary causation and their doctrine of legal causality. As I have stressed again and again, they believe that ordinary causal ideas are embodied in the law. But it seems clear that Hart and Honoré either do not believe or else do not show that all of the common sense notions they discuss are relevant to the law. For example, although they argue at some length that particular causal judgments in interpersonal transactions are not defended by appeal to even loose generalizations and although this idea seems important in their analysis of ordinary common sense causal thinking, it plays a negligible role in their analysis of legal causality. On the other hand, the voluntary intervention principle, which they argue operates in common sense thinking, plays a major role in their views on legal causality.

One must also distinguish what is peripheral in their analysis of common sense causal thinking from what is not. As we have seen, they argue that there is a central notion of causality (a human action that manipulates or changes some object in the environment) and they maintain that other ideas are based on this. Yet the importance of this thesis to their other views on common sense causality is not clear. It seems possible to reject their account of the central notion of causality and yet accept their other ideas. To be sure, if their central notion of causality is accepted, it may give some unity to the other ordinary notions of causality they analyze by showing their historical or logical connection to the central notion. But it seems possible to achieve unity in other ways.

In what follows let us consider some of Hart and Honoré's ideas about common sense causality as empirical hypotheses to be tested and let us specify when possible what the consequences of the rejection of these hypotheses would be for Hart and Honoré's overall scheme. When appropriate I will suggest that their ideas might be interpreted not just as empirical hypotheses but as policy proposals or even as statements of logical connections.

The Central Notion

According to Hart and Honoré, the central notion of causality in common sense thinking is based on the bodily manipulation of an inanimate object that brings about certain changes in the object. This central notion has been developed and extended to include cases of one natural event, for example, the wind, causing another natural event, for example, damage to a tree, as well as cases of one human action, for example, threat, causing another human action, for example, compliance with the threat. One way of understanding the thesis that the central notion of causality in common sense thinking is based on the bodily manipulation of an inanimate object that brings about certain changes in the object is to suppose that Hart and Honoré are putting forth the following historical hypothesis:

> (H_1) Historically all of our concepts of causality evolved from the central notion of causality.

I have just said it is unclear just how important (H_1) is to Hart and Honoré's overall theory. It would seem that (H_1) could be rejected and that all of their other theses about common sense causality would survive. However, (H_1) does provide a unified account of our ordinary causal notions in that it asserts an historical connection between the various common sense causal notions, bringing them together under one basic idea and its extension. If (H_1) is rejected, the connections between the various causal notions specified by Hart and Honoré remain unclear and some other unifying ideas must be sought. Is there any reason to accept (H_1)? Even if one admits linguistic intuition as a reliable method of verifying theses about ordinary usage this would hardly verify (H_1). After all, (H_1) is not about contemporary usage, but about its historically distant origins. Thus, present-day linguistic intuition seems irrelevant. Unfortunately, it is not clear that there is historical evidence to support (H_1).

It may be argued, however, that to interpret Hart and Honoré's thesis as (H_1) is to misunderstand them. In particular, it may be urged that they intend their view as a logical thesis, not an historical one. Thus it might be argued that in order to possess the concept of one natural event's causing another natural event, or to possess the concept of one human action's causing another human action, one must have the concept of a human action's bringing about some change in an inanimate object. This suggests the following logical thesis:

> (L_1) A logically necessary condition of having any notion of causality is having the central notion of causality.

But (L_1) is not obviously true. One can imagine a group of people who believe that floods and other natural events intervene in the natural course of events, but not that humans do. Indeed, they might believe that what would seem to us as an intervention and its result, for example, striking a sharp blow to the nose and a nose bleed, was in fact the result of some natural occurrence associated with the nose bleed, for example, the wind or the position of the sun. To be sure, such views sound strange to us but they are completely coherent.

Still another possible interpretation of Hart and Honoré's thesis is the psychological one that people learn the central notion first and then extend it in various ways. However, Hart and Honoré provide no evidence to support this hypothesis.

Other interpretations are perhaps also possible, but we need not pursue them here. As indicated above, despite providing a unifying idea for the various common sense notions of causality analyzed by Hart and Honoré, the central notion may well be rejected without great loss. I suggest that it should be or else that the authors should clarify its status and the evidence for it.

Attributive and Explanatory Contexts

Recall that, in their critique of Mill, Hart and Honoré claimed that he did not distinguish between attributive and explanatory contexts. In the explanatory context one is puzzled about why or how something happened and a causal explanation relieves one's puzzlement. But in the attributive context one may understand why something occurs and yet be puzzled about what harm can be attributed to some agent. This puzzlement in the attributive context, they say, is generated by a factor in the situation, in addition to the agent's action, that has some of the characteristics by which common sense distinguishes causes from mere causal conditions.

Some commentators on Hart and Honoré's work have been puzzled by the distinction between explanatory and attributive contexts. Martin Golding doubts that it is "anywhere clearly drawn,"[48] and John Mansfield believes that it really comes down to what seems to be an insignificant difference: in the explanatory context thought starts with a later puzzling event and moves backward to an earlier event, namely the cause of the later event; in an attributive context thought moves forward from an earlier to a later event (attributed to the earlier one).[49] I agree that Hart and Honoré's two contexts are puzzling but not for the reasons given by Golding and Mansfield.[50] Whatever unclarity there is in Hart and Honoré's distinction, they seem to be committed to the following existential hypothesis:

(H_2) There are contexts in using ordinary causal notions in which one understands why some harm occurred but does not know whether to attribute it to a particular agent A's action that is part of the context.

Consider a typical case of causal attribution. A lights a match; a fire starts. B arrives on the scene and pours gasoline on the fire just before it is about to go out. The fire then spreads and burns down C's house. The key question in the context of attribution is whether A or B caused C's house to burn down—that is, whether C's house's burning down should be attributed to A or to B. Clearly the presence of B's action in the chain of events raises questions and creates doubts. What is puzzling about this example is that on Hart and Honoré's view the presence of B's action in the chain of events also raises questions in the explanatory context.

Look at this case from the explanatory point of view. Suppose we know that C's house has burnt down and we want to know why. After tracing the causal chain back to B's action, the question arises if in order to explain what happened the cause should be traced back to A's action. It would seem that the presence of B's action raises problems in both contexts. The example cannot therefore be a clear confirmatory instance of (H_2).

Indeed, it is difficult to imagine a confirmatory instance of (H_2) if one is using the term "understand why" in the common sense way Hart and Honoré seem to have in mind. For, in that way, to understand why something occurs involves picking out the cause from among mere causal conditions. But to distinguish a cause from a mere causal condition would seem to be tantamount to deciding in cases like the above whether A's action or B's action or neither was the cause of the harm. This in turn is tantamount to attributing the harm to either A's or B's action or neither.

In the case under consideration, in order to pick out the cause from among mere causal conditions one might appeal to the voluntary intervention principle. If B's action was voluntary, the causal chain is broken. We would explain the harm to C's property in terms of B's action, but not A's action. This amounts to attributing the harm to B. If, on the other hand, B's action was not completely voluntary, we would explain the harm by tracing the causal influence through B to A; this would amount to attributing the harm to A. If the above story was changed slightly, however, and the fire took place in a laboratory situation (normally free from oxygen) after oxygen escaped into the laboratory, one might explain the harm by citing the presence of oxygen; in this case one would not attribute the harm to either A or B.

It would seem, therefore, that unless further clarification is made, the attributive context is, on Hart and Honoré's account, simply a special case of the explanatory context in which human action and some subsequent harm is involved. In explaining why some harm occurred in this special case, one must decide whether to attribute it to some particular human action. One might, of course, explain something in common sense terms—why there was a landslide—yet not attribute the result to anyone because no human actors were involved. (The landslide was caused by heavy rainfall.) One might explain some harm in common sense terms and not attribute the harm to anyone because, although human actors were involved, the cause was not a human action. (The oxygen leaked into the laboratory and caused the fire.) But if a particular human action is the explanation of the harm, it is difficult to see why the harm would not be attributed to this action; the explanation in this case would involve attribution. If, on the other hand, the explanation of the harm does not involve a human action, how could the harm be attributed to a human action?

Naturally, if one accepts a different view on common sense causality from that of Hart and Honoré, an account that does not always involve picking out the cause from among mere causal conditions, confirmatory instances of (H_2) abound. In this case explaining why something occurred might just involve telling a simple or complicated causal story. In such a causal story one would not have to decide what is the cause and what is not; consequently one would not attribute the cause to any particular agent. We have already told such a story above: "A lights a match and a fire starts; B comes on the scene and pours gasoline on the fire just before it is about to go out; the fire spreads and burns down C's house." In obvious common sense terms one understands what has happened: if this story is true, one has explained what has happened. As I understand Hart and Honoré's account, the above simple causal story would not be considered explanatory since the cause of the harm was not selected.

I conclude that Hart and Honoré's distinction between the explanatory and attributive contexts is not what they seem to suppose. Since in any case it seems to play a relatively minor role in their thought, without further clarification it cannot be considered helpful.

Defense of Particular Causal Judgments

As we have seen, Hart and Honoré argue that in ordinary causal thinking causal judgments are defended, not by citing statements of invariable sequences, but by citing broader, less specific generalizations, ones that tend to be platitudinous. Thus, if one says that A's blow to B's nose causes B's nose to bleed, one defends this claim by citing some broadly framed generalization asserting, for example, that striking someone's nose a hard blow commonly brings about bleeding. Further, Hart and Honoré say that in order to justify one's judgment that A's blow caused B's nose to bleed it is necessary to distinguish this case "from counterexamples or cases outside the known limits of any generalization used."[51]

Further, Hart and Honoré also argue that to defend particular causal judgments in interpersonal transaction cases one does not use even broadly framed generalizations. Hart and Honoré's views here have some affinity with those traditional theories that make a sharp distinction between the explanation of human behavior and explanation in other contexts. This distinction is often invoked to differentiate between explanations in the natural sciences in which some particular event is subsumed under a generalization and explanations in the social sciences where no generalization is used but where empathetic understanding is appropriate.[52] Hart and Honoré do not appeal to empathetic understanding but they do maintain that in interpersonal transaction contexts one cites the actor's reasons to explain his or her action. They argue, moreover, that an appeal to reason R to explain actor A's behavior does not commit one to justifying one's claim that A acted because of R by reference to a loose generalization. Thus, they claim that the statement that one person did something because, for example, another threatened him carries no "implication or covert assertion that if the circumstances were repeated the same action would follow."[53]

Hart and Honoré's views are complicated. For example, they think that an actor's reasons and generalizations are connected in some way. They admit that a possible reason of an actor "is not independent of how in a general very broad sense most people act. If a person said he left the room 'because Caesar died in 44 B.C.' we should not understand him" and "we recognize as a reason for action (and therefore as a given person's reason on a particular occasion) something which is relevant to the promotion of some purpose known to be pursued by human beings and so renders an action eligible by human beings as we know them." The concept of a reason, they say, "therefore *presupposes* that, in general, human beings respond to certain situations in such ways as fleeing from danger, or conforming with social rules or conventions etc." Yet they say "this presupposition of broad similarity in human behavior . . . does not mean that, when on a particular occasion we assert that a person acted for a particular reason (e.g. to avoid threatened danger) we are committed to any assertion that, if the circumstances were repeated, the same action would follow."[54]

As I pointed out, although Hart and Honoré's distinction is apparently important for their theory of common sense causality, it plays no significant role in their views on legal causality. Thus even if Hart and Honoré's views about causal generalization are wrong or unjustified, they might still be correct about the law. Further, their views about causal generalization are independent of their other views about common sense causality. So rejection of their views on generalization does not entail rejection of their entire theory of common sense causality.

One hypothesis suggested by Hart and Honoré's statement about the use of loose generalizations in non-interpersonal transaction contexts is this:

(H_3) In cases of non-interpersonal transactions, in defending the causal judgment that A caused B, it would always be appropriate to cite a generalization of the form "Things of type A will commonly bring about things of type B."

One might have two reservations about the formulation of (H_3). One problem is that it is unclear if Hart and Honoré are committed to the phrase "always be." However, since they do not explicitly cite any exceptions or qualifications to their views, the "always be" seems plausible. The other reservation is that even if they do maintain that it is always appropriate to justify the particular causal judgment that A is the cause of B by citing a loose generalization, it is not completely clear they maintain that a loose generalization of the type specified in (H_3) would always be appropriate. Unfortunately, they do not cite any examples to illustrate their views. However, (H_3) is not an implausible interpretation of their theory.

Hart and Honoré seem to think that it is impossible to state any correct strict generalization that could be used to justify a particular causal judgment, and they also seem to assume that the following hypothesis is correct:

(H_4) In cases of non-interpersonal transaction, in defending the causal judgment that A causes B, it would always be inappropriate to cite a strict generalization of the form "Things of type A invariably bring about things of type B."

As we have seen, in interpersonal contexts Hart and Honoré argue that no generalization—either strict or loose—can be cited to justify the particular causal judgment that X acted because of reason R although they admit that reasons for action presuppose some broad similarity in human reaction. This suggests that they assume the further empirical hypothesis:

(H_5) In cases of interpersonal transactions, in defending the causal judgment that A caused B, it would never be appropriate to cite either a loose generalization of the form "Things of type A will commonly bring about things of type B" or a strict generalization of the form "Things of type A will invariably bring about things of type B."

However, their idea that a reason for action presupposes broad similarities in human reactions is perhaps best understood as a logical thesis specifying a logically necessary condition for someone's having a reason, rather than an empirical hypothesis, about what it would be appropriate to say in ordinary speech. Ordinary usage would be relevant to such a logical thesis because the latter would purport to describe the logical implications of our ordinary concept of having a reason. Consider, then, the thesis:

(L_2) In a situation S in order for a person X to do A because X believes S has property P it is logically necessary that in general people do A in situations with property P.

Hart and Honoré seem to maintain that in order for someone to flee from a situation because he or she believes it is dangerous (that is, the danger of the situation is the person's reason for fleeing), it is logically necessary that in general people must flee from dangerous situations. Yet they maintain that it would not be appropriate in interpersonal transactions to cite the loose generalization "people commonly flee from dangerous situations" to justify a particular causal judgment, for example, the causal judgment that Jones fled from the scene because he thought Smith, who was present and who had threatened Jones, was dangerous.

Empirical hypotheses (H_3)-(H_5) as well as logical thesis (L_2) can be questioned. Consider (H_3)—in cases of non-interpersonal transactions, in defending the causal judgment that A caused B, it would always be appropriate to cite a generalization of the form "Things of type A will commonly bring about things of type B." Although knowledge of loose generalizations usually aids and facilitates making particular judgments, one need not defend the statement that A caused B by saying that events of type A commonly bring about events of type B. In fact, such a loose generalization might be false and yet the particular causal judgment could be correct.[55] Suppose one says that A's striking B a sharp blow to the nose caused B's death. This could be a true causal statement yet it would not be true that striking someone a sharp blow to the nose commonly causes death. Thus this loose generalization could not be used to defend this particular causal judgment. Special knowledge of the circumstances of the blow rather than some loose generalization might in this case justify the particular causal judgment.

(H_4)—in cases of non-interpersonal transaction, in defending the causal judgment that A causes B, it would always be inappropriate to cite a strict generalization of the form "Things of type A invariably bring about things of type B"—seems dubious too. Although citing a loose generalization is often appropriate and citing a strict generalization is often inappropriate in defending particular causal judgments, this is not always so. Consider the case in which we know that a strict generalization relevant to defending a particular causal judgment is true. Then it would be inappropriate to defend the particular causal judgment, for example, that A's cutting off B's head caused B's death, by citing the loose generalization, for example, that cutting off someone's head commonly brings about death. Since we know that decapitation invariably leads to death, to defend a particular causal judgment by reference to it would make little sense. Hart and Honoré seem to believe that it is impossible to make correct statements of invariable sequences. But the true statement "Cutting off someone's head invariably brings about death" shows that this is not so.

(H_5)—in cases of interpersonal transactions, in defending the causal judgment that A caused B, it would never be appropriate to cite either a loose generalization of the form "Things of type A will commonly bring about things of type B" or a strict generalization of the form "Things of type A will invariably bring about things of type B"—seems also to be dubious. If one says, for example, that A's threat of death caused B to give A his wallet, it seems quite appropriate in defending this judgment to cite the loose generalization that death threats commonly induce people to give up their wallets.

Indeed, one wonders why in an interpersonal transaction context the particular causal judgment A causes B does not implicitly assume some strict generalization although one might not know how to state it precisely. Hart and Honoré's thesis that we are not committed in interpersonal transaction contexts to the generalization that X will act for a particular reason in the same circumstances seems either trivially true or unintelligible depending on how it is interpreted. If by the "same circumstances," one means the same external circumstances, then the thesis is certainly true. After all, X may respond differently to the same external circumstances given different goals and beliefs about these circumstances. But given that the psychological circumstances are also the same, Hart and Honoré's thesis is difficult to understand. If X has the same beliefs and goals, if X is just as rational in both cases, and so on, why does X act to avoid danger in one case and not in the other? Hart and Honoré do not say why.

The logical thesis (L_2)—in a situation S in order for a person X to do A because X believes S has property P it is logically necessary that in general people do A in situations with property P—may also be questioned. If the human race, for example, because of genetic damage caused by radiation, began not to flee from danger, this would hardly undermine our concept of fleeing from danger as a reason. Surely people could still understand someone who has escaped radiation damage when they cited such a reason to explain their fleeing from danger. In this case, citing a loose generalization that people commonly flee from danger in order to defend the explanation would be inappropriate since the generalization would be wrong. But, as I argued above, citing such a generalization is not always appropriate.

The Stage-Setting Exclusion Hypothesis

It will be recalled that Hart and Honoré claim that certain outside factors that intervene in a causal situation break the causal chain between some wrongful act and subsequent harm and that one such factor is an abnormal condition. However, an abnormal condition that exists at the same time as the wrongful act does not break the causal chain but merely sets the stage before the actor comes on the scene. Thus Hart and Honoré can be interpreted as proposing an hypothesis about common sense causal thinking:

(H_6) In common sense causal thinking, a condition that exists at the same time as act A is never considered to break the causal connection between A and some subsequent harm.

Hart and Honoré offer no evidence to support (H_6). Furthermore, my linguistic intuition, at least, suggests that (H_6) is mistaken. Consider an example suggested by Feinberg.[56] Because of the prior existence of a segregation law a protest march results in a race riot. Let us suppose that from some relevant point of view the existence of the segregation law is abnormal. According to (H_6) one could not argue that the prior existence of the segregation law broke the causal connection between the march and the subsequent harm. To be sure, reasonable people might disagree over the cause of the riot. But it does not seem to be in accord with common sense thinking to exclude *a priori* the idea that the protest march was not to blame because of the prior existence of the law.

One could, of course, treat the stage-setting exclusion hypothesis, not as a factual thesis about ordinary usage, but as a policy about what should be allowed to break the causal chain. This policy could be stated as follows:

> (P_1) A condition that exists at the same time as act A should never be considered as breaking the causal connection between A and some subsequent harm.

However, the application of (P_1) to particular cases would be condemned by many on grounds of utility and social justice. Consider the protest march. Many people would maintain that it would be wrong to say the protest caused the riot; they would maintain that in all fairness the blame should be put on the prior segregation laws. Furthermore, they would maintain that, fairness aside, it is wrong on grounds of utility to blame the march rather than the laws. By blaming the march, they would insist, one would discourage protest marches, which in general have great utility for society. On the other hand to blame the segregation law would induce people to change the laws and that would have a beneficial effect on society.

If (H_6) is not true, then Hart and Honoré cannot argue, as they do, that (H_6) specifies a common sense way of thinking that is embodied in the law. They may, of course, still be correct that a stage-setting exclusion principle does operate in the law. But they could not support this by an appeal to common sense; common sense and the law would be in conflict. Further, if there is a stage-setting principle in the law, this principle could not be justified on policy grounds since the objections raised to (P_1) would apply. Without common sense or policy considerations to support it, a stage-setting exclusion principle in the law would have no reason to exist.

One might suppose that Hart and Honoré could have no reason to maintain that the stage-setting exclusion idea exist in common sense thinking. Should they not argue then that when voluntary human action is not at issue any abnormal factor, whether it sets the stage or comes on the scene later, breaks the causal chain? Should they not maintain:

> (H_7) When voluntary human intervention is not at issue in ordinary causal thinking, any abnormal condition—either one that exists at the same time as A or one that intervenes between A and B—breaks the causal chain between A and B.

But (H_7) is false. Some abnormal conditions that exist at the same time as A do not break the causal chain. Suppose person X is a diabetic (the abnormal condition of diabetes sets the stage). X is taken care of by a nurse N, who negligently fails to administer insulin, and X dies. X would not have died but for the prior condition of diabetes; yet this condition does not break the causal chain. N's wrongful action is the cause of X's death.

The crucial question is why some prior existing abnormal conditions do break the causal chain and some do not. However, this is just to say that the presence of an abnormality is not the whole story in determining when a causal chain is broken and that other factors must be taken into account. Thus Hart and Honoré could not easily give up (H_6) and accept (H_7). The diabetes case and the race riot case show that the situation is complex. Sometimes a stage-setting abnormal factor breaks the causal chain and sometimes it does not. If this point is granted, Hart and Honoré's neat characterization of common sense causal thinking in terms of abnormal factors breaking the causal chain seems to collapse.

The Abnormal Factor Intervention Hypothesis

As we have seen, Hart and Honoré argue that in ordinary causal thinking there are two basic criteria (abnormality and voluntary human action) that enable one to distinguish the cause of an event from mere causal conditions and permit one to say whether some factor broke the causal chain between some human action and some subsequent harm. Moreover, Hart and Honoré restrict the abnormality criterion to abnormal factors that come after the harmful human action. Hart and Honoré believe that the two basic criteria also play an important role in causal thinking in the law. With respect to the abnormality criterion they stress that what is considered abnormal may vary from context to context and may depend on one's point of view. Although we have found reasons to reject (H_7), a more moderate hypothesis specifying that, if voluntary human intervention is not at issue, then any abnormal factor that intervenes in the situation after the initial action breaks the causal chain may be correct. Consider:

> (H_8) Where voluntary human intervention is not at issue in ordinary causal thinking, any abnormal factor that intervenes between A and B breaks the causal chain between A and B.

This hypothesis is surely one of Hart and Honoré's major theses. It is crucial to their analyses of common sense causal notions and crucial to their thesis that ordinary concepts of causality are embodied in legal thinking.

Nevertheless, (H_8) seems incorrect. Consider the Case of the Incompetent Poisoner. Suppose Jones attempts to poison his senile aunt by putting arsenic in her nightly Ovaltine. Because of his incompetence, his efforts continue to be unsuccessful: sometimes he forgets to put the poison in the drink; sometimes he spills the glass; sometimes he puts the glass beyond her reach on her bed stand. In short, failure and bungling the job are normal in this context. Nevertheless, one night an abnormal event occurs. A strange and unprecedented wind comes through the window and pushes the glass on her bed stand so it is within her reach; she drinks the poison and expires. Nevertheless, the freak wind—the abnormal event—does not break the causal chain; Jones' action was still the cause of his aunt's death. So (H_8) is incorrect; consequently Hart and Honoré cannot argue that insofar as the law embodies the ideas of (H_8) it is based on common sense causal thinking.

One could, of course, construe Hart and Honoré's view not as an empirical hypothesis about ordinary causal language, but as a policy, namely:

> (P_2) Where voluntary human intervention is not at issue in ordinary causal thinking, any abnormal factor that intervenes between A and B should be considered to break the causal chain between A and B.

But (P_2), like (P_1), seems inadvisable on grounds of both justice and utility. It is, first of all, unfair that Jones should not be considered the cause of his aunt's death despite the freak breeze. Further, allowing Jones to go free might well encourage other bungling criminals to try, whereas requiring Jones to take responsibility would discourage such attempts.

THE VOLUNTARY INTERVENTION HYPOTHESIS

Voluntary intervention is another common sense factor that Hart and Honoré say is to break the causal connection between an act and subsequent harm. They claim, however, that it does not hold in the context of interpersonal transactions where a person persuades, induces, or entices (in contrast to advising or facilitating) another person. In these contexts, they say, causal chains can be traced through the intervening human action. But in non-interpersonal transactions, voluntary intervention does break the causal connection. Their idea can be formulated as the following hypothesis:

> (H_9) In non-interpersonal transaction contexts, voluntary intervention breaks the causal chain between an act A and subsequent harm.

In non-interpersonal transactions in ordinary life there seem to be situations where the voluntary intervention principle does not hold, however. Indeed, Feinberg considers several hypothetical counterexamples to (H_9).[57] In one, which he calls the Ingenious Suicide, Mr. Blue wants to commit suicide but cannot bring himself to take his own life. He knows that another person, Manley Firmview, will kill anyone who says so and so to him. Mr. Blue does say so and so to Mr. Firmview, and Mr. Firmview calmly shoots Mr. Blue. Feinberg argues that Mr.

Blue's remarks to Mr. Firmview were the cause of Mr. Blue's death despite the fact that Mr. Firmview's action was a deliberate voluntary action. In this case, the causal connection was not blocked; voluntary human action did not act as a barrier through which the cause could not be traced.

One might be inclined to discount Feinberg's counterexample by saying that it is a case of an interpersonal transaction where, according to Hart and Honoré, the human intervention principle does not hold. But this would be a mistake. X does not coerce or advise Y to do anything. Indeed X does not even suggest or imply that Y should do anything. X just says so and so and Y reacts. Nor is it clear that this can be assimilated to the type of borderline case Hart and Honoré discuss.

Another counterexample cited by Feinberg is the Case of the Foolhardy Bank Teller. Jones is depositing money in a bank when a robber enters, draws his gun, and warns that if anyone moves, he or she will be shot. When a bank teller rashly dives toward the floor the robber shoots and the ricocheting bullet injures Jones. Assuming that the bank robber was fully aware of what he was doing and that the bank teller was negligent in causing an unreasonable risk to the customers, Feinberg maintains that the bank teller's action and not the action of the robber is the cause of Jones' injury; this is despite the fact that the robber's action is a voluntary intervention in the causal chain that led from the action of the bank teller to the injury of Jones.

Feinberg's counterexamples seem to show that (H_9) is not a correct account of common sense causal thinking. Consequently, then, (H_9) cannot be used to argue that common sense causal ideas are embodied in the law. Hart and Honoré do argue, however, that the common sense voluntary human intervention principle is embodied in the law. Support for this principle will have to be found outside of common sense.

Perhaps the existence of a voluntary intervention principle in the law should be justified in terms of policy. Consider:

(P_3) In non-interpersonal transaction contexts in the law, voluntary intervention should break the causal chain between act A and subsequent harm.

However, the correctness of this policy is by no means obvious. In the case of the Foolhardy Bank Teller, one might argue on grounds of justice and utility that in tort law the teller's bank, not the bank robber, should be held liable for Jones' injury. First of all, it seems to be unfair to hold the robber responsible for Jones' injury since Jones would not have been shot but for the bank teller's reckless action. Moreover, on grounds of utility it might be maintained that holding the bank responsible will encourage this and other banks to put pressure on employees to be more careful. In addition, it would be absurd on practical grounds to hold the bank robber liable for damages. He has long since fled and could probably not pay damages even if he were to be caught. On the other hand, the bank is able to pay for damages for it can always pass the cost on to its customers.

Conclusion

I have argued in this chapter that Hart and Honoré's attempt to formulate our common sense causal notions and to show that some of these are the basis for legal causality is unsuccessful. On general methodological grounds, their appeal to linguistic intuitions to establish hypotheses about common sense causal notions is unwarranted. Further, their very appealing to these linguistic intuitions raises certain doubts about their particular claims. Moreover, I have argued that if, instead of proposing empirical hypotheses about common sense linguistic usage, we interpret Hart and Honoré as proposing policies about the use of certain causal notions, their views are dubious because the policies are dubious.

Although I have defended Hart and Honoré against Nowell-Smith's criticism that the particular common sense notions they consider are based on policy considerations, I have argued that more can be said by way of rehabilitating the modern view that policy considerations are basic to all causal judgments in the law, including those founded on common sense. Hart and Honoré's critique of the modern theory seems conclusive if the latter is given one of its usual interpretations:

(A) All causal judgments in the law are disguised judgments of policy.

But there are other ways to formulate the theory and they are not open to Hart and Honoré's criticism. Moreover, even if Hart and Honoré are correct that many of the causal judgments in the law are based on the sort of common sense judgments they have suggested, it might still be useful to look for policy considerations lurking behind causal judgments. We have already found it useful to try to make positions more plausible by reformulating them as programs defined by methodological rules. The modern theory of causality can be reformulated in this way too. It can be interpreted, at least in part, as a program for legal scholars who are investigating legal causation. Consider, then, the following methodological rule to guide scholarly research:

(CM_1) Assume that all legal causal judgments in fact rest directly or indirectly on policy considerations.

Whether or not this is a fruitful rule depends on whether (CM_1) in fact directs researchers to the discovery of hidden policy considerations in the making of actual causal legal judgments. These could be direct and obvious ones such as those in the New York laws limiting liability for damage due to someone's negligently causing a fire. Or they could instead be very indirect and subtle as, for example, are the sorts of considerations raised by Nowell-Smith. Indeed, they could be even more indirect and general than those he suggests. For example, someone might argue that there is an implicit policy that one should have causal notions in the law that are easy to understand and reflect our intuitive notions of justice; common sense notions, it may be argued, are easy to understand and do reflect our intuitive notions of justice; consequently, they are found in the law.

The modern theory can also be analyzed normatively. Instead of interpreting it as saying that all causal judgments in the law in fact rest on policy considerations, we can interpret it as saying that they should rest on such considerations. In one form this view would argue that causal judgments in the law should be analyzed as tacit policy recommendations. Expressions of the form:

(1) X is the legal cause of Y.

would be understood to mean:

(2) It is a good policy to hold X legally responsible for Y.

As Hart and Honoré point out, (2) would not work as a general analysis since X may be an inanimate object, for example, a storm, that cannot be held responsible. But the normative implications of the modern theory could be more broadly understood. After all, there might be policy considerations involved in deciding that certain entities, for example, storms, should not be held responsible. For example, if storms are held responsible, there might be no way to collect damages and this would be undesirable on policy grounds. On the other hand, there might be good policy reasons for pursuing the idea that storms are acts of God and, consequently, holding that God is responsible for the damage to victims of storms. Victims of storms could collect damages from God's secular representatives, churches. A tax on churches could be used to pay for victims of storms and other "acts of God." This idea suggests another rule to guide legal policy makers:

(CM_2) Assume that all legal causal judgments should be based directly or indirectly on policy considerations.

Even if one decides that common sense causal considerations should play an important part in the law, according to (CM_2) this decision itself should rest on policy considerations. As indicated above, such considerations could be very general and very indirect: for example, one consideration could be that common sense causal language is easy to understand and may embody our intuitive notion of justice. So understood, (CM_2) would politicize causality in the law, but not in the crude way that seems to be assumed by most versions of the theory.

(CM_1) (Assume that all legal causal judgments in fact rest directly or indirectly on policy considerations) and (CM_2) together capture the spirit of the modern theory but would seem to be free of its major problems. (CM_1) would be directed to legal scholars and researchers and its fruitfulness would be determined by how well it furthers the discovery of hidden policy considerations. (CM_2) would be directed to judges and legislators and it would be evaluated by how well it provides a rationale for causal judgments in the law. It would force judges to provide a rationale for their use of causal language in their decisions and legislators to provide one in their use of causal language in formulating the law.

It should be noted that (CM_2) is compatible with judges' and legislators' introducing causal notions into the law that are rather different from the common sense notions analyzed by Hart and Honoré. There would be no reason, *a priori*, that a legal expert ought not to use scientific notions of cause in certain contexts. The decision of whether or not to do so would depend on whether certain policy considerations were furthered by the use of such notions. Moreover, in order to make intelligent judgments about the use of causal judgments in the law—whether commonsensical or otherwise—it would be necessary to have certain relevant factual information. Thus, in order to know whether the use of common sense causal language has a certain effect specified by the policy, empirical investigation would be necessary.

Chapter

4

Theory of Legal Definition and Elucidation

HART'S ANALYSIS OF a legal system, of judicial interpretation, and of legal causality are all based on his notion of elucidation. In his most mature work he distinguishes this notion from definition. In this chapter I concentrate on Hart's theory of definition and elucidation both because it is interesting in its own right and because it provides added critical insight into his theory of law.

Definition in "The Ascription of Responsibility and Rights"

In his well-known paper "The Ascription of Responsibility and Rights,"[1] Hart gives a theory of the definition of legal terms that contrasts in interesting ways with his later ones. The main purpose of Hart's paper, however, is not to expound a theory of legal definition, but to argue that the "philosophical analysis of the concept of a human action has been inadequate and confusing."[2] Hart argues that this confusion arises at least in part because action sentences of the form "He did it" are not primarily descriptive but ascriptive. Just as the function of sentences of the form "This is his" is to ascribe rights in property, the function of sentences of the form "He did it" is to ascribe responsibility. His purpose, then, in considering legal definition, is to throw light on the analysis of the concept of human action.

In response to criticisms Hart has abandoned the major theses of this early paper, saying "its main contentions no longer seem to me defensible, and . . . the main criticisms of it made in recent years are justified."[3] However, although the critics of this early paper have pointed out serious problems with his ascriptive account of human action, they have not drawn attention to problems with his theory of legal definition, which is relatively independent of his theory of human action. So unless independent reasons are given why the main contentions of his theory of definition, in contrast to his theory of action, are in error Hart's abandonment of his early theory of legal definitions seems unwarranted. Unfortunately, Hart has not supplied us with these independent reasons. As a result, his rejection of this earlier theory of definition appears to be an overreaction to criticism and his later theory of legal definitions, which conflicts with his earlier theory on many points, as a consequence appears arbitrary. However, as I will show in what follows, there are very good reasons why his theory of legal definitions should be rejected. In the light of these reasons, moreover, his later theory of legal definition is plausible. Whether the reasons I cite are in fact the ones that persuaded Hart to give up his theory we may never know. The point to note, however, is that a critique of his earlier theory of definition has not been given and is badly needed both in its own right and as rationale for his later theory.

Perhaps the most important thesis about legal definition in Hart's paper on responsibility and rights is that legal concepts are defeasible; that is, legal claims can be defeated or reduced by various recognized exceptions or mitigating factors. For reasons that will be examined later, Hart believes that the defeasible nature of legal concepts means that they cannot be defined by specifying sufficient conditions. A secondary thesis running throughout the paper is that legal language, like action language, is not descriptive but ascriptive. Closely connected with both of these theses is the idea that judges' decisions are not based on deductive or inductive inferences.

The approach to legal definition Hart takes in his paper is deeply indebted to that of British analytic philosophers of the time. The view that philosophy is an activity devoted to eliminating philosophical puzzles caused by linguistic confusions was expounded by Wittgenstein, among others,[4] and certainly influenced Hart's approach. In fact, the whole purpose of Hart's paper is to eliminate philosophical puzzles caused by linguistic confusion. Furthermore, the idea that there are functions of language besides a descriptive one was a common tenet in British analytic philosophy circles in 1948: indeed, Hart explicitly cites J. L. Austin's notion of performatory utterances[5] as an example of a non-descriptive language use. Finally, Hart's thesis against the possibility of giving legal definitions in terms of necessary and sufficient conditions was not unexpected. The idea that ordinary language is loose and vague and cannot be fitted into traditional linguistic molds was an essential part of the Oxford "revolution" in philosophy.[6] In one respect, then, Hart is simply applying the view of Oxford ordinary language analysis to legal language.

Vagueness, Defeasibility, and Sufficient Conditions

According to Hart, "the decisive stage in the proceedings of an English law court is normally a *judgement* given by the court to the effect that certain facts . . . are true and that certain legal consequences . . . are attached to those facts."[7] Consequently, such a judgment is a "blend of facts and law."[8] Now there are several characteristics of the legal element in these blends that "make the way in which facts support or fail to support legal conclusions, or refute or fail to refute them, unlike certain standard models of how one kind of statement supports or refutes another."[9]

It may look as if the judge in applying the law simply determines whether facts come within the scope of a rule defining the necessary and sufficient conditions of, for example, contracts, trespass, or murder. But this would, according to Hart, be a disastrous oversimplification and distortion. First, in common law the judge is not supplied "with explicitly formulated general criteria defining 'contract,' or 'trespass.'" Instead the judge decides cases "by reference to past cases."[10] This means that legal concepts are not only vague but that the quest for a definition of a legal concept "cannot be answered by the provision of a verbal rule for the translation of legal expressions into other terms or one specifying a set of necessary and sufficient conditions."[11] To be sure, general statements on the effect of the past cases can be specified. However, if they are not to mislead, answers to the question "What is trespass?," or "What is a contract?," must take "the form of references to the leading cases on the subject, coupled with the use of the word 'et cetera.'"[12] More important, legal concepts have another characteristic "which makes the word 'unless' as indispensable as the word 'et cetera' in any explanation or definition of them."[13] The application of legal concepts can be challenged. On the one hand, one can challenge the facts on which they are based; on the other, one can bring up certain other facts in the present case that indicate that the legal claim should not succeed or should be reduced to a weaker one. These other facts bring the case under some recognized exception. Thus, the legal claim "Jones murdered her husband" may be reduced to manslaughter if provocation is shown. In contract law, the claim "Jones has a valid contract with Smith" may be defeated if it is shown that Jones signed the contract under duress.

Legal concepts are thus defeasible concepts; that is, legal claims can be defeated or reduced by various recognized exceptions or mitigating factors. This property of legal notions is sometimes obscured by "providing a general formula which seems to meet the demand"[14] of a theorist for the specification of necessary and sufficient conditions. Thus, in criminal law some jurists have offered a general theory of the mental element in a crime (*mens rea*). But this approach to definition obscures rather than clarifies. For what is meant by the mental element is only to be understood by considering certain defenses or exceptions—a mistake of fact, accident, duress, insanity, and so on—that either exclude liability altogether or reduce it. Thus, the general formulae are explained by these heterogeneous defenses; they are not explained by the general formulae.

Since legal concepts such as contract, trespass, or murder are defeasible, it is wrong to suppose that the meaning of such concepts can be captured with a statement specifying the conditions under which contract, murder, or trespass are held to exist. Whereas such statements would have to express "necessary and sometimes sufficient conditions" for the application of them, they "could not express conditions which are always sufficient."[15] Further, an attempt to specify the meaning of legal concepts in a general formula would fail since such a formula could not account for their composite character, a blend of fact and law.

According to Hart, this feature of legal concepts has a special relevance to what judges do. A judge decides whether, for example, a contract is valid or not only on the basis of the actual facts and arguments before the bench, not on an ideal basis.[16] Moreover, the judge does not make deductive or inductive inferences from the facts. Hart concludes that what the judge does "may be either a *right* or a *wrong* decision,"[17] but it is not true or false. In short, judicial decisions are not descriptive statements. The facts are not related to a legal conclusion as statements of facts are related to descriptive statements. Rules of law are "not linguistic or logical rules but . . . rules for deciding."[18]

Of course, outside of courts of law, legal language might be used in a different way. Sometimes one might use legal language descriptively, and in these cases statements containing legal concepts would be true or false. For instance, the statements "My contract with Smith is in the wastepaper basket" and "My father made his will today" are used to describe and are either true or false.

Hart's Argument Evaluated

According to Hart, although it may be possible to specify necessary conditions for the application of a legal concept and conditions that are "sometimes sufficient," it is impossible to specify conditions that are always sufficient. Why does Hart hold this view? Several reasons are suggested by his words but none of them seems compelling.

First, as I have shown, Hart argues that given the use of precedent in common law, legal concepts are not embodied in clear general rules. Accordingly, answers to the question, "What is a contract?," must refer to leading cases of the past coupled with the use of the term "etcetera." It is unclear, however, why the open-endedness of common law procedures would affect a clear specification of a sufficient, but not a necessary, condition for the application of legal terms.

Furthermore, it is not obvious why the open-ended quality of common law procedure should be a bar against specifying either necessary or sufficient conditions for the application of legal terms. As we know, Hart allows that to some extent judges create the law. According to Hart this is true in the non-standard application of terms used in a legal rule. Thus, the judge decides whether for the purpose of the rule that no vehicles are allowed in the park a scooter is a vehicle. It seems a natural extension of this creative view of a judge's role that a judge could create definitions of law in cases where the legal terms were vague and unclear. Some of these creations might well specify necessary and sufficient conditions for the application of a term. Naturally, such definitions of legal concepts would be put forth with the understanding that they might be revised by later courts as new social problems arose.

When we look at them in this way there is nothing wrong with legal definitions specifying necessary and sufficient conditions as long as we realize that they are tentative and subject to revision as the common law changes. Hart's emphasis on the impossibility of this type of definition seems to obscure the fact that definitions in common law are subject to revision.

Second, the major thrust of Hart's argument seems to be based on the defeasibility of legal concepts and not on their common law precedent foundation, that is, on the need for the "unless" clause rather than the "etcetera" clause. But why should the defeasibility of legal concepts mean that no generally sufficient conditions for the application of legal concepts can be specified?

One possibility is that the number of exceptions that defeat a legal claim is unlimited or perhaps unknown. If this were the case, then it would be impossible to specify when all exceptions failed to occur and it might be argued that, therefore, no sufficient conditions could be specified. It would be impossible to complete a formula of the following kind: "If there is no duress and no undue influence and no fraudulent misrepresentation and . . . , then there is a valid contract." But Hart nowhere does claim that the list of exceptions is endless or unknown. Indeed, his words suggest that he believes that the exceptions, although numerous, are specifiable and, indeed, that they have been specified in, for example, treatises on contracts.

Yet even if all the exceptions were unspecifiable, would this mean that it would be impossible to specify a generally sufficient condition? Not necessarily, for one would specify as a part of the sufficient condition of the presence of a contract "the presence of no well-recognized exceptions." Of course, the meaning of this phrase would not be self-explanatory but would have to be learned by studying cases; further, its meaning would not be completely exhausted by this study since the study would be endless. However, this would be as true of the necessary conditions of a contract as of the sufficient conditions. Thus, an acceptance and an offer are supposed to be necessary conditions of a contract. But "acceptance" and "offer" are not self-explanatory terms and a study of cases is needed to understand what they mean, for their meaning is not obviously exhausted by a study of cases.

Third, in the context of specifying a sufficient condition, Hart speaks at times of the heterogeneity of the exceptions. This suggests that perhaps the reason he believes that a sufficient condition is impossible to specify is that the exceptions are heterogeneous. But it is unclear why this should matter. So long as the exceptions are known they can be listed, and given this list one could generate the needed sufficient condition by specifying the negation of the exceptions. Furthermore, what is heterogeneous and what is not is not an absolute notion. What may seem like a hodgepodge of various exceptions without an adequate theory can be given unity in terms of some more comprehensive theory. Hart, of course, seems to reject all such theories as misleading. He speaks of the "pursuit of the will-o'-the-wisp" of a general formula by which "legal theorists have sought to impose a spurious unity . . . upon these heterogeneous defences."[19] Thus, in criminal law, Hart argues, general formulae in terms of foresight and voluntariness are merely summaries that express the absence of various exceptions. The exceptions in criminal law are not evidence of the lack of *mens rea* but criteria for the absence of responsibility.

Whether Hart is correct in terms of all existing general formulae of his day is unclear since he does not even begin to review these formulae critically. Furthermore, theories that have appeared after his paper was published that might provide a unity that is not spurious could not have been considered by Hart. One can say, at least, from our present perspective that Hart has not proven the lack of unity among exceptions.

Fourth, in a footnote[20] Hart seems to admit that it would be possible to specify necessary and sufficient conditions for legal concepts. However, he seems to believe that such specification would be empty. Thus, in referring to the difficulty in specifying necessary and sufficient conditions for the existence of a contract he says, "It could, of course, be done vacuously by specifying as the necessary and sufficient conditions of contract, consent and other positive conditions and the negative of the disjunction of the various defences."[21]

But the reasons why Hart claims that this procedure is vacuous are quite unclear. The resulting statement would hardly be trivial or unilluminating. It would not be like a tautology that said, "A contract exists when necessary and sufficient conditions for a contract are present." The statement Hart had in mind would specify the usual positive conditions of a contract as well as the absence of all exceptions. To be sure, if it was correct, the definitional statement would be a tautology and since all tautologies are vacuous in that they make no factual claims this definitional statement would be so too. But in this sense all correct definitional statements that specify the meaning of terms are vacuous. Presumably, this is not what Hart had in mind.

Finally, still another reason given by Hart to justify his claim that specifying a sufficient condition for a legal concept is impossible is that any such attempt at specification "could not convey the composite character of these concepts nor allow for the distinctive features due to the fact that the elements in the compound are of distinct logical types."[22]

Hart maintains that legal judgments are a "blend" of fact and law but what does this metaphorical talk of "blend" and "composite" really come down to? On one plausible interpretation, a legal judgment, for example, "Jones has a valid contract with Smith" or "Jones trespassed on Smith's land," is a blend of fact and law if it follows from statements of fact and rules of law; that is, the antecedent of a rule specifies some factual circumstance and the consequent of the rule some legal effect. Thus, the judgment

(1) Jones has a valid contract with Smith

follows from the conjunction of:

(2a) Jones and Smith signed a conventional formula of a contract with full and free consent in May, 1944
(2b) There were no well-recognized exceptions in the circumstances
(3) If the parties sign a conventional formula of contract with full and free consent and there are no well-recognized exceptions in the circumstances, then the partners have a valid contract.

Statement (2b) could be replaced by a conjunction of statements specifying the absence of all recognized exceptions if these were finite and knowable. Appropriate changes could be made in (3). In general, on this interpretation[23] any legal judgment C follows from D, a descriptive statement, and R, a rule of law in the form of a hypothetical whose antecedent is a descriptive statement, D, and whose consequence, C, is a legal prescriptive statement.

It is important to notice that there is nothing in this construal that would prevent one from specifying a sufficient condition for a legal notion. Indeed, the antecedent of R does precisely this. However, there is some reason to suppose that Hart would object to a construal of legal decisions involving inductive or deductive reasoning.

So far as I can discern them, Hart's reasons for rejecting both deductive and inductive reasoning are not persuasive. He argues that timeless conclusions of law, for example,

(1) Jones has a valid contract with Smith

do not follow from statements of temporal facts, for example, from

(2a) Jones and Smith signed a conventional formula of a contract under full and free consent on May 1, 1944.

Of course, Hart is correct. Statement (2a) does not entail statement (1). Indeed, even if one added (2b) this would still be true: (2a) and (2b) do not entail (1). But, of course, statements like (1) do not follow from statements of fact—temporal or otherwise—unless they are combined with rules of law such as (3).[24]

As we have seen, Hart maintains that since judges literally decide on the basis of the facts before the bench whether a contract or trespass does or does not exist, they are neither describing the facts nor making a deductive or inductive inference. This may well be true. Deciding whether or not a contract exists may not be the same thing as describing the facts or making an inference. But this admission is compatible with saying that a decision is based on an inference and descriptions of facts. Something similar is true in applied science. Deciding whether to perform surgery or build a bridge is not the same thing as describing the facts and making inferences related to the decision. But descriptions of the facts and inferences are used in deciding; indeed, the description and inference are the basis for the decision.[25]

After all, a judge who used descriptive statements (2a) and (2b) and inferences based on (2a) and (2b) and (3) would still have decisions to make. First, he or she would have to decide whether (3) was an appropriate rule in this case, and whether (2a) and (2b) were true. Second, given a positive answer to the questions previously mentioned, he or she would have to decide whether (1) should be the holding of the court. This latter decision would be tantamount to determining whether the court should be bound by the implication of the facts and laws that were previously decided. This decision might be an easy one for most judges to make, but it is a decision nevertheless.

One can conclude that Hart has not shown that legal concepts cannot be defined in terms of necessary and sufficient conditions. Nor has he shown that legal statements are not based on logical inferences. I have argued in detail that Hart's arguments are incorrect for two basic reasons. First, unless his arguments are refuted, Hart's later account of definition will seem unjustified and even irrational. For, as I will show next, his later account of definition assumes some of the very things he had previously argued were impossible. One would like to know that the above arguments could have been given to justify his radical change of approach. Second, the giving of definitions in terms of necessary and sufficient conditions can be an illuminating and fruitful approach to philosophical analyses; they have proved to be useful in other areas of philosophy and it would be surprising if they could not also be used in the analysis of legal concepts. In showing that Hart's argument from the impossibility of necessary and sufficient condition analyses in legal contexts is not adequate, my critique thereby gives one some hope that this familiar type of definition may prove to be an illuminating and fruitful approach to the law.

Definition in the Inaugural Lecture

In his Inaugural Lecture, "Definition and Theory in Jurisprudence,"[26] delivered at Oxford University in 1953, Hart expounded a theory of definition in many respects strikingly different from the one he proposed earlier in "The

Ascription of Responsibility and Rights." The basic insight of Hart's 1953 theory is that legal terms cannot be defined in isolation, but only in the sentence in which they appear. In giving a contextual theory of definition Hart specifies truth conditions for the application of the sentence and also gives an account of the function of legal sentences. In so doing he seems to give up some of the main theses about legal definition that he held in his earlier paper: the truth conditions specified by Hart seem to be intended as a sufficient condition for the application of legal sentences; moreover, his analysis assumes that legal sentences are true or false and that some sentences of law, for example, "Jones has a legal right," are based on logical inferences. These are precisely the ideas that he denied in 1948.

Rejection of Traditional Approaches

According to Hart, there are questions that are posed inside and outside the law that have generated philosophical puzzlements. For example, inside the law one might ask "What is a corporation?" or "What is a right?" Outside the law one might ask "What is time?" One's puzzlement would not be relieved, according to Hart, if one knew the dictionary definitions of "corporation," "right," and "time" or if one knew how to use these terms correctly. In the law there are, according to Hart, two reasons for this. First, one might know the definition of a term and not know the principles behind the term's application. Second, words like "right" or "corporation" do not have "the straightforward connection with counterparts in the world of fact which most ordinary words have."[27]

Moreover, Hart maintains that the traditional method of definition does not relieve this puzzlement. The traditional method is to find synonyms that can be substituted for the word to be defined. This attempt at definition usually proceeds as follows: one specifies the general classification to which the thing the word describes belongs and one then goes on to describe the specific difference that marks it off from other species of the same general kind. However, this way of defining is helpful only when one is not puzzled about the general classification. Thus, if one is clear on what a corporation is, then there is no problem in using the traditional method to define a college. One would distinguish a college from other types of corporations. But if the notion of corporation is itself puzzling, the traditional method is not helpful for one does not know how to classify "corporation."

Indeed, Hart argues that the traditional method of definition can be misleading since it can encourage belief that "corporation," "right," and so forth describe persons, qualities, processes, and events. Then when it becomes difficult to find what these words stand for, certain devices are used to explain away the difficulty. Some people end up saying that the words stand for complex empirical future facts; others that they stand for nothing, that the terms refer to fictional entities; still others that they refer to non-empirical facts. According to Hart, the use of traditional definitional methods in jurisprudence has generated theories and schools of jurisprudence that "fall disquietingly often into a familiar triad."[28] Thus, with respect to the question, "What is a right?" the American realist argues that "right" is a term by which one describes the probable behavior of courts and officials. The Scandinavian realist maintains that a right is nothing real at all; it is a fictional power. Someone holding the older traditional rights theory argues that rights have an objective reality existing independent of the behavior of human beings. Other theories are of little help, indeed can bring about confusion. To the lawyer these theories "stand apart with their heads . . . in the clouds," and the use of such terms as "right" and "corporation" are "neutral between competing theories."[29] For example, it is one thing to ask for a definition of "corporation" and quite another to plead a political course connected with corporations. Yet controversy over the nature of the corporation in terms of, for example, fictional or realist theories of the corporation have confused logical and political criteria.

The elucidation of legal terms, Hart maintains, could be accomplished "without entering a forbidding jungle of philosophical argument" by using "methods properly adopted to their special character."[30] Hart does not mean to suggest by this that the elucidation he attempts in his lecture is not philosophical. He does, however, mean to reject an approach to such issues in which large and controversial theories play a crucial role.

Analytic Philosophy Background

In rejecting traditional approaches to definition Hart is not breaking new philosophical ground; rather he is applying the methods and insights of the philosophical analysts of his day to jurisprudence and, perhaps even more important, using the theories of definition of earlier philosophers, most notably Bentham.

First, Hart is suspicious of the idea that in all cases there is a clear correlation between individual legal words and objects and properties in the world. Outside the law this view had already been criticized: Wittgenstein had attacked the picture theory of language[31] and Austin had taken to task the view that language mirrors world.[32] Hart is also suspicious of bringing theory to bear on philosophical issues in law. Hart maintains that what is wrong with some definitions in jurisprudence is their confusion with traditional jurisprudential theories. A suspicion of traditional theories was also a recurring theme in Oxford analytic philosophy. Indeed, until the late 1950's the approach of Oxford analysts was piecemeal, unsystematic, and non-theoretical.[33]

It should be noted, however, that there is at least one respect in which Hart's Inaugural Lecture departs from the views of the British analytic philosophers who influenced him. Hart seems to believe that there is something anomalous about legal language that causes philosophical puzzles. He claims that legal words do not have "the straightforward connection with counterparts in the world of fact which most ordinary words have and to which we appeal in our definition of ordinary words."[34] Yet the very philosophers who influenced Hart argued that many ordinary terms do not have a straightforward connection with the world of facts. They would, therefore, certainly have rejected the view of ordinary language that Hart seems to presuppose in his Inaugural Lecture. Interestingly enough, in "The Ascription of Responsibility and Rights" Hart himself argues that action terms do not describe. These, however, are terms found in ordinary language.

If dictionary definitions miss the point in relieving puzzlement concerning the question of what is a right, and the traditional theories confuse issues, how does Hart think one should proceed in elucidating the concept of a legal right? He argues that one must not focus on the single word "right" but must consider instead whole sentences in which the term plays a characteristic role. Thus, one might consider the sentence "You have a right," rather than the word "right."

This approach to definition was not completely new in either jurisprudence or contemporary analytic philosophy. Hart points out that Bentham many years before argued that one must never consider legal words alone; rather, they should be considered in whole sentences in which they play their characteristic role.[35] He does not, however, mention Russell's notion of the incomplete symbol. According to Russell, such symbols are words that have no significance in isolation from sentences in which they are used. This is because there are not objects in the external world to which they correspond and to which one appeals in explaining them.[36] In a paper defending his Inaugural Lecture Hart does point out, however, that Gottlob Frege advocated specifying the meaning of number words by considering propositions in which these words appeared.[37]

Truth Condition Analysis

According to Hart, in concentrating on sentences rather than on single words, one considers the conditions under which sentences containing the terms "corporation," "right," and so on are true. By specifying these conditions one provides a partial elucidation of, for example, the concepts of legal right or corporation. I will call this aspect of an elucidation a truth condition analysis.

With respect to legal rights one truth condition is plain from the start. In order for the statement "A has a legal right to be paid $10 by B" to be true, there must be a legal system "with all that this implies by way of general obedience, the operation of sanctions of the system, and the general likelihood that this will continue."[38] So one condition that must hold for "X has a legal right" to be true is:

(a) There exists a legal system.

However, Hart stresses that when one says "A has a legal right to be paid $10 by B" one is *not* explicitly stating that a legal system exists. Another condition specified by Hart is:

(b) Under the rule or rules of the system some other person Y is, in terms of the events that have happened, obliged to do or abstain from some action.

Now as Hart points out in a footnote[39] (b) is a truth condition of "X has a right" only when "right" is understood in *one* sense, namely, the correlative duty sense.

A third condition specified by Hart is:

(c) This obligation is made by law dependent on the choice either of X or of some person authorized to act in his behalf so that Y is bound to do or abstain from some action only if X (or some authorized person) so chooses or alternatively only until X (or such person) chooses otherwise.

Some interpretive questions can be raised about the truth condition aspect of this analysis. First, are these conditions individually *logically* necessary and/or jointly *logically* sufficient for the truth of "X has a legal right"? Certainly, Hart never speaks in these terms and it would not seem in keeping with his purpose of elucidation to require this. After all, Hart's purpose is to relieve the philosophical puzzlement of people who understand how to use a legal term. To relieve this puzzlement, Hart specifies under what conditions sentences that contain the term "right" are true and how such sentences function. Given this purpose it is surely not necessary that these truth conditions hold in all logically possible worlds or that the function be the same in all logically possible legal systems.

There is another reason to suppose that Hart does not intend that the truth conditions specify logically necessary conditions. Two years after his Inaugural Lecture, Hart defended his theory of definition against an attack made by Jonathan Cohen in an Aristotelian Society Symposium, "Theory and Definition in Jurisprudence." Hart stressed that, in the definition of legal systems, although there are many criteria for saying that a legal system exists, very few are logically necessary.[40] So, given Hart's purpose and given his subsequent comments on his Inaugural Lecture, it is reasonable to conclude that he does not intend the truth conditions to specify logically necessary or logically jointly sufficient conditions of "X has a right."

The next question is whether these conditions hold for all uses of the sentences or whether they hold only for all standard or characteristic uses of the sentences, and thus whether even in our world sentences of the form "X has a right" could sometimes be true when these conditions do not hold. There are two reasons to think that Hart has in mind standard or characteristic uses of the sentences. First, in his Inaugural Lecture he wants to consider words like "right" and "duty," as well as the names of corporations, not alone but "in examples of typical contexts where these words are at work."[41] Second, in the 1955 Symposium in which he defends his Inaugural Lecture against Cohen, he says that some criteria for the application of the term "legal system" are necessary, but "the rest form a sub-set of criteria of which everything called a legal system satisfies some but only *standard* or *normal* cases satisfy all."[42] Considered in this way, Hart has the rather modest goal of specifying truth conditions for the standard or typical uses of expressions such as "X has a right" in our language.

Finally, one may raise the question of whether Hart is interested in specifying *necessary* as well as sufficient conditions for this standard usage. Given the way he formulates his analysis it seems as if he is specifying sufficient conditions. Thus his formulation "X has a right if . . ." suggests that he intends these conditions to specify a sufficient condition for the standard use. (He does not say "X has a right only if . . . ," which would indicate he intends to specify a necessary condition.) This need not be interpreted to mean that he intends to specify a *logically* sufficient condition for the characteristic usage. It should be noted, however, that Hart's analysis of "X has a right" as opposed to the formula itself seems to specify logically necessary conditions if the appropriate interpretation is given to the relevant term. For example, if "right" is understood in the duty correlative sense, condition (b) specifies a logically necessary condition; if "right" is understood in a sense of right that is capable of being waived, condition (c) specifies a logically necessary condition. However, it would be a mistake to suppose that this indicates that Hart believed in general that truth conditions in an elucidation must specify logically necessary conditions. Hart's statement in 1955 indicates that he did not intend this and, indeed, there is nothing in his Inaugural Lecture to suggest such an interpretation.

The Function of Legal Right Statements

In order to elucidate legal rights, Hart goes beyond specifying the truth conditions for "X has a right." It is also important, he says, to understand the distinctive function of "X has a right" as it is used in legal discourse. So, in addition to specifying the truth condition of "X has a right" in elucidating a legal right we must also specify the distinctive function of statements like "A has a right to be paid $10 by B."

This aspect of Hart's analysis was not new in English philosophical circles of the 1950's. As I have already mentioned, at Cambridge Wittgenstein had stressed understanding the use of expressions in unraveling philosophical puzzles while at Oxford J. L. Austin was analyzing performative utterances, statements such as "I promise" that do not state a fact but have a different function. British philosophy above all was alive to uses of language. It is not surprising then that, in analyzing legal language, Hart should consider the elucidation of legal concepts to consist in part in specifying the use or function of these expressions in legal contexts.

According to Hart, one of the distinctive functions of a statement such as "A has a right to be paid $10 by B" is that of being drawn as a conclusion of law. This statement is a consequence of the conjunction of two types of statements: (1) legal rules, for example, of contract law, and (2) a statement of certain facts relevant to the case. Although Hart does not put his point this formally, it is clarified in the following. Let:

(C) = A has a legal right to be paid $10 by B
(R_1) = If (D), then (C)

and let (D) be some descriptive statement specifying the condition associated with making a contract, for example, signing a certain type of document under full and free consent. Now (D) and (R_1) entail (C). However, when some person P asserts that (C), P is not asserting (D) or (R_1); rather P is drawing a conclusion (C) from (D) and (R_1), although (D) and (R_1) remain unstated. According to Hart, when P says (C), P is drawing a conclusion of law from unstated premises like (D) and (R_1), and not stating that (D) and (R_1) are true. This is so whether P is a judge acting in an official capacity or a lawyer discussing a case informally with a client. If P is a judge acting in an official capacity, (C) is authoritative; if P is not a judge, then (C) is not authoritative and may have to be retracted in light of official pronouncements. But in either case a conclusion of law is being drawn.

However, at other times in his lecture Hart does not say that in stating (C) one is drawing a conclusion of law. He says rather that in stating (C) one is using (C) to "draw a conclusion of law in a particular case which falls under such rules."[43] The thesis that (C) is used to draw a conclusion and the thesis that (C) is a conclusion of law are not necessarily incompatible since (C) could *both* be a conclusion drawn from unstated premises like (R_1) *and* (D) and used to draw a further, perhaps unstated conclusion from other rules.[44] Let:

(R_2) = If (C), then (M)

and let (M) be some deontic prescriptive statement, for example,

B ought to pay A $10 under condition X.

Thus (C) and (R_2) entail (M). So (C) can be used in drawing a conclusion of law as well as being a conclusion of law.

Nevertheless, although Hart's two different claims, one about a conclusion and the other about a premise, can be made compatible, they cause a certain confusion and make it unclear exactly what his thesis is. At least three possible interpretations come to mind. Hart could mean that in *every* case in which a statement like (C) is used in a legal context, the speaker draws (C) as a conclusion of law and uses (C) to draw a further conclusion of law. Let us call this the strong interpretation. On the other hand, Hart could mean that in every case in which a statement like (C) is used in a legal context the speaker is drawing (C) as a conclusion of law, but only in some of these cases is the speaker using (C) to draw any further conclusion of law. Let us call this the weaker interpretation.

There is still another interpretation, however, and it is the most plausible one. Under this third interpretation Hart's thesis is that a statement of the form "X has a right" is used *characteristically* as a conclusion drawn from other legal rules and descriptive statements or as a premise, in combination with other premises, to draw further conclusions of law in a particular case. This interpretation is presupposed by Hart's reference to standard or characteristic uses of sentences containing "right" in his Inaugural Lecture. Let us call this the characteristic interpretation.

Hart's Theory Evaluated

The first thing to note in evaluating Hart's theory is that his general approach to definition in terms of truth conditions and the function of legal language could be correct but his particular analysis of, for example, "X has a legal right" mistaken. Thus, even if one refutes his analysis of "X has a legal right," one has not refuted his general approach. Still, if his particular analysis is refuted and Hart has produced no other analysis that applies his general idea, one can at least claim that his approach has not been proven. Further, if there are problems with his particular analysis that may plausibly be supposed to affect other analyses using this approach, one may be skeptical of his general approach until a particular analysis is produced that meets these problems. In what follows, Hart's particular definition of "X has a legal right" will be criticized and one problem will be mentioned that may affect other analyses following this general approach.

Hart admits that his analysis applies only to the first (duty correlative or claim) sense of right distinguished by Hohfeld. However, he argues that the same form of analysis can be used for other types of rights (liberty, power, and immunity). Indeed, he argues that this type of analysis will show what unifies all these different senses of rights: "The unifying element seems to be this: in all four cases the law specifically recognizes the *choice* of an individual either negatively by not impeding or obstructing it (liberty and immunity) or affirmatively by giving legal effect to it (claim and power)."[45] Thus the most important aspect of Hart's analysis of legal rights is condition (c), namely that this obligation is made by law dependent on the choice either of X or of some person authorized to act in his behalf so that Y is bound to do or abstain from some action only if X (or some authorized person) so chooses or alternatively only until X (or such person) chooses otherwise.

One might easily suppose that Hart's analysis is incorrect since not all legal rights seem to be waivable. For example, it may be argued that I have a right not to be murdered but the obligation not to murder me is not based on my choice. However, there is good reason to suppose that Hart would not accept this counterexample. In his later writings he argues that it is unnecessary and confusing to suppose that the criminal law, in contrast to the civil law, contains legal rights. His reason seems to be that to say that some person has a legal right in the criminal law, for example, the right not to be murdered, is to say no more than that other people have an obligation not to murder the person.[46]

In his Inaugural Lecture Hart says: "If there are rights which cannot be waived, these will require special treatment."[47] Later he came to believe that there were such legal rights, rights that could not be unified by the concept of choice. In particular, in "Bentham on Legal Rights" he singles out the legal rights recognized by the constitutions of certain countries by bills of rights that are "essential for the maintenance of the life, the security, the development, and the dignity of the individual" as rights that cannot be unified under the choice theory.[48] Hart seems to admit that such rights do not just need "special treatment"; rather, the choice theory must be rejected as a general account of rights. Thus, in order to save Hart's analysis from counterexamples, one must restrict the legal rights at issue to ones that can be waived. But this restriction makes (c) trivially true.

One way that Hart might meet the above criticism is to argue that although some legal rights can be waived this is not the standard or common legal use of the expression "X has a right." The problem with this response, however, is that it is not clear how one determines the standard legal use of an expression. Determining this would seem to be a job for empirical science; it cannot be known *a priori*. But Hart provides no evidence that this is the standard use of "X has a legal right."

This is not to say that a scientific investigation of whether the standard or common use of the expression "X has a legal right" entails "X is waivable" would be simple. But it would not be impossible or beyond the scope of present-day empirical science. One approach to the problem would be to obtain a representative sample of the uses of "X has a legal right" from law journals, trial transcripts, legal briefs, and the like. A panel of legal experts would then subject the sample to the following sort of analysis: In each particular case where "X has a legal right" is used, the panel would ask, "Given the context, is it plausible to suppose that 'X is a legal right' entails that X is waivable?" If it was found that in the vast majority of cases the answer was yes, this would be a good reason to suppose that the standard use of "X has a legal right" is what Hart adopts. As far as I know no such evidence is available. At best, then, if Hart's is a claim about the standard use of "X has a legal right" it should be considered a hypothesis in need of empirical backing.

Depending on what interpretation one gives Hart's thesis concerning the function of legal statements such as "X has a right," it seems to be either false or unjustified. Consider the strong interpretation. A lawyer might conclude "A has a right to be paid $10 by B" and yet not use this statement to draw any further legal conclusions for a number of reasons. The speaker might suddenly die before any further inference could be made or the speaker might not know the legal rule that is needed to draw deontic prescriptive conclusions (in terms of the example above, the speaker might not know R_2).

One can also think of cases in which the weaker interpretation is false. A poorly informed lawyer might state, "A has to be paid $10 by B" on the basis of pure speculation; this lawyer might not derive the statement from unstated legal and descriptive statements.

Whether or not Hart's thesis under the characteristic interpretation is correct is difficult to tell since in order to support it one needs evidence of the actual use of legal language that at present we do not have. An alternative hypothesis to Hart's thesis is that sentences of the form "X has a right" do not have a characteristic use but are used in a variety of different ways depending on the context. For example, when said to a judge "X has a right" may be used to protest ("I have a right to cross-examine the witness"), to concede ("You have a right but in the circumstances don't insist on it"), to speculate ("If you have a right, then we will have a strong case").[49]

Now it may be argued that these cases do not show that Hart's thesis is incorrect, for even when one protests or concedes one is drawing a conclusion of law. Indeed, one may protest by drawing "X has a right" as a conclusion of law. This is true, but it is also true that in order to protest by using "X has a right" one need *not* draw this statement as a conclusion of law or use it to draw a conclusion of law. To repeat: empirical evidence, not *a priori* reasoning, is needed to establish Hart's thesis (interpreted as the *characteristic* use of "X has a right") and to eliminate alternative hypotheses.

One might argue that such evidence is available since the use of expressions of the form "X has a right" are duly recorded in the case reports found in law libraries. However, the use of expressions of the form "X has a right" in such literature may not be a representative sample of the way they are used in more informal contexts, ones in which such expressions may occur much more frequently. Furthermore, a relevant statistical analysis of the use of statements of the form "X has a right" in case materials has yet to be done. It is worth noting that Hart does not cite one case in his lecture in which a statement of the form "X is right" is used to draw a conclusion. Even if he did, it is one thing to exhibit examples of such a use and quite another to show that such a use is characteristic and typical.

Again, although the empirical investigation of legal language would not be easy, in principle it seems possible and, indeed, well within the scope of present-day empirical science. I suggested above one research design to investigate whether the standard uses of expressions of the form "X has a legal right" have certain implications. A similar design might be used to investigate whether the characteristic function of "X has a right" is either as a conclusion drawn from other legal rules and descriptive statements or as a premise, in combination with other premises, is used to draw further conclusions of law. Again a representative sample of uses of "X has a legal right" would be analyzed by a panel of experts. If it turned out that "X had a legal right" was very often used in the way Hart indicated, Hart's analysis would gain support. Without this kind of support Hart's analysis remains speculative.

In any case, another point that Hart hardly mentions in his lecture is worth noting. Suppose Hart is correct and that typically a lawyer or judge draws a conclusion of the form "X has a right" from legal rules and descriptive statements. This drawing may involve a great deal of interpretation and construction of the rules involved. Legal rules are often ambiguous and vague; in order to derive anything from them, they need to be interpreted and sometimes these interpretations are controversial. Now in this case, at least, a statement of the form "X has a right" is hardly "the tail-end of a simple legal calculation,"[50] as Hart in one place maintains, unless by "simple legal calculation" Hart is referring to derivations that occur *after* the controversial interpretation is given. But if this is what Hart means, his account is oversimplified. In fact, in cases in which a controversial interpretation is involved, a statement of the form "X has a right" is the tail-end of a controversial legal construction, one small part of which involves a logical calculation.

Now it should be emphasized that Hart is quite aware of the ambiguities and vagueness of legal language. For example, he discusses these problems at some length in the PAS Symposium in which he defends his Inaugural Lecture against Cohen's attack. Yet despite this keen awareness, Hart does not deal with the problem being raised here. Although he recognizes that judges make law and is opposed to mechanical jurisprudence, he still speaks in his lecture about statements of rights being the tail-end of "simple legal calculation." In "hard cases" statements of rights, however, are hardly the tail-end of "simple legal calculation."

Of course, one must not overemphasize the relevance of this point to Hart's thesis. In particular, it is important not to draw unwarranted inferences about the elucidation of legal concepts from the fact that sometimes drawing legal conclusions involves legal interpretation and construction. For example, Cohen argues that since legal language is vague and ambiguous controversial moral and political theories are needed to draw statements of the form "X has a right" from legal rules and descriptive statements.[51] This means that certain controversial theories must be included in the elucidation of the concept of a legal right. For example, consider the implicitly prescriptive theory (T_1), "A judge decides correctly when he uses sources of the law entirely as his conscience dictates and legal rights are claims so regulated." Translated into explicitly prescriptive form, (T_1) becomes "A judge should decide by using sources of the law entirely as his conscience dictates and legal rights should be claims so decided." If (T_1) were embraced many problems of legal interpretation would be solved, for it would provide guidance to judges in deciding hard cases where legal language is vague and ambiguous. But, as Hart points out, it does not follow that in order to understand the concept of a legal right one must *include* this theory in the elucidation of the concept.

Indeed, to include it would generate a serious problem for there are theories incompatible with (T_1). Consider (T_2), "The law of the state is the will and morality of the dominant economic class and legal rights are the claims so regulated." Translated into an explicit prescriptive form this becomes "The law of the state should be the will and morality of the dominant class and legal rights should be claims so regulated." (T_2) would also provide guidance in hard cases. But which theory, (T_1) or (T_2), should be included in our elucidation of legal rights? Clearly, both cannot be since they are in conflict and the choice of either one without further argument seems arbitrary.

Hart's point against his critics, a point that seems quite correct, is that it is a mistake to include such theories in a definition of legal terms even if they are important in legal decision making. His elucidation of legal rights needs correction, not by building controversial theories into elucidation, but by stressing that legal inferences may involve controversial interpretations of legal rules. In fact, Hart does stress this in his later writings.[52]

So far I have argued that Hart's particular analysis of "X has a legal right" has serious flaws. Although this does not undermine his general approach, until a viable analysis of a legal concept is produced using Hart's general approach, one can at least conclude that Hart's general approach has not been proven.

But can one go further? Do some of the problems found in Hart's particular analysis suggest that there would be similar problems in any analysis using this approach? I believe that there is one such problem with the truth condition aspect of Hart's analysis. This problem is epistemological or methodological: How does one determine the standard or normal uses of a legal expression since the standard or normal uses of legal expressions are what Hart seems to be talking about?

It would seem that finding the standard or normal uses of expressions is a job for linguistic science. Philosophers of law may suggest hypotheses based on their linguistic intuitions, but the verification of these hypotheses is an empirical matter. So any approach that stresses the specification of truth conditions for the standard use must be based on empirical research that is not yet done.

Much the same sort of thing can be said of the functional aspect of Hart's analysis. The most plausible interpretation, as I have already mentioned, is that he is talking about the characteristic function of legal expressions. Again it would seem that, in order to know what this characteristic function is, empirical research would be needed. Yet such research is not yet available. For all we know there may be rather different characteristic functions of the same legal expression in different legal contexts. This has yet to be determined.

Although I have proposed a possible experimental design for investigating some of Hart's claims about legal language, this should only be considered a tentative suggestion.[53] More adequate designs can and should be made by social scientists in cooperation with philosophers of law and legal scholars. My general point is that, although the empirical investigation of the sorts of claims about legal language that Hart has made would not be easy, it would be well within the scope of present empirical science. There exists even now a vast amount of empirical research on legal language. Unfortunately, none of the presently available research seems directly relevant to evaluating Hart's claims.[54]

Hart's lack of concern about how his claims regarding legal language could be confirmed and his apparent ignorance of empirical data on legal language is not surprising. John Austin, to his credit, did seem aware of some of the difficulties his methods posed and suggested ways of investigating ordinary language, for example, the extensive use of tape recorders and an occurrence analysis of locutions found in dictionaries.[55] His suggestions were undeveloped at best, however, and he did not attempt to integrate his ideas in any systematic way with linguistic science. In fact, most Oxford ordinary language analysts have ignored the problems surrounding the confirmation of their claims. A few have actually maintained that empirical investigation is completely unnecessary.

On those occasions when an argument has been given to support the thesis that empirical investigation is unnecessary, it has been rather weak.[56] For example, in perhaps the most extensive defense available of the armchair methods of ordinary language analysis, Stanley Cavell maintains that, since a native speaker is the *source* of the linguist's empirical data about the native's language, that speaker does not need empirical data to support claims about his or her own language.[57] As Jerry Fodor and Jerrold Katz point out,[58] however, just because a native speaker is the source of a linguist's data it does not follow that the native speaker's claims (the meta-linguistic comments the speaker makes) about his or her own language are correct. Now Cavell admits that a native speaker's claims about the history of the language, the sound system, and special study of the morphology of the dialect do need empirical support. But it is difficult to see why empirical support would be needed, for example, in the case of knowledge claims about the sound system and not in the case of knowledge claims about the semantics of the language since, in light of our present evidence, both sorts of claims are known in a similar way.[59] Hart has not taken Cavell's tack and actually defended armchair methods. He uses such methods uncritically. One observer has claimed that ordinary language philosophy is dead.[60] Whether or not this is so, the call from within[61] and from without[62] the legal profession to integrate linguistic philosophy with linguistic science can scarcely be ignored.

Definition in the Concept of Law

Hart's basic thesis on definition in *The Concept of Law* is that definitions can neither clarify the concept of law nor solve the philosophical puzzlement connected with legal concepts. Although he rejects definition he advocates elucidation that is guided by theoretical and practical criteria where conflicting conceptions of the law are at issue as a means of clarification and the relief of puzzlement. Appeals to linguistic usage to settle disputes are deemed to be inadequate. Interesting comparisons can be made with this theory of definition and his earlier ones.

Definition and Elucidation

As we know in *The Concept of Law* Hart does many things: he elucidates the concept of law, gives a new theory of natural law, proposes a theory of judicial interpretation. He also expounds a new approach to legal definition that I will discuss here in virtual abstraction from these other issues. Although Hart's elucidation of the concept of law itself may be considered one of the results of applying this new approach to the concept of law, it can and should be separated for analytic purposes from his general approach to elucidation. After all, it may be correct while the particular results he achieves using it may not be.

In *The Concept of Law* Hart argues[63] that there are three recurrent issues in jurisprudence. How does law differ from and how is it related to orders backed by threats? How does legal obligation differ from and how is it related to moral obligation? What are rules and to what extent is law an affair of rules? In order to answer these questions traditional jurisprudence has searched for a definition of law. At least the most familiar forms of definition, says Hart, have done little to resolve the persistent difficulties and doubts connected with these questions.

Hart maintains that definition is primarily a matter of drawing lines and the need for drawing lines "is often felt by those who are perfectly at home with the day-to-day use of the word in question."[64] As he did in his Inaugural Lecture, Hart points out that a person may know how to use a term and yet feel puzzled about what the term means. A definition might supply the latent principles governing the use of a term and exhibiting relationships between the types of phenomena to which we apply the word and those to which we do not. Thus, according to Hart, a definition does two things at once: it provides a formula translating the word into other well-understood terms and it locates the kind of thing to which the word is used to refer.

However, Hart argues as he did in his Inaugural Lecture that it is not always possible to give this form of definition (*per genus et differentiam*) and that even when it is possible, this form of definition is not very illuminating. If, for example, one is unclear on the properties of the genus, a definition in terms of genus and differentiam is hardly illuminating. Indeed, this is precisely what is wrong with a definition of law in terms of rules of behavior: the notion of rule is unclear.

The traditional form of definition is also based on the false assumption that all instances of general terms signify common characteristics that can be stated. But the ordinary use of an expression may be "open" in that it does not *forbid* the extension of the term to cases "where only some of the normally concomitant characteristics are present."[65] For example, in defining the term "law" this openness would result in borderline cases, for example, primitive law and international law.

Furthermore, instances of general terms are sometimes linked together in ways that are not captured by a traditional definition. Thus they may be linked by analogy, as when one speaks of the foot of a mountain and the foot of a person. They may be linked by different relations to some central element, as when one uses the term "healthy" to apply not only to a man but to his complexion and his morning exercise; the central element is the man's health, his complexion is a sign and his exercise a cause of the central element. Instances of a term may also refer to different constituents of a complex activity, as when "railway" is used to refer not only to trains, but to lines, stations, porters, and companies, all of these elements in a complex system.

Now Hart argues that although there are other types of definitions besides the very simple traditional form, "nothing concise enough to be recognized as a definition" could provide a satisfactory answer to the three recurrent issues mentioned above: "The underlying issues are too different from each other and too fundamental to be capable of this sort of resolution."[66] Nevertheless, says Hart, the instinct that brought those questions under a request for a single definition has not been misguided for it is possible to "isolate and characterize" a central set of elements that forms a common part of the answer to all three questions. What these common elements are, Hart assures us, will emerge in the course of the argument of his book.

Thus, in *The Concept of Law* Hart rejects all attempts to give a definition of law and says that he will instead elucidate the concept of law. It is by elucidation, not definition, that he thinks an improved analysis of the concept of law will be achieved. This approach to definition should be contrasted with that in Hart's Inaugural Lecture. There he also speaks about elucidating certain kinds of legal concepts, but an elucidation seems to involve giving a certain kind of definition appropriate to the subject matter.

At various points in *The Concept of Law* Hart discusses borderline cases in which legal theories have been in doubt over the application of "law" and "legal system." One such case is that of an immoral system of rules, for example, the system existing in Germany during World War II. Figures such as Bentham and Austin have argued that so long as such systems meet the formal requirements for a legal system they are such despite the evil character of the rules. Other theorists in the natural law tradition, however, have been interpreted to maintain that a system is not a legal system without at least a minimum moral content.

According to Hart, "we cannot grapple adequately with this issue if we see it as one concerning the properties of linguistic usage."[67] Indeed, Hart seems to believe that the Bentham-Austin conception is justified on linguistic grounds and the natural law concept is not. But he refuses to argue for the Bentham-Austin concept on these grounds. Rather he argues on theoretical and practical grounds that what has to be evaluated are the comparative merits of a wider way (the Bentham-Austin view) and a narrower way (the natural law view) of classifying legal rules. Thus Hart argues: "If we are to make a reasoned choice between these concepts, it must be because one is superior to the other in the way in which it will assist our theoretical inquiries, or advance and clarify our moral deliberations, or both."[68] He goes on to give various reasons for preferring the wider conception.

International law is a second case where doubts have been raised over the application of the term "law." Although "law" has been applied to it for over 150 years, doubts and perplexities have remained about whether such application is appropriate. In international law there is no international legislature, no courts with compulsory jurisdiction, and no centrally organized sanction. This means that international law lacks secondary rules. Consequently, Hart maintains that the question "Is international law really law?" cannot be "put aside."[69] However, he does not attempt to justify the use of the term "international law" by appeal to usage or to dismiss such usage because international law lacks secondary rules. Instead, he says that he will inquire into the details of the doubts about international law and, as in the case of World War II Germany, consider whether the "common wider usage that speaks of 'international law' is likely to obstruct any practical or theoretical aims."[70]

Hart does not say very much about the distinction between practical and theoretical aims. In defending the wider conception of law he gives what are presumably practical reasons. He believes that such a view would make people more clear-sighted in confronting the official abuse of power and would also prevent them from oversimplifying the variety of moral reasons to which iniquitous laws give rise. There might be other practical reasons also for preferring one view of "law" or "legal system" over another in controversial applications. For example, some views may be easier to understand or teach than others and some may be more psychologically satisfying than others.

Although Hart speaks of theoretical considerations, exactly what he means is a little unclear. He may, however, have had in mind such considerations as simplicity and explanatory power, coherence with well-supported sociological and historical theories, coherence with plausible moral and political doctrines. Again it should be stressed that practical and theoretical considerations, whatever they may be, come into play only in disputed cases, ones where a clear application of the term is lacking.

Evaluation of Hart's View

There are two basic problems with the views on definition and elucidation contained in *The Concept of Law*. First, Hart's attempt to distinguish between definition and elucidation seems inadequate. Second, although Hart introduces theoretical and practical considerations in evaluating different conceptions of law, these play a very limited role in his analysis. In a more adequate approach to the analysis of legal terms such considerations would play a larger role.

What is the difference between definition and elucidation? A major obstacle to answering this is that it is not clear what Hart means by "elucidation." At one point he contrasts definition and elucidation in terms of their conciseness.[71] According to this suggestion definitions are concise whereas elucidations are not. In other places Hart contrasts definition and elucidation by saying that definitions provide a rule according to which the correctness of the use of the words can be established. Apparently the elucidation of a concept does not do this. His purpose, he says, in elucidating the concept of law is not to provide a rule of reference according to which the correctness of the use of the word "law" can be tested but to advance legal theory by providing an improved analysis of the distinctive structure of a legal system and a better understanding of the resemblances and differences between law and the related social phenomena of coercion and morality.[72]

The first suggested difference between definition and elucidation is puzzling because it is not obviously correct that definitions must be concise. Cicero said explicitly that definition should be concise and Aristotle's account implies conciseness. But the thesis has been denied by others. John Dewey, for example, thought the whole of his logic was an expansion of the definition of inquiry and Santayana regarded his definition of beauty as constituting the whole of his book *The Sense of Beauty*. This controversy about the conciseness of definition is discussed by Richard Robinson in his well-known treatise, *Definition*,[73] a book Hart cites in another context in *The Concept of Law*.[74]

Moreover, even if definitions are concise this should not mean that someone could not provide a definition as a partial answer to a controversial philosophical question, an answer that would need to be complex and long. A *complete* answer, one would have thought, would involve explaining and elaborating the terms in the definition, something that goes beyond the definition *per se*. Consider, for example, the question "What is knowledge?" Someone might give a concise answer: knowledge is true, justified belief. Although this might provide a partial answer to the question, for philosophical purposes amplification would be needed. At a minimum one would need to spell out what is meant by "truth," "justified," and "belief." On this view, then, definitions are not opposed to elucidation; definition is simply one aspect of an elucidation. But apparently Hart believes that he has elucidated the concept of law *without* giving a definition.[75]

The second way Hart contrasts definition and elucidation is also puzzling. One would have thought that given his stated purpose of elucidating the concept of law, one aspect or part of his elucidation would consist of giving a definition. How is one to understand the resemblances and differences between law, coercion, and morality as types of social phenomena unless one knows what law is, and how can one know this without some definition of law? Naturally, more would be needed than a definition of law; one would need to have definitions of morality and coercion. But in this case definition is simply one aspect of an elucidation, not something separate as Hart seems to imply.

If one looks at what Hart does in elucidating the concept of law and not at what he says about elucidation, perhaps one will see more clearly what he means by an elucidation and how elucidation and definition can be compatible. Hart attempts to clarify the concept of law by doing all of the following:

(a) Contrasting law with a related notion, for example, morality.
(b) Showing how various aspects of the concept of law fit together, for example, the connection between rule and interpretation.
(c) Contrasting clear cases of law, for example, municipal legal systems, with debatable cases, for example, international law.
(d) Critically evaluating leading theories of what the law is, for example, Austin's theory.

One might abstract and generalize from these considerations and characterize an elucidation of a concept as follows:

An elucidation of a concept C is an extended and detailed attempt to clarify C by doing most of the following things: showing the connection of C to closely related concepts, contrasting clear cases of C and borderline cases, showing how various aspects of C are related to one another, and critically evaluating alternative analyses of C. Hart's treatment of legal causality is certainly an elucidation in this sense. Hart and Honoré show the connection between the concept of legal causation and the ordinary concept of causality; they show how aspects of the concept fit together, for example, abnormality and breaking of the causal chain; they criticize alternative analyses of the concept of legal causality, for example, the modern theory. Furthermore, Hart's theory of judicial interpretation seems to be one aspect of his elucidation of the concept of law.

Given this account of elucidation it seems clear that a definition of law, for example, in the sense advocated in Hart's Inaugural Lecture, and an elucidation are compatible. For example, one can define "legal system" and define "morality," thereby contrasting law and morality.

Whatever Hart's view in *The Concept of Law* on the exact relation between definition and elucidation a new element seems to have entered his approach to philosophical analysis. For the first time he maintains that theoretical and practical considerations should enter into decisions concerning borderline cases. Conflicting analyses concerning borderline cases are not to be judged in terms of whether they are in accord with linguistic usage—even if the usage is known and clear—but in terms of their theoretical and practical implications. These practical and theoretical considerations may provide grounds for a change of usage.

It is not clear, however, whether Hart believes that these practical and theoretical considerations are part of an elucidation.[76] It would seem that the resolution of borderline cases *via* practical and theoretical considerations should be one aspect of an elucidation. After all, since Hart considers an elucidation as advancing legal theory by providing an improved analysis it may well be necessary to settle controversies over borderline cases. In any event, I will take the resolution of borderline cases by considering practical and theoretical issues to be one aspect of an elucidation.

One may well wonder if the consideration of practical and theoretical implications of an analysis coheres with the views on definition Hart expounded in his 1948 paper "Ascription of Responsibility and Rights" and his Inaugural Lecture. Certainly, no theoretical or practical considerations seemed to enter into the 1948 paper. There Hart argued that since legal concepts are defeasible, necessary and sufficient considerations cannot be specified for their application. I have questioned this idea, but even if his view is true, Hart does not seem to consider the possibility that for theoretical or practical reasons it might be useful to specify necessary and sufficient conditions for legal terms.

It is not completely clear why Hart held the position on definition he did in the 1948 paper. Perhaps he recognized the difference between an elucidation and a definition and restricted himself to talking about the definition of legal terms. Or perhaps he did not have the notion of an elucidation at that time. Whatever the reason, at that point in his philosophical development Hart seemed willing to specify rules of usage—the very thing he claims not to be doing in *The Concept of Law*.

Hart speaks of elucidation for the first time in the 1953 Inaugural Lecture, but he does not there differentiate elucidation from definition. Indeed, he appears to be giving an elucidation of legal concepts by giving a certain kind of definition of these terms. Although he rejects mixing theory and definition, he does not consider the possibility that one's concept of legal right or corporation might be preferred on practical or theoretical grounds. Indeed, he seems to oppose the idea that political considerations should enter into legal definitions.

As I have argued, Hart was no doubt correct in maintaining that the statement of a theory should not be part of a definition. But it is one thing to suggest this and quite another not to consider the utility of a definition for theoretical and practical purposes. Of course, in one sense Hart does consider the practical utility of his definition, for he argues that his definition of "right" and "corporation" will relieve puzzlement. But he seems to be assuming that the underlying principles of ordinary usage will be made clear in his definition, and he does not seem to consider the possibility that the underlying principles may be confused and in need of revamping in the light of theoretical or practical considerations—in other words, that ordinary usage should be changed in terms of these considerations. In short, the practical considerations Hart does consider are of a very limited kind.

Even in *The Concept of Law* Hart's conception of the function of practical and theoretical considerations seems to be limited to the reconciliation of conflicting analyses over a few borderline cases. He does not explicitly entertain the idea that even where there is no controversy over borderline cases, practical and theoretical considerations should inform his analyses. Given his professed purpose of providing an improved analysis of the concept of a legal system, this seems strange. The question can be immediately raised, improved in relation to what? Given certain scientific or practical goals one analysis may be preferable to another even if there is no controversy over borderline cases.[77]

One can only speculate about why Hart restricts the function of practical and theoretical considerations as he does. One reason might be his great faith in the power of the study of ordinary linguistic usage to reveal reality. He often quotes J. L. Austin with approval: "We are using a sharpened awareness of words to sharpen our perception of the phenomena."[78] However, one might argue that the study of legal language cannot reveal reality insofar as this language is confused, that one can only see things clearly by changing confused concepts in the light of theoretical and practical considerations.

Another reason why Hart minimizes the theoretical and practical dimensions of analysis may be his belief that there is wide agreement and lack of controversy over the use of legal language; thus it is only necessary to use such considerations in a few borderline cases. But there may in fact be much wider disagreement over legal terminology and far more controversy than Hart thinks. The thesis that disagreement is *not* widespread is, after all, an empirical one for which empirical evidence is needed, evidence he does not supply.

Definition and Reduction

Now that I have surveyed and assessed Hart's views on legal definition it may be useful to relate my conclusions to the account of Hart's theory of legal definitions given by G. P. Baker.[79] According to Baker, Hart's quest for legal understanding is guided by two principles: first, that it is possible to give genuine explanations of legal concepts and legal statements; second, that legal concepts and statements are irreducible, that is, that they can be shown to be logically equivalent to non-legal concepts and non-legal statements. Baker agrees with the first of Hart's principles. However, for all three of Hart's major works on definition he shows that Hart's views are compatible with reductionism; thus he argues that Hart has failed to establish his second principle.

My analysis of Hart's theory of definition and elucidation is compatible with Baker's criticism. First, insofar as Hart fails to show in his 1948 paper that specifying a sufficient condition for legal concepts is impossible, he fails to show that specifying a sufficient condition for legal concepts in non-legal terms is impossible. Such a specification would provide a reduction of legal terms to non-legal terms in one sense of "reduction." Second, in his Inaugural Lecture Hart allows that specifying a sufficient condition for legal statements is possible. However, nothing he says there seems to rule out the possibility that the sufficient condition must be in non-legal terms. Thus the reduction of a statement like "X has a legal right" to non-legal terms is not shown to be impossible. Finally, in *The Concept of Law*, although the concept of an elucidation is unclear, nothing Hart says rules out the possibility of giving a definition as part of an elucidation, for example, in terms of necessary and sufficient conditions. Furthermore, these necessary and sufficient conditions presumably could be specified in non-legal terms.

Moreover, as I have stressed, in allowing theoretical and practical considerations to be relevant in decisions over borderline cases, Hart opens the door for theoretical decisions to enter into elucidation where borderline case decisions are not at issue. One theoretical consideration that might be important in constructing a legal elucidation is that of reduction. An elucidation permitting the reduction of legal to non-legal concepts may be commended on grounds such as coherence with well-supported sociological and historical theories. One excellent way to show the coherence of legal concepts or statements with sociological or historical theories would be to show that these concepts or theories are reducible to the sociological or historical theories.

However, even if Hart had succeeded in showing that legal concepts and legal statements are irreducible in the sense Baker specifies—that is, as not logically equivalent to non-legal concepts and non-legal statements—he would not have shown that legal concepts and legal statements are not reducible in some weaker sense. As I have argued elsewhere, there are a variety of reduction relations logically weaker than logical equivalence.[80]

The upshot of this comparison with Baker is that Hart's different views on legal definition are compatible with the reduction of legal terms and legal statements to non-legal terms and non-legal statements although Hart was opposed to reduction. This is true whether reduction is interpreted in terms of logical equivalence or of some logically weaker relation.[81]

Conclusion

I have traced Hart's theory of legal definition over a thirteen-year period. Although there have been significant changes in it, it is important not to overlook the continuities in his thought. Down through the years Hart's theory of legal definition has been strongly indebted to the assumptions about language and philosophy of British analytic philosophy, especially those of his colleagues at Oxford. Unfortunately, like his colleagues, Hart has pursued the study of language in virtual isolation from any scientific or empirical approach to language. This armchair *apriorism* has been a notable feature of British analytic philosophy and pervades Hart's approach as well. Even his use of theoretical and practical criteria in *The Concept of Law* can perhaps be traced to the more systematic orientation among some of his colleagues in the late 1950's.[82] However, he has remained through the years an ordinary language philosopher. Pragmatic and theoretical considerations play only a very small role in his mature thought and almost none in his earlier thought. Understanding of the actual use of legal language has remained, for him, the basic goal of definition or elucidation.

Hart has continued to stress the importance of definition and elucidation in the philosophy of law. Clarification of legal language has played an essential role in his thought. This is in keeping with the orientation of British analytic philosophy and also with the tradition of analytic jurisprudence with which he identifies.

For many students of Hart's philosophy his neglect of a scientific approach to legal language and his minimal use of theoretical and practical considerations in evaluating legal concepts can only be seen as a limitation of his thought and an obstacle to achieving an adequate analysis of legal notions. Despite these limitations, however, no one else has shown philosophers so well the subtleties of legal language; no one has shown lawyers so well the potential of philosophical analysis.

Part II

Law and Morality

Chapter

5

Theory of Punishment

HART'S *Punishment and Responsibility* (1968) is a collection of previously published essays. The theory of punishment contained in this volume is related to his other work on the law in ways that he does not spell out. Hart's attempt to define punishment is based on the theory of definition presented in his 1953 Inaugural Lecture and his theory of punishment is connected with the definition of a legal system he gives in *The Concept of Law*. Part of the minimum content of natural law, Hart says in that book, is the use of sanctions. Since having the minimum content of natural law is a necessary condition of a legal system, the existence of punishment is a necessary condition of a legal system. Moreover, a key element of the definition of a legal system that can be extracted from that work is that the legal system has a monopoly over physical sanctions. Hart's theory of punishment is concerned with the meaning and justification of physical sanctions.

In addition, in *Causation in the Law* Hart and Honoré are critical not only of the attempt to assimilate causal judgments to policy judgments but of a special case of this: the attempts to assimilate judgments of causality concerning the commission of a crime to policy considerations. Hart and Honoré stress that policy considerations sometimes enter into the decision of whether someone is guilty of a crime and consequently should be punished. They cite as a clear policy consideration used in criminal law the rule that, if the accused is guilty of murder, the victim's death must supervene within one year and a day from the infliction of a wound.[1] But they argue that nothing is gained by supposing that in every case policy considerations are important. Indeed, they tend to maintain that questions of criminal liability are based on our ordinary common sense notions of causality embodied in the criminal law and not on policy considerations. Thus criminal guilt and consequently punishment are often related to ordinary causal judgments.

Finally, Hart's theory of punishment is connected with his views on legal interpretation. As we have seen, Hart's mature position is that, although judges have discretion, their decisions are constrained by policy, principles, and other general legal standards. Now some of these constraining factors would also be relevant to the question of whether someone should be punished. Suppose Jones testifies falsely against Smith and Smith is convicted and hanged. Suppose we then learn of Jones' perjury. Should Jones be punished? In his defense Jones appeals to what he claims is a valid rule of law: a defendant is not guilty of homicide when death is caused by false testimony given in a court of justice.[2] The judge must decide whether this rule is valid and consequently whether Jones should be punished. One policy consideration that might restrain the judge's decision is that informants should not be discouraged from giving evidence in murder trials. There might, however, be other policies or principles that pulled the judge in the other direction.

In his theory of punishment Hart describes himself as attempting to tread "the middle way."[3] By this he means that he attempts to combine retributive and utilitarian elements in his overall scheme. He insists not only "on the restriction of punishment to an offender, but also on the general retention of the doctrine of *mens rea*, and allows some place, though a subordinate one, to ideas of equality and proportion in the gradation of the severity of punishment."[4]

Above all, Hart emphasizes that an adequate theory of punishment is complicated. It is not enough to realize that

> a plurality of different values and aims should be given as a conjunctive answer to some *single* question concerning the justification of punishment. What is needed is the realization that different principles . . . are relevant at different points in any morally accepted account of punishment. What we should look for are answers to a number of different questions such as: What justifies the general practice of punishment? To whom may punishment be applied? How severely may we punish? In dealing with these and other questions concerning punishment we should bear in mind that in this, as in most other social institutions, the pursuit of one aim may be qualified by or provide an opportunity, not to be missed, for the pursuit of others. Till we have developed this sense of the complexity of punishment . . . we shall be in no fit state to assess the extent to which the whole institution has been eroded by, or needs to be adapted to, new beliefs about the human mind.[5]

According to Hart, advocates of traditional retributivist and utilitarian theories usually have attempted to answer very different questions about punishment. In so doing they have failed to see that these theories provide appropriate answers to one question and not another; they have failed to see that an adequate account of punishment must combine retributive and utilitarian elements. Hart's stress on the importance of distinguishing different questions in his theory of punishment is typical of his approach to moral philosophy in general. In Chapter 8 we will find him constantly separating different questions in debating Devlin on the legal enforcement of morality. This clear separation of questions is, of course, typical of the Oxford analytic approach, which teaches that much philosophical confusion will be avoided if one gets clear on precisely what question is at issue.

Hart believes in discussions of punishment that it is important to distinguish three different questions:

(1) What does "punishment" mean?
(2) What are the general justifying aims of punishment?
(3) How should punishment be distributed?

Under the distributive question, he says, we should distinguish two further questions:

(3a) Who should be punished? (liability)
(3b) How much should the offender be punished? (amount)

In order to determine in what sense Hart's theory is a combination of utilitarianism and retributivism, it is necessary to have some understanding of the latter. Hart provides us with a statement of retributivism in its extreme form. A retributivist theory of punishment asserts three things:[6]

(A) A person may be punished if and only if he has voluntarily done something wrong.
(B) A person's punishment must in some way match, or be the equivalent of, the wickedness of the offense.
(C) The justification for punishing people under such conditions is that the return of suffering for moral evil voluntarily done is itself just or morally good.

Although Hart does not provide us with an equivalent statement of an extreme utilitarian theory of punishment, it is not difficult to construct one on the basis of his writings:

(A′) A person may be punished if and only if punishing the person maximizes social utility.
(B′) The extent and type of a person's punishment must maximize social utility.
(C′) The justification for punishing people is the maximization of social utility (correction, prevention, deterrence, and so on).

The Definition of Punishment

Hart defines the "standard or central case"[7] of punishment in terms of five elements:

(1) It must involve pain or other consequences normally considered unpleasant.
(2) It must be for an offense against legal rules.
(3) It must be of an actual or supposed offender for his offense.
(4) It must be intentionally administered by human beings other than the offender.
(5) It must be imposed and administered by an authority constituted by a legal system against which the offense is committed.

He relegates to the position of substandard or secondary cases the following "among many other possibilities":

(a) Punishments for breaches of legal rules imposed or administered otherwise than by officials (decentralized sanctions).
(b) Punishments for breaches of non-legal rules or orders (punishment in a family or school).
(c) Vicarious or collective punishment of some members of a social group for action done by others without the former's authorization, encouragement, control, or permission.
(d) Punishment of persons, otherwise than under (c), who neither are in fact nor are supposed to be offenders.

One general question is that of the relationship, if any, of Hart's analysis of punishment to his theories of legal definition described in Chapter 4. He expounded this definition of punishment in 1959, when his Inaugural Lecture was behind him and *The Concept of Law* was yet to come.

The brevity of Hart's analysis indicates that he does not take his analysis of punishment to be an elucidation of the sort proposed in *The Concept of Law*. That Hart's analysis of punishment can be assimilated to the type of definition outlined in his Inaugural Lecture is not completely clear, however. Certainly, Hart does not explicitly attempt to analyze a sentence in which the term "punishment" appears by specifying truth conditions and the function of this sentence in legal discourse. But perhaps by a slight reworking Hart's definition can be construed as at least in part in accordance with the model of the Inaugural Lecture. Consider the following:

X is given punishment P by Z for Y if:
(1) P involves pain or other consequences normally considered unpleasant.
(2) Y is an offense against a legal rule.
(3) X is an actual or supposed offender.
(4a) Z administers P intentionally.

(4b) Z is a human being.
(4c) Z is not identical with X.
(5) Z is an authority constituted by a legal system against which Y is committed.

If we use the Inaugural Lecture as our model, the function of an expression of "X is given punishment P by Z for Y" remains unclear. Nor is it completely clear if Hart intends (1)–(5) as necessary as well as sufficient conditions for the truth of "X is given punishment P by Z for Y." (Following the model of the Inaugural Lecture, I have construed (1)–(5) as sufficient conditions.)

In any case, it is difficult to understand why Hart thinks that the standard or central cases of punishment are confined to punishment in *legal* systems. No reason is given for this contention. Indeed, earlier well-known analyses, for example, Antony Flew's,[8] did not restrict punishment in the primary sense to either legal or moral offenses and Hart says that he is simply drawing on that work.[9]

Not only does Hart's view that the standard cases of punishment are legal ones conflict with the earlier analyses on which he purports to be relying, but it seems implausible on independent grounds. Dictionary definitions do not identify punishment with legal punishment, and it seems highly unlikely that we learn the concept of punishment from legal contexts. After all, children learn the concept of punishment before they are even aware of legal systems. It is possible, of course, that the standard cases of punishment do not play a crucial role in learning the concept of punishment, but there is a presumption that they do, and, without independent evidence, Hart's thesis seems implausible.

There is at least one peculiar implication of Hart's analysis that also casts doubt on his analysis. According to (2) above, in order for there to be a punishment in the standard case, the punishment must be for an offense and *not* simply for a supposed offense. According to (3), in order for there to be a punishment it must be a punishment of an actual *or* a supposed offender. These two conditions, combined with the other conditions, imply that if public officials inflict pain on an innocent person supposing him or her to be guilty of an actual crime, they are punishing the person. But if they inflict pain on an innocent person supposing him or her to be guilty for what they wrongly suppose was a crime, they are not punishing the person in the standard sense of punishment. It is possible, of course, that the standard sense of punishment has this implication, but this seems unlikely.

In any case, Hart uses what he believes are substandard cases to prevent what he calls the "definitional stop"[10] in discussions of punishment. The definitional stop works in this way: Critics of a utilitarian theory of punishment have argued that, since it justifies punishment by reference to beneficial social consequences, then, if the punishment of an innocent person were to have beneficial consequences, it would be justified. Some utilitarians have tried at this point to defend their theory by arguing that it is logically impossible to punish an innocent person since the definition of punishment involves punishing someone for committing an offense. This "definitional stop" is what Hart attempts to capture in the second condition (Y is an offense against a legal rule) and the third condition (X is an actual or supposed offender) of what he takes to be standard or central cases of punishment.

Hart maintains that the definitional stop strategy fails to satisfy critics of utilitarian theories of punishment and that it would prevent us from investigating "the rational and moral status of our preference for a system of punishment under which measures painful to individuals are to be taken against them only when they have committed an offense."[11] Hart's argument seems to be that people who are persuaded by the definitional stop fail to notice that there are substandard uses of punishment in which punishment of the innocent is not a contradiction in terms. Once they realize the existence of these substandard cases, the force of the definitional stop will be removed.

But even if there are no substandard cases of punishment surely the definitional stop will not work where punishment of the innocent is not a contradiction in terms. And, if punishment of the innocent is a contradiction in terms in all cases of punishment, it could still be argued that utilitarians are committed to inflicting pain on an innocent person if this is socially beneficial. Whether this is called punishment or something else hardly seems to matter. Thus Hart's reliance on substandard cases to block the definitional stop seems unnecessary.

The General Aim of the System of Punishment and the Liability of Punishment

Hart believes that it is important to distinguish two aspects of a theory of punishment: the general justifying aim of punishment and the liability of punishment, that is, who may be punished. This distinction is relevant to the two classical theories of punishment—retributivism and utilitarianism—in that he believes that retributive theories fail to provide a general justifying aim.[12] These theories either avoid the question of justification altogether or are disguised forms of utilitarianism. Thus Hart rejects (C) above, namely:

(C) The justification for punishing people under such conditions is that the return of suffering for moral evil voluntarily done is itself just or morally good.

According to Hart, the reason for having criminal law is to announce to society that certain actions are not to be done and to secure that fewer crimes are committed. The general justifying aim of a system of punishment is closely connected with this reason, for it is to help assure conformity to the requirement of the criminal law. The general justification of a system of punishment, in other words, is that it deters people from breaking the law.[13] Thus Hart believes that utilitarians, not retributivists, provide the general justifying aim of punishment. In short, he accepts (C′) above,

(C′) The justification for punishing people is the maximization of social utility (correction, prevention, deterrence, and so on).

Hart insists, however, that even if retribution is not part of the general aim of punishment, it can provide an answer to the liability question—the question of who should be punished. Recall (A) above:

(A) A person may be punished if and only if he has voluntarily done something wrong.

Assumption (A) can be understood as entailing three propositions that are important to an understanding of Hart's position:

(A_1) A person may be punished for doing X only if he or she has done X.
(A_2) A person may be punished for doing X only if the person did X voluntarily (the person had the requisite *mens rea* when doing X).
(A_3) If a person may be punished for doing X, then the person in doing X is morally wrong.

Assumption (A_1) puts a clear restriction on who can be punished and is, according to Hart, a necessary supplement to utilitarianism. This restriction illustrates his idea that sometimes the aim of a social institution must be restricted by principles that limit the unqualified pursuit of these aims.[14] Hart's theory of punishment, then, is a utilitarianism modified by a retributive principle regarding who can be punished. In terms of the two models stated above, Hart accepts (A_1) and (C′).

Two questions can be raised about Hart's views on (A_1) and (C′): Is utilitarianism, as he conceives it, an adequate account of the justifying aim of punishment? Or to put it in the terms introduced above, is (C′) correct? Does retributivism alone entail that the innocent must not be punished? Or to put it in the terms introduced above, does (A′), combined with relevant factual information, entail (A_1)?

For one thing, some critics have argued that Hart's theory gives no account of the apparent appropriateness of punishment where the deterrence of others is not a plausible objective. For example, Richard Wasserstrom argues:

> Thus, the punishment of persons such as Goering or Eichmann, and indeed the punishment of war criminals generally, is probably not justifiable on the grounds that this deters the rest of us from committing crimes of war. And, as Hart himself suggests, even if some case for deterrence could be made out, it hardly seems to get to the heart of the issue. Whatever the legitimate objections to the punishment of someone like Eichmann may have been, the objections did not turn at all on the presence or absence of a possible deterrent effect.[15]

Wasserstrom suggests alternative retributive general aims. In particular, punishment may be a community's social mechanism where an offender can best achieve expiation of wrongdoing or else a means by which unjust enrichment of the offender is stopped.

Could a utilitarian theory of punishment answer these objections? It is by no means clear to me that the punishment of war criminals could not be justified in large part on grounds of deterrence. Of course the deterrence is not aimed, as Wasserstrom suggests, at "one of us," who has very little opportunity to commit war crimes. One major aim, however, would be to deter people in positions of great power from committing such crimes.

Wasserstrom is surely correct that any legitimate objection one might have had to Eichmann's punishment would not have been in terms of the presence or absence of the deterrent value of the punishment. But this hardly rebuts Hart's theory that the general aim of punishment is deterrence. There were special circumstances in Eichmann's capture and trial that one might have objected to on non-deterrent, but nonetheless utilitarian, grounds. A utilitarian can maintain that the way a *particular* criminal is punished is unjustified on utilitarian grounds and still maintain that the general practice of punishing criminals is justified on grounds of deterrence.

Furthermore, an expanded utilitarian theory may be able to handle Wasserstrom's retributive scruples; that is to say, Hart's utilitarian justification may take too limited a view of utilitarianism. Thus, the punishment of criminals may encourage and reinforce certain aspects of common sense morality that in turn have desirable consequences. For example, the Nuremburg Trials reinforced and encouraged the very retributivist principles found in ordinary morality that Wasserstrom has pinpointed and these views may themselves be desirable on utilitarian grounds. If people believe that offenders go unpunished, this will cause and spread unhappiness and discontent. By indicating that offenders do not go unpunished, the punishment of Goering can be said to have been indirectly conducive to human happiness.

Philosophers who, like Wasserstrom, have retributive predilections about the general justifying aim of punishment might ponder the following hypothetical case. Suppose the Nuremburg Trials had been held in secret and that the punishment of the war criminals found guilty at the trial had been secret as well; in other words, suppose that no one knew of the trial and its results except the defendants, counsels, and judges. Would they still believe that the punishment of the war criminals was justified? This is to be doubted. It is only when the results of such a trial are widely known that their punishment seems justified. This certainly suggests that the justification of punishment in this case at least is based on the consequences of punishment, deterrent or otherwise.

In the second place, a broadly conceived utilitarianism can block justification for punishing the innocent. For if innocent people are punished, it is likely that great anxiety and social unrest would result that in most circumstances would outweigh any deterrent value such punishment would have. So, it would seem that punishing the innocent can be condemned on straight utilitarian grounds and that no retributivist supplement is needed.

Hart's answer to these utilitarian rejoinders is problematic. He argues first that in extreme cases people might think it right to punish innocent people, but that this would be resorted to "with the sense of sacrificing an important principle. We should be conscious of choosing the lesser of two evils, and this would be inexplicable if the principle sacrificed to utility were itself only a requirement of utility."[16] However, utilitarianism can explain why the choice is between the lesser of two evils. There is nothing in the utilitarian position that prevents one from seeing that some action justified on utilitarian grounds nevertheless causes some evil. Indeed, it is perfectly consistent with utilitarianism to say that what should be done has more evil than good so long as the action has less evil than any alternative action. In such a case a utilitarian might well speak of what should be done as the lesser of two evils. Consider the following two choices as the only ones open to legal authorities. Let us suppose the numbers in parentheses indicate units of utility and the total represents the correct utility assessments connected with each choice.

(1) Deter a great amount of crime (20) but cause a great amount of anxiety by punishing innocent people (−25). Total: −5
(2) Deter no crime by not punishing innocent people (−6) but do not cause any anxiety (0). Total: −6

Given the above assumptions, choice (1) could be spoken of as the lesser of two evils and would be the preferred choice on utilitarian grounds.

In punishing to deter crime, utilitarians certainly would feel a sense of sacrificing something. After all, utilitarians believe that pain and suffering are evils: they do not want to bring evil about and, if it were possible, they would not bring it about; however, when they must, they bring it about only for a greater good or lesser evil. Regret because one has brought about pain and suffering for the larger good is an emotion that is not only compatible with a utilitarian orientation but may even be justified on utilitarian grounds, in that having such an emotion may have utilitarian value. In punishing the innocent utilitarians would certainly realize that they were causing anxiety in the general populace and as a consequence would feel regret; indeed, they might act as if a great sacrifice had been made for the prevention of crime.

Hart also argues that the justification of not punishing the innocent cannot be utilitarian because, when immoral laws are involved, punishing people who do not break the laws would be a "*special* iniquity."[17] But again it seems that the utilitarian has an easy response: punishing the innocent would add further evil to an already evil system; it would cause anxiety and worry.

Suppose there was a law forbidding people from speaking against the government. Suppose Jones who was innocent of breaking the law was punished under the law. There would indeed be a special iniquity in this but this iniquity could be explained on utilitarian grounds. In addition to the evil of laws forbidding people from speaking against the government, punishing Jones, an innocent person, would cause further evil by generating anxiety and worry.

Theory of Excuses

We have already seen that Hart's utilitarian theory of punishment is limited by one retributivist restriction, namely (A_1): A person may be punished for doing X only if he or she has done X. Hart also accepts as a restriction on utilitarianism (A_2): A person should be punished for doing X, only if the person did X voluntarily (the person had the requisite *mens rea* when doing X).[18]

Hart believes that the best way to understand *mens rea* in the law is negatively —that is, by specifying the excusing conditions that must be present if someone who commits a crime is not to be punished. An historical point must be made here. In "The Ascription of Responsibility and Rights," Hart argued that *mens rea* was a defeasible concept: "What is meant by the mental element in criminal liability (*mens rea*) is only to be understood by considering certain defenses or exceptions."[19] Roughly speaking the defenses and exceptions specified in that article are what Hart calls excuses in papers on punishment appearing in the late 1950's. To be sure, in these papers the focus is different. In his earlier article *mens rea* was used to elucidate the defeasibility aspect of his theory of definition. In the later paper *mens rea* plays a crucial role in his theory of punishment. In both instances, however, *mens rea* is to be understood negatively.

Hart argues that the justification of excuses in a legal system cannot be understood in utilitarian terms, for one must appeal to independent principles of justice and fairness. Bentham's well-known utilitarian defense of excuses is refuted by Hart as follows: Bentham argues that the punishment of people who could not have helped doing what they did, that is, people with excuses, could not be effective. For if they could not have helped doing what they did, their punishment could not be a threat to them. Consequently, the punishment of people who had excuses are cases "unmeet for punishment."[20] Hart maintains correctly that this argument is a *non sequitur*. Bentham may be correct to suppose that the *threat* of punishment will not deter *people with excuses*. But the *actual* punishment of people with excuses may well deter *people without excuses* from committing crimes, indeed deter them more than if people with excuses were not punished. As Hart points out, "any increase in the number of conditions required to establish criminal liability increases the opportunity for deceiving courts or juries by the pretence that some condition is not satisfied."[21]

Hart considers another utilitarian counterargument to his thesis that a utilitarian theory of excuses is impossible. Utilitarians might hold that in societies, including our own, where the principle that punishing involuntary conduct is wrong and is engraved in popular mores to punish people who could not help doing what they did would result in social disturbances and unhappiness. He has two objections to this but it is not clear if either one succeeds.[22] Hart argues that there are workable legal systems with strict liability for relatively minor offenses but not for major crimes. In such systems there is no social disturbance and unhappiness that can be appealed to in showing the utilitarian disadvantages of a system without excuses. He also objects that "we do not dissociate ourselves from the principle that it is wrong to punish" those who could not help doing what they did "by treating it as something merely embodied in popular *mores* to which concessions must be made sometimes."[23] We condemn legal systems where they disregard the principle that people should be punished for what they could not help doing even if there are no popular mores against punishing these people.

Surely the first reason Hart gives provides no argument against utilitarianism. Just because a workable system of punishment is possible with strict liability for minor crimes it does not mean that a working system is possible in which strict liability is imposed for major crimes. A utilitarian in perfect consistency can argue that a mild infringement of popular morality will not cause serious social upheaval whereas a strong infringement of popular morality will.

Hart's second reason seems irrelevant to justifying excusing conditions in a system like ours where excusing conditions *are* embodied in popular mores. Furthermore, Hart provides no evidence that we (who are the "we" anyway?) would condemn legal systems that disregard the principle that people should be punished for what they could not help doing when there are no popular mores against punishing these people.

Hart rejects a full-blown retributivist account of excusing conditions as well as an extreme utilitarian one. Thus, he dismisses (A_3): If a person may be punished for doing X, then the person in doing X is morally wrong. On this view, one he associates with Jerome Hall, a professor of criminal law, a criminal must have moral culpability to be punished; if an excusing condition can be shown to be present, the criminal does not have moral culpability and consequently should not be punished.[24] First, Hart maintains that Hall's view does not correspond to the way the law is actually practiced. So, if it is meant to describe how the law actually works, it is wrong. Some acts are crimes but not morally wrong, for example, driving on the wrong side of the road. So it is mistaken to associate legal responsibility for a crime with moral guilt. Hart also argues that if Hall's position is meant to be a recommendation for an ideal system of law where all crimes are morally wrong acts, his position cannot be refuted since it merely represents a moral preference.

But there is, of course, another interpretation of Hall's view. Hall might have meant to analyze the central or core idea behind excusing conditions. But, then, that there are some cases in which criminal acts are not morally wrong would be of small consequence. As Wasserstrom has pointed out, Hart himself argued in "Positivism and the Separation of Law and Morals" and later in *The Concept of Law* against the idea that in a philosophical analysis one must specify essential properties. He now seems to have forgotten this and assumes that Hall is committed to some essentialist view.[25]

Furthermore, it is difficult to see why Hart believes that if Hall's view represents a moral preference it cannot be refuted. In his other writings Hart does not hesitate to argue against moral views; there he does not suppose that moral preferences are beyond criticism. Indeed, it would seem *prima facie* that there are strong arguments against any system of criminal law that requires every criminal act to be morally wrong. Since such a system could not have criminal laws regulating which side of the street one drives on, it would be quite undesirable.

How then does Hart justify excuses? He argues that "it is unfair and unjust to punish those who have not 'voluntarily' broken the law."[26] He seems to give two basic rationales for this contention.[27] First, he maintains that, if there were no excuses allowed in a legal system, there would be undesirable consequences: our power of predicting what will happen would decrease because we could not predict very well if we would do something by mistake or accident, our choices would condition what befalls to a lesser extent than our own choices now do, and we would suffer sanctions without having obtained satisfaction. Second, Hart argues that there are advantages to a legal system with excuses:

> First, we maximize the individual's power at any time to predict the likelihood that the sanctions of the criminal law will be applied to him. Secondly, we introduce the individual's choice as one of the operative factors determining whether or not these sanctions shall be applied to him. He can weigh the cost to him of obeying the law—and of sacrificing some satisfaction in order to obey—

> against obtaining that satisfaction at the cost of paying 'the penalty.' Thirdly, by adopting this system of attaching excusing conditions we provide that, if the sanctions of the criminal law are applied, the pains of punishment will for each individual represent the price of some satisfaction obtained from breach of law.[28]

One crucial point that should be noted at the outset is that it is unclear why Hart believes that his justification for a theory of excuses is not utilitarian. One important type of utilitarian theory is ideal utilitarianism, where the goal is to maximize a variety of different values. A superficial look at Hart's rationale for excuses indicates that he argues in terms of consequences: a system without excuses has bad consequences; a system with excuses has good consequences. A closer look suggests that he assumes that predictive power, free choice, and getting satisfaction from one's choices are values that are maximized in legal systems with excuses. Whether for Hart such values are intrinsic or instrumental is unclear but that is no matter. On one *prima facie* plausible reading, Hart is giving an ideal utilitarian justification of a legal system of excuses.[29]

The difficulty with this type of justification, however, is that it seems to constitute only part of the story. Even if Hart is correct that a legal system with excuses maximizes *these* values, one with excuses may not maximize *other* important values.[30] Thus, the disadvantages may cancel out any advantage that a system of excuses might have. For example, a legal system without excuses may have much more deterrent value than a system with excuses.

For this reading of Hart to make sense, we must assume that he rates the values of predictive power, free choice, and getting satisfaction from one's choices higher than deterrent value. Instead of saying that the general utilitarian aim of punishment is limited by some retributive principle, perhaps he should say that the general aim of punishment, namely deterrence, should be balanced against other important values.

That Hart's justification for this theory of excuses is based on utilitarian considerations and not on independent principles of justice and fairness, as he claims, is suggested by another consideration. Some of the advantages claimed for a system with excuses seem to have nothing to do with justice and fairness. For example, his claim that such a system would decrease our ability to predict shows nothing about the unfairness of the system; nor does the fact (if it is one) that the individual's power to predict what sanctions of the criminal law will be applied is maximized by a system of excuses indicate something about the fairness of the system. Indeed, the ability to predict shows something about the utility of the system, not its fairness or unfairness.

Aside from the issue of whether or not Hart's justification of excuses is basically utilitarian there is the problem that some of the claims made by Hart are not obviously true.[31] For example, although it is true that a system of criminal law without excusing conditions would *decrease* our ability to predict when we would get punished, it is also the case that it would *increase* our ability to predict that if we got punished we would be tried for a crime. In such a system we would know with certainty that excuses would not work and consequently we would know more accurately than we do now the outcome of the trial. So it is quite uncertain whether our overall predictive capacity would be decreased in a system with no excuses. Similarly, it is unclear if our overall ability to predict the likelihood that sanctions of the criminal law would be applied to us is increased in a system with excuses, for in some respects it is increased and in other respects it is decreased.

Hart is no doubt correct in supposing that in a system of criminal law without excuses there would be cases in which people suffered sanctions without obtaining satisfaction. Suppose that by accident a person kills someone. Since there are no excuses, the person is punished. However, since the victim was not the person's enemy, not someone the person wished to kill, he or she has obtained no satisfaction. What Hart does not seem to take into account is that given a legal system with excuses a person may obtain illicit satisfaction without any sanction. For example, one may deliberately kill one's enemy, use the insanity defense, and get off. So whether the total amount of satisfaction associated with punishment is increased or decreased in a system of criminal law with excuses is by no means certain.

It is also correct for Hart to assume that in a criminal law system without excuses there would be cases in which choice would not condition what befalls someone. A person kills someone by accident; since there are no excuses the person is punished. One could certainly speak in this case of the person's choice not conditioning what befell him or her. But what Hart fails to note is that in a system of law with excuses a person's choice may not condition what befalls him or her either. A person may deliberately kill someone and even expect to be punished for the act and yet get off because of the insanity defense. In this case, too, one may well speak of what happened as the person's choice not conditioning what befell the person. Whether there is an *overall* increase in cases in which people's choices condition what befalls them is uncertain.

Still, it might be argued that there is a crucial difference in the two cases. In a criminal law system with excuses a potential lawbreaker can weigh the chances of being punished by taking into account the likelihood that some defense, for example, the insanity plea, will succeed. But it might be maintained that in a system without excusing conditions, no such calculations are possible. Yet is there a crucial difference after all? In a system of criminal law *without* excuses people can weigh whether to act or not in terms of the likelihood of their making a mistake, having an accident, and so on. For example, one might estimate the probability of shooting someone by accident. This probability would then be combined with other probabilities in order to arrive at the overall estimate of being punished in a system without excuses because of something not conditioned by choice. Let us call this probability P_1. Now let P_2 be the probability that in a legal system with excuses, for example, the insanity defense will succeed even when the person is in fact guilty and expects to be punished. P_2 will thus be an estimate of the probability in a system that has excuses of something happening to a person that is not conditioned by his or her choice. It is not obvious that P_1 is any less knowable than P_2.

Punishment of Negligence

What is the relation between Hart's theory of excuses and his views on the punishment of negligent conduct? In most systems of criminal law certain negligent behavior is punishable. For example, in England driving without due care and attention is a summary offense although no harm is involved. In other jurisdictions there are criminal laws against causing bodily harm by negligence. Insofar as Hart attempts to justify such laws he does so in terms of their deterrent value.[32]

He argues that it is too restricted a view of deterrence to suppose that the punishment of negligent conduct cannot have a deterrent effect. It is true, Hart argues, that the threat of legal punishment could not deter some inadvertent, unthinking behavior on some particular occasion. For the actor is, by hypothesis, not deliberately weighing the possibilities of punishment. Nevertheless, Hart points out that these threats of punishment could nevertheless deter criminal behavior in that punishment for negligence may well cause a person not to be negligent at some later time. As Hart puts it, the threat of punishment is something that causes a person to "exert his faculties, rather than something which enters as a reason for conforming to the law when he is deliberating whether to break it or not."[33]

Hart is at great pains to argue that legal punishment for negligence is significantly different from punishment for strict liability. In the case of negligence, the person could have taken precautions and could have acted with due care. The negligent person, in other words, could have avoided doing what he or she did. But in the case of strict liability punishment may be handed out even if the person could not have avoided doing what he or she did. Consequently, some of the arguments against punishment for strict liability do not apply to punishment for negligence.

But in terms of the scheme of justification of excuses developed by Hart and outlined above, the punishment of negligent behavior would seem to have disadvantages. For although negligent action in some sense is action in which one could have done differently, it is not behavior one has deliberately chosen. Presumably, then, all of the disadvantages Hart claims for a system of punishment without excuses would apply.[34] For example, our powers of prediction would be decreased since we cannot predict very well if we will do something negligently. The mere fact that we could have acted differently if we had thought does not mean that we deliberately chose to do the action. It would seem, then, that Hart should be opposed to the punishment of negligence for the same reasons that he is opposed to a system of punishment without excuses. Indeed, it would seem that Hart should allow the state of mind of a negligent person to be an excusing condition recognized by law. But Hart seems to argue that punishment for negligence is justified on deterrent grounds and, that at least in some situations, the state of mind of a negligent person should not be an excusing condition.

Whether or not there is any way to reconcile this apparent conflict in Hart's theory is unclear. One possibility would be to argue that the advantages of punishing negligent behavior outweigh the disadvantages, that although the punishment of negligent behavior would somewhat decrease our power of prediction, it would deter future negligent conduct, and that this deterrence is more important than the decrease in predictive powers.

There are some problems with this suggestion, however. First, it is unclear that increased deterrence in the case of negligence is more important than decreased predictive value. Second, and more important, this argument, if pressed, cuts very deep. Consider the implications of this suggestion when it is applied to conduct that people could not help. Punishing such conduct might have deterrent value that might be said to outweigh any resulting disadvantages. For example, punishing the criminal acts of insane people might deter people from doing certain criminal acts. It might either deter other insane people or (which is more likely) deter people who are not insane but who think that they can get off on the insanity defense. This deterrence may be deemed to have great value and outweigh any disadvantages, for example, loss of predictive power, that result from not allowing the insanity defense. So it would seem that if this defense of Hart's theory is allowed, it might undercut the general justification of excuses he gives.

Treatment and Punishment

If it is difficult to reconcile Hart's account of the punishment of negligent behavior with his overall theory, his views on mental abnormality as a legal defense seem even harder to reconcile with it. Hart's views on mental abnormality as a legal defense can only be understood in the context of his critique of Lady Wootton's proposal concerning the appeal to *mens rea* in criminal law.[35] Wootton proposes that the criminal law should not be considered a system of punishments, but rather a system of social control that is completely forward-looking and is not concerned with the guilt of the offender in the traditional sense.

Criminal law procedure should, on Wootton's view, have two stages. In the first stage, the state would establish only if someone actually committed an act forbidden by the law. If the person was found to have done the proscribed act, in the second stage the state might do various things with the offender: for example, give the offender treatment; or, if treatment was not appropriate but the offender was still dangerous, confine the offender to a "place of safety" so that he or she could not bring about further social harm; or, if the offender was no longer dangerous, release him or her.

Wootton apparently does not consider the second stage of criminal law procedure to be punishment since the offender's treatment is not based on any consideration of responsibility in the traditional sense. On Wootton's scheme, people are, of course, responsible for what they do in the sense that they bring about certain consequences of their action, but offenders are not responsible in the sense of having a certain mental state when they act and being culpable because of this state.

It is perhaps worth noting that, according to Hart, putting someone in a place of safety against the person's will is a punishment in the central sense of the term. None of Hart's conditions of the normal meaning of punishment entails that in order to punish someone he or she must have a particular mental state. Clearly, Wootton is operating with a more restricted sense of punishment than is Hart. This is not to say that the mental state of the offender is completely irrelevant in Wootton's system, for it may enter into the decision of what to do with an offender. For example, knowledge that an offender has paranoid delusions may be relevant to whether the person should receive treatment or simply be confined.

Now Hart rejects Wootton's proposal in its extreme form that no consideration of *mens rea* be used in the criminal law. However, he accepts a modified—what he calls a moderate—version of her proposal.[36] He advocates the view that all considerations of mental abnormality be removed from the criminal law. This would entail that no defense of mental abnormality should be allowed in criminal law proceedings. Presumably Hart would allow, as Wootton would, an appeal to mental abnormality in the second stage of criminal procedure where the question is what the state should do with the offender.

Given his reasons for rejecting Wootton's more extreme position and his reasons for preferring a system of excuses the crucial question is whether Hart can consistently maintain this moderate position. Hart has three misgivings about Wootton's extreme position. His first one has to do with individual freedom. Without *mens rea*, Hart argues, there will be increased occasions for "official interference with our lives." For example, without *mens rea* in criminal assaults, "every blow, even if it was apparent to a policeman that it was purely accidental or merely careless and therefore not, according to present law, a criminal assault, would be a matter for investigation . . . and the condition if serious treated by medical or penal methods."[37] This will lead to the increased discretion of prosecuting authorities and will consequently decrease people's power to predict what will happen to them if they accidentally or carelessly strike someone.

The difficulty with this argument is that it applies to Hart's moderate position as well. Since no defense of mental abnormality is allowed on that position, every criminal act, for example, the jaywalking of a person with the mental abnormality of somnambulism, would be "a matter for investigation and if the condition is serious enough" treated by psychiatric methods. This, in turn, would lead to increased discretion by psychiatrists and other mental health professionals and consequently to a decrease in people's powers to predict what will happen to them if, for example, they jaywalk while sleepwalking. Offhand, however, it is not obvious that not being able to predict accurately what will happen to you if you jaywalk in your sleep is less undesirable than not being able to predict what will happen to you if you strike someone accidentally.

Hart's second misgiving about Wootton's extreme proposal is that compulsory medical treatment and imprisonment are to be considered alternative forms of social hygiene. Which one the state should use will depend on what their probable effects will be and not on the responsibility of the offender. On moral grounds Hart objects to this on the grounds that it is wrong to imprison an offender in order to deter him or her (or other potential offenders) unless the offender could have done otherwise. On sociological grounds he argues that, if imprisonment is not considered a form of punishment for a crime for which the offender is responsible, the law will lose an important element of its deterrent force. This is because imprisonment in our present system is an act "expressing the odium, if not the hostility, of society for those who break the law."[38] If imprisonment is not a form of punishment but a form of social hygiene, this function will be lost.

Again, these objections seem to apply to Hart's moderate version as well. A habitual criminal with an untreatable mental abnormality might be imprisoned for deterrence considerations, yet the person might not be able to help doing what he or she was imprisoned for. Further, if a person with an untreatable mental abnormality is imprisoned after conviction this would seem to undercut the standard function of imprisonment stated by Hart, namely that of "expressing the odium, if not the hostility, of society for those who break the law." Consequently, Hart's proposal would lessen the deterrent force of imprisonment. Thus Hart's sociological objection applies to his own moderate proposal.

Hart's third misgiving concerns the implication he draws from Wootton's proposal that no definition of criminal offense must contain any reference to mental elements. He argues that there are some harmful activities that can only be identified by mental elements, for example, attempted crimes, that should be criminal offenses. But on Wootton's extreme view, there could be no criminal code with a law against, for example, attempted murder since the definition of attempted murder must contain reference to an intention to murder.

Once more, the problem Hart discerns in Wootton's proposal occurs also in his more moderate proposal. One type of mental abnormality is intoxication. With all mental abnormality eliminated, so presumably is the crime of driving while intoxicated. Thus, on Hart's own proposal there could be no criminal code with drunk-driving laws.

One of Lady Wootton's major rationales for making the criminal law completely forward-looking and eliminating all consideration of *mens rea* is an epistemological one. She is skeptical that we are able to know a person's inner thoughts and impulses; consequently we are unable to know if a person does have the requisite *mens rea* to be legally excused for what he or she has done. Although he rejects the overly strong form in which Wootton states her case, Hart is sympathetic with this thesis. Dismissing Wootton's claim that it is impossible in principle to know someone's inner thoughts and impulses, he maintains instead that it is sometimes possible to know whether a person could not have helped doing something. However, Hart admits that such cases are rare and are not typical of what the courts face. Indeed, Hart says that the debate before the courts over whether the accused could have controlled his or her behavior seems often "very unreal."[39] The evidence is not only conflicting but has often a remote bearing on the issue of whether the accused could control his or her behavior at a particular time. In view of these essentially epistemological problems Hart says he prefers the moderate form of Wootton's doctrine where only mental abnormality is excluded as a defense in criminal law.

A crucial question can be raised here about whether Hart has overgeneralized the solution to the problem. One plausible way of reading him is that in many criminal law cases the difficult epistemological problem is not that of having no knowledge of the abnormal mental states of the accused in general, but rather that of not having knowledge of whether the accused has the incapacity to conform his or her behavior to the law. If this is the basic problem, then the solution would seem to be not to allow incapacity to conform to the law on a particular occasion as an excusing condition. It would be unnecessary to exclude from the criminal law *all* excuses in terms of mental abnormality.

After all, mental abnormality is a wide category including everything from somnambulism to intoxication, everything from not knowing the difference between right and wrong because of a defect of reason resulting from a disease of the mind to epileptic seizure. Now not being able to conform one's behavior to the law may be one aspect of some types of mental abnormality but it is certainly not characteristic of all.

Furthermore, Hart's view may be an overgeneralization even if only incapacity to conform to the law is at issue. For it seems fairly clear that in certain types of mental abnormality one can have great confidence that someone cannot conform his or her behavior to the law in a particular instance. For example, suppose a person in an epileptic seizure thrashes about and injures an attending nurse. One can have great confidence that he or she could not have helped doing this; indeed, one can have more confidence in a case such as this than in many cases where no mental abnormality is at issue but where knowledge of *mens rea* is crucial.

On practical grounds it is not clear that the law could allow as a defense in the case of epileptic seizure the incapacity to conform one's behavior to the laws without allowing it as a defense in more typical cases that come before the court. However, Hart does not consider this issue. Rather he advocates ruling out not only all defenses in terms of incapacity to conform to the law but all defenses in terms of mental abnormality. Given the problem as he states it, at the very least Hart might have considered some finer distinctions and a less restrictive approach.

The Amount of Punishment

Hart admits that a general utilitarian aim primarily determines the amount or severity of punishment, but he says that three principles of justice also enter into fixing the amount of punishment. First, justice requires that certain mitigating circumstances be allowed to lessen the penalty for people who have special trouble in following the law. Second, there is what Hart calls the "hazy requirement" of justice that like cases be treated alike.[40] Third, there is the requirement of justice that offenses of different gravity should not be punished with equal severity.

Hart does not believe that this third principle of justice can be derived from either a utilitarian or a retributivist theory of punishment. He is skeptical that it can be derived from the latter since, despite what some retributivists think, he doubts that "there is for each crime a penalty 'naturally' fitted to its degree of iniquity."[41] He believes that at best, in common sense thinking, there is a very rough correlation between types of crimes and appropriate punishments and that no precise correlation is possible.

Why does Hart believe that only a very rough correlation between the severity of punishment and crime is possible? He says that in many cases it makes no sense to suppose that the criminal should be punished by having done to him what he did. For example, it makes no sense to punish a forger by forgery. Furthermore, once we go beyond this crude version of retributivism things become difficult. There are no units to measure wickedness, no units to measure severity of punishment. He might have added that, even if there were such units, there would be no way of translating units of wickedness into units of severity of punishment in order to get an equivalence.

There are even difficulties, Hart points out, in merely rank-ordering crimes in terms of wickedness and punishment in terms of severity. Once the ranking is complete, moreover, there is the problem of determining a starting point: "Our starting point or base of comparison must be a crime for which a penalty is fixed otherwise than by comparison with others."[42] Hart argues also that it is not clear whether the seriousness of a crime is to be determined by the subjective evil intention or by the objective harm done. And finally, he asks, if subjective factors are to be taken into account, how are they to be weighted? How can one take into account motive, opportunity, temptation, and so on?

Because of these problems Hart argues that only those types of crimes loosely representative of actual individual crimes can be roughly correlated to appropriate punishments and that only a rough discrimination between intentional and unintentional injury can be taken into account in fixing punishment. What is unclear, however, is whether, given the way Hart has characterized the retributive theory of punishment, a precise correlation between crimes and punishment is needed. Recall (B):

> (B) A person's punishment must in some way match, or be the equivalent of, the wickedness of the offense.

This characterization seems compatible with there being a *rough* equivalence between the severity of punishment and the wrongness of the crime. Interpreted in this way (B) would seem to entail this third principle of justice.

Further, one common interpretation of (B) entails the first principle of justice, namely that it requires certain mitigating circumstances. It is commonly supposed that the wickedness of an act depends in part on the degree of voluntariness of an act. A person who breaks the law but has great difficulty in bringing his or her behavior into conformity with the law is less morally culpable than someone who breaks the same law and has no problem in bringing his or her behavior into conformity with it. The second principle of justice—treat like cases alike—also seems to be implicitly contained in (B). If two people commit the same crime with the same *mens rea* and the same criminal background, (B) would entail that they should be given the same severity of punishment. Thus there is a *prima facie* case that Hart's three principles of justice can be derived from the retributivist theory outlined above.

Hart rejects a utilitarian justification of the third principle as well as a retributivist one, yet the justification that he actually gives for it seems utilitarian in spirit. He argues that unless legal penalties are graded in such a way that they are an approximate match of our common sense intuitive notions of what is an appropriate punishment, there will be undesirable consequences. He says: "For where the legal gradation of crimes expressed in the relative severity of penalties diverges sharply from this rough scale, there is a risk of either confusing common morality or flouting it and bringing the law into contempt."[43] Presumably a similar utilitarian justification can be given for the first and second principles of justice. Both of these principles are, he supposes, enshrined in our common sense morality and if the law sharply diverges from them "there is a risk of either confusing common morality or flouting it and bringing the law into contempt."

Although, according to Hart, the law should take into account the retributive principle of justice reflected in common sense morality, and although these principles may be to a certain extent justified indirectly on utilitarian grounds, still it would be a serious mistake to rely on these principles exclusively in fixing the amount of punishment. First, there is nothing sacrosanct about the community's scale of value. Some common sense evaluations might rest on an inadequate appreciation of the facts. Moreover, the law should not passively reflect the common view but "actively help to shape moral sentiments to rational common ends."[44] Second, it is naive to think that there is some homogeneous social morality to appeal to in fixing the degree of punishment. Our society is a pluralistic one and, in attempting to reflect the common morality in fixing sentences, judges may be merely projecting their own moral beliefs onto a morally heterogeneous community. Although these two points raise very different issues, they indicate that utilitarian considerations play a decisive role in Hart's thinking. The first suggests that he believes that, although going against common sense morality may have undesirable consequences in some cases at least, such consequences can be outweighed by desirable ones. But, then, on utilitarian grounds going against the retributive principles embedded in common sense morality is justified in some cases. The second point indicates that he supposes that sometimes what people think is society's morality is, in fact, only the morality of some small articulate sub-group. So going against what is thought to be society's morality may have far fewer undesirable consequences than was at first expected. So again, Hart can be interpreted as saying that on utilitarian grounds it is sometimes desirable to go against retributive principles embedded in what is thought to be common sense morality.

Although Hart is sensitive to the tension in a legal system between the more modern, forward-looking goals of utilitarianism (deterrence, rehabilitation) and the traditional principle that the punishment should fit the crime, he does not attempt to explain in any systematic way how these two approaches can be brought into harmony. At times he mentions some specific possibilities for reconciling utilitarianism and retributivism, but he does not endorse these. Most of the time he seems content simply to describe the tension.

One possible way he mentions to reconcile the two views is to view retributivist concerns about appropriate punishment as relevant only to setting the maximum penalty and utilitarian considerations as relevant to setting a penalty *within* this maximum.[45] But clearly this cannot be a general solution for reconciling the two approaches. Suppose on retributive grounds that the maximum penalty for rape is thirty years and that the average person believes that any longer sentence for rape is too strict. Now, suppose it is shown that on deterrent grounds a one-year sentence and a large fine is no less effective than a more severe penalty. But the average person may be opposed to such a lenient penalty. So if a rapist was given the light sentence and his trial was well publicized, then there might well be such a public outrage that the law would be held in contempt. There might then be good utilitarian reasons not to have this be a general way of reconciling the two views.

The Death Penalty

Hart's views on the death penalty are basically an application of his more general views on punishment. Although, as we have seen, Hart does not normally utilize social science information, in his discussion of the death penalty he cites empirical studies, evaluates the relevance of statistics, and generally shows a good grasp of the empirical issues involved.

Hart advocates what he refers to as a "cautious utilitarian"[46] theory with respect to the death penalty. It is utilitarian since he urges that the death penalty be judged in terms of social consequences, which he acknowledges are based on "a question of fact."[47] Rejecting both the view that the death penalty is never justified because it is "something absolutely evil"[48] and the view that the death penalty is something that morality demands as a uniquely appropriate means of retribution for the worst of crimes, his utilitarianism is cautious. It is, of course, a utilitarianism qualified by a principle of fairness. Although he believes that only utilitarian considerations can justify a general system of punishment containing the death penalty for certain crimes, he holds that non-utilitarian considerations enter into the justification of the application of this system to particular individuals. Thus, a principle of fairness prevents punishment from being inflicted on a person who has not broken the law.

For Hart, the crucial question in the case of the death penalty is, "What is the weight and character of the evidence that the death penalty is required for the protection of society?"[49] He considers two main evidential approaches to be relevant to this question: statistical and common sense ideas concerning "the strength of fear of death as a motive in human conduct."[50]

Hart points out several drawbacks with statistical types of evidence. Statistical comparison between the murder rate in countries that have abolished the death penalty and countries that have not is "practically useless"[51] since the countries compared are very different in so many relevant variables. He points out that even evidence that compares the murder rate in countries before the death penalty is repealed and after it is repealed is of limited value. First, in many countries in which the death penalty has been abolished it was not used for many years prior to the time of abolition. Second, even if one could precisely determine when the death penalty ceased to be a serious threat, the crucial question is whether abolition has had long-term effects. Typically, statistical evidence does not tell us this.

In Hart's opinion the most impressive evidence about the effects of the death penalty is obtained where "one of a bloc of several neighbouring states of similar population and similar social and economic conditions has abolished or introduced the death penalty for murder while others have not changed it."[52] When comparisons have been made between fairly homogeneous states, the results "suggest" that the murder rate in "such states are conditioned by factors operating independently of the death penalty."[53] But, Hart stresses, "There is, however, too little of such evidence to justify a positive inference."

He argues that "the most important lesson" to be drawn from a "dispassionate survey"[54] of statistics is the need to distinguish between two ideas:[55]

(1) There is no evidence from statistics that the death penalty is a superior deterrent to imprisonment
(2) There is evidence that the death penalty is not a superior deterrent to imprisonment.

Hart holds that (1) is justified and that (2) is not. He points out that critics might argue that (1) is too cautious a view.[56] It would be justified if one confined the evidence to single countries for it is possible in any given case where the murder rate fell or stayed the same that some independent cause tending to produce a fall in the murder rate was operating. But the critic might argue that this independent cause theory is very improbable when we include all the cases of countries in which the murder rate stayed the same or fell after abolition, that it is unlikely that in all these cases there is an independent cause that masks the effects of abolition.

However, Hart challenges this argument by maintaining that in many cases the murder rate was already declining *prior* to official abolition. Consequently some causes tending to lower the murder rate were already operating, and there is, then, nothing improbable in supposing that such causes were operating after abolition. What evidence is needed to make the independent cause hypothesis unlikely, according to Hart, are cases where the murder rate was *not* declining prior to the abolition of the death penalty and remained stable or declined after abolition. But this is precisely the evidence that is lacking.

Hart's judgment that (1), not (2), is the proper position to take seems as correct today as it was when he wrote "Murder and the Principles of Punishment: England and the United States" in 1958 (reprinted in *Punishment and Responsibility*). Although recent developments concerning the evidence for the deterrent value of the death penalty are complicated and cannot be easily summarized, several points can be made. In 1975 some stunning and sophisticated work by Isaac Ehrlich using econometric techniques was reported that seemed to show that the death penalty was effective. However, Ehrlich's research has been strongly criticized and his results have been rejected by well-known and highly respected social scientists.[57] The debate between Ehrlich and his critics is still going on. As Hugo Bedau, an expert on the subject, says:

> If one must draw the balance sheet at the present moment, it appears that despite the introduction of econometric techniques, the negative judgment on the deterrent superiority of the death penalty over long-term imprisonment reached a generation ago by Sellin and other criminologists has not been seriously undermined or contradicted.[58]

The non-statistical evidence for the deterrent value of the death penalty, according to Hart, really amounts to the alleged truism that "men fear death more than any other penalty, and that therefore it *must* be a stronger deterrent than imprisonment."[59] Hart undermines this view by pointing out that, although *after* he has been convicted, a murderer may well dread death much more than life imprisonment this may be irrelevant to the potential murderer. The death penalty for the potential murderer may mean "a not very high probability of death in the future. And futurity and uncertainty, the hope of an escape, rational or irrational, vastly diminishes the differences between death and imprisonment as deterrents, and may diminish it to vanishing point."[60]

Furthermore, according to Hart, "in all countries murder is committed to a very large extent either by persons who, though sane, do not in fact count the cost, or are so mentally deranged that they cannot count it."[61] Hart concludes his critique of the non-statistical evidence in this way:

> One day, indeed, the still young sciences of psychology and sociology may confirm the speculation that the fear of death has the potency thus claimed for it, or perhaps that the death penalty has had some unique influence in building up and maintaining our moral attitude to murder. But we certainly cannot take this to be established, and those who base their advocacy of the death penalty on this rough 'common-sense' psychology must seriously consider psychological theories that run in other directions. For at present, theories that the death penalty may operate as a stimulant to murder, consciously or unconsciously, have some evidence behind them. The use of the death penalty by the state may lower, not sustain, the respect for life. Very large numbers of murderers are mentally unstable, and in them at least the bare thought of execution, the drama and notoriety of a trial, the gladiatorial element of the murderer fighting for his life, may operate as an attractive force, not as a repulsive one. There are actual cases of murder so motivated, and the psychological theories which draw upon them must be weighted against the theory that the use of the death penalty creates or sustains our inhibitions against murder.[62]

Hart does not specify what evidence available to him in the late 1950's supports the theory that the death penalty encourages murder. But in any case, in 1977 some evidence was produced that indicated that each execution "adds roughly three more to the number of homicides in the next nine months of the year after the execution."[63] Whether this finding will stand up under examination remains to be seen.

The conclusion Hart draws is that there are three factors that make it appear that the death penalty and "the mode of its use in England" are *prima facie* evil and therefore should only be retained in order to minimize murder or because it serves "some other valuable purpose which other punishments could not serve."[64] The three factors are: (1) "*prima facie* the taking of a life, even by the State, with its attendant suffering not only for the criminal but for many others, is an evil to be endured only for the sake of some good; (2) the death penalty is irrevocable and the risk of an innocent person being executed is never negligible, and (3) the use of the death penalty in England was possible only at the cost of constant intervention by the Executive after the courts had tried and sentenced the prisoner to death."[65] Hart points out that the first two factors are clearly applicable to the death penalty in the United States and that there is "some analogy to the third factor in the possibility, inescapable in the United States, and sometimes realized, of long periods intervening between the sentence of death and its execution."[66]

These factors lead Hart to believe that the onus of proof is on the advocates of the death penalty to show positive evidence that it is effective. Since they cannot show this, he concludes that the death penalty should not be maintained. However, it seems to me that some of the factors specified by Hart are of dubious validity. First, the taking of a life by the state may bring about far less suffering, all things considered, than a life sentence in prison. Some murderers have no friends or relatives who will suffer because of their death; moreover, the death penalty itself may be painless. On the other hand, what with homosexual rape, brutal guards, and the like, life in prison may bring about far more suffering.

Moreover, the third factor, the administrative cost of executive interference, must be balanced against others not mentioned by Hart. There is, for example, the cost of maintaining prisoners for long periods of time when there is no death penalty. Surely it would be necessary to argue that administrative costs of interference outweigh the costs of maintenance before the argument can have any force. It is certainly not self-evident that the administrative costs of executive interference do outweigh maintenance costs.

This leaves factor (2), the possibility of mistakenly executing innocent people. No doubt this consideration should carry a good deal of weight and, for many, it is decisive. Still, there is another consideration suggested by Hart's statement that given these three factors the death penalty should be retained only if there is some positive evidence that it minimizes murder or because it serves "some other valuable purpose which other punishments could not serve." For there is one purpose that the death penalty serves that other punishments cannot serve. It serves the purpose of satisfying the belief that certain crimes deserve the death penalty. The value of this purpose is, of course, a matter of controversy. Nevertheless, recent public opinion polls indicate that for certain crimes the public supports the death penalty by a margin of two to one.[67] As I noted above, Hart argues that, unless legal punishments are graded in such a way that roughly approximates to an intuitive notion embedded in our common sense morality, "there is a risk of either confusing common morality or flouting it and bringing the law into contempt."[68] The public opinion polls referred to here suggest that the death penalty for certain crimes does indeed roughly correspond to many people's intuitive notion of morality. As we have seen, Hart qualifies the use of common sense principles of morality in fixing punishment. If common sense views rely on an inadequate appreciation of the facts, the law should not reflect common sense but should reshape it. The crucial question, then, is what the basis of the public's preference for the death penalty is. Although opinion polls indicate that the public believes in the deterrent value of the death penalty—despite the lack of evidence indicating it has deterrent value—there is also evidence that many people who advocate the death penalty would still do so even if it were shown to have no deterrent value. The evidence thus suggests that many people who advocate the death penalty do it from a basically retributivist point of view.[69]

If this is true, then it may be that Hart's qualification of the utilization of common sense morality would not be applicable. The evidence available suggests that the public preference for death may not be based on an "inadequate appreciation" of the facts of deterrence. Whether this preference is based on an inadequate appreciation of *other* facts is at the present time something we do not know.

Hart would be well advised in the light of these considerations to argue that factor (2), that is, the possibility of giving the death penalty to an innocent person, is of fundamental importance and outweighs any advantage that might result from satisfying the public's desire for retribution, and/or that given our present legal system the death penalty is irrational, random, and capricious in its application. This latter argument is not one that Hart uses although it has played a large role in recent abolitionary literature and has considerable merit.[70]

Conclusion

Hart seems to have underestimated the resources and power of utilitarianism. At times he has failed to see that a plausible utilitarian answer was possible or to rebut adequately a utilitarian counterargument. Just as he has tended to underestimate the power of utilitarianism criticisms of his theory, he also seems not to have appreciated the complexity of the utilitarian arguments upon which he relies. As a result it is unclear if some of the conclusions he draws from utilitarian considerations are valid. Thus in his defense of a system of legal excuses he uses basically utilitarian arguments, yet he does not take into account the benefits involved in a system without excuses or the disadvantages of a system with excuses in arriving at his conclusion.

As we have seen, Hart attempts to tread a middle path and provide a mix of utilitarian and retributive theories. His complex position seems fragile, however, and many of his distinctions appear to be untenable. For example, his attempt to distinguish his position from Wootton's collapses on examination; the reasons he gives for rejecting Wootton's theory are applicable to his own. Further, on examination his allegedly non-utilitarian defense of excuses seems basically utilitarian; moreover, his position on the punishment of negligent behavior seems to be untenable given his theory of excuses.

Yet, if Hart's answers to the different questions he distinguishes concerning punishment are not free from problems, it is his lasting contribution to have clearly seen that there are different kinds of questions and that different answers may be appropriate to them. Furthermore, even if Hart is wrong that retributive answers are necessary for certain questions concerning punishment and even if, despite what Hart says, utilitarian theory broadly conceived can provide adequate answers to all the different questions he distinguishes, his approach forces utilitarians to work hard to show the relevance of their theory to the different questions.

Chapter

6

Natural Rights and Natural Law

COMMENTATORS ON HART'S work have tended to ignore his theory of natural law.[1] Two possible reasons for this neglect suggest themselves. In the first place Hart bases his theory on propositions so obvious that they seem beyond challenge. Moreover, the content of his natural law doctrine is so minimal as to seem uncontroversial. Yet Hart's theory of natural law is not uncontroversial since the argument he uses to establish the minimum content he gives to natural law is problematic.

Furthermore, Hart's views on natural law warrant our attention, for they are intimately connected to other aspects of his thought. As we saw in Chapter 2, his theory of natural law is an essential part of the definition of a legal system that can be extracted from *The Concept of Law*. Hart supposes that in order to have a legal system the laws in the system must contain the minimum content of natural law. In addition, his theory of natural law is related to his theory of punishment, for one aspect of the minimum content of natural law is that laws must provide sanctions if they are not obeyed.

Besides a theory of natural law, Hart holds what may be called a theory of natural rights. As we will see here, he argues that, if there are any moral rights at all, there is a natural right of all men to be free. It has been claimed that this view of natural rights forms the basis of a critical principle that Hart uses in his debate with Devlin,[2] namely that the use of legal coercion by any society needs justification because it is *prima facie* objectionable.[3] It is also claimed that this principle is connected with his theory of punishment.[4] Thus it is as important to examine his theory of natural rights as it is his theory of natural law.

It should be noted that Hart's theories of natural rights and natural law are independent of one another from both a logical and a functional point of view. The two theories are logically independent in the sense that one can accept either one and without contradiction reject the other. The two theories are functionally independent in the sense that they play different roles in Hart's system. For example, his theory of natural rights plays no role in explicating his concept of law whereas his theory of natural law does. On the other hand, his theory of natural law does not even appear to play any role in justifying his view that coercion is *prima facie* evil. Whether his theory of natural rights plays such a role remains to be seen but it is at least not initially implausible to suppose that it could.

There is another important difference in the two positions. With respect to natural rights, Hart's argument is purely hypothetical. He argues that, if there are any moral rights, then there is a natural right. But with respect to natural law, although he argues hypothetically that, if people want to survive, then laws must have a minimum content, he also asserts that people do want to survive.

Historical Background

As a moral basis of the law, the doctrine of natural law goes back at least to the Stoics. In the Middle Ages it was refined by such thinkers as St. Thomas Aquinas and for many today it remains a viable approach to the morality of the law. Although there have been significant differences among thinkers who have been called natural law theorists down through the ages, there have also been significant similarities, ones that justify our speaking of a common approach. All natural law theorists maintain that positive law must be judged by criteria bearing a close analogy to a legal code—in particular, criteria capable of being formulated as a set of rules or precepts against which the particular positive laws of a society can be judged. Moreover, these rules or precepts must form a consistent set. They also agree that the set of precepts by which positive laws are to be judged are grounded in something wider, more fundamental and permanent, than the conventions or custom of humankind. They call this something "nature" and give various interpretations of it. Finally, natural law theorists sometimes maintain that those particular positive laws failing to meet the requirements of natural law are not properly speaking laws at all.[5] It is this third characteristic of natural law theory that has sharply distinguished natural law theory from the theory of legal positivism advocated by John Austin that "the existence of law is one thing, its merit and demerits another."

Now one of the basic problems of traditional natural law theory has been an epistemological one. How is one to know the sets of precepts against which positive law is to be evaluated? How can one distinguish what is in accord with natural law and what is not? One common approach to the epistemological problem has been to appeal to reason: what is in accord with reason is in accord with natural law. But then the question arises of what is in accord with reason. An answer often given to this question is that whatever is in accord with reason is self-evidently true. It is at this point, however, that an epistemological problem arises, for history indicates that self-evidence is an unreliable guide to truth.

Everything from the divine right of kings to the flatness of the earth has at some time been thought to be self-evidently true. Indeed, what appears self-evident to one person appears dubious or even false to another.

Although Hart is opposed to natural law theory in its traditional form, he proposes[6] a theory that he believes rescues what is valuable in the traditional natural theory. In order to see clearly the differences between Hart's theory and traditional forms of the doctrine of natural law let us contrast his view with St. Thomas Aquinas'. Since Aquinas' views are typical of many natural law theories, this comparison should be instructive.

One obvious difference between Hart's theory and traditional ones such as Aquinas' lies in the postulated goal or aim of law. Hart postulates the simple goal of the survival of human beings whereas traditional theories postulate more exalted ends. Thus Aquinas maintained that the end of law was the common good.[7] Presumably this benefit includes more than simple survival.

Another difference is that of the content of natural law. For Hart, law must contain rules restricting violence, requiring mutual forbearance, governing the use of property, enabling obligations to be created, and specifying sanctions for lawbreakers. Traditional natural law theories include more. To be sure, Aquinas speaks of the natural tendency of humans to preserve their own lives,[8] and this may be translated into human laws as rules restricting violence and requiring mutual forbearance. But Aquinas' natural law principles go beyond Hart's restrictions, for the former also speaks of the natural tendency of men to engage in sexual intercourse and educate their children, and he argues that men have a natural inclination to know the truth about God, to shun ignorance, and to avoid offending others. Although it is less than clear exactly how these natural inclinations are to be translated into rules that form part of human law, it seems obvious that the content of human law in Aquinas' system must go beyond Hart's rules, which are aimed only at preserving a viable society. Connected with the very limited content of Hart's natural law theory is a related difference between Hart's theory and Aquinas' theory. Hart's theory, unlike Aquinas', is *obviously* compatible with legal systems that are not morally good but are also morally iniquitous.

A third difference between the two addresses the question of knowledge. Aquinas argues that the basic principles of natural law are self-evident, at least to "the wise,"[9] that is, to people who understand the meaning of terms used in stating the principles. This is not Hart's position. He argues that given certain simple truisms and the goal of self-preservation, certain minimum content of law is a "natural necessity,"[10] but he does not claim self-evidence even for the simple truisms, let alone for the minimum content of law.

One last difference relates to the application of natural law. According to Hart, the minimum content of natural law may apply only to a small sub-group in a society, whereas Aquinas seems to believe that natural law, at least in principle, must apply to all men. To be sure, he admits that special circumstances might arise that would dictate an exception.[11] Despite this qualification, however, it is plausible to suppose that natural law principles have a wider application in Aquinas' system than in Hart's, and this seems to be true for traditional theories in general.

Given these differences between Hart's theory and traditional conceptions of natural law it may well be doubted that Hart's should be called a natural law theory. It may be said that it is merely a thesis about the need for a minimum content of positive law for any legal system whose subjects are human beings with certain physical and psychological characteristics and a concern to survive and that to refer to it as a natural law theory is misleading.

There are, however, some fundamental similarities between the traditional natural law doctrine of, for example, Aquinas and Hart's theory that make the application of the term "natural law" seem not completely inappropriate. Although critical of the grandiose constructions of traditional natural law theory, Hart seems to see himself as capturing in his own theory what is valuable in the older views. To be sure, he rejects appeals to self-evidence; however, he believes that the premises of his argument are based on certain obvious facts of human nature and the world. Moreover, although he believes that the minimum content of natural law may apply only to a small sub-group in a society, he still seems to think that it applies to some sub-group in *every* society. Thus, despite their differences, Aquinas and Hart suppose that their respective theories apply to all societies. Furthermore, although Hart's theory is compatible with great moral iniquity, it does have some moral content; it is not compatible with all forms of moral iniquity. For example, it would forbid the free exercise of violence against all groups in society. At the same time, Aquinas' theory may actually be compatible with moral iniquity although not to the same degree as Hart's theory and in not as obvious a way. One can imagine a society that meets Aquinas' natural law conditions yet has great injustices and moral wrongs. Finally, Aquinas argues that a positive law in conflict with the precepts of natural law is not really a human law, but rather a perversion of law.[12] In Chapter 1 I argued that despite the fact that Hart's natural law thesis is about natural, and not logical, necessity, since Hart defines a legal system partly in terms of having the minimum content of natural law, a system that did not have this minimum moral content would not be a standard case of a legal system.

Ancient and medieval legal thinkers seem to have been mainly concerned with duties rather than rights, duties of humans to their king or their God. Since the seventeenth century, however, problems connected with rights have played an important role in discussions of the law.[13] Legal and political thinkers in the seventeenth and eighteenth centuries argued that human beings have natural rights that should be safeguarded by the state and enshrined in positive law. Indeed, lists of such rights were drawn up in the American Bill of Rights and the

French Declaration of Rights,[14] and these were used both to guide the government and as a tool in criticizing its activities.

Although there have been many different conceptions of natural rights, as with natural law theory there are significant similarities that justify speaking of a common approach. There is in natural rights theory, as in natural law, an analogy to rights in a positive legal code. In particular, natural rights have to be capable of being specified in terms of a list against which legal rights in a positive legal code can be evaluated, for a legal system that failed to incorporate these natural rights would be judged morally faulty. Moreover, the rights against which positive legal rights are to be judged are grounded in something more basic and permanent than convention or custom, namely nature. As with natural law, various interpretations of "nature" are given by different theorists. Further, in most instances natural rights theorists maintain that these rights are held equally by all humans and that they are inalienable and absolute: inalienable in the sense that they cannot be waived or given up; absolute in the sense that the claims of natural right cannot be defeated by some stronger claim.

The traditional epistemological problem of natural law theory is inherited by natural rights theory. How can one tell what our natural rights are? How can we distinguish legal rights based on natural ones from legal rights merely based on custom and tradition? The appeal to self-evidence—as manifested in the American Bill of Rights' phrase "We hold these truths to be self-evident"—is problematic and suspect given the various and conflicting historical claims made in its name.

Although Hart does not propose a traditional natural rights theory he does argue for a moderate natural rights thesis.[15] In his 1955 paper "Are There Any Natural Rights?," he argues that, "if there are any moral rights at all, it follows that there is at least one natural right, the equal right of all men to be free."[16] According to Hart, to say that someone has this right is to say that in the absence of certain special conditions that are consistent with the right's being an equal right "any adult human being capable of choice (1) has the right to forbearance on the part of all others from the use of coercion or restraint against him save to hinder coercion or restraint and (2) is at liberty to do (i.e., is under no obligation to abstain from) any action which is not one coercing or restraining or designed to injure other persons."[17]

Why does Hart maintain that the equal right of all men to be free is a natural right? Hart's answer is that because it is possessed by men *qua* men and not only as members of some society or people standing in some special relation to one another; and because it is not created or conferred by people's voluntary action as other rights are. According to Hart, except for the right to be free and rights that are particular exemplifications of that right, rights are created or conferred by voluntary action.

Hart points out that his thesis is much more modest than traditional theories of natural rights. It is conditional, not categorical, in that he maintains that *if* there are moral rights then there must be at least one natural right and he does not commit himself to the thesis that there are moral rights. Hart's hesitation to affirm his thesis categorically is apparently based on his belief that it is possible for there to be moral codes that do not contain the concept of right. These codes would be based on moral notions such as good, bad, right, wrong, wise, foolish. In such systems there would be no equal right for all people to be free. It seems clear that in formulating his thesis hypothetically Hart wants to remain morally neutral. He sees himself engaged in the logical exercise of unpacking what is involved in the concept of moral right, rather than arguing that there should be this or that moral right.

A second way in which Hart's thesis is more modest than those of traditional natural rights theories is that, although it specifies that all men are equally entitled to be free, "no man has an absolute or unconditional right to do or not do any particular thing or to be treated in any particular way."[18] Restraint of any action may be justified in special circumstances that are consistent with the general principle. Consequently, Hart says that his argument will not show that men have any right that is absolute except the equal right of all to be free.

Yet another respect in which his theory is different from traditional ones is one that Hart does not mention. As we have seen, natural rights are traditionally based on a particular epistemology; they are said to be self-evident at least to all rational men. Hart does not claim that the natural right of men to equal freedom is self-evident; he only claims that the right follows or is logically presupposed by the assumption of any moral rights at all. That it does follow is a logical presupposition Hart attempts to show by argument. His argument is *a priori* and nonempirical and at least in this respect has some similarity to traditional views of natural rights. But he need not claim and, as far as I can see, does not claim that it is self-evident that, if there is any moral right, then there is at least one natural right.

A final way in which Hart's theory differs from traditional theory is that he advocates only one natural right. As we shall see, he attempts to show that other rights, for example, the right to worship as one pleases and the right to say what one wants, are based on this one natural right. Thus, given his attempt to derive all natural rights from one basic natural right, his views have a unity and coherence that traditional natural rights theories with their lists of rights do not have.

There is, however, at least one significant similarity between Hart's theory and traditional views of natural rights. Its one basic natural right, the right to be free, places his account squarely in the tradition of liberal individualism into which classical natural rights theories from Locke to Jefferson also fall. These latter used natural rights as a bulwark against repressive governments in order to protect individual liberty and as a justification for revolution.

The view of natural rights under discussion here is to be contrasted with a common view of rights held today.[19] Today various "human rights" to some positive benefit are asserted and not merely to freedom from various interferences. Thus the 1948 U.N. Universal Declaration of Human Rights says that everyone as a member of society "has a right to social security" (Article 22) and "to a standard of living adequate for the health and well-being of himself and his family, including food, clothing, and housing" (Article 25). It has been suggested that such assertions do not entail that the government or anyone else has a duty to provide such services: these assertions are merely statements of basic human needs and people as such have claims to these services even if "there should temporarily be no one in the corresponding position to be claimed against."[20] Clearly neither Hart's natural rights nor classical natural rights are human rights in this sense.

Natural Law

Hart's Argument Expounded

Hart's argument for a natural law with minimum content is based on what he calls "simple truisms." These are:

(T_1) Human beings are vulnerable to physical attack.
(T_2) Human beings are approximately equal in mental and physical abilities.
(T_3) Human beings have limited altruism.
(T_4) Human beings have limited resources.
(T_5) Human beings have limited understanding and strength of will.

Hart argues that things could have been different, that (T_1)–(T_5) are not logically necessary truths. For example, humans could have been built so as not to be vulnerable to attack from members of their own species and people might have been more like angels than they are. But although these things are logically possible, in our world human beings are vulnerable and are not angels.

Further Hart assumes that

(W) Humans want to survive.

This is a contingent fact about human nature. This too could have been different, but in our world survival is a basic human desire. Survival, then, is a minimum goal for human law. As Hart puts it, "Our concern is with social arrangements for continued existence, not with those of a suicide club."[21]

Given truisms (T_1)–(T_5) and the goal of survival, Hart argues that a certain minimum content of law is a "natural necessity." This minimum content is specified by Hart as follows:

(V) Laws must have restrictions on the free exercise of violence.
(M) Laws must be based on mutual forbearance.
(P) Laws must regulate the use of property.
(D) Laws must provide for the creation of obligations.
(S) Laws must provide for sanctions if they are not obeyed.

What precisely is the connection between (T_1)–(T_5) and (W) on the one hand, and (V), (M), (P), (D), and (S) on the other? Hart does not claim that the facts specified by (T_1)–(T_5) and (W) cause the rules of law to have the content specified by (V), (M), (P), (D), and (S). The connection is rational, not causal. The facts specified by (T_1)–(T_5) "afford a *reason* why, given survival as an aim, laws and morals should include a specific content. The general form of the argument is simply that without such a content laws and morals could not forward the minimum purpose of survival which men have in associating with each other."[22]

Hart stresses that the causal connections between certain child-rearing practices and the successful function of the law are not what he is concerned with. "Connexions of this sort . . . are not mediated by *reasons*; for they do not relate the existence of certain rules to the conscious aims or purpose of those whose rules they are. Being fed in infancy in a certain way may well be shown to be a necessary condition or even a *cause* of a population developing or maintaining a moral or legal code, but it is not a *reason* for their doing so."[23] According to Hart, causal connections do not rest on truisms but are established by the sciences through observation and where possible experimentation.

Given this rational connection between the goal of survival, the truisms, and the minimum content of law, one can speak of the minimum content of law as a "natural necessity." By this term Hart wants to contrast his position with two others. Hart is not saying that it is logically necessary for law to have this minimum content. This would make the connection too strong, for given a different world in which the truisms (T_1)–(T_5) did not hold and given the aim of survival, laws without minimum content might be rational. Or given a different world in which people did not want to survive and the truisms (T_1)–(T_5) still held, it would not be rational to have laws with the minimum content required by Hart's theory. Nor is Hart just saying that as a matter of fact most legal systems have rules with minimum content. This makes the connection too weak, for, given the truisms and the goal of survival, it is rational for the legal system to have rules with minimum content.

However, Hart is not claiming that it is a natural necessity that the laws governing every group in society must have this minimum content. He argues that this minimum content may be extended to "different ranges of persons"[24] in different societies. In a slave society, for example, laws governing slaves would not have this minimum content. Hart's position seems to be that given

(1) (T_1)–(T_5) and (W)

it is a natural necessity that

(2) For every society there is at least one group in the society whose laws have minimum content (specified by (W), (M), (P), (D), and (S) above)

and that there is a rational connection between (1) and (2).

Hart's Argument Explicated

Hart is surely correct that (T_1)–(T_5) and (W) provide a reason why (2) should be true. If this were all Hart is saying when he speaks of a rational connection between (1) and (2), there would be no disagreement. Hart's thesis would be uncontroversial and rather uninteresting. After all, (T_1)–(T_5) and (W) might be one among many reasons for (2), and not a very important reason at that. So in taking this as well as other reasons into account it might not be rational (all things considered) to suppose that (2) should be true.

However, Hart seems to be saying more than this. He says that the "general form of the argument is simply that without such a content laws and morals could not forward the minimum purpose of survival."[25] He also says that given (T_1)–(T_5) and (W) laws with minimum content are a "natural necessity." How can this stronger interpretation of Hart be understood?

One suggestion is that Hart is saying that (1) is a conclusive reason why (2) should be true. By "conclusive reason," I mean this. Assume:

(R) People are rational.
(K_1) People know that (1).
(N) People are not prevented from carrying out their plans.

Then to say that (1) is a conclusive reason why (2) should be the case is to say that (R) and (K_1) and (N) entail (2)[26] and that (1) is true.

We may assume that (1) is true since (1) consists of the truisms (T_1)–(T_5) and the uncontroversial (W). To say that the conjunction of (R) and (K_1) and (N) entails (2) is to say that the statement

(3) If (R) and (K_1) and (N), then (2)

is a necessary truth.

It is important that what I am saying not be confused with the claim that

(3′) If (1), then (2)

is a necessary truth. It is clearly not. Furthermore, it is important to see that my explication does not conflict with Hart's insistence that (2) is a natural necessity given (1) and not a logical necessity. Statement (3), not (2), is logically necessary on the present interpretation and the claim that (3) is logically necessary is compatible with the claim that (2) is not.

This explication of Hart makes good sense of two rather obscure statements of his mentioned above: (a) Given (1), (2) is a natural necessity but not a logical necessity. (b) There is a rational (but not a causal) connection between (1) and (2). Statement (a) is simply an elliptical way of calling attention to the idea that (2) is neither logically necessary nor accidentally true. Statement (2) is a nomological statement that allegedly follows from (R) and (K) and (N). Statement (b) is an elliptical way of calling our attention to the idea that rational people with knowledge of (1) will construct societies with certain kinds of laws if they are not prevented. It does not mean that the facts described by (1) cause societies with laws of a certain kind to be constructed.

Hart's Theory Evaluated

Given this interpretation, Hart's argument is wrong, for (2) is not a logical consequence of (R) and (K_1) and N. One can imagine a case in which the conjunction of (R) and (K_1) and N is true but (2) is false. Put less formally, Hart is mistaken to suppose that rational people who knew that (1) would construct societies with laws with a natural law minimum content unless they were prevented from doing so. It is important to see that I am not attacking Hart's truisms. I will question the truth of (3), not (1).

Consider a world in which people have a desire to survive, where (T_1)–(T_5) hold true, where people are rational and know that they want to survive and know that (T_1)–(T_5), but where human nature is such that laws with the minimum content specified above are not the best way to further survival. Suppose, for example, that in this world positive reinforcement is a much more effective way of getting people not to break the law than the use of sanctions and that people know this. Indeed, suppose that in this world it is well known that the use of sanctions would so outrage the population that it would indirectly cause civil strife. So far from sanctions' inducing obedience to law, they would cause disobedience. Thus (R) and (K_1) and (N) do not entail (2) and consequently (1) cannot provide a conclusive reason why (2) should be true.

This suggests another interpretation of the relationship of (1) to (2). Since

(R) and (K_1) and (N) combined do not entail (2) straightaway, perhaps R and (K_1) and (N) in combination with other premises entail (2). What would these other premises be? Consider:

> (4) In all societies sanctions are the most effective ways to prevent people from breaking the law

and

> (K_2) People know that (4).

Then we can say that (1) and (4) together provide a conclusive reason for

> (2′) Every society has at least one group of people in the society governed by laws with sanctions for breaking the law.

This means only that the conjunction (R) and (K_1) and (K_2) and (N) entails (2′) and that (1) and (4) are true.

The trouble with this suggestion is that it is by no means clear that (4) is true. In fact, some psychologists such as B. F. Skinner have maintained that positive reinforcement is more effective than sanctions.

When Hart contrasts causal and rational connections he seems to be suggesting that rational connections, unlike causal connections, rest upon truisms and that evidence from the social sciences is not needed to establish them. But on the present interpretation evidence that presumably is not available is needed to establish (4). Thus, (1) and (4) combined cannot provide a conclusive reason why (2) should be true, since (4) is dubious.

Could a similar argument be used against other aspects of the minimum content of natural law? I believe so. Consider rules governing property. (R) and (K_1) and (N) in conjunction do not entail

> (2″) For every society there is at least one group of people in the society that has rules governing its use of property.

Consequently, (1) cannot provide a conclusive reason why (2) should be true.

To see this, imagine a world in which people have the desire to survive and in which (T_1)–(T_5) hold, but in which psychological, sociological, and economic factors different from ours are present. Consider a world of pacifist communists. They believe that the land and material goods belong to no one or perhaps to everyone. Anyone can help themselves to anything, including what anyone produces. Everyone is expected to do their share, but if some people do not, that is something the others believe one must live with. These people believe that it is far better that people should help themselves without doing their share than that there should be rules forbidding their behavior. In such a society there would be no institution of property, at least as Hart seems to understand it. There would be, to use Hart's example, no rules "excluding persons generally other than the 'owner' from entry on, or the use of the land, or from taking or using material things."[27]

Could people survive in this society? It may be suggested that they could not; that without rules to stop them, people would want more and more, would acquire more land and more material goods in their insatiable greed; that their uncontrolled greed, given limited resources, would make survival in this world impossible. But in the world I am imagining people are not greedy. This seems to be quite compatible with Hart's truisms. Thus, the truism that human beings have limited altruism refers to people's desire to inflict violence on one another, not to their greed. In fact, one can imagine that, given people's psychological make-up, in this world rules regulating property might cause such greed that no sanctions could stop it. So, rather than furthering survival, rules of property might hinder it.

Consider, however, the following:

(5) People are greedy in all social and economic systems.
(6) Because of limited resources, uncontrolled greed makes survival impossible.

Let us suppose:

(K_3) = People know that (5) and (6).

Then it might be argued that (R) and (K_1) and (N) entail (2″) and, consequently, that (1), (5), and (6) combined provide a conclusive reason why (2″) should be true.

But even if one accepts (6), the truth of (5) is by no means obvious. Some theorists have suggested that greed is a function of the social and economic system people live in and that those who lived in a non-capitalistic system would not be greedy. Whether this is true or not remains to be shown, of course, but the important point for our discussion is that the truth of (5) is not known. Consequently, the fact that (1) and (5) and (6) combined provide a conclusive reason for (2) and (5) is dubious.

Consider now the laws restricting the free exercise of violence. Again we may question if (1) is a conclusive reason why it should be the case that

(2‴) Every society has at least one group of people in the society governed by laws restricting the free exercise of violence.

Do (R) and (K_1) and (N) entail (2‴)? I think not. One can imagine a society in which there are no laws forbidding the free exercise of violence (just as in our society there are no laws forbidding people from hurting other people's feelings or being impolite) and yet the chance of survival is close to ours. In this imaginary society, of course, people are in general opposed to violence and take steps to protect themselves from it. Someone who desires to hurt or kill someone else might be deterred from doing so by private self-defense measures. But there would be no laws against violence and people in this society might well be appalled at the very idea of such laws. (Compare people's reaction in our society to the very idea of laws forbidding hurting other people's feelings or being rude.)

What would be the individual survival rate in such a society? I imagine a society in which the survival rate is close to ours. I construct this imaginary society in such a way that makes this possible. First, in such a society everyone is trained in self-defense from childhood; people are always armed. Housing and clothing are designed with self-defense in mind. People who attack others can be fairly well assured that they will meet stiff and sophisticated resistance. Second, people in such a society are psychologically prepared for violent attack and are determined to defend themselves. Third, people in this society have a sophisticated defense technology. For example, they might have metal detectors built into their clothing to warn them that someone with a gun is nearby.

It might be argued that the above considerations neglect the possibility of many people banding together in order to hurt or kill some individual person, that self-defense training and weapons would be powerless against large numbers of violent people working in unison. However, there is nothing in this imaginary society, as I have conceived it, that necessitates people's protecting themselves individually.

A defender of Hart may argue that, once this last step is taken, Hart's point must be granted. For if groups band together for mutual protection there must be rules restricting the free exercise of violence among members of this group. This is tantamount to granting (2‴). Consequently (1) *is* a conclusive reason for (2‴) once the need for mutual protection societies is granted. However, there is nothing inevitable about large groups of people banding together to hurt individuals. Whether violent people work individually or in groups is a function of certain psychological and sociological factors operating in a particular society. In the society I imagine violent people are always loners. This is compatible with Hart's truisms.

Moreover, even if large numbers of people are needed to protect someone from group violence it does not follow that a mutual protection society is essential.

If I have ten people to protect me and my house from my enemies, who have banded together to kill me, it is not necessary that my ten guards and I form a mutual protection society. My guards may protect me just because they are getting good pay and not because I will protect them in turn. There need be no rules restricting the free exercise of violence in order to hire bodyguards. The bodyguards know, of course, that if they attack me or one another they will not get paid, and that if I attack them they will no longer want to protect me. Such restraint is not based on rules, but on economic advantages. Whatever may be the case in ours, I assume that in this society considerations of economic advantages are paramount.

The above considerations suggest other premises that need to be added to (1) to provide a conclusive reason. Consider:

(7) In every society, there is no adequate individual self-protection against group violence.
(8) In every society there will be group violence.
(9) In every society without a public police force the only adequate protection against group violence is mutual protection sub-societies.

If

(K_4) People know that (7), (8), and (9)

then we could say that (1), (7), (8), and (9) provide a conclusive reason for (2‴). But, for the reasons given above, even if one accepts (7), (8) and (9) are not obviously true. Consequently, it is not clear that (1), (7), (8), and (9) do provide a conclusive reason for (2‴).

Could Hart Meet the Criticism?

Can Hart's theory be reformulated to meet my objections? The various reformulations that suggest themselves either trivialize his theory or else are implausible.

One proposal has in a way already been considered. Hart might say that (1) provides *a* reason why (2) should be the case but not a conclusive reason. Given this formulation of his position, my criticism that rational people who believe (1) would not necessarily bring about (2) if they were not prevented would be irrelevant. Since rational people would simply take (1) into account in constructing their laws, their laws would not necessarily have the minimum content specified by Hart.

The problem with this suggestion is that it trivializes Hart's thesis. Who would want to deny that (1) is something rational people would take into account in constructing their laws? But, of course, rational people take all sorts of things into account in constructing their laws. Statement (1) may have no particular significance and may have little importance.

Another proposal would be to say that only under *some* conditions would rational people who know (1) construct societies with laws with minimum content unless they were prevented. In our terms the claim would be that

(3″) There is some condition C such that if (R) and (K_1) and (N) and C, then (2).

Such a claim would be trivial since C could be (2) itself, consequently (3″) would be the barest tautology.

Yet another suggestion would be to specify condition C in some particular way. But how could it be so specified without granting the very point raised above, namely that (R) and (K_1) and (N) entail (2) *only* given certain particular assumptions about the society in which people live and the psychological motivations of the people and so on? More importantly, this would be to give up Hart's major idea that the minimum content of natural law is based on truisms and the desire to survive; it would undercut completely the generality of his theory and his own perception of it. As I have stressed, Hart intends his theory to apply to all societies—not just societies of a certain kind—and to all people—not just people motivated in certain ways—for which (1) holds true. He envisions his theory as being in the tradition of natural law theory, which certainly had these broad and general aims.

Finally, it might be proposed that (1) would provide rational people with a *prima facie* conclusive reason for (2). Rational people who knew (1) would have conclusive reasons to construct laws with minimum content unless there were special and abnormal circumstances that prevailed in their society. Thus on the assumption

(A) There are no known abnormal or special circumstances prevailing in any society

the following would be entailed:

(3‴) If (R) and (K_1) and (N) and (A), then (2).

The trouble with this suggestion is that it is unclear why it is supposed that the circumstances that might induce rational people not to construct laws with minimum content are special or abnormal. The hypothesis that reinforcement and not sanctions is the most effective way to prevent people from breaking the law is not dependent on any special or abnormal circumstances. Furthermore, what one takes to be special or abnormal may vary from one perspective to another. A society of pacifist communists may appear abnormal to us. To them our society of aggression and capitalism would appear abnormal.

I conclude that the suggestion that Hart could easily meet the above criticism is implausible.

Natural Rights

Let us turn now to Hart's theory of natural rights. After explicating it, I will point out several problems with his analysis. In particular I will argue that Hart's attempt to be morally neutral is unsuccessful, that his attempt to link having a right with limiting other people's freedom and having a choice is a mistake, and that his attempt to show that moral rights presuppose natural rights fails. I will also raise the question of whether his 1955 view on natural rights is consistent with his later criticisms of rights theories.

Explication of Hart's Theory

In "Are There Any Natural Rights?" Hart argues that there is a close connection between having a right and the justified limitation of one person's freedom by another. First, if I have a right, then others require a special justification for limiting my freedom. For instance, if I have a right to speak, then others require a special justification for stopping me from speaking. Second, if I have a right, then I have a justification for limiting the freedom of others. For instance, if I have a right to speak, then I have a justification for limiting another's freedom to stop me from speaking. It should be clear that these two points are different and are logically independent. Others may need a special justification for limiting my freedom when I have a right. But from this it does not follow that I have justification for limiting another's freedom if I have a right.

In any case, what does limiting someone's freedom amount to? At times Hart seems to assume it involves using coercion. At one place he says that "the most important common characteristic of this group of moral concepts [justice, right, and obligation] is that there is no incongruity, but a special congruity in the use of force or the threat of force to secure that what is just or fair or someone's right to have done shall in fact be done; for it is in just these circumstances that coercion of another human being is legitimate."[28]

Hart believes that there is a close relation between right and choice, but contrary to the usual assumption he also believes that there is no close connection between right and benefiting from the performance of duty. He uses the following example to illustrate these points: In return for some favor X promises Y that X will look after Y's aged mother. Because of X's promises Y has a right, but Y's mother has no right because of X's promise. Yet Y's mother, not Y, will be the beneficiary of X's fulfilling his obligation created by the promise made to Y. Y in this situation has a choice. He can demand that his claim against X be fulfilled or he can waive his claim and release X from his promise. Y is in a position to determine and limit X's behavior.

That Hart maintains that all rights are waivable is not completely clear, but his words suggest that he does think so. He says that what makes it appropriate to speak of a person's having a right is that the person can determine by his choice how another person shall act.[29] Further, he objects to saying that animals and babies have rights in the usual sense.[30] Presumably this is because they are not capable of choice, not because there is no transaction or agreement in the case of animals or babies. As we shall see there is no transaction in the case of general rights either and yet Hart allows these as general rights.

Hart distinguishes two types of rights: special and general. Special rights arise out of special transactions between individuals or special relations in which they stand to each other. Examples are rights created by acts of promising, authorizing a person, for example, a physician, to act in your behalf, rights created by natural relations, for example, between parent and child, and rights that arise out of situations of mutual forbearance, for example, in a political society.[31] The person with a special right has some special justification for interfering with another's freedom that other people do not have.

General rights are not based on some special relation or transaction between individuals, but are possessed by all persons capable of choice. These rights are asserted defensively when some unjustified interference is anticipated or threatened. Although Hart gives no list, he cites two examples: the right to say what one thinks and the right to worship as one pleases. These rights do not arise from any promise, authorization, natural relation, or mutual forbearance. Although Hart does not call them natural rights, he maintains that these general rights "directly invoke" the natural right that all men equally have the right to be free whereas special rights indirectly involve this natural right.[32]

What does Hart mean by "invoke" here? It means at least to presuppose or assume. In other words, Hart is maintaining that general rights presuppose the natural right that men equally are free and that special rights presuppose this natural right as well. To refute Hart, then, one must show that there could be some special or some general rights without this natural right.

What is Hart's argument that general and special rights presuppose that all persons equally have the right to be free? Unfortunately, his exposition of it is truncated. What follows, therefore, is my reconstruction of his argument.

Let us consider general rights using an example of Hart's, namely the right to say what one wants. Suppose we say defensively:

(1) I have a right to say what I want.

Now, (1) generalized becomes:

(2) All persons have a right to say what they want.

According to Hart, (2) is simply a special case or a particular exemplification of

(3) All persons equally have the right to be free.

One wonders, however, how one gets from (1) to (3).

Recall that (3) is supposed to be presupposed by (1). Consider the step from (1) to (2). Clearly (1) does not entail (2), for a generalization is not presupposed by an instance of it. Perhaps what is involved here is the tacitly accepted premise:

(1a) I am not different in morally relevant respects from other persons.

This premise combined with another that is possibly analytic, namely

(1b) If I am not different in morally relevant respects from other persons and I have the right to say what I want, then all persons have the right to say what they want

entails (2).

Now consider the step from (2) to (3). Clearly (2) does not entail (3). On the contrary, (3) seems to entail (2) as a special case and a special case of P does not entail P. However, the following premise may be tacitly assumed:

(2a) With respect to freedom people's acts of saying what they want are not different in morally relevant respects from other acts that they do.

This premise combined with what may be the analytic truth

(2b) If with respect to freedom people's acts of saying what they want is not relevantly different from other acts that people do, then all people equally are free

entails (3).

Now let us consider special rights. Using an example of the right created by a promise, let us now consider special rights. Suppose:

(1) Jones freely promises to give Smith item B.

Then:

(2) Smith has a right to be given item B by Jones.

According to Hart, from (2) follows:

(3) Smith has a right to interfere with Jones' freedom in order to obtain item B.

But if (3) is true, then according to Hart:

(4) Jones freely chooses to create Smith's right to interfere with Jones' freedom.

But if (4) is true, then according to Hart:

(5) Jones has a right to be free.

Then presumably Hart must suppose one can generalize that

(6) All men have the right to be free.

There are a number of steps in this argument that need to be filled in. First consider the inference from (1) to (2). Clearly (1) does not entail (2) straightaway. After all, item B may not be something that Smith has the right to provide Jones with. So one must add:

(1a) Jones has a right to provide item B to Smith.

Given (1) and (1a), (2) seems to follow. Whether (3) follows from (2) depends, however, on the truth of the following premise:

(2a) If Smith has a right to be given item B by Jones, Smith has a right to interfere with Jones' freedom in order to obtain item B.

Whether or not (2a) is true we will consider presently. For now let us agree that given (2) and (2a), (3) follows. Statement (4) then seems to follow from the earlier premises if one grants what appears to be an analytic truth:

(3a) If X freely promises something to Y, and this promise creates a right for Y, and X knows this promise creates a right for Y, then X freely chooses to create a right for Y.

And also the additional premise:

(3b) Jones knew Jones' promise to Smith would create a right for Smith to interfere with Jones' freedom in order to obtain item B. Presumably the all-important move from (4) to (5) is justified if the following premises are granted:

(4a) If Jones freely chooses to create Smith's right to interfere with Jones' freedom, then Jones freely creates an obligation to allow Smith's interference with Jones' freedom.

(4b) If Jones freely creates an obligation to allow Smith's interference with Jones' freedom, then Jones has in the absence of this free creation a right to be free from Smith's interference.

(4c) If Jones has (in the absence of this free creation) a right to be free from Smith's interference and the free creation of the obligation toward Smith is not different in morally relevant respects from other free creations of other obligations, then Jones in the absence of the free creation of obligation has the right to be free.

(4d) The free creation of an obligation toward Smith is not different in morally relevant respects from other free creations of other obligations.

Statement (5) and the additional premise:

(5a) Jones is not relevantly different from other persons combined with the premise that may be an analytic truth:

(5b) If Jones has the right to be free in the absence of a free creation of obligation and Jones is not relevantly different from other persons, then in the absence of the free creation of obligation all men equally have the right to be free

seem to entail (6) where (6) is understood to hold in the absence of the free creation of obligation.

Evaluation of Hart's Theory

Moral Neutrality and the Analysis of Rights

As I mentioned earlier Hart apparently wishes to remain morally neutral in his analysis; he does not want to take a stand on the existence of moral rights; he prefers simply to analyze what the concept of moral right entails. Thus he seems to be putting forth the following thesis:

(A) For any moral system S, if S assumes any moral rights, then S assumes the natural right, namely the equal right of men to be free.

However, at one point he says something that suggests a weaker thesis: "I think that the principle that all men have an equal right to be free, meager as it may seem, is probably all that political philosophers of the liberal tradition need have claimed to support any program of action even if they have claimed more."[33] This suggests:

> (B) For any moral system S in the liberal tradition, if S assumes any moral right, then S assumes the natural right, namely the equal right of men to be free.

It is important to recall that both (A) and (B) are *a priori* truths; they are established by conceptual analyses, not empirical inquiry. Counterexamples to them can be actual historical cases or hypothetical ones. Moreover, since Hart wishes to remain morally neutral the term "moral system" is used descriptively, not morally. No theory whether the moral systems at issue are correct or acceptable or even not morally outrageous is presupposed in (A) and (B).

Let us consider (A). One obvious *prima facie* counterexample to (A) is that of a racist moral code, for example, a Nazi or white supremacist one.[34] In such a code one might suppose that Jews or Blacks would not have equal rights to freedom and that this would not just be under the special circumstances mentioned by Hart. Nazis, for example, might maintain that only people with Aryan blood are moral agents and have rights and duties toward one another, that Aryans could treat non-Aryans in the same way they would treat animals.

How might Hart attempt to meet such an example? When he considers a related matter he mentions two possible strategies.[35] First, one might interpret "moral code" in (A) descriptively and argue that any justification a Nazi or white supremacist who interferes with the freedom of others may have is not a *moral* one. On this approach Nazis or white supremacists could not have a *moral* code that allows interference with the freedom of Jews or Blacks. Admitting that he does not show that such a Nazi or racist code is not a moral code, Hart quickly drops this idea.

Of course "moral code" in (A) could be used normatively and not descriptively. Then Hart could argue that Nazis or white supremacists do not have a correct or acceptable moral code; that is, "moral code" in the normative sense does not apply. But in so doing he would not be remaining morally neutral.

Hart's second way of meeting the *prima facie* counterexample would be to argue that Nazis or white supremacists cannot claim a moral *right* to interfere with Jews or Blacks, although they might claim this on other moral grounds. Thus Hart says:

> Claims to interfere with another's freedom based on . . . the general character of the parties ("We are Germans; they are Jews.") even when well founded

> are not matters of moral right or obligation. Submission in such cases even when proper is *not due* to or *owed to* the individuals who interfere; it would be equally proper whoever of the same class of persons interfered. Hence other elements in our moral vocabulary suffice to describe this case, and it is confusing here to talk of rights.[36]

Since Hart ascribes duties to Jews in the above passage he is presumably assuming that Jews are moral agents. But this need not be assumed in the present example. On the contrary, in this example Nazis have rights with respect to Jews, but Jews have no corresponding duties. Nazis in other words have liberties toward Jews; they are under no obligation to refrain from treating them in certain ways. Jews, of course, have no right to be free. If they did, this would conflict with the Nazis' right to treat them as they pleased.

But even if Hart could show that Nazis or white supremacists had no moral *right* to interfere with the freedom of Jews or Blacks, this would hardly be sufficient to show that Jews or Blacks have a right not to be interfered with. In general, it does not follow that, if X has no right to do A with respect to Y, then Y has a right to have X refrain from doing A. Jones may have no right to deface the "Mona Lisa," but it does not follow that the "Mona Lisa" has a right to have Jones refrain from doing this.

Again Hart could rule out the Nazi or white supremacist counterexample by assuming the correctness of some particular code and interpreting (A) normatively and not descriptively. But in doing so Hart would be giving up his moral neutrality.

The problem with Hart's position can be seen in a more direct way by considering the derivation of the natural right of persons to equal freedom from the general right of saying what one wants. It was noted above that in order to derive

> (2) All persons have a right to say what they want

from

> (1) I have a right to say what I want

one must assume

> (1a) I am not different in morally relevant respects from other persons.

But in a Nazi code (1a) is precisely what one could not assume. Aryans and Jews would have morally relevant differences in this code. The derivation flounders at the first step. Since in the Nazi code some people do not have general rights, it certainly cannot be the case that these people have a natural right, the right to equal freedom, since general rights are supposed to be particular instances of this natural right.

We can assume that thesis (A) is mistaken. But what about thesis (B)? Historically, "liberalism" has meant many different things. There are the English, French, German, and American varieties of liberalism, each with its own ideology. It is doubtful—and certainly Hart has not shown this—that (B) is true for all varieties of liberalism. Thus Maurice Cranston writes of German liberalism:

> In the nineteenth century a new school of liberalism, which was first and foremost nationalistic, arose in Germany. The freedom it stood for was the freedom of Germany and the condition of the realization of this national freedom was the unification of Germany. Thus, whereas the old Lockean liberals were against the state, the new national liberals wanted to create a greater state. The French declaration of 1789 proclaimed the rights of *man*; the German liberals inspired in 1846 a declaration of the rights of the German people.[37]

It hardly seems likely that (B) holds true for German liberalism. It would seem that in order to prevent (B) from being refuted by historical counterexamples, (B) would have to be restricted to some particular varieties of liberalism. The crucial question is whether the criterion of restriction could be specified without presuming the natural right of all persons to equal freedom as part of the criterion. If this could not be done, (B) as modified would be trivially true. It would be true of all moral codes in a liberal tradition (characterized by assuming the natural rights of all men to equal freedom) that, if these codes assume any moral rights, they assume the right of all men to equal freedom, but it would be trivial.

Seen in the light of varieties of liberalism (B), as it stands, is probably false and needs to be restricted in a way that does not make it trivially true. Hart has not provided this restriction. Whether he could is unclear.

RIGHTS AND INTERFERENCES

As we have already seen, Hart argues that there is a close connection between having a right and the justified limitation of one person's freedom by another. He seems to maintain that, if I have a right, then others require a special justification for limiting my freedom and I have a justification for limiting the freedom of others. This second assumption does not follow from the first; moreover, as we have also seen, Hart seems to associate limiting someone's freedom with using coercion against that person.

Hart's second assumption plays a crucial role in his derivation of the natural right of equal freedom for all men. As I have reconstructed and illustrated the argument, in the derivation of the natural right from the special right of a person to be given some item B, the following premise is assumed:

> (2a) If Smith has a right to be given item B by Jones, Smith has a right to interfere with Jones' freedom in order to obtain item B.

But is (2a) true?[38] One naturally thinks that if someone has a moral right to be given some item, that person is justified in demanding and insisting on this item and may be justified in complaining to the giver or even denouncing the person for failure to live up to his or her duty. But it is one thing to say this and quite another thing to say that one is justified in using coercion, physical threats, and the like to obtain this item. In short, (2a) seems to be incorrect for moral rights. What may be true is a thesis holding for legal rights:

> (2a′) If Smith has a legal right to be given item B by Jones, Smith has a right to insist that officials of the legal system interfere with Jones' freedom in order to obtain item B.

(2a′) seems much more plausible than (2a), but Hart seems to assume (2a) and not (2a′) in his basic argument.

In a footnote Hart modifies his basic position as follows:

> Here and subsequently I use "interfere with another's freedom," "limit another's freedom," "determine how another shall act" to mean either the use of coercion or demanding that a person shall do or not do some action. . . . I think it is enough for present purposes to point out that having a justification for demanding that a person shall or shall not do some action is a necessary though not a sufficient condition for justifying coercion.[39]

This seems inconsistent, however, with the general tenor of his argument that there is a special congruity between the concept of right and the use of force and that the analysis of legal rights has value for the elucidation of rights outside of legal contexts because of the intimate connection between legal rights and the use of coercion. The idea put forth in the footnote just quoted that limiting another's freedom may only involve demanding that some person act or not act does not fit very well with Hart's stand on coercion and on the close connection between moral rights and legal rights. Nor does it make good sense in terms of the concept of limiting someone's freedom, for it is unclear how merely demanding something limits anyone's freedom.

Perhaps the conclusion we should draw from Hart's work here is that legal rights and moral rights are less closely related than he indicates. We must recognize, moreover, that it is misleading to speak of a justified limitation of someone's freedom in referring to both moral rights *and* legal rights since in the case of moral rights Hart uses this expression in a much broader sense than he does in the case of legal rights; in the former case his use is incompatible with merely demanding.

RIGHTS AND CHOICE

As we have seen, Hart argues that there is a close connection between right and choice. If one has a right against someone, one can either waive one's claim or insist on one's claim. This aspect of Hart's theory is similar to his earlier analysis of legal rights in his Inaugural Lecture and is subject to a similar objection. In that lecture he makes the legal obligation created by the right dependent on the choice of the right holder or the person authorized to act for the right holder. The person with an obligation to the right holder is bound to do or abstain from some action only if the right holder or some authorized person so chooses or chooses otherwise.

In Chapter 1 I pointed out that not all legal obligations correlative with rights are dependent on the choice of the right holder. A similar point can be made with respect to moral rights. Certainly in many systems of morality, if I have a moral right to worship as I please, I cannot waive this right. In our legal system this moral right has become embedded *via* the U.S. Constitution. Our constitutional right to freedom of worship is not waivable. Yet the right to worship as one pleases is considered by Hart to be a general right, one that is a special case of the right of all men to be free. Elsewhere in his writing Hart has admitted that the choice theory of rights does not provide a general account of all legal rights.[40] But it is important to see that it does not even seem to account for all the *moral* rights discussed in his paper "Are There Any Natural Rights?"

The issue of the waivability of rights raises the whole question of the relationship among special rights, general rights, and the natural right of men equally to be free in Hart's system. It should be noted that my reconstruction of Hart's argument assumes that the natural right of all men equally to be free can under special circumstances be set aside. Unless this is assumed, it is difficult to make sense of Hart's argument. Because of one's right to be free one can promise something that creates an obligation that limits one's freedom. Hart, however, mentions no explicit restrictions on the ability of people to limit their own freedom through free choice.

On the other hand, Hart says that the natural right of men to be free is not created by voluntary action. Does this imply that it could not be destroyed by voluntary action? Could we sell ourselves into slavery? As we have also seen, he claims that the equal right of all men to be free is absolute. Does this suggest that there are some built-in limitations on how much and in what respect one can limit one's freedom *via* voluntary agreement?

One can only conclude that there is a tension in Hart's account between his emphasis on free choice in the exercise of rights and his thesis about natural rights, rights that are not created by free choice.

DUTY CORRELATIVE RIGHTS, LIBERTY RIGHTS, AND NATURAL RIGHTS

In his paper Hart makes a distinction between rights that create correlative duties and rights that do not. Rights of the latter type are called liberties. To say that one has a liberty to some act means one has no obligation to refrain from doing this act. According to Hart, in the realm of competition liberty rights and not duty correlative rights are what is relevant.

One crucial question that arises is whether liberty rights are warranted in Hart's derivations of natural rights—that is, whether Hart has shown that, if there are any moral rights, there is at least one natural liberty. He certainly believes that he has shown more. He believes that he has shown that, if there are any moral rights, then there is at least one natural duty correlative right of men to equal freedom.[41]

In the analysis above we saw that in order to carry off Hart's derivation premise (4a) and (4b) must be assumed. (4a) seems unobjectionable. But

(4b) If Jones freely creates an obligation to allow Smith's interference with Jones' freedom, then Jones has in the absence of this free creation a right to be free from Smith's interference

is dubious if "right to be free" is understood in the sense of duty correlative right. What seems to be justified is a different premise, namely:

(4b′) If Jones freely creates an obligation to allow Smith's interference with Jones' freedom, then Jones has in the absence of this free creation no obligation to allow Smith's interference.

But from (4b′) it can only be inferred that Jones has in the absence of a free creation of obligation a liberty right to be free from Smith's interference. (Recall that having a liberty right to do A means having no obligation to refrain from doing A.) Nothing follows about Jones' having a duty correlative right. But since (4b) is false, the rest of Hart's derivation collapses.

THE VARIETY OF MORAL RIGHTS

One of the salient features of Hart's thesis is the claim that, if there are *any* moral rights, then there is at least one natural right, namely the equal right of all men to be free. As we have seen, Hart attempts to show that this thesis is true for what he calls special and general moral rights. So far we have questioned his derivation of the right of all men equally to be free from the assumption of certain moral rights. To summarize my criticism: First, Hart's thesis interpreted descriptively fails in the case of Nazi or white supremacist moral codes and, even if his thesis is restricted to moral codes in the liberal tradition, it is either probably false or possibly empty. Second, a premise in Hart's derivation linking the rights of someone and the justification of coercion seems dubious. Third, another premise of Hart's argument is unjustified since he mistakenly seems to assume that a duty correlative right is assumed whereas only a liberty right is assumed. Fourth, although this aspect of Hart's argument may not be as essential to his derivation as the other aspects mentioned, it is not the case for all moral rights that the right holder has the power to waive the right; thus Hart's choice theory does not even apply to all the rights he considers in his article, let alone to other rights.

Even if the above criticisms are invalid, Hart has not made out his case. There are a variety of different things claimed as rights and he has not begun to show for all the different types of rights that, if any rights are assumed by a moral code, then there exists the natural right of men equally to be free.[42] A variety of rights has been assumed in moral systems in the Western tradition that Hart does not mention: a right to be told the truth, a right to gratitude for benefits done, and a right to assistance. It is quite unclear that these rights presuppose the right of men equally to freedom. They seem to be based neither on a free creation involving a promise or authorization nor on mutual restriction that is characteristic of political rights and obligations.

Indeed, Hart does not even show this for all the special rights he discusses. Consider the special right created by natural relations between parents and children, for example, the right of parents to obedience by the child. Hart does not even try to show that this right presupposes the natural right of men to be free and it is difficult to see how this could be shown given the drift of his argument. In the case of special rights created by promises, consent, or authorization the claim to interfere with another person's freedom is justified because a person has, in the exercise of his equal right to be free, freely chosen to create this claim. But in the case of parents' right to obedience from their children, it hardly seems plausible that children have freely created this claim against them in the exercise of their right to be free. Nor is it clear how this special right of parents to their children's obedience is to be justified in the way political rights are justified, that is, by mutual restrictions that are designed to bring about an equal distribution of freedom.

NATURAL RIGHTS AND COERCION AS *PRIMA FACIE* OBJECTIONABLE

It has been supposed that there is a connection between Hart's view on natural rights and his view expressed in his later writing that coercion and punishment are *prima facie* objectionable. But what is this connection and can his views on natural rights provide a justification for his later views?

Consider the following argument:

(1) If there are any moral rights at all, there is at least the equal right of men to be free.
(2) If there is at least one natural right, the natural right of men to be free, then coercion is *prima facie* objectionable and to be tolerated only for the sake of some countervailing good.
(3) There are moral rights.

---

(4) Therefore coercion is *prima facie* objectionable and to be tolerated only for the sake of some countervailing good.

I can find no evidence that Hart actually assumes this argument, let alone that he actually gives it. Nevertheless, it does seem a natural way to link his argument for natural rights to his later views.

Unfortunately, however, the above argument has serious problems. As we have seen, premise (1) is dubious because Hart's attempt to derive the existence of the right to be free from the existence of moral rights is based on several questionable premises. Furthermore, at least in his paper on natural rights, he does not even assert premise (3), let alone argue for it, and it is unclear that he assumes moral rights in a categorical manner in his other writings.[43] Moreover, it is one thing to assume the existence of these rights and quite another to argue for their existence. I am not aware that Hart has ever explicitly argued categorically for moral rights.

Indeed, his recent writing suggests that he is rather skeptical of arguments for human rights and the "new faith" in natural rights. Asserting that the human rights found in the work of such philosophers as Robert Nozick and Ronald Dworkin are presented in forms that are, in spite of "much brilliance, in the end unconvincing,"[44] Hart gives the impression he does not think that human rights or natural rights exist. But rejection of the existence of rights—in particular of human or natural rights—does not in the end seem to be Hart's position. Despite his skepticism about their philosophical foundation, Hart says "a theory of rights is urgently called for. . . . So the protection of a doctrine of basic human rights limiting what a state may do to its citizens seems to be precisely what the political problems of our own age most urgently require."[45]

Hart's position, then, can be characterized as follows: On the one hand, he does not argue for (3) above and is skeptical of arguments that have been given. On the other hand, he believes that there are moral rights although his belief cannot at present be based on any sound argument. Even in his latest writing

Hart does not deny that humans have the right to be free, the only natural right he considered in his earlier paper. Nor has he ever denied that humans have other natural rights.

If this is, indeed, Hart's position, then we must conclude that his views on natural right lend no support to his views on the *prima facie* evil of coercion. The question therefore remains of how Hart could justify his thesis that coercion is *prima facie* evil. It is not implausible to suppose that he could attempt to justify it on utilitarian grounds by arguing that there is good reason to suppose that in most instances coercion brings about more harm than good; hence generally there is a presumption that coercion is evil. This presumption could only be rebutted by showing that coercion contributes to some countervailing good.

THE CONTENT OF THE EQUAL LIBERTY PRINCIPLE

So far I have refrained from considering critically the content of the equal freedom principle itself. The content of this principle does have very peculiar implications, however—indeed, so peculiar that it seems to reflect on Hart's attempt to derive the equal freedom principle from the existence of moral rights. Once these implications are spelled out one cannot but suspect that there is something wrong with the derivation itself.

We should recall that Hart specifies two aspects of the equal freedom rights. First, any adult human being capable of choice has the right to forbearance on the part of others from the use of coercion or restraint except to hinder coercion or restraint. I take this to mean that one has a right to demand that others not coerce or restrain one except when one uses coercion or restraint against others. Second, any adult human being capable of choice is under no obligation to abstain from some action that is not one coercing or restraining or designed to injure other persons. I take this to mean that one has no obligation not to do something except when one is coercing or restraining or deliberately injuring other people. Thus Hart believes that although people have a right to be free this is compatible with restraint in special circumstances, the very circumstances specified above.

However, Hart's view of the special circumstances seems extremely narrow. Indeed, his special circumstances seem compatible only with a very limited type of government, the caretaker type of the libertarian. Consider the first aspect of the principle. The government uses coercion or restraint in order to get people to pay taxes, enforce building codes, wear motorcycle helmets, and so on; these restraints and this coercion are not based on people's use of coercion or restraint against others. To be sure, the government's use of coercion may be wrong and libertarians and anarchists have argued that they are. But libertarianism and anarchism are very controversial positions and in his later writings Hart rejects them.[46]

The second aspect of the equal liberty principle seems equally implausible, for it excludes a variety of different duties many people believe that they have. People believe that they have an obligation not to abstain from paying their taxes, not to abstain from giving to charity, not to abstain from going to the aid of others in distress if they can do so without injury. None of these obligations involves abstaining from coercing, restraining, or injuring people and so on. Again, people could be wrong about their duties. But if they are, the reason they are should be explained. Furthermore, it is unclear that Hart would reject all of the abovementioned duties. He surely believes that people have an obligation to not abstain from paying their income tax.

ARE HART'S EARLIER AND LATER VIEWS ON NATURAL RIGHTS COMPATIBLE?

Although in his later work Hart has been skeptical of recent theories of rights, he seems to think that a viable theory of rights is needed. Furthermore in his later writings he raises problems about natural rights. One may well wonder if these problems affect his earlier views.

To a certain extent Hart seems to be sympathetic with Bentham's critique of natural rights. The latter offered two basic criticisms of natural rights that Hart claims have taken "a firm root in English political theory."[47] First, Bentham argued that, unlike legal rights, where there is an objective way of determining whether someone has a right, there is no way of settling the question of whether someone has any natural rights. There is simply no agreed-on test. Bentham also argued that insofar as rights are represented as absolute in form, hence allowing no exceptions, they are impossible to reconcile with the powers of government; they are anarchical. On the other hand, if they allow for exceptions they are nugatory, "empty guides both to legislators and their subjects."[48]

Hart disagrees with Bentham that advocates of natural rights are advocating either something that is impossible (rights with no exceptions) or something that is nugatory (rights with exceptions). Arguing that "there is certainly more to be said about the relationship between basic human rights and other values than he allows," he maintains that, "in spite of recent work, I do not think we yet have a satisfactory theory showing how respect for such rights is to be combined with the pursuit of other values."[49]

Does Hart's theory of natural rights escape Bentham's criticisms? Consider Bentham's first argument. Hart does not, of course, provide any test of either natural or moral right, except the conditional one that he can derive the equal right of all men to be free from any moral right. So *if* we establish some moral right, Hart claims he can show by logical argument that there is the right of all men to be free. As we have seen, this derivation is unsuccessful. So Hart in fact is unsuccessful in providing any test of right, even a conditional one.

Consider Bentham's second criticism. As we have seen, the equal liberty principle leads not to anarchy but to a very minimal state. Hart's equal liberty principle allows the state to use coercion or restraint against a person only if the person is using coercion or restraint against others; in all other cases the person has a right to forbearance from the state. Although such a position is perhaps not impossible in some absolute sense, it is impossible to reconcile with the powers of presently existing governments. Furthermore, it seems to be a position that Hart objects to. He rejects such a limited view of the state. Although Hart disagrees with Bentham's analysis to some extent, he maintains that natural right theory provides no account of how respect for such rights is to be combined with the pursuit of other values. He provides no account of how the protection of the right to freedom can be combined with the need for taxation, the paternalistic interest of the government (for example, a law requiring motorcycle helmets), and the furthering of legitimate state interest (for example, regulating building construction).

It is significant, I believe, that, although Hart's paper on natural rights is one of his most reprinted works, he himself does not refer to it in his later writings.[50] Although he did not explicitly reject[51] the major thesis of this paper until 1983, it seems clear that in his more mature thought Hart has implicitly repudiated most of its major ideas. The only idea he seems to retain is the hope that a viable natural rights theory can be developed.

CATEGORIZING HART'S ETHICAL THEORY

Hart's position on natural rights indicates the difficulties one encounters when one attempts to characterize Hart's ethical position in any simple way. As we saw in the last chapter, Hart is not a utilitarian on all questions connected with punishment. Although his rejection of a full-scale utilitarianism in his theory of punishment does not entail the conditional theory of natural rights developed during the same period, it is consistent with this theory. His recent hope that a viable moral theory based on rights can be developed surely suggests that he believes that it would capture an important aspect of morality that utilitarian theory cannot. Needless to say, his perceptive criticisms of different forms of utilitarianism[52] indicate that he is keenly aware of the problems of utilitarianism. On the other hand, his criticisms of the rights-based theories of Dworkin and Nozick,[53] his recent explicit rejection of his own conditional theory of natural rights,[54] his partial sympathy with Bentham's objections to natural right theories, and his belief that a viable rights-based theory has yet to be developed all indicate his awareness of the problems of any theory of natural rights.

William Frankena has characterized an ethical theory as a *mixed deontological theory* if it recognizes the principle of utility as well as some other ethical principle or principles not based on utility.[55] Perhaps from the very beginning of his career to the present Hart's ethical theory, although never fully articulated, is best described as a mixed deontological one. The difference between his earlier and more mature views is perhaps that now Hart is much less sure than he once was about the content and justification of non-utilitarian principles, especially those based on natural rights. Hart's recent skepticism over the foundation of natural rights has not affected his ethical arguments in his other works, however. He does not explicitly appeal to natural or moral rights in arguing against Devlin in *Liberty and Morality*. In the index to *The Concept of Law* "right" refers to legal rights, and in *Punishment and Responsibility*, although Hart may assume that some retributivist principles could be based on a belief in moral rights, he does not say explicitly that his own retributivist views are.

Conclusion

Hart's conception of natural law is problematic. His claim that, given certain truisms and the goal of human survival, at least one group in every society must have laws with a particular minimum content is not substantiated. Although the truisms Hart specifies and the goal of human survival provide *a* reason for having laws with minimum content, Hart's thesis is much stronger than this. He maintains that human survival cannot be furthered given these truisms without laws with certain minimum content. In other words, Hart claims that the goal of survival and the truisms provide a conclusive reason for having one group in every society with laws with survival content. I have shown that this is incorrect since societies can be imagined that are perfectly consistent with Hart's truisms and the goal of survival but that do not have any group with laws with minimum content. The attempt to strengthen Hart's theory by allowing other premises to be added to ones specifying the truisms and the goal of survival might provide conclusive reasons if these other premises were true. But, as I have argued, the difficulty is that these added premises do not seem to be truisms; indeed, their truth may well be doubted. Further, the attempt to meet my criticisms by various modifications of Hart's theory does not work.

Hart's natural law theory actually plays a relatively minimal role in his thought. He can, I believe, drop this element of his work without serious loss. Although in his natural law theory he links survival with having sanctions, there is no reason to believe that punishment could not be more plausibly justified in a straightforward utilitarian way. Indeed, Hart attempts to do this in his more systematic effort to justify punishment. In that effort natural law really plays no direct role. Nor does Hart utilize his theory of natural law in his debate with Devlin. To be sure, Hart's theory of natural law does seem to play a role in the definition that can be extracted from his concept of law. But this aspect of his definition seems mistaken and can in any case be dropped without loss. Indeed, the only place in his thinking that his theory of natural law plays any significant role is in the debate with Fuller. As I will show in the next chapter, this theory does not strengthen Hart's argument; indeed, it concedes too much to Fuller.

Hart's theory of natural rights also has serious problems. One crucial question is whether his failure to provide a viable, non-traditional theory of natural law and natural right really matters to his major philosophical views. As I have suggested, the principle that coercion is *prima facie* evil—an idea that, as we shall see, Hart utilizes in his debate with Devlin—can be justified in other ways. Moreover, in neither his debate with Fuller nor his debate with Devlin does he explicitly utilize a natural rights approach.

Chapter

7

The Connection Between Morality and Law: The Hart-Fuller Debate

HART IS A legal positivist in the sense that he believes that it is crucial to separate the question of what the law is from the question of what the law ought to be. His legal positivism is evident in his analysis of the concept of law and of a legal system. For, according to his analysis, it is possible to have a law or legal system that is evil. Hart believes that it is a fundamental confusion—a confusion associated with natural law theory—to argue that simply because a rule or system of rules is evil it is not a law or a legal system.

Attempting to distinguish his brand of legal positivism from early varieties, for many years Hart debated this point with Lon Fuller—a modern advocate of natural law theory. Although, in general, Hart had the better of the debate, Hart's position and Fuller's are actually much closer than is usually supposed. Moreover, there is a fundamental conflict in Hart's views between his rejection of natural law theory and his acceptance of some minimal connection between morality and law.

Background to the Debate

One of the major controversies in the philosophy of law pits legal positivists against advocates of natural law theory. Legal positivism, a position traditionally associated with Jeremy Bentham and John Austin, advocates three major theses. The first is that what the law is and what the law should be are distinct questions. According to positivism, from the fact that some rule is a valid rule of law in a legal system nothing follows about whether the rule is moral or immoral. Both Bentham and Austin believed that many laws were evil and should be changed, but they thought that nothing but confusion resulted from supposing that if a rule is immoral it is not a law. Bentham and Austin also argued that it is important to analyze legal concepts such as a legal system, rule, right, and so on. And finally they maintained that laws are commands of a sovereign whom the populace habitually obeys.

Natural law theorists reject the positivist view that what the law is and what the law ought to be are separate questions. They maintain instead that the validity of the law and the morality of a law are connected. Traditional natural law theorists, for example, Aquinas, often maintained that the principles of natural law specify substantive moral principles of God discoverable by reason that human laws must meet. Although it is dubious that all traditional natural law theorists have actually claimed that evil rules could not be laws, natural law theory has sometimes been interpreted as having this implication. In fact, traditional natural law theorists have usually held a more subtle and complex view of the relation between law and morality.[1]

H. L. A. Hart accepts two of the three tenets of classical legal positivism. He certainly believes that the questions of what the law is and what the law ought to be must be separated and he maintains that iniquitous governments can still be governments of laws. In fact, Hart is the best-known advocate in contemporary philosophy of law of the separation of law and morality. Further, he maintains that it is important that legal philosophers analyze legal concepts. Indeed, as we have seen in earlier chapters, he himself has provided analyses of key legal concepts. However, Hart rejects the command theory of law adopted by Austin and Bentham. As we saw in Chapter 1, the concept of a legal system has nothing to do with the command of a sovereign.

If Hart is the best-known contemporary representative of legal positivism, Lon Fuller is the best-known contemporary critic of legal positivism and advocate of natural law theory. To be sure, since Hart rejects the command theory of early legal positivists, it would be a mistake to identify his views completely with classical legal positivism. Similarly, although Fuller holds the view that morality and law cannot be separated from legal validity and in this respect advocates a natural law approach, it would be a mistake to suppose that his views can be completely identified with traditional natural law theory. For example, Fuller rejects the view that natural laws are moral principles of God discoverable by reason. Further, whereas traditional natural law theory, according to Fuller, has been primarily concerned with substantive natural law principles, such as principles about marriage, birth control, and the like, Fuller is concerned with procedural questions of natural law, such as whether laws are clear, possible to follow, consistent, and so on. Perhaps the difference in approach between Fuller and traditional natural law theories can be illustrated in this way. A traditional natural law theorist would reject as a law a rule requiring women to be sterilized since it conflicts with a divine principle, the allegedly self-evident truth that the human species should propagate. Fuller would reject the rule as a law if, for example, the rule was hopelessly unclear or secret, not for any substantive religious reasons. Now it may seem that the controversy between modern-day legal positivists like Hart and modern-day natural law theorists like Fuller is a trivial semantic issue with no practical import over the meaning of the word "law." However, nothing could be farther from the truth.

To understand the practical import of the controversy consider the case of Nazi Germany. A natural law theorist would argue that the rules called "laws" in Nazi Germany were not really laws, that they were too iniquitous to be laws. In contrast, a legal positivist would maintain that Nazi Germany had laws, although very evil ones. These positions have very different implications. Indeed, after World War II some legal scholars in Germany rejected legal positivism for practical reasons. Gustav Radbruch, for example, rejected his earlier legal positivism in the light of the Nazi experience. According to Hart, Radbruch concluded from "the ease with which the Nazi regime had exploited subservience to mere law . . . and from the failure of the German legal profession to protest against the enormities which they were required to perpetuate in the name of law, that 'positivism' . . . had powerfully contributed to the horrors."[2] Radbruch came to believe that the principle of humanitarian morality was part of the concept of legality and that no statute could be law unless it conformed to these principles. Radbruch's doctrine meant that lawyers and judges should denounce statutes that did not meet humane purposes not only as immoral but as not legal.

Hart tells us that after the war German courts applied Radbruch's theory of law to cases in which local war criminals, informers, and spies under the Nazi regime were punished. The persons accused claimed in defense that under the Nazi law enforced at the time of their alleged crimes what they had done was not illegal. But using a Radbruchian approach, the courts argued that the rules on which the defendants relied were not laws because they were in conflict with the fundamental principles of morality—that is, with natural law.

Thus in one grudge informer case, a woman who wanted to get rid of her husband denounced him to the authorities for insulting remarks he had made against Hitler while he was on leave from the German army. According to Hart, what the man said was in apparent violation of Nazi statutes. The husband was arrested and sentenced to death, but instead of being executed he was sent to the front. After the war the wife was prosecuted by a West German court for depriving a person of his freedom, an offense under the German Criminal Code of 1871, which was still in force. The wife argued that the husband was denied freedom pursuant to Nazi statutes; consequently she was innocent of committing a crime. The court held that the woman was guilty of depriving her husband of liberty and that the Nazi rules were not legally valid since they were inconsistent with sound moral principles—that is, with natural law.

Although Fuller concentrates on procedural questions in natural law and rejects Radbruch's appeal to a higher law, he believes that there is a serious question of whether Nazi Germany had a rule of law since the Nazis made extensive use of retroactive legislation and "secret laws." Fuller's position, no less than the traditional natural law one, is that it is doubtful that German war criminals could claim in their defense that they were merely following the law. Outlining the situation in German legal scholarship at the time of Hitler's rise to power, he argues that the acceptance of legal positivism in pre-Nazi Germany "made smoother the route to dictatorship."[3] Fuller notes, in particular, that German scholars took legal theories very seriously and "banned from legal science any consideration of the moral ends of law," thus rejecting all natural law ideas. Fuller believes that considerations such as these make it plausible to suppose that "the attitudes prevailing in the German legal profession were helpful to the Nazis."[4]

The alleged connection between the rise of Naziism and the acceptance of legal positivism is one kind of attack that defenders of legal positivism must meet. But this argument does not exhaust the criticism raised against it. Some critics have attempted to show that the separation of law and morality is impossible. Moral considerations must enter into law, they argue, *via* judicial interpretation and no other way. Other critics have maintained that, even if the separation of law and morality is possible, it is pernicious, for it results in amoral or even immoral attitudes toward the law.

It is not surprising that Hart and Fuller should have debated the issue of the separation of law and morality: whether such separation is possible, whether it is pernicious, whether it aided the rise of Nazi Germany. Nor is it surprising that the debate has become the most famous one in contemporary philosophy of law. What is perhaps surprising, however, is that it lasted more than a decade. In 1958 the *Harvard Law Review* published a paper by Hart entitled "Positivism and the Separation of Law and Morals"[5] together with a critical response by Lon Fuller entitled "Positivism and Fidelity to Law—A Reply to Professor Hart."[6] In *The Concept of Law* Hart returned to the theme of the separation of law and morals and attempted to answer Fuller's attack.[7] Fuller's book *The Morality of Law*, in which Hart's stand on the separation of law and morality was criticized, appeared in 1964.[8] The debate continued when Hart reviewed Fuller's book in the *Harvard Law Review* in 1965.[9] In a 1969 revised edition of his book Fuller replies to Hart.[10] Meanwhile other philosophers of law had joined in the controversy, some taking sides with Hart and others with Fuller.[11]

Hart's contribution to the debate was threefold. He showed that the command theory of law should be detached from the other tenets of classical legal positivism. Given this detachment he was then able to argue for some of the major insights of classical legal positivism and in so doing to keep alive and revitalize the views of Bentham and Austin. Finally, he was able to relate the traditional issue of the separation of law and morality to contemporary problems such as non-cognitivism in ethics and interpretation in judicial decisions. As a result the issue of the separation of law and morality became more sharply defined and was better defended than it ever had been. Indeed, Hart raised the discussion to a new level.

Hart's Defense in the *Harvard Law Review*

Hart's general strategy in defending the separation of the question of what law is from the question of what the law ought to be is first to present the reason classical legal positivists like Bentham and Austin gave for the separation and then to answer particular objections that have been raised against the separation. In setting forth the reasoning of the classical legal positivists he attempts to place legal positivism in historical perspective by approaching the problem of the separation of law and morals "as part of the history of an idea."[12] Hart points out that the architects of early social reform of the late eighteenth and early nineteenth centuries were utilitarians. Bentham and Austin, two of the best known, stressed the need to distinguish law as it is from law as it ought to be, and they criticized natural law thinkers for blurring this distinction. Hart argues that at the present time the situation is reversed: the separation between law and morals is held to be superficial and wrong, and some critics have even claimed that it weakens resistance to state tyranny and absolutism. The term "legal positivism" in one of its various senses refers to the "sin, real or alleged,"[13] that advocates separation.

Why, Hart asks, did the great social reformers insist on a separation? For Austin, the fundamental principles of morality were God's commands, "to which utility was an 'index.'"[14] There was also the accepted morality of a social group, which he called "positive morality." Austin insisted, however, that something could be law and yet be in conflict with both the fundamental principles of morality and positive morality. Bentham characterized morality in terms of utility, not God's commands, but also insisted on this distinction. Both theorists' reason for the separation of law and morality "was to enable men to see steadily the precise issues posed by the existence of morally bad law, and to understand the specific character of the authority of a legal order."[15]

According to Hart, Bentham wanted to avoid the extreme both of the anarchist who refuses to obey a law just because it is a bad law and of the reactionary who believes that just because something is law it ought to be obeyed. Bentham's view was "to obey punctually; to censure freely."[16] But he realized that there could come a time when the state's laws were so evil that they had to be resisted. Without the clear separation of law and morals the complexity of the facts to be considered in the decision to obey the law would be overlooked.

Of course, classical legal positivists like Austin and Bentham never denied that the development of legal systems was influenced by moral opinions or that moral principles might be incorporated into the law or a constitution by an explicit legal provision. They only insisted that it could not follow from the fact that a rule violated a standard of morality that it was not a law nor that because a rule was morally desirable it was a law. After this doctrine was expounded by Austin, Hart argues, it dominated English jurisprudence for many years and it was assumed "as something that enables lawyers to attain a new clarity."[17] Moreover, in the United States men like John Chipman Gray and Oliver Wendell Holmes, acknowledging their debt to Austin, insisted on the separation of law and morals.

In attempting to defend the separation of law and morality against particular objections, Hart proceeds in the typical analytic fashion of separating out different questions and making necessary distinctions.

One common objection to legal positivism is that laws cannot always be plausibly understood as commands. To reject the thesis of the separation of laws and morality because of the implausibility of the command theory is, however, a mistake, Hart insists. Indeed, the three doctrines of legal positivism are separate. One might well advocate with perfect consistency the separation of laws and morals and also an analytic study of legal concepts without advocating the command theory of law, and in fact this is precisely what Hart does. Outlining the serious problems connected with the command theory of law in *The Concept of Law*, he makes the point that its refutation leaves the doctrine of the separation of law and morality untouched.

In his 1958 paper Hart hints at the view of the nature of law he comes to advocate in *The Concept of Law*. He says there that the foundation of a legal system is based on the acceptance of certain rules, not on the notion of command. However, he insists that these rules need not be morally acceptable, nor need these rules be accepted on moral grounds. The social acceptance of rules might be "motivated only by fear or superstition or rests on inertia."[18] Consequently, Hart argues, any objection against the separation of law and morality that turns on the rejection of the command theory would be misplaced. Since he rejects the command theory and in any case shows it to be detachable from the separation thesis, no refutation of the command theory can affect the thesis of the separation of law and morality.

Another objection leveled against legal positivism turns on what Hart calls the problem of the penumbra. Recall the legal rule forbidding one to take a vehicle into the public park. It is clear that it forbids automobiles, but a question arises about bicycles, roller skates, and toy automobiles: Are these vehicles for the purpose of the rule? According to Hart, an ordinary term has a settled meaning but there will be a penumbra of debatable cases to which the term neither obviously applies nor obviously does not apply. In such cases the judge must make a decision on something beside deduction from a rule.

Critics of legal positivism argue that the "something beside" is a consideration of what ought to be done. Thus a judge in deciding whether a bicycle should be allowed in the public park must make a moral judgment about what the law should be. But then the legal positivists are wrong. Because of their rigid formalistic view of judicial decision making they overlook the necessary connection between law and morals.

Hart denies that the legal positivists were formalistic. Austin, Hart shows, was alive to the vagueness and open character of language and, indeed, argued that judges should legislate in penumbra cases. Hart argues that if the utilitarian distinction between law and morality is to be shown to be wrong by reason of the error of formalism, the point must be restated. One must not merely show that "a judicial decision to be rational must be made in the light of some conception of what ought to be, but that the aims, the social policies and purposes to which judges should appeal if their decisions are to be rational, are themselves to be considered as part of the law in some suitable wider sense of the 'law', which is held to be more illuminating than that held by the Utilitarians."[19] In this wider sense of "law," instead of saying that judges legislate in the penumbra, we say that social policies that guide judges are there for them to discover, that the judges only are "drawing out" of a rule the social policy that, as it were, is latent within it.

Hart rebuts this argument as follows. First, he says, it is important not to think in too simple-minded a fashion about "ought." Ought judgments can occur from many different points of view, not all of which are moral. Thus a wider conception of law in which social purposes are considered part of the law need not be restricted to social purposes that are morally desirable. Hart points out that a Nazi legal system could be imagined in which judges did not make mechanical decisions. Judges in such a system might make intelligent and purposive decisions in terms of what ought to be done from the point of view of Nazi goals. (They might in fact believe that they were discovering the law and not making it.) But, granting the assumption that the Nazi purposes were not moral, in such a system law and morals would not be necessarily connected. Second, Hart argues that the invitation to revise it by including in the concept of a legal rule various aims and purposes in terms of which penumbra cases are decided should be refused. One can describe the judicial process in less mysterious ways, he claims, by saying that laws are incurably incomplete and that we must decide the penumbral cases by social aims. Furthermore, the proposal obscures the importance of clear cases and tends to make it seem as if all legal questions are like those of the penumbra.

The next criticism Hart considers derives from the views of legal scholars like Gustav Radbruch who lived through the Nazi experience in Germany. Radbruch maintained that the acceptance of legal positivism in Germany contributed to the rise of Naziism, but Hart argues that Radbruch was naive to suppose that "insensitiveness to the demands of morality and subservience to state power in a people like the Germans should have arisen from the belief that law might be law though it failed to conform with the minimum requirement of morality."[20] He points out that in other times and places, for example, in eighteenth-century England, legal positivism was associated with an enlightened liberal attitude. This suggests, he says, that special conditions in Germany in the 1930's made the separation of law and morals acquire a sinister character. Moreover, according to Hart, Radbruch has only "half digested the spiritual message of liberalism which he is seeking to convey to the legal profession."[21] After all, people like Austin and Bentham never believed that because a rule was a rule of law it should be obeyed. This is not part of legal positivism.

As far as the case of the Nazi grudge informer is concerned, Hart argues that there were alternative solutions for the court and legislature to have taken that would have been preferable. In order to punish the wife it was not necessary to declare the Nazi rules illegal because of their failure to meet certain natural law principles. One obvious alternative would have been to have enacted some retrospective law. Despite the use of odious retrospective legislation, such a course of action would have had merits of candor. The approach recommended by Radbruch, Hart suggests, hides the moral dilemma and substitutes for clarity and plain speech (something can be law and yet be evil) a controversial philosophical position (no evil statute is really law).

The next criticism Hart considers is that, while it may be argued that the separation of law and morals is correct when we are speaking about individual laws, this separation does not hold when we are talking about the legal system as a whole. Hart is prepared to admit that certain things true of legal systems may not be true of laws taken separately. For example, although there need be no sanction associated with each individual law, there could be no legal system without some sanction. According to Hart, there are in fact two ways in which a legal system as a whole may be necessarily connected with morality. The first was discussed at length in the last chapter. In his 1958 paper Hart sketches the theory of the minimum content of natural law that he then elaborated in *The Concept of Law*. He argues that, given certain obvious but contingent facts about human beings and their desire to survive, a minimum moral content of law is a natural necessity. The second way that a minimum moral content is necessarily attached to legal systems is through the use of general rules. By the use of general rules legal systems assure a formal principle of justice: similar cases are to be treated similarly. However, as he points out, such a necessary overlap between morals and laws will not satisfy critics of legal positivism. This is because a legal system can have a minimum natural law content and formal justice and still be morally oppressive. There could, for example, be slave societies that meet this minimum requirement. Hart apparently does not believe that any more of a connection between legal systems and morality can be shown.

The final argument against legal positivism Hart considers is that the separation between law and morals is based on some subjective or non-cognitive theory of morality. Some critics perhaps believe, he says, that if there is no sharp separation between fact and value—if man's ultimate purpose is something one discovers and not something one chooses, if morality is not just a matter of non-cognitive preference or a subjective postulate of the will—then the sharp distinction between law and morality cannot be maintained. However, Hart points out that this is not the case. Even if ethical statements are rationally defensible, indeed even if they are identical with factual statements, laws could still be immoral. If moral judgments are cognitive and objective, then the only thing that follows is that the immorality of law is rationally demonstrated. Hart concludes that "something further or more specific must be said if disproof of 'non-cognitivism' or kindred theories in ethics is to be relevant to the distinction between law as it is and law as it ought to be."[22]

Saying "No one has done more than Professor Lon Fuller of Harvard Law School in his various writings to make clear such a line of argument," at this point in his defense of legal positivism Hart considers Fuller's position.[23] As expounded by Hart, Fuller's position is this: In many instances judges in making decisions in the penumbral area do not seem to be legislating in terms of social goals. Rather they seem to be elaborating a rule in a natural way, "implementing a 'purpose' which it seems natural to attribute (in some sense) to the rule itself rather than to any particular person dead or alive."[24] Hart admits that Fuller's description is true in some cases of legal decisions. But he argues that such cases are rare[25] and that descriptions of judges' legislating in terms of social purposes frequently seem more accurate, and, furthermore, that even if Fuller's description is accurate, this does not mean there cannot be immoral laws. Hart points out that the natural elaboration and working out of the purpose of a rule is compatible with immoral legal codes; indeed judges may be elaborating the code by working out its immoral purpose.

Fuller's *Harvard Law Review* Paper and Hart's Response

Fuller's Arguments

Fuller's arguments in his *Harvard Law Review* paper are directed at undermining Hart's contention that law and morality are separate. His arguments are not easily summarized since they are not all of a piece and are directed at various aspects of Hart's position. Thus he brings up objections to Hart's view of law and morality, he attempts to refute Hart's analysis of the Nazi experience, he attempts to refute Hart's detachment of the command theory of law from the separation of law and morality, he argues for the internal morality of the law—a type of procedural natural law theory—and he attempts to establish the connection of morality and law *via* the notion of judicial interpretation. In general, Fuller reacts to Hart's paper in piecemeal fashion rather than attempting to develop a systematic approach.

In his preliminary comments, Fuller maintains that Hart's chief contribution is to pose the question clearly: How best can we define and serve the ideal of fidelity to law? In the remainder of his discussion of Hart, Fuller seems to assume that Hart advocates fidelity to law. Fuller admits that Hart does not believe we have an obligation to follow immoral laws, for example, those immoral statutes that were enacted during the Nazi regime. But he insists that Hart assumes fidelity to the law even in the case of Nazi statutes since "he considers that a decision to disobey them presented not a mere question of prudence or courage, but a genuine moral dilemma in which the ideal of fidelity to the law had to be sacrificed in favor of more fundamental goals." Fuller argues that it was unwise to pass such a judgment "without first inquiring with more particularity what 'law' itself meant under the Nazi regime."[26]

Fuller then argues that although Hart's thesis is that law and morality are separate, Hart does not specify what law is. This poses a problem, he argues, since legal positivists have had different views of law. How, Fuller asks, can one in concrete and practical terms have fidelity to the law if the meaning of law is unclear? A stipulative definition of law will not do since it will not help one to achieve fidelity to law in time of trouble. Hart's position, Fuller concludes, is incomplete.

According to Fuller, Hart, like other legal positivists, uses morality in a very broad sense to include "all sorts of extra legal notions about 'what ought to be', regardless of their sources, pretensions, or intrinsic worth."[27] But toward the end of Hart's paper, Fuller notes, he argues that some systems of what ought to be cannot be called moral. Fuller seems to think that the distinction Hart makes between various systems of what ought to be and an acceptable system is not in keeping with "the prevailing tenor"[28] of his thought or, he hints, with legal positivism generally.

Fuller also raises a critical point against Hart's view on morality and law. Hart, he says, assumes that evil aims have as much coherence and inner logic as good ones. Fuller denies this. Maintaining that when "men are compelled to explain and justify their decisions, the effect will generally be to pull their decisions toward goodness, by whatever standards of ultimate goodness there are,"[29] he finds incongruous the idea of legal systems with "a possible future in which the common law would 'work itself pure from case to case' toward a more perfect realization of iniquity."[30]

Fuller next makes a number of assertions all aimed at showing that legal positivism is not as effective a protection against the infusion of what he calls "immoral morality" as higher law or natural law principles. He questions whether a judge or a political regime bent on realizing evil would be more likely to use the rhetoric of "law is law" than the rhetoric of natural law. Although he does not give examples of what he means, one supposes that he has this sort of thing in mind: Suppose a regime wanted to eliminate some minority group. Fuller seems to believe that it would be more likely to pass statutes making persecution of the minority legal while arguing that these should be obeyed since "law is law," than in passing such statutes and justifying their obedience by appeal to natural law.

As we have seen, Hart separates the question of the validity of the command theory of law from that of the separation of law and morality and argues that, although the command theory is mistaken, the thesis that law and morality are distinct is not affected. Fuller challenges this, saying, "I do not think any mistake is committed in believing that Bentham and Austin's error in formulating improperly and too simply the problem of the relation of law and morality was part of a larger error that led to the command theory of law."[31] According to Fuller, had Austin given up the command theory, as he was tempted to do, this would have involved his giving up the separation of law and morality; indeed, since the whole object of Austin's lectures was to separate law and morals, he resisted this temptation.

Why does Fuller believe that giving up the command theory would lead to the merger of laws and morals? His argument seems to be that had Austin given up the command theory he would have had to embrace a theory like Hart's that assumes some fundamental accepted rules as the basis of the legal system. However, in order to be effective the fundamental rules of a legal system must be accepted on moral grounds, on what people believe to be right and just. But, in this case, there is indeed a merger of law and morality.

Fuller also argues that there is an "internal morality" to the law. Contrasting this with the "external morality" of law, that is, the acceptance of the basic goals of the system on moral grounds, he sees the internal morality of law as the morality of order, a functioning order. For example, for a system of rules to be effective the rules must be clear and unambiguous. Thus, having clear and unambiguous rules is one requirement of the internal morality of law. Elsewhere,[32] Fuller specifies eight requirements that constitute the inner morality of the law. Rules should be (1) general, (2) made known or available to the affected party (promulgated), (3) prospective, not retroactive, (4) clear and understandable, (5) free from contradiction. Furthermore, they should not (6) require what is impossible or (7) be too frequently changed, and (8) there should be congruence between the law and official action. A system that has rules that meet these requirements is sometimes said to follow the principle of legality or to follow the rule of law.

Fuller argues that Hart almost completely neglects the internal morality of the law. Hart admits that laws have some formal principles of justice built into them. But, according to Fuller, he "quickly dismisses this aspect of law as having no special relevance to his main enterprise."[33] This dismissal is a complete mistake, Fuller says; in fact, it is because of this neglect that Hart fails to notice that morality and law are merged.

Fuller maintains that Hart's analysis of the situation in Nazi Germany and his recommendations with respect to it are mistaken. Rather than declare that these Nazi statutes were never law, Hart recommends the enactment of retroactive laws in order to punish grudge informers who acted under the Nazi statutes with impunity. Against Hart, Fuller raises the following points:

First, Hart "seems to assume that the only difference between Nazi law and, say, English law is that the Nazis used their law to achieve ends that are odious to an Englishman."[34] This is not true. The Nazis made extensive use of retroactive legislation if it suited their purposes; thus, in the Nazi regime the internal morality of the law, the morality of order, is gone.

Second, Hart's analysis of the grudge informer case is inaccurate. The actual facts of the case indicate that under one statute the husband could not have been prosecuted without a dubious interpretation of it that was widely used by the German court and that under another statute he could not have had the death penalty imposed upon him without another dubious interpretation. It is implausible that the legal meaning of the statute is determined by these dubious interpretations of the German court. Hart is committed to the view that the legal meaning of the statute would be determined by these interpretations.

Finally, Hart is unfair to Gustav Radbruch, for Radbruch was perfectly aware that he was facing a moral dilemma. The question is how the dilemma should be stated. Hart's statement of the dilemma is as follows: "On the one hand, we have an amoral datum called law, which has the peculiar quality of creating a moral duty to obey it. On the other hand, we have a moral duty to do what we think is right and decent. When we are confronted by a statute we believe to be thoroughly evil, we have to choose between those two duties."[35] But this statement is meaningless since no clear meaning is given by legal positivism to the obligation of fidelity to the law.

According to Fuller, Hart's views on judicial interpretation are also incorrect. In Hart's theory judges make decisions in the penumbra in the light of social purposes, while purposes do not enter into their interpretations in the core. Fuller objects to this account. Arguing that it assumes that judges interpret words in isolation whereas they really interpret whole sentences or even paragraphs, he holds that even in unproblematic cases where the interpretation of a single word is at issue purposes are involved. Thus, if the rule "No vehicles are allowed in the park" seems to apply easily in some cases, it is because whether "the rule be intended to preserve quiet in the park, or to save carefree strollers from injury, we know, 'without thinking,' that a noisy automobile must be excluded."[36]

Further, Fuller maintains that Hart's position suffers from a mistaken theory of the nature of language, one that ignores or minimizes the speaker's purposes and the structure of languages. According to Fuller, philosophers who stand at the very head of modern developments in logical analysis, for example, Wittgenstein, Russell, and Whitehead, have rejected this theory. Thus Fuller implies that Hart, an analytic philosopher, has a theory of judicial interpretation that is not consistent with the theory of language assumed in modern analytic philosophy.

Fuller concludes by saying that "the dominant tone of positivism is set by a fear of purposive interpretation of the law and legal institutions."[37] Positivism has this fear, Fuller thinks, because it believes that legal interpretations if pushed too far pose a threat to freedom and human dignity.

Hart's Reply

In *The Concept of Law* Hart does not attempt a point-by-point refutation of Fuller. Indeed, Fuller's name is only mentioned in passing in a footnote and Fuller himself is referred to, and then not by name, only once elsewhere.[38] In what follows, therefore, I will present what I believe Hart's reply would have been had he chosen to respond to Fuller's particular points. In most cases, what Hart would have said is rather easy to determine since Fuller's critique seems either to be based on misunderstandings and confusions or to have been answered in Hart's *Harvard Law Review* paper itself.

Fuller makes a great deal of Hart's alleged advocacy of the ideal of fidelity to the law, but it is doubtful that Hart does advocate such an ideal. As far as I can tell, he never uses the expression "fidelity to the law" or the equivalent one of "loyalty to the law." Nor does he speak even of a *prima facie* obligation to obey the law. On the contrary, Hart believes that disobeying immoral laws such as those that prevailed in Nazi Germany need not result in the sacrifice of any particular value.

To be sure, in the context of certain decisions facing the German court after the war Hart does speak of a moral dilemma. But the dilemma is not what Fuller supposes. It is a dilemma, not concerning the sacrifice of disobeying evil laws in terms of other important values, but concerning whether the court should pass retrospective laws (a disvalue) in order to secure a grudge informer's punishment (a value). Hart advocates that this dilemma should be clearly faced. He does not maintain that disobeying Nazi laws necessarily poses any moral dilemma.

However, there is nothing in Hart's view that would prevent Hart from admitting that on a particular occasion one would show respect for the laws of a particular legal system. After all, one might have independent reasons to suppose that a particular legal system is in general just. If one did, then this might create a rebuttable presumption that one should not disobey the laws of this system. Indeed, there is one passage in Hart that suggests this interpretation.[39] But from this nothing follows about a general *prima facie* duty to obey the law.

Fuller, as we have seen, maintains that Hart's view of the law is unclear, that we cannot have fidelity to the law if the meaning of the "law" is unclear and a stipulative definition of "law" is not helpful. As I have suggested, when he criticizes the command theory Hart does hint at a definition of law, one he develops in detail in his book *The Concept of Law*. Hart, of course, never claims in his 1958 paper that the meaning of law is given by a stipulative definition. In any case, since fidelity to the law is not at issue for Hart, the major presupposition of Fuller's criticism is mistaken.

Fuller maintains that Hart's distinction between various systems of what ought to be and an acceptable system is not in keeping with the prevailing tenor of his thought or, he hints, with legal positivism generally. However, early in his *Harvard Law Review* paper Hart points out that Austin makes a distinction between positive morality, that is, commonly accepted systems of what is good and bad, and an acceptable moral system based on God's command. Surely a similar distinction is implicit, if not explicit, in Hart's own thinking right from the start.

Recall that Fuller maintains against Hart that evil aims do not have as much coherence as good ones and that if judges are required to justify their decisions they will be "pulled" toward goodness. Hart would argue that Fuller gives no argument for his position. One can surely imagine a system of law with evil purposes whose judges work out the details of the law in relation to those purposes, justifying and explaining their decisions in light of them. Why Fuller thinks that this justification and explanation would tend to improve matters is a mystery. But let us suppose Fuller is correct. Still it does not follow from this that evil laws are impossible. For even if the justification and explanation of decisions would tend to pull decisions toward goodness, the laws that resulted from such decisions might still in balance be evil. At best, Fuller's thesis would only show that *in the long run* a system of law in which decisions are justified and explained could have no evil laws. But, as Lord Keynes once remarked, in the long run we'll all be dead.

Whether or not Fuller is right that it is more likely that a regime determined to eliminate some minority group would appeal to positivism to justify repressive laws than to natural law theory depends on historical evidence that he does not supply. One would have to look carefully at the rhetoric and propaganda of repressive regimes and see what sorts of justification they tended to give. As far as Nazi Germany is concerned, there is some evidence that Hitler appealed to what may be fairly called natural law principles to justify his doctrine of racial purity, one plank in his anti-Semitic program. Thus in *Mein Kampf* Hitler says, "just as little as Nature desires a mating between weaker individuals and stronger ones, far less she desires the mixing of a higher race with a lower one." Moreover, he argued that lowering the standard of the higher race is "sinning against the will of the Eternal Creator."[40] Of course, detailed historical scholarship would have to be mustered to show that such natural law-type arguments were used directly to justify laws against Jews in Germany. But it is not implausible in the light of the above quotation to suppose that they were. Whether this type of justification has been used in other times and other places I do not know.

There are a number of objections that can be raised against Fuller's argument that rejection of the command theory would lead to a merger of law and morality, some of which are made by Hart. It should be recalled that Fuller maintained that if the command theory is rejected, the fundamental rules of the legal system must be accepted on moral grounds. However, even if the fundamental rules of a legal system are accepted on moral grounds, that is, on what people believe to be the principles of right and justice, it does not follow that they are *acceptable* on moral grounds. People could be completely wrong about what is right and just. So, at most, Fuller's argument shows that there is a merger between law and *positive* morality, not a merger between law and true principles of right and justice.

Moreover, as Hart points out, people might accept the fundamental rule of law on grounds other than positive morality, for example, out of fear or ignorance, and follow the rule out of habit. Hart makes this last point clearly enough and Fuller, as far as I can tell, makes no explicit attempt to refute it. How then can Fuller's implicit argument be constructed? Perhaps in this way: Hart only points out the *possibility* that people might accept the fundamental rules on grounds other than those of positive morality. Although this is possible, in point of fact for a legal system to be *effective* people must accept the fundamental rules on moral grounds (positive or otherwise).

If this formulation of Fuller's argument is correct, he must be assuming the following:

> (1) In order for a legal system to be effective, the fundamental rules of the system must be accepted on moral grounds (positive or otherwise).

Condition (1) is, of course, a factual proposition and Fuller supplies no evidence or argument for it. On the other hand, Hart really supplies no evidence to refute (1). The citing of hypothetical cases in which people embrace the fundamental rules of the system for other than moral reasons, positive or otherwise, does not show that (1) is false. What is needed in order to refute Fuller is historical evidence, cases of legal systems that were effective and in which the basic rules of the system were embraced out of fear, out of habit, and so on. Does the case of Nazi Germany supply such historical evidence? It is interesting to note that, whatever answer Fuller might give to this question, he has a problem. Suppose he answers, "No, Nazi Germany cannot serve as a counterexample to (1) because the positive morality in Germany was such that the fundamental rules of the system were compatible with the positive morality of the German people." Although (1) is saved from a counterexample in this way, Fuller would seem to be admitting that an evil legal system is possible, a system based on an evil positive morality. On the other hand, if the answer is yes, then (1) is false and the basic rules of a legal system do not have to be based even on a positive morality.

What does Hart say to Fuller's point on the internal morality of law? Hart, as we have seen, is at pains to show that, even though the law has considerations of formal justice built into it, it can still be evil. Not surprisingly, he says the same thing about Fuller's "internal morality" of the law:

> If social control of this sort is to function, the rules must satisfy certain conditions: they must be intelligible and within the capacity of most to obey, and in general they must not be retrospective, though exceptionally they may be. This means that, for the most part, those who are eventually punished for breach of rules will have had the ability and opportunity to obey. Plainly these features of control by rule are closely related to the requirement of justice which lawyers term principles of legality. Indeed one critic of positivism has seen in these aspects of control by rules, something amounting to a necessary connexion between law and morality, and suggested that they be called 'the inner morality of law'. Again, if this is what the necessary connexion of law and morality means, we may accept it. It is unfortunately compatible with very great iniquity.[41]

The one critic of positivism Hart mentions is clearly Fuller. How would Hart defend his analysis of the situation in Nazi Germany against Fuller's attack? With respect to Fuller's point that Hart failed to take into account the lack of the internal morality of the law in Nazi Germany, Hart would point out that we can imagine an evil system of law that does not have secret laws, that we can imagine retroactive laws that do not disregard the other aspects of what Fuller calls the "internal morality of the law." So, even if we admit that the German system is not a legal system, it is still not established that evil laws are impossible.

With respect to the grudge informer case, Hart would certainly disagree that he is committed to the view that the legal meaning of the statute would be determined by some dubious interpretation of the Nazi court. If the situation is as Fuller describes it, then the German court and legislature after the war had several options, among them:

(a) Accept the Nazi court's interpretation, allow that the wife's action in denouncing her husband fell under the German statute, and pass retroactive legislation in order to punish the wife.
(b) Accept the Nazi court's interpretation, allow that the wife's action of denouncing her husband fell under the German statute, declare the

German law (given the Nazi interpretation) invalid on natural law principles, and punish the wife according to relevant law.

(c) Reject the Nazi court's interpretation, argue that the wife's action of denouncing her husband did not fall under the German statute, and punish the wife according to relevant laws.

It is important to note that alternative (c) makes it unnecessary to pass retroactive laws or declare the Nazi statutes invalid on natural law principles. Scholarship noted by Hart in *The Concept of Law*[42] indicates that the German court chose something very close to alternative (c). At the time Hart wrote his 1958 *Harvard Law Review* paper, however, he was not aware of the detailed facts of the case; consequently he chose alternative (a). In *The Concept of Law* he came to believe that his earlier analysis should be taken to refer to a hypothetical, not an actual, case. Suppose, for example, that the wife's action of denouncing her husband fell under the Nazi statute *without* dubious interpretation by the Nazi court. Then option (c) would not be plausible. The only plausible choices would be (a) and (b); Hart's argument for (a) over (b) then applies.

Hart would reject Fuller's other critical point regarding the case of the Nazis. Fuller says that Hart gives no clear meaning to his claim that there was a dilemma facing German intellectuals between fidelity to evil laws and the duty to do what is right. According to Fuller, this is because Hart gives no clear meaning to the idea of fidelity to the law. He assumes that Hart believes that there is a general moral duty to obey the law, that there is fidelity to the law. But, as we have seen, this is not so. Hart would certainly deny Fuller's contention that the acceptance of legal positivism by German legal scholars was instrumental in the rise of Naziism. He would point out that Fuller must show more than that the attitudes prevailing in German the legal profession were helpful to the Nazis. He must show, and he does not, that these attitudes were brought about or encouraged by the doctrines of legal positivism. Legal positivism does not advocate passive acceptance of the law but actively encourages moral criticism of the law. Austin, for example, certainly did not think that "any considerations of moral ends" should be banned from the law. That German scholarship perverted Austin's thinking should be evident. But it is well to recall that any doctrine can be perverted. (As I mentioned above, Hitler seemed at times to appeal to natural law ideas.) Further, Fuller does not show that Austin would have approved of the German legal scholars' attitudes toward moral criticism in pre-war Germany. What would Hart say to Fuller's criticism that Hart's theory of interpretation assumes that single words are interpreted in isolation and speakers' purposes are crucial in understanding language?

The first thing to notice about Fuller's criticism is that, even if it were valid, it would not affect the outcome of the controversy between them over the relationship of law and morals. With perfect consistency Hart could grant all of Fuller's points on interpretation and yet insist that there could be evil laws. He could point out that the purposes used in interpreting language that Fuller makes so much of could be evil.

Second, it is certainly not clear that Hart is committed to the view that all legal interpretations consist in interpreting single words. Hart's example of the interpretation of "vehicle" in the rule "No vehicles are allowed in the park" was meant *simply* as an example; as far as one can tell it was not meant to epitomize all legal interpretations. In *The Concept of Law*, for example, Hart considers the problems of interpreting "vague standards and precedents," not single words.

Furthermore, Hart does not deny that purposes are involved even when a single word, for example, "vehicle," is involved in the clear application of a statute. What he denies is that judges make choices in terms of social purposes in these clear cases. Obviously purposes come into the formulation of rules in the first place. A rule that forbids vehicles in the park is based on certain legislative purposes, for example, preserving peace and quiet in the park. Such a purpose determines the clear application of the rule. Obviously motor cars, buses, and motorcycles would be clear cases, given these purposes. Fuller is correct that purposes determine what is a clear case and that judges automatically apply the rule to these clear cases because they have these purposes implicitly in mind. Indeed, Hart makes the same point in *The Concept of Law*.

Hart would certainly argue that Fuller's thesis that legal positivism is afraid of interpretation is completely unjustified. Fuller admits that Bentham is an exception to his claim that legal positivism is afraid of interpretation, and it is unclear why Austin is not one as well since, as we have seen, Austin's views are very similar to Bentham's. Austin thought that judges should have the discretion to legislate in terms of social purposes, that laws should be formulated in terms of utility. Hart advocates that judges should decide cases in the penumbra in terms of social purposes, and he explicitly acknowledges that laws are created with social purposes in mind. Positivism's fear of purposive interpretation seems to be a figment of Fuller's imagination.

As far as the Hart-Fuller debate in the *Harvard Law Review* is concerned, then, the outcome can be simply stated: Fuller's critical points do not touch Hart's thesis. In some instances, Fuller seems to have misinterpreted Hart. In others his argument leaves Hart's thesis unaffected. But the debate does not end there.

Fuller's *The Morality of Law*

In 1964 Fuller's *The Morality of Law* appeared. In this book Fuller sets his many criticisms of Hart's legal philosophy in the context of a systematic view of the relation of law and morality.

In *The Morality of Law* Fuller makes two key distinctions: one between a morality of duty and a morality of aspiration and one between the internal and the external morality of the law. The morality of duty, according to Fuller, lays down basic rules without which an ordered society is impossible. A morality of aspiration is a morality of excellence, of the fullest realization of human potential. The law cannot require persons to fulfill their potential, says Fuller, but it can require someone to do their duty. On the other hand, one does not reward or praise people for doing their duty although, according to Fuller, one may reward or praise people for fulfilling their potential.

As Fuller conceives it, the inner morality of the law is a procedural version of natural law. Affirmative and creative in nature and difficult to realize in terms of duty, the inner morality of the law, Fuller concludes, must remain largely a morality of aspiration and not of duty. The external morality of the law, on the other hand, specifies the substantive aim of the law. Although Fuller does not say so explicitly, these substantive aims must often embody certain parts of the morality of duty; that is, they must specify what people in a society must or must not do in order to have an ordered society.

Although Fuller believes that over a wide range of issues the law's internal morality is indifferent to the substantive aims of the law, he does not think that every substantive aim is compatible with the internal morality of the law. He cites Hart as an example of someone who believes that the internal morality of the law is compatible with all substantive aims. As evidence of this view, Fuller quotes a passage from *The Concept of Law* that was cited above:

> Indeed one critic of positivism has seen in these aspects of control by rules, something amounting to a necessary connexion between law and morality, and suggested that they be called 'the inner morality of law'. Again, if this is what the necessary connexion of law and morality means, we may accept it. It is unfortunately compatible with very great iniquity.[43]

He then comments on this passage as follows:

> Certainly one could not wish for a more explicit denial of any possible interaction between the internal and external morality of law than that contained in this last sentence. I must confess I am puzzled by it. Does Hart mean merely that it is possible, by stretching the imagination, to conceive the case of an evil monarch who pursues the most iniquitous ends but at all times preserves a genuine respect for the principles of legality? If so, the observation seems out of place in a book that aims at bringing "the concept of law" into closer relation with life. Does Hart mean to assert that history does in fact afford significant examples of regimes that have combined a faithful adherence to the internal morality of law with a brutal indifference to justice and human welfare? If so,

> one would have been grateful for examples about which some meaningful discussion might turn.[44]

Fuller concludes that, "while Hart recognizes in passing that there exists something that may be called an internal morality of the law, he seems to consider that it has no significant bearing on the more serious concerns of jurisprudence."[45]

Using the example of racial discrimination in South Africa, Fuller argues for the thesis that the internal morality of the law is not neutral between good and evil substantive aims. According to Fuller, because of the lack of any uniform basis of race classification the racial laws of South Africa are unclear and, consequently, they are in conflict with one aspect of the inner morality of the law, namely that laws should be stated in clear terms. As another example of an unclear law that is presumably not neutral with respect to substantive aims of the law, Fuller cites Israel's Law of Return:

> Finally, by a bitter irony the Israeli High Court of Justice has encountered well-nigh insoluble problems in trying to give some simple and understandable interpretations of the Law of Return. . . . On December 6, 1962, a divided Court held that a Roman Catholic monk was not a Jew for purposes of this law. His counsel argues that, being of Jewish parentage, he was by rabbinical law still a Jew. The Court conceded that this was true, but said that the question was not one of religious law but of the secular law of Israel. By that law he was no longer a Jew because he had embraced the Christian religion.[46]

In his review of Fuller's book in the *Harvard Law Review* Hart remarks, "he takes me seriously to task for having said that respect for the principle of legality is unfortunately 'compatible with great iniquity'; but I cannot find any cogent argument in support of his claim that these principles are not neutral as between good and evil substantive aims."[47] Hart's comments, however, do not directly respond to Fuller's question specified above. Recall that Fuller questioned whether Hart's thesis that the principles of legality can be found to exist in legal systems with evil aims was a hypothetical one or if it was based on actual historical examples. If the former, Fuller seems to find it incompatible with the aims of *The Concept of Law*; if the latter, Fuller wants Hart to cite actual historical cases.

As far as one can tell Hart does not cite any examples of legal systems with evil substantive aims in which the principle of legality is followed. One assumes that Hart's is not an historical thesis. Given the major aim of his book—the elucidation of the concept of law—it seems clear that Hart is making a conceptual point, not an historical one. The use of hypothetical examples in conceptual analysis is commonplace. Indeed, Hart uses various hypothetical examples in *The Concept of Law* to make conceptual points.[48] In short, I can find nothing in

Hart's use of hypothetical reasoning that is in conflict with the aims of *The Concept of Law*.

Hart finds Fuller's argument having to do with South African racial laws "patently fallacious."[49] The example "shows only that the principle that laws must be clearly and intelligibly framed is incompatible with the pursuit of vaguely defined substantive aims, whether they are morally good or evil."[50] Thus he maintains that nothing Fuller has said has shown that there could not be clearly defined laws with evil substantive aims. He does not cite historical examples of this kind of legal system; his point is conceptual and hypothetical.

The case of Israel's Law of Return cited by Fuller is one in which the law has a morally good substantive aim even though the aim is too vague to be achieved through clear rules. Turning the example against Fuller, he says:

> Do not the South African and Israeli statutes taken together show the ethical neutrality both of clarity and unclarity? Indeed, in order to purge the author's argument of its fallacy, we need the additional premise that good ends are essentially or peculiarly determinate and bad ends are essentially vague and indefinable and so cannot be achieved by clear laws. I do not know whether the author would subscribe to this view, but I do not.[51]

He concludes by saying that it is "quite generally true that a regime bent on monstrous policies will often want the cover of secrecy and vague, indefinable laws if it is not certain of general support for its policies or finds it necessary to conciliate external opinion. But this is a matter of the varying popularity and strength of government, not of any necessary incompatibility between government according to the principles of legality and wicked ends."[52]

There is one final critical point raised by Hart that should be noted. Fuller insists on calling the principle of legality "the inner morality of the law," but Hart in his review rejects this label as based on a confusion between purpose and morality. He argues that every activity, for example, poisoning, has internal principles ("for example, avoid poisons, however lethal, if their shape, color, or size is likely to attract notice"). But to call such principles of poisoning "the morality of poisoning" would "simply blur the distinction between the notion of efficiency for a purpose and those final judgments about activities and purposes with which morality in its various forms is concerned."[53]

Fuller's Last Word

Fuller seemed to have the last word in the debate. In 1969 in the revised edition of *The Morality of Law*, he added a chapter entitled "A Reply to My Critics" in which he returns to his debate with Hart. Choosing not to answer Hart's detailed criticisms, he traces instead the differences between his critics' views and his own to basic and fundamental differences in how they conceive the law. Fuller summarizes his position as follows:

> I have tried to show that our differences on this issue stem from a basic disagreement about law itself. This disagreement I have attempted to express by contrasting a view of law that sees it as an interactional process and one that sees in it only a unidirectional exercise of authority. My reviewers have, of course, criticized a number of positions on specific issues taken in my book that I have left unmentioned and undefended here. I believe that most, though not all, of these disagreements on subsidiary matters have their origin in the same fundamental divergence in starting points that I have just examined at length. This is particularly true of my critics' rejection of the suggestion that governmental respect for the internal morality of law will generally be conducive toward a respect for what may be called the substantive or external morality of law.[54]

Fuller refers interested readers to a 1965 defense of his position published in the *Villanova Law Review*.[55] Before we examine this defense we must consider the thesis that differences between Hart and Fuller can be traced back to Hart's rejection and Fuller's acceptance of an interactional view of the law. What might Hart say about this?

By an interactional view of law Fuller presumably means one in which lawmakers and citizens interact in a certain way. The law emerges as a collaborative effort between the lawgiver and the subject, the purposes of one affecting how the other responds. Such a view emphasizes voluntary cooperation and mutual confidence between the government and its citizens rather than hierarchical authority.

Fuller's presentation of this interaction view of the law is quite sketchy. Nevertheless, two points should be noted. The first is that Hart would surely wonder whether the view is meant to describe how the law actually operates or how ideally it should operate. If the former, he might well say that the view seems dubious in that many legal systems cannot be accurately described in Fuller's interaction terms. Although the government and citizens may interact in some ways, this could hardly be described in terms of voluntary cooperation and collaborative effort.

But even if a legal system could be characterized in Fuller's terms, Hart might ask why this means that the internal and external morality of the law must be in harmony. Could not the government and citizens cooperate in bringing about substantive evil ends? Could not this cooperation take place in a context of a legal system that does not employ the rule of law? As far as I can tell, nothing Fuller says refutes the logical possibility of affirmative answers to these questions.

To be sure, in the *Villanova Law Review* paper we find Fuller denying that he is talking about logical possibilities: "I have never asserted that there is any logical contradiction in the notion of achieving evil, at least some kinds of evil, through means that fully respect all the demands of legality."[56] Stressing that in his debate with his critics it is important to distinguish between logical consistency and "what may be called motivational affinity or compatibility in the pursuit of similar ends,"[57] he quotes himself as saying "that it is possible, by stretching the imagination, to conceive the case of an evil monarch who pursues the most iniquitous ends but at all times preserves a genuine respect for the principles of legality."[58] He says that he is "not interested here in telling a good tale, but in examining the prosaic facts of life."[59]

With respect to Hart's objection to the use of the phrase "the inner morality of the law," Fuller insists that Hart's poisoning example is inappropriate and that the question is not, as Hart implies, just that of the efficacy of purpose. Here again he argues that his differences with Hart are the results of different general concepts of the law, in particular that his interaction view of the law would yield a judgment different from Hart's. Fuller's attempt to trace his differences with Hart to some different general view of the law seems no more plausible here than it did in *The Morality of the Law*.

Appraisal of the Debate

A review of the Hart-Fuller debate leaves one with the lingering suspicion that, despite several papers, chapters of books, reviews, and many thousands of words, if their positions were clarified Fuller and Hart would not be in as much disagreement as they suppose.[60] In retrospect what does it all come to?

One thing is clear: Fuller and Hart seem to agree that

> (1) It is logically possible that a government can pursue evil goals with a legal system that follows the rule of law.[61]

Hart has consistently maintained this and Fuller's comments in 1965 indicate that this is his position as well. So if we are to find serious disagreement in this debate it will not be in (1).

Fuller seems to maintain a factual thesis concerning the relation between the rule of law and the pursuit of evil aims. He never states it clearly but it may perhaps be formulated as follows.[62]

> (2) It is more likely that a government that pursues evil aims will not follow the rule of law than that it will.

He seems to give at least two types of arguments for (2). First, he cites historical cases, for example, Germany and South Africa, that have pursued evil aims and have not followed the rule of law, and he implies that there are no historical counterexamples to (2). Second, he suggests that it is plausible to suppose that (2) is true because of "motivational affinity." I take this to mean that, given our background knowledge of political history and human motivation, it is likely that governments with evil aims will not follow the rule of law. Governments with evil aims want to suppress negative opinion, control behavior, and the like, and not following the rule of law usually has a closely related motivation.

It is not clear that Hart would disagree with (2). Coming closest to addressing this issue in a passage already quoted in which he seems to admit (2) with perhaps only small qualifications, he says that whether or not a government pursues evil ends *via* a system that does not follow the rule of law "is a matter of varying popularity and strength of government."[63] But this qualification may well be compatible with (2). For although it might be the case that very popular and strong evil governments would not need to abuse the rule of law to hold power and conciliate external opinion, it is unlikely that evil governments would be both powerful and popular. At best, perhaps Hart's words suggest the following revision of (2):

(2′) For governments that are neither popular nor powerful given that they are pursuing evil ends it is more likely that they will not follow the rule of law than that they will.

It is not obvious that after reflection Fuller would reject (2′). So it is at least plausible that no sharp disagreement can be found between Hart and Fuller concerning (2) or its variants.

Although Hart and Fuller never clearly distinguish (1) from a different thesis, (3), there is no reason to suppose they would not both agree to

(3) It is logically possible that a government can pursue good goals with a system that does not follow the rule of law.

As we have seen, Hart cites the Israeli system as an example of one that pursues good aims that at least in part conflict with the stipulation of the rule of law that laws be clear. There is no reason to suppose that on reflection Fuller would not agree to (3) since, as he admits, he is not talking about mere logical possibilities. But I believe that Fuller would maintain:

(4) It is more probable that a government that pursues good aims will by and large follow the rule of law than that it will not.

Hart might well agree to (4) and indeed he might even admit that Israel's legal system *by and large* does follow the rule of law. So, again, the controversy between Hart and Fuller is not likely to be centered around (3) and (4).

It would be a mistake, however, to suppose that Fuller is just putting forth an empirical-historical thesis about the relation between the rule of law and the aims of government. He also seems to be making a logical or conceptual point:

(5) A system in which the rule of law is seriously and consistently abused is not a legal system.

It is because of the abuse of the rule of law in Nazi Germany that Fuller believes that the system in Germany was not a legal system. Hart, as we have seen, seems to admit (5).[64] He says "we may accept"[65] that there is a connection between the inner morality of the law—the principle of legality—and the law. This seems to suggest that a system without the principle of legality would not be a legal system. He only wishes to insist that a system in which the principle of legality is operating could be evil. But this is quite compatible with (5).

One problem with this interpretation of Hart, of course, is that he seems to reject the idea that the Nazi system should not be considered a legal system. Fuller uses (5) as a reason for saying Nazi Germany's system was not a legal system. Another problem is that Hart rejects the natural law approach to law on theoretical and practical grounds, yet (5) in part seems to assume this approach. It remains to be seen if Hart's views are consistent on this matter.

What about Hart and Fuller's disagreement over the label "the inner morality of the law"? Although Hart rejects this label in his review of Fuller's book, in *The Concept of Law* he is less dismissive. He finds, "in the bare notion of applying a general rule of law, the germ at least of justice"; further he finds a "minimum form of justice" in the rule of law and does not reject Fuller's term "the inner morality of law." He only wishes to insist that a system could have the rule of law and still be evil.[66] How then might one understand Fuller's point so that Hart would agree? Consider:

(6) Whether or not a system follows the rule of law is relevant in determining whether it is a just system.

On this view, following the rule of law is a just-making property of a system analogous to good-making or right-making properties of an action; it is one property that would be considered in order to tell whether a system was just or whether one system was more just than another. Such a view would be logically compatible with an evil, unjust system that follows the rule of law, a point that both Hart and Fuller insist on. But it would be compatible with the further point explicitly acknowledged by Hart in *The Concept of Law* although seemingly rejected in his review of Fuller's book that the principle of legality has a moral dimension; it would acknowledge the presence of the rule of law as morally relevant.

Are Hart's Views Consistent?

Two potential problems are generated by the interpretations just given. The first is that Hart accepts (5), linking serious abuse of the rule of law to the non-existence of a legal system. But, as we have seen, he seems to reject the natural law approach according to which the Nazi system would not be considered a legal system because of its immorality. This problem of interpretation can be posed more formally as follows. Hart accepts:

> (5) A system in which the rule of law is seriously and consistently abused is not a legal system.

He seems to accept:

> (7) Nazi Germany had a legal system.

Fuller has argued that

> (8) Nazi Germany consistently and seriously abused the rule of law.

Premises (5), (7), and (8) are inconsistent. One way of Hart's getting out of this problem is to deny (8). Indeed, he never really attempts to address the issue of whether the rule of law was consistently abused in Nazi Germany. He admits, of course, that the Nazi system was an evil system, but he does not focus on the alleged rule of law abuses. On this interpretation the disagreement between Hart and Fuller would be over a factual historical matter and not over any particular theoretical doctrine of law or morality; it would be over whether (8) was true. If, however, it could be shown that (8) is true, in order to be consistent Hart would have to give up either (5) or (7). But Hart seems firmly committed to (5); thus the obvious candidate for him to give up would be (7).

The acceptance of (5) poses the second problem of interpretation. As we saw in Chapter 4, Hart argues that whether we adopt the natural law or the legal positivist theory of whether iniquitous rules are laws is not just a matter of English usage concerning the word "law"; the decision is based on the comparative merits of a wider and narrower concept of rules and should be based on theoretical and practical grounds. Hart argues that there is nothing theoretical to gain from the natural law approach. He says:

> It seems clear that nothing is to be gained in the theoretical or scientific study of law as a social phenomenon by adopting the narrower concept; it would lead us to exclude certain rules even though they exhibit all the other complex characteristics of law. Nothing, surely, but confusion could follow from a proposal to leave the study of such rules to another discipline, and certainly

> no other history or other form of legal study has found it profitable to do this. If we adopt the wider concept of law, we can accommodate within it the study of whatever special features morally iniquitous laws have, and the reaction of society to them.[67]

He also argues that from a practical point of view the natural law perspective would not make people more clear-headed and would not be likely to "lead to a stiffening of resistance to evil."[68]

What is curious about Hart's position is that, if it is taken seriously, it would seem not only to undermine (5) but to undermine his minimum natural law position. This position can be stated as follows:

(9) A system that does not have the content of the minimum natural law is not a legal system.

Thus Hart's reasons for preferring legal positivism and rejecting natural law seem like reasons for rejecting both (5) and (9). There would surely be theoretical disadvantages in saying that a system that did not follow the rule of law or that did not have a minimum natural law content was not a legal system. Some such system may have very similar characteristics to systems that do have minimum natural law content or to ones that follow the rule of law. Hart's words certainly come back to haunt him. "Nothing but confusion could follow from a proposal to leave the study of such rules to another discipline." If we adopt a wider concept of law that would include systems that did not follow the rule of law and that did have a minimum natural law content, we could study whatever "special features" make these systems morally objectionable and the reaction of society to them.

Furthermore, Hart's restrictions do not seem to have a practical advantage. There is no reason to suppose that, if people thought that a system that did follow the rule of law or that did not meet minimum natural law requirements was not a legal system, this would make them more clear-headed or stiffen their resistance to evil. I conclude that there is a serious tension in Hart's thought between the reason he gives for rejecting traditional natural law theory and his acceptance of some minimal conceptual connection between law and morality. This tension has never been noticed, let alone addressed, by Hart.

Is the Rule of Law a Relevant Moral Consideration?

As we have seen, there is a plausible way of reading Hart's position in *The Concept of Law* that suggests that he would accept:

(6) Whether or not a system follows the rule of law is relevant in determining whether it is a just system.

But, as we have also seen, in his review of Fuller's book Hart seems to reject (6). There he argues that the rule of law or the principle of legality is not morally relevant but is only relevant to the efficiency of the system.

The reasons Hart gives in his review, however, do not seem adequate to reject (6). Granted he argues that a poisoner may follow certain principles to accomplish his aims and that this shows nothing about the morality of these principles. He also maintains that the examples of South African and Israeli law together show that unclear rules are ethically neutral. However, if Fuller is correct, the law is relevantly different in its aim from the activity of poisoning; thus Hart's example would be irrelevant to showing that the principles of legality are not relevant to the morality of the law. Second, the examples of South Africa and Israel do not seem to refute (6). For although unclear laws may be found in both evil and good legal systems, the existence of unclear laws may still be morally relevant in determining the justice or injustice of these systems. Consider an analogous case. Suppose pain is found in two situations, one good, the other evil. This would hardly show that the existence of pain is irrelevant in judging whether the situations are good or evil. What Hart must show, but does not, is that unclear laws, retroactive laws, laws that are impossible to follow, and so on are completely irrelevant to judging whether, for example, the South African or Israeli system is unjust.

Ronald Dworkin's critique of Fuller is more cogent than Hart's and is one that Hart might well accept. Dworkin argues that laws not fulfilling the requirements of the rule of law—what he calls "badly drafted statutes"—might be "put to uses having terrible moral implications, but that depends on the uses to which the statute is put, not merely the bad drafting."[69] Indeed, he argues that sometimes inconsistent and vague legislation is morally desirable since the enforcement of evil laws would be hindered. Dworkin's distinction between the lack of the rule of law and the use to which this lack is put is an important one: it is the use to which the lack is put that is directly relevant for moral appraisal. But there is a weaker position Fuller could retreat to that captures much of what he was getting at and it may be one that Hart, even in his tough and critical mood, could accept.

Although the absence of the rule of law is not itself morally relevant, the absence of the rule of law may be a fairly reliable indicator or predictor of whether this absence will be used for unjust purposes. Thus consider the following thesis, one Fuller surely would accept:

(10) It is more likely that a government with the absence of the rule of law will use this absence for unjust purposes than for just purposes.

Hart and even Dworkin might well accept this too. However, Fuller might even wish to assert a stronger claim than (10). For (10) is compatible with the possibility that the absence of the rule of law will not usually result in unjust use. Consider:

(11) It is more likely that a government with the absence of the rule of law will use this absence for unjust purposes than not.

Clearly Dworkin rejects (11). He claims that "in the normal, everyday cases of poor legislative draftsmanship, no particular immorality is involved,"[70] although he supplies no evidence of this clearly factual thesis. Whether Hart would reject (11) is unclear.

In any case Dworkin and, I believe, Hart would accept:

(12) The use by the government of the absence of the rule of law for unjust purposes is relevant in determining whether the system is just.

Given (11) one can more easily predict from the fact that some system lacks the rule of law that this will be used for evil purposes than that it will not; given (12) this prediction is relevant for determining whether the system is just. So, although the lack of the rule of law is not itself morally relevant, it is, on this interpretation, a good prediction of something that is.

In sum, although Hart is right that (6) is incorrect, his arguments are inconclusive; Dworkin, on the other hand, seems to be correct and for the right reason. Yet Fuller still may have a point that does not seem to be appreciated by either Hart or Dworkin, namely that the absence of the rule of law may be a good indicator that it will be put to evil use. Of course, the tenability of this position depends on the truth of (10) and (11), and these propositions are by no means self-evident. Still, on this interpretation the differences (if any) that remain between Hart and Fuller are based on factual considerations capable of objective determination. Further, neither Fuller nor Hart provides any historical, psychological, or sociological evidence that would be very relevant in deciding the issue; empirical claims thus go begging for empirical evidence.

Chapter

8

The Legal Enforcement of Morality: The Hart-Devlin Debate

HART ENGAGED IN another debate on a question concerning law and morality, this time with Lord Patrick Devlin, a distinguished judge. The most widely cited contemporary debate on the legal enforcement of positive morality between sophisticated jurists, the particular issue they debated was whether private homosexual behavior between consenting adults should be outlawed. However, this was a special case of a larger issue, namely whether the law should enforce the positive morality of society. Hart took the liberal position in the debate, arguing that private homosexual behavior should not be outlawed, while Devlin took the conservative position that it should be. A variety of different moral and legal arguments were marshalled by the two men, and their various exchanges took place over approximately an eight-year period.

The Hart-Devlin debate is important to us for a number of reasons. Once again we see Hart's analytic and critical powers in action as he makes distinctions and clarifies and criticizes arguments. Further, although Hart's normative position is roughly in the Millian tradition, he rejects some of the significant aspects of Mill's view. To be sure, although Hart goes beyond Mill's view that the state has the right to interfere with human action only if it harms others, his additions to Mill's doctrine are not developed in any detailed way. Yet he does present a sketch of a social philosophy, if not a systematically developed theory.

As we shall see, Hart bases his key arguments against Devlin on factual premises. He argues that empirical evidence is lacking to support Devlin's case. Yet, although Hart makes clear the importance of empirical evidence, his references to it are vague and unspecific; indeed, he makes no attempt to cite relevant evidence. Thus, although the Hart-Devlin debate is largely based on different empirical assumptions, Hart does not appeal to concrete empirical evidence to argue his theses. Only in 1967, after the debate was over and Devlin had come to believe that legal restrictions on private homosexual behavior should be repealed, did Hart rise above the controversy and specify clearly what evidence would be relevant in settling things.

Historical Overview

In order to understand the controversy over the legal enforcement of morality it is necessary to consider the background to the Hart-Devlin debate. For our purposes here the controversy over the legal enforcement of morality can be said to have begun with the publication in 1859 of John Stuart Mill's celebrated essay *On Liberty*.[1] Mill was interested in providing an answer to the question: What are the limits of individual freedom? Mill's answer was that the individual should have unlimited freedom so long as his or her action did not harm others. This principle laid down by Mill—sometimes referred to as the harm principle—was supposed to be justified on utilitarian grounds. Mill maintained that only a society operating with it would provide conditions for the adequate development of individual personality.

Mill's views were criticized by his contemporaries, the most famous of whom was Sir James Fitzjames Stephen, a distinguished historian and commentator on the criminal law. The major purpose of Stephen's book *Liberty, Equality and Fraternity*,[2] published in 1873, was to refute the theses Mill argued for in *On Liberty*. Stephen rejected the harm principle as being an adequate test to determine when society can intervene in human affairs. In particular, he maintained that immoral conduct could be regulated by law even if it did not harm others.

This controversy over law and morality was dormant in England until the publication of the Wolfenden Report in 1957.[3] This report was the work of a committee, chaired by John Wolfenden, that was formed to consider the existing laws on homosexuality and prostitution in England and recommend changes. The Wolfenden Report recommended that homosexual behavior in private between consenting adults should no longer be punishable by law; it also recommended that acts of prostitution should not in themselves be illegal, although public solicitation should be. Millian in tone and substance, the report argued that there was a distinction between matters of private morality and public order, decency and harm to others: matters of private morality were no concern of the law; in matters of public order and decency and where harm to others was involved, the law had a legitimate concern.

In 1959 Lord Patrick Devlin delivered the Maccabaean Lecture in Jurisprudence to the British Academy. Entitled "The Enforcement of Morals,"[4] this lecture was an attack not only on the rationale of the Wolfenden Report but also on the report's Millian assumptions. In the same year Hart gave a talk on the BBC criticizing Devlin's position. Entitled "Immorality and Treason,"[5] it was published in *The Listener* and then in 1963 was expanded into a small book entitled *Law, Liberty, and Morality*.[6] After the appearance of Hart's book Devlin delivered lectures in which he criticized Hart's views. These lectures along with his original one were published in 1965 under the title *The Enforcement of Morals*.[7] Oddly enough, for all intents and purposes the debate between Devlin and Hart ended that same year when Devlin signed a letter in the *Times*[8] reversing the position he had held on the legal enforcement of positive morality concerning private homosexual behavior. Nevertheless, in 1967 Hart published "Social Solidarity and the Enforcement of Morality" in the *University of Chicago Law Review*,[9] in which he discussed in some depth the evidential issues that had separated him from Devlin. Meanwhile, other philosophers of law had entered the debate, some taking the side of Mill and Hart, some taking the side of Stephen and Devlin.[10]

Devlin's Maccabaean Lecture

Devlin's argument that the law should attempt to enforce positive morality about homosexuality is basically conservative. On one central meaning of the term, a person is conservative who is hostile to radical change.[11] This type of conservatism comes through clearly in Devlin's Maccabaean Lecture, where he argues that private homosexual behavior threatens society and for this reason should be outlawed. He also attempts there to refute the liberal position of the Wolfenden Report by arguing that principles expressed in the report conflict with existing criminal law. In both his arguments Devlin assumes the value of the *status quo*, in the first case in relation to society, in the second in relation to the criminal law. His conservatism is tempered to some extent, however, in that he maintains that, although conflict between a principle and existing criminal law constitutes a reason for rejecting the principle, it is not a conclusive reason.

Two other conservative themes are to be found in Devlin's thought. One is that human affairs are very complicated; various aspects of society are connected in an organic way such that a change in one part of society has far-ranging ramifications in another. For this reason, change must be slow and gradual. Another is a suspicion of abstract reason and the belief that more good comes out of the use of habit and instinct than rational thought.[12]

Both tendencies are manifested in Devlin's work. On one plausible interpretation of his Maccabaean Lecture, he argues that there is a close organic connection between the positive morality of a society and society itself, so that legalizing homosexual behavior would undermine our most cherished social institutions and structures. In this lecture and in his later writings he is also suspicious of abstract rationality, appealing instead to the judgment of the ordinary man who does not reason at all and that man's instinctive reactions.

In the beginning of his lecture Devlin states that he will not be concerned with the practical conclusions of the Wolfenden Report but with the general principles on which the recommendations are based. He says that although he starts with the feeling that the report's complete separation of crime from sin might be disastrous for the criminal law, he will not rest with this feeling but will try to justify it by cogent argument. His standpoint will be that of a "strict logician."[13] Devlin first considers whether the view put forth in the Wolfenden Report that law should not punish immorality as such is consistent with the principles of English criminal law. This, he believes, is one way of testing the report's basic principles, though by no means a conclusive one. Society has the right to "overturn even fundamental conceptions if they are theoretically unsound. But to see how the argument fares under the existing law is a good starting-point."[14]

Presumably what Devlin is getting at here is that there is a presupposition that a moral principle is unsound if it is inconsistent with principles of the criminal law. So, if a critic of the criminal law assumes some principle that is in conflict with the principles of criminal law, this presumption shifts the burden of proof onto the critic. To put it in another way, in case of a conflict there is a *prima facie* case that the critic is wrong. More formally stated the argument is this:

(1) If moral principle P conflicts with the principles of criminal law, then there is a *prima facie* case that P is wrong.
(2) The principle that no immorality as such should be punished conflicts with the principles of criminal law.

---

(3) Therefore, there is a *prima facie* case that the principle that immorality as such should not be punished is wrong.

Devlin cites examples in the criminal law in which it appears that immorality as such is being punished: suicide, incest, duelling, euthanasia, and murder by consent. These crimes, Devlin says, cannot be explained in terms of Mill's harm principle since they involve the consent of the victim.[15] The only explanation for them is to suppose that the criminal law is punishing immorality as such. Premise (2) thus seems to be a conclusion of another implicit argument, namely:

(2a) If suicide, incest, duelling, euthanasia, murder by consent are crimes, then the punishment of those crimes could not be justified under the harm principle.
(2b) If the punishment of these crimes could not be justified by the harm principle, then this punishment could only be justified by the principle that immorality as such should be punished.
(2c) If the punishment of crimes could only be justified by the principle that immorality as such should be punished, then the principle that no immorality as such should be punished conflicts with the criminal law.
(2d) Suicide, incest, duelling, euthanasia, murder by consent are crimes.

---

(2) Therefore, the principle that no immorality as such should be punished conflicts with the principles of criminal law.

On the basis of this argument Devlin believes that he has established a *prima facie* case against the basic assumption of the Wolfenden Report. But he does not let his case rest there. On the contrary, he goes on to consider directly reasons why the criminal law should enforce morality as such.[16] And finally he asks if society has the right to pass judgments on matters of morality, that is, if there ought to be a public morality.

Addressing this last issue, Devlin argues that the existence of a public morality is necessary for the very existence of society. In order to have any structure, society must have public morality. Indeed, public morality partially defines society. Thus, for example, monogamy is part of our society's public morality; it constitutes part of the structure of the society in which we live. If monogamy is rejected and replaced by polygamy, it would no longer be *our* society. Devlin concludes from this that society has the right to pass moral judgment on non-monogamous marriages, that is, to condemn polygamy morally, since its very existence is at stake. It is not a question that can be left to individual judgment.

Concluding that society has the right to pass moral judgment about immoral behavior, Devlin asks if it has the right to use the weapon of law to enforce this judgment. He has no trouble in answering yes. Society has the right to protect itself and, given this right, it has the right to pass laws that aid in that protection.

Drawing an analogy to illustrate his point, Devlin says that society cannot tolerate treason, for, since it is aimed at aiding enemies of the government, the very existence of the government is at issue. Whether someone engages in an act of treason or not is not something that can be left to individual judgment. In a similar way, society cannot tolerate affronts to public morality since they might well overthrow the moral structure of society. Thus whether or not someone's behavior conflicts with public morality cannot be left to individual judgment.

His argument can be stated more formally as follows:

(1) Society has a right to protect itself from destruction.
(2) If society has a right to protect itself from destruction, then it has a right to enforce laws to protect itself.
(3) If society has the right to enforce laws to protect itself, then it has a right to enforce laws against immorality.

---

(4) Therefore, society has the right to enforce laws against immorality.

So far Devlin has argued that society has the right to enforce morality as such and punish immorality as such. But what is the test of immorality? How can one tell that a piece of behavior or action is immoral according to the public morality? The test, he says, is the reaction of the "reasonable man." The reasonable man is not necessarily the rational man, for the reasonable man "is not expected to reason about anything."[17] The reasonable man is the average man in the street—

the man on the Clapham omnibus, the typical person in a jury box. Thus, Devlin gives, as it were, an operational definition of public morality:

> Behavior B is immoral in society S if and only if, when reasonable men in S contemplate B, they consider B immoral.

What, according to Devlin, would constitute the destruction of society that immoral practice might bring about? He is not very clear on this point. On one very strong interpretation of what he says, he seems to believe that a society S is destroyed when there is any change in its moral institutions. For example, one change in legal-moral institutions of our society over the past several years is the legalizing of abortion. On this strong interpretation, this change brings about the destruction of the society existing before legalization.

This strong interpretation is made more plausible if it is combined with the factual assumption that any change has wide ramifications affecting the basic institutions of the society. Thus, it may be argued that the change in abortion law has wide ramifications in that it affects people's view of the sanctity of life, the institution of marriage, the sexual freedom of women.

A weaker interpretation of Devlin's position is that he believes that society is destroyed when there is a *basic* change in the moral institutions, one that, as it were, redefines society. For example, if polygamy became the basic form of marriage, it might be maintained that the present society would no longer exist since monogamy is now the marital standard. Similarly, if homosexuality became the basic form of sexual behavior, our society would no longer exist, it might be said, since heterosexuality is its basic form of sexual behavior. But suppose 20–30 percent of all sexual behavior was homosexual or lesbian and that homosexual and lesbian marriages were legally permitted and constituted 10–15 percent of all marriages. Suppose homosexual and lesbian couples were allowed to adopt children. Would this be such a basic change that it would constitute the destruction of our present society? This is unclear, and Devlin says nothing to clarify the situation.

We have seen that Devlin argues that society has the right to enforce morality as such and punish immorality as such and that he has suggested a test for immorality. But it is one thing to say that society has the *right* to enforce morality and another thing to say that society *should* enforce morality. Devlin argues that there is no general rule for deciding when society should enforce morality, that it all depends on the circumstances and involves the balancing of several factors. On the other hand, there are no fixed boundaries where the law cannot interfere.

One of the factors to be taken into account in this decision is the right of the individual to freedom. However, this right must be balanced against the integrity of society: the law should strive for the maximum of individual freedom consistent with the integrity of society. Another factor to be taken into account is shifts in public feeling. The law should work slowly and always be alert to these shifts. A change in the law based on present public opinion may turn out to be premature if public sentiment changes in the next generation; the law may suddenly find itself without strong backing. Furthermore, privacy should be respected as far as possible. It may have to give way in order to preserve society, however. Still another factor to be taken into account is the difficulty of enforcement. Adultery that breaks up marriage, for example, is as destructive to the fabric of society as homosexuality or bigamy, but the difficulty of enforcement militates against making it a criminal offense except in the "worst manifestations."[18]

Still there comes a time, according to Devlin, when *ad hoc* balancing stops, when the limits of tolerance have been surpassed and society must act. This time is not passed when the majority disapproves of a practice as immoral for "there must be a real feeling of reprobation." The test for when the limits of tolerance have been surpassed is when society feels "intolerance, indignation and disgust."[19] This is not determined by rational argument. It is simply a feeling that reasonable men have toward a practice when they consider it calmly and dispassionately.

Devlin suggests the following test, which I will call the Disgust Test, of when a practice should be regulated by law:

> Immoral behavior B should be made illegal if, when reasonable men in society S contemplate B calmly and dispassionately, they feel intolerance, indignation, and disgust.

The Disgust Test provides a sufficient condition of when a society should make a practice illegal, but not a necessary condition. There could be other cases in which a practice judged immoral by reasonable men should be made illegal. These cases presumably would be decided by *ad hoc* balancing, that is, by balancing the dangers of the immorality of the practice against the factors considered above.

Devlin seems to admit that the reaction of the reasonable man can change from generation to generation. Presumably at one time the reasonable man did not feel intolerance, indignation, and disgust at what the reasonable man does today, for example, at cruelty toward animals. Presumably the reverse can also happen. What was an object of disgust for the reasonable man in the past may not be one for the reasonable man today.

Devlin gives no indication that he believes that such a change has occurred with respect to homosexual behavior. Indeed, he certainly seems to assume that the reasonable man of today feels indignation, intolerance, and disgust toward homosexuals, just as the reasonable man of the 1930's did.

What is the relationship between society's right to self-protection and the feelings of intolerance, indignation, and disgust that provide a test of when society should make immorality as such illegal? There is a gap here in Devlin's argument that needs to be filled in. The general idea must be that, when reasonable men have such feelings, unless society acts through its laws it is in grave danger of destruction. Devlin's argument, it will be recalled, was that society has the right to protect itself, including the right to protect itself from immorality. Presumably this right should be exercised when there is imminent danger of destruction. So Devlin's argument from survival connects with his test of the limits of tolerance only on the assumption that feelings of intolerance, indignation, and disgust indicate grave dangers of societal destruction.

Considered in this way, Devlin's argument for outlawing homosexual behavior can be simplified and reformulated as follows:

(1) If when reasonable men in society S contemplate immoral behavior B calmly and dispassionately they feel indignation, intolerance, and disgust toward B, then society S is in grave danger of destruction by immoral behavior B.
(2) If society S is in grave danger of destruction from immoral behavior B, then society S's right to protect itself should be exercised by outlawing B.
(3) When reasonable men in our society contemplate homosexual behavior calmly and dispassionately, they feel indignation, intolerance, and disgust.

---

(4) Therefore, our society's right to protect itself should be exercised by outlawing homosexual behavior.

Clearly the crucial premise in this argument is (1). Whether it is true or false, of course, will depend on what "destruction of society" means. As we have seen, what Devlin means by this is not clear.

Hart's "Immorality and Treason"

In Hart's first criticism of Devlin, which appeared in *The Listener* in 1959 under the title "Immorality and Treason," he defends a liberal point of view in which private homosexual behavior should not be outlawed. But in what sense is Hart's point of view liberal? In the classical meaning of "liberalism" associated with J. S. Mill, liberalism is a view advocating freedom for the individual so long as that freedom does not harm others. Hart argues that Mill's harm principle is too simple a ground for interfering with liberty, and he suggests that there are "multiple criteria," not a single criterion, for determining when human liberty may be restricted.[20] In *Law, Liberty, and Morality*, these other criteria become clear. He allows that the law may interfere when a person's action is harmful to him or herself as well as to others or is an affront to public decency. The latter criterion could justify interference with public homosexual or heterosexual behavior whereas the former could justify interference in self-regarding harmful action such as drug abuse.

In going beyond the classical liberal position of Mill, Hart's position is compatible with the broader view of liberalism adopted today. Today the term "liberalism" has come to apply to the advocacy of such state intervention as is necessary to free individuals from poverty.[21] Liberalism in this sense of the state's giving people freedom from poverty is compatible with large-scale welfare programs and state socialism. It seems also, however, to be compatible with the state's giving people freedom from their own irrationality in harmful self-regarding actions and from offensive public conduct.

Although Hart does not embrace completely the simple liberalism of Mill, he believes that Devlin's conservatism has far worse problems. Hart is not critical of Devlin's test of public morality, the test of what reasonable men feel. What he challenges is Devlin's reliance on the Disgust Test. He says:

> For him [Devlin] a practice is immoral if the thought of it makes the man on the Clapham omnibus sick. So be it. Still, why should we not summon all the resources of our reason, sympathetic understanding, as well as critical intelligence, and insist that before general moral feeling is turned into criminal law it is submitted to scrutiny of a different kind from Sir Patrick's? Surely, the legislator should ask whether the general morality is based on ignorance, superstition, or misunderstanding; whether there is a false conception that those who practise what it condemns are in other ways dangerous or hostile to society; and whether the misery to many parties, the blackmail and other evil consequences of criminal punishment, especially for sexual offenses, are well understood. It is surely extraordinary that among the things which Sir Patrick says are to be considered before we legislate against immorality these appear nowhere.[22]

Hart says earlier:

> But with all its simplicities the liberal point of view is a better guide than Sir Patrick to clear thought on the proper relation of morality to the criminal law: for it stresses what he obscures—namely, the points at which thought is needed before we turn popular morality into criminal law.[23]

Hart also gives a *reductio ad absurdum* argument against Devlin's Disgust Test. It would, he says, justify the harming of old women for witchcraft and the punishment of those for association with people of a different race or color if "these things were viewed with intolerance, indignation and disgust."[24] Hart points out that although people may no longer have strong feelings about witchcraft, in some countries today they still feel intolerance, indignation, and disgust when different races associate. So Devlin's theory would seem to justify present-day segregation and other odious racial laws.

It will be recalled that Devlin draws an analogy between treason and immoral sexual behavior to support his argument. Questioning its appropriateness, Hart claims that private subversive activity is a contradiction in terms since subversion means overthrowing the government and this is a public activity. Homosexual behavior between two adults in private can be made to "*seem* like treason only if we assume that deviation from a general moral code is bound to affect that code, and to lead not merely to its modification but to its destruction."[25] But Hart says that there is "ample evidence"[26] that people will not abandon morality, will not think any better of murder, cruelty, and dishonesty merely because some private sexual practice that they abominate is not punished by laws.

In terms of our analysis of Devlin's position and argument, where then is Hart's attack directed? It seems clear that his main attack is directed at the Disgust Test and, in particular, against the alleged connection between it and the destruction of society; in other words, at premise (1) of the simplified and reformulated argument of Devlin.

(1) If when reasonable men in society S contemplate immoral behavior B calmly and dispassionately they feel indignation, intolerance, and disgust toward B, the society S is in grave danger of destruction by immoral behavior B.

Hart maintains that (1) is false. It should be noted that he does not explicitly deny that society has a right to defend itself against destruction. He does not even explicitly deny that immoral behavior could under certain circumstances lead to the destruction of society; nor does he explicitly deny that society should at certain times exercise the right to self-protection—premise (2) in the above argument. What he denies is that there is any evidence that private homosexual behavior toward which the average man may well feel indignation, intolerance, and disgust would lead to the destruction of society. Indeed, he suggests that all the available evidence indicates just the opposite.

Hart does, of course, go on to point out the absurd consequences of the use of the Disgust Test and to argue that critical intelligence involving the evaluation of evidence must be used in order to determine whether a practice would lead to society's destruction. But his main point is that (1) is false.

It is not completely clear what interpretation Hart gives Devlin's notion of the destruction of society. He seems to interpret Devlin in the strong sense discussed above, namely that any change in morality would result in the destruction of society. Apparently he attributes this strong thesis to Devlin because the latter also maintains that changes in one aspect of morality have wide ramifications throughout the system. Hart's criticism, then, is that there is no evidence that private homosexual behavior between consenting adults would have these wide ramifications. Presumably, even if Devlin should be interpreted in the weaker sense, Hart's critique would apply: Hart would simply argue that there is no evidence that not punishing homosexual behavior would result in basic changes in society's moral institutions.

What then is the basic difference between Hart and Devlin as manifested in Devlin's 1959 lecture and Hart's short piece in *The Listener*? It would seem that their basic disagreement is over the use of the Disgust Test and that this disagreement turns on the factual issue of whether when society is really in grave danger the Disgust Test is positive. I say this because it would seem that if Devlin could show a positive result on the Disgust Test for private homosexual behavior and could also show that this result would likely lead to society's destruction, then Hart, at least the Hart of the *Listener* article, would not deny Devlin's conclusion that private homosexual behavior should be outlawed.

If the basic issue between Devlin and Hart is really a factual one, it is surprising and unfortunate that factual evidence does not play a larger part in the debate.[27] Devlin cites no evidence to support his claim while Hart vaguely refers to, but does not produce, "ample evidence" showing that Devlin's thesis is wrong.[28]

Devlin's "Law, Democracy, and Morality"

In 1961 Devlin delivered the Owen J. Roberts Memorial Lecture, which was published in the *University of Pennsylvania Law Review* in 1962.[29] This lecture is important because in it Devlin attempts to answer some of Hart's criticisms by appeal to democratic principles. Although much of Devlin's 1961 lecture repeats arguments and positions from his 1959 lecture, this tack was not explicitly to be found in the Maccabaean Lecture.

How does Devlin answer Hart's criticism that lawmakers and judges must appeal to critical intelligence and sympathetic understanding and not the gut feeling of the person in the jury box? Devlin questions whether the moral opinion of the trained and educated is really better than that of ordinary men. He points out that educated men using reason have been unable to agree on what moral laws should be, and he hints that such an appeal to educated opinion is undemocratic and elitist. The lawmaker "will assume that the morals of his society are good and true; if he does not, he should not be playing an active part in government. . . . His mandate is to preserve the essentials of his society, not to reconstruct them according to his own ideas."[30] However, Devlin is not consistent.

Elsewhere in his lecture he says the lawmaker has "a wide discretion in determining how far he will go in the direction of the law as he thinks it ought to be."[31] Even a judge, according to Devlin, will "move toward the law as he thinks it ought to be," and although the judge is "tethered" to the law he is "not shackled to it."[32] Naturally, it is difficult to make sense of these seemingly conflicting pronouncements. It seems clear, however, that the discretion allowed the legislator and judge in Devlin's later statement is compatible with the critical intelligence advocated by Hart.

Is Devlin's defense against Hart's attack successful? Hart's views on critical morality need not be identified with the morality of "educated men." In fact, Hart never mentions education in discussing critical morality. His position can well be interpreted as follows: legal force should not be given to the moral views of men, ordinary or educated, if such views are based on prejudice and gut feeling; in order to be given legal force, the views of men must be based on principled reflection.

Whether Hart believes that such principled reflection always leads to consensus on a given issue is not clear. However, by arguing that the moral views of educated men are often different on a given issue Devlin does not show that principled reflection does not lead to consensus on that issue. Moreover, even if principled reflection does not always lead to consensus, one should remember that people's unreflective moral opinions do not always agree either. Indeed, Devlin gives no reason to suppose that there is wide agreement over the evil of homosexuality at the gut level.

Recall that Hart also argued that Devlin's appeal to the Disgust Test would justify the segregation of races today and witchhunting in bygone times. What is Devlin's answer to this charge? Devlin does not deny it; rather, he appears to think that this is part of the price one pays for democracy. He argues that except in matters having to do with morality no one—at least no advocate of democracy—would object that the majority will must prevail. Here many people wrongly think that educated opinion on morals is better than majority rule.

But this extreme majoritarian view of Devlin's seems to conflict with his claim in the Maccabaean Lecture that the law must allow the maximum individual freedom consistent with the integrity of society. It also seems to accord ill with the principles of those modern democracies that recognize minority rights.

As I mentioned above, however, the major difference between Devlin in the Maccabaean Lecture and Hart in "Immorality and Treason" seems to be a factual one. Hart points out that Devlin cites no evidence to support the claim that positive results in the Disgust Test indicate that society is in grave danger. Devlin does not even try to meet this objection in the present lecture. He again argues that society may legislate to preserve itself and that it is necessary to preserve the integrity of society to enforce the ideas of right and wrong of the majority. He cites no evidence, however, to show that unless the ideas of the majority are enforced the integrity of society will not be preserved.

Hart's *Law, Liberty, and Morality*

In 1963 Hart's *Law, Liberty, and Morality*, a work based on the Harry Camp Lectures at Stanford University, appeared. In these lectures Hart expands and elaborates his critique of Devlin.

Principles of Critical Morality

The question he addresses in the lectures is, "Is it morally permissible to enforce morality as such?" As Hart notes, this is a question *about* morality, but it is also one *of* morality. In order to make this point clear, he invokes a distinction used by the classical utilitarians between "positive morality," the morality actually accepted and shared by a given social group, and the general moral principles used in the criticism of actual institutions. These general principles are principles of "critical morality." The question Hart raises, then, is one of critical morality about the legal enforcement of positive morality.

According to Hart, Devlin sees the issues in this way as well. Devlin bases his affirmative answer to the question "Is it morally permissible to enforce morality as such?" on a general principle of critical morality, namely that it is permissible for any society to take steps to preserve itself. Hart's interpretation of Devlin is correct, for Devlin assumes the following premise:

(1) Society has a right to protect itself from destruction.

Hart has serious reservations about this principle of critical morality. As he puts it:

> We might wish to argue that whether or not a society is justified in taking steps to preserve itself must depend both on what sort of society it is and what the steps to be taken are. If the society were mainly devoted to the cruel persecution of a racial or religious minority, or if the steps to be taken included hideous tortures, it is arguable that what Lord Devlin terms the "disintegration" of such a society would be morally better than its continued existence, and steps ought not be taken to preserve it.[33]

Whether in his subsequent lectures Devlin has a response to this criticism remains to be seen. This criticism is new, however; Hart did not raise it in "Immorality and Treason."

Hart is not just critical of Devlin's principles of critical morality; he puts forth principles of critical morality of his own. One important such principle is this:

(2) The use of legal coercion by any society calls for justification as something *prima facie* objectionable to be tolerated for the sake of some countervailing good.[34]

Now some commentators on Hart see a connection between (2) and Hart's argument considered in Chapter 6 that, if there are any moral rights, there is at least one natural right, the right of all men to be free.[35] However, in *Law, Liberty, and Morality*, Hart makes no explicit appeal to natural rights to justify this principle and, in fact, attempts to justify it by basically utilitarian arguments. For example, he argues that the administration of punishment without special justification is wrong since punishment involves inflicting pain on the individual and results in hardship to his or her family and also that the threat of punishment may impede the exercise of an individual's free choice. This latter consequence is either bad in itself or has bad consequences. Thus, the threat of punishment may frustrate people's ability to experiment and so to discover what is valuable to them. In the case of laws against private homosexual behavior, it may adversely affect peoples' emotional lives and personalities.

Hart suggests several other principles of critical morality that should be interpreted as specifying when society is justified in using legal coercion for the sake of some countervailing good.

(H) *The Harm Principle*: Society *via* law has the right to forbid action of an individual that harms others.

(P) *Legal Paternalism*: Society has the right *via* law to forbid an action of an individual that causes harm to the individual.

(O) *The Public Offense Principle*: Society has the right *via* law to forbid an action of an individual that is a public affront to decency.

These three principles should be contrasted with what Hart calls "legal moralism," a principle that he attributes to Devlin and that he rejects:

(M) *Legal Moralism*: Society has the right *via* law to forbid an action that conflicts with the society's positive morality.

It should be noted that (1), namely that society has a right to protect itself from destruction, is used by Devlin to justify (M). If society has a right to protect itself from destruction, it has a right to forbid action that conflicts with its positive morality if such action will destroy society.

There is a way to understand Devlin's legal moralism so that it becomes a special case of the harm principle. To do this we must distinguish two kinds of harm principle. The *individual harm principle* is identical with (H) above; the *institutional harm principle*[36] can be stated as follows:

(H′) *The Institutional Harm Principle*: Society has the right *via* law to forbid actions of an individual that harms some institutional practice or regulatory system that is in the public interest.

Devlin can be interpreted as advocating (H′). Maintaining that actions that are in conflict with positive morality may threaten significant institutions of society, for example, marriage, the family, and indirectly society itself, he holds that society has a right to outlaw such actions. On this interpretation both Hart and Devlin agree about the moral principle at issue. The controversy is over whether certain actions harm certain institutions of society, that is, whether the institutional harm principle applies in a particular case. Unfortunately, although this interpretation makes a great deal of sense in understanding the debate, neither Hart nor Devlin adopts it.

ALTERNATIVE EXPLANATIONS

It will be recalled that Devlin uses the consistency argument to try to establish a *prima facie* case that immorality as such should be punished. Arguing that morality as such is enforced in areas of law not concerned with sexual morality, he cites examples of laws against euthanasia and suicide and says they can only be explained as laws punishing immorality as such. Hart argues that, if Devlin is correct that the law in these cases can only be explained as designed to enforce morality, then Devlin's argument has considerable force. Indeed, even people who would tend to be sympathetic with Mill might be swayed toward Devlin's views on the legal enforcement of morality.

But, arguing that Devlin's interpretation of these examples is dubious, Hart gives alternative explanations. In the terms being used here, he challenges the following premise:

(2b) If the punishment of these crimes (suicide, incest, duelling, euthanasia, murder by consent) could not be justified by the harm principle, then this punishment could only be justified by the principle that immorality as such should be punished.

For example, according to Hart there is another explanation of why the law does not accept the consent of the victim in murder or assault cases. The law may be operating on (P), the principle of legal paternalism, a policy designed to protect individuals against themselves. He points out that (P) has long been recognized in the law; Mill, for one, clearly distinguished it from (M), legal moralism, although he was opposed to both.

An alternative explanation using (O), the public offense principle, is also available, he says. In defending Devlin, Eugene Rostow[37] uses the example of the legal prohibition against bigamy to argue that the law enforces morality as such. Hart argues, as he did in the case of murder by consent, that Rostow's explanation of the law of bigamy as the legal enforcement of morality is not the only one. After all, in many legal districts a man and woman can live together "in sin" and the law will not interfere. The law only forbids there being a marriage. The purpose of bigamy laws, Hart implies, may be the protection of religious sensibilities, the protection against public nuisance. The ceremony of marriage if one partner is already married could be considered by many as an affront to public decency. So bigamy law, according to Hart, does not provide good evidence that the law enforces morality as such. Consequently, neither Devlin nor his defenders can use such a law to build a *prima facie* case that the law should enforce morality as such.

Mill's critic, Stephen, argued that certain facts about the criminal law can only be explained by supposing that the law enforces morality as such. Hart provides an alternative explanation of these facts as he does of the ones cited by Devlin. Hart finds the following argument in Stephen's writings: In determining the degree of punishment for a crime the moral wickedness involved in the crime is relevant. But if the object of legal punishment were simply to prevent harm (as Mill thought) this would not be true. Stephen concludes from this that it is appropriate that the law enforce morality as such.

According to Hart, this argument is a *non sequitur*. It does not follow from the fact that the law should make gradations of punishment in terms of moral wickedness that the object of such punishment is to enforce morality as such. Hart brings up an argument considered in Chapter 5 above, namely that there might be good utilitarian reasons why legal punishment should be graded in terms of moral wickedness. For example, if legal punishment were not graded, it might confuse moral judgments and bring the law into disrepute. Further, principles of justice that are widely accepted require morally distinguishable offenses to be treated differently and morally similar offenses to be treated the same. Hart considers that, "if in the course of punishing only harmful activities we think it right . . . to mark moral differences between different offenders, this does not show that we must also think it right to punish activities which are not harmful."[38]

Critique of Legal Moralism

In defending his liberal position Hart not only gives alternative explanations to that of legal moralism of why the law makes certain actions crimes but attacks legal moralism directly. He distinguishes two varieties of legal moralism. What Hart calls the moderate position holds the principle of legal moralism on the grounds that immorality may threaten the existence of society. Since society has a right to protect itself, society has a right to enforce morality as such. This moderate position, attributed at least under one plausible interpretation by Hart to Devlin, is identical with the argument for survival outlined above.

Hart calls the second variety of legal moralism the extreme position. On this version of legal moralism, attributed by Hart to Stephen and, under one interpretation, to Devlin, the enforcement of morality has not only instrumental but intrinsic value. Enforcing morality is valuable in preserving society and valuable in itself.

Hart's major criticism of Devlin's position interpreted as moderate legal moralism is similar to one he made in "Immorality and Treason." Arguing that Devlin believes that any change in morality would have wide-ranging effects on the whole of a society's morality, that morality is a seamless web, Hart maintains that Devlin cites no evidence to support his position and argues that there is much evidence to refute it although he does not say what this evidence is. There is one difference between Hart's earlier critique and his critique of Devlin here, however. The former was related directly to the Disgust Test. He argued that there was no evidence that a positive result of the Disgust Test showed that society was in grave danger. In *Law, Liberty, and Morality* the Disgust Test is not mentioned. Hart argues that there is no evidence that morality is a seamless web and, in particular, that "those who deviate from conventional sexual morality are in other ways hostile to society."[39]

In any case, one must understand that under the present interpretation of Devlin

(I) The preservation of morality is necessary for the preservation of society

is a factual statement. The trouble, according to Hart, is that Devlin cites no facts to support (I).

Hart also argues that Devlin sometimes moves from the proposition

(a) Some shared morality is essential to the existence of any society

to

(b) Society is identical with its morality.

Whereas (a) is true, he says, perhaps is even a necessary truth, (b) is absurd. This is shown by considering what follows from (b). If (b) were true, then we could not say that the morality of a given society has changed. One would have to say that one society has disappeared and another has taken its place.

Let us call the move from (a) to (b) the Identity Fallacy. I can find no evidence that Devlin commits the Identity Fallacy and, as we shall see presently, Devlin himself denies making the move from (a) to (b) and argues that his theory is different from (b).

In any case, if Devlin is interpreted as holding (b) above, then according to Hart

(I) The preservation of morality is necessary for the preservation of society

is a necessary truth, since society is identical with its morality. Here no factual evidence is needed to support (I). On this interpretation Devlin holds a variant of what Hart calls extreme moral legalism since enforcement of morality is valuable in order to preserve morality and valuable in itself.

Hart critically considers two other arguments for extreme legal moralism. He deals quickly with the argument from retribution, namely that the punishment of immorality is justified not by results but by the wickedness of the crime. As we saw in Chapter 5, Hart maintains that retributivism is only plausible in answering certain questions concerning punishment, for example, who should be punished. Endorsing there the retributivist principle that only people who commit some criminal act should be punished, he rejects the retributivist principle that only people who have done some moral wrong should be punished. In *Law, Liberty, and Morality* Hart continues to accept only some retributivist principles. In particular, he argues that a retributive justification of punishment is only plausible when there is a victim. In victimless crimes like homosexual activity between consenting adults the retributive theory rests on nothing but "the implausible claim that in morality two blacks make a white: that the evil of suffering added to the evil of immorality as its punishment makes a moral good."[40]

Stephen seems to appeal to retributive considerations in arguing for his extreme form of legal moralism. But, according to Hart, Stephen sometimes appeals to a different sort of consideration to justify his views, one Hart calls the denunciation element. Stephen's argument from denunciation can be reconstructed in the following way:

(1) If an overwhelming majority of the community universally condemns a practice, then there should be an appropriate way to express the community's disapproval of the offender.

(2) If there should be an appropriate way to express the community's disapproval of the offender, then the community's disapproval should be expressed through punishment.

(3) There is an overwhelming majority of the community in England and the United States that universally condemns immoral sexual behavior.

---

(4) Therefore, the community in England and the United States should express their disapproval of immoral sexual practices by punishment.

Now Hart criticizes this argument on two different grounds, which are tantamount to attacking premise (2) and premise (3). Consider premise (3). He argues that there may have been an overwhelming majority condemning immoral sexual practices in "mid-Victorian England" but it would be "sociologically naive" to assume this uniformity today. Even when "there is lip service to an official sexual morality," this does not mean that there may not be "mutually tolerant morality," and "even where there is some homogeneity of practice and belief, offenders may be viewed not with hatred or resentment but with amused contempt or pity." Stephen's doctrine and "much" of Devlin's view, according to Hart, "hover in the air above the *terra firma* of contemporary social reality."[41] Stephen's and Devlin's views reflect the outlook of English judges, not contemporary society.

Hart also argues against premise (2). Pointing out that "the normal way in which moral condemnation is expressed is by *words*," he asks "why a solemn public statement of disapproval would not be the most 'appropriate' or 'emphatic' means of expressing this. Why should a denunciation take the form of punishment?"[42]

Hart considers the possibility that Stephen means by "appropriate" expression of moral disapproval one that "is effective in instilling or strengthening in the offender and in others respect for the moral code which has been violated."[43] If this is what Stephen means, then his position is open to the objection that there is no evidence that legal enforcement of morality is effective in this way. For example, practices like incest or homosexual behavior are ones for which most men feel "aversion and disgust."[44] In these cases, according to Hart, it is "fantastic"[45] to suppose that, if the state did not punish incestuous and homosexual behavior, the majority of people would engage in such practices. Furthermore, according to Hart, this assumption of the effectiveness of the punishment of homosexuality conflicts with the experience of countries where homosexual behavior is not legally punished. (Hart does not say what these countries are or exactly what these experiences have been.)

Let us suppose, Hart says, that Stephen is correct; let us suppose that an overwhelming majority of people do violently disapprove of immoral sexual practices and that unless immoral sexual practices are punished the prevalent morality would be radically changed. The question then is, What can be said to support the claim that the preservation of the moral *status quo* is of sufficient value to "offset the cost in human misery which legal enforcement entails"?[46] He considers "three propositions concerning the value of preserving social morality which are in perennial danger of confusion."[47] The first proposition is that all moralities contain certain universal values such as freedom, safety of life, protection from deliberate harm. These values are worth protecting, but it does not follow from this that sexual morality would have to be enforced by the law to preserve these values; if sexual immorality spreads, it does not mean that these values are adversely affected.

The second proposition is that social morality contains certain formal values. These formal values involve an impersonal standpoint in which general rules are applied impartially to oneself and others. But although these formal values are worth preserving, it does not follow that society's moral code—in particular its sexual moral code—is worth preserving or that changing this code would undermine these formal values.

The third proposition is mere moral conservatism, the view that "the preservation from change of any existent rule of a social morality, whatever its content, is a value and justifies its legal enforcement."[48] This view, according to Hart, is just a pure dogma unless it is based on some theory, for example, Burke's or Hegel's. If it were based on a theory, then it would be subject to rational criticism. Moral conservatism will "stand or fall with the general theories deployed in its support."[49] But Stephen has no general theory. In fact, some theorists like Burke who were anxious to defend the positive morality of a society would have been opposed to its legal enforcement. For Burke, the value of established institutions was their slow evolution and development as a result of men's adaptation to changing conditions. To use the law to maintain the moral *status quo* would be "artificially to arrest the process which gives social institutions their values."[50]

Stephen also seemed to assume wrongly that legal enforcement is the only way to preserve morality. But Mill emphasized the appropriateness of discussion, advice, and argument to influence people's opinions on moral matters. Mill did not teach moral indifference; he was only opposed to coercion. The techniques of discussion, advice, and argument leave the individual "the final judge."[51]

The last argument for moral legalism that Hart criticizes is the one based on the principles of democracy that Devlin presented in the Owen J. Roberts Memorial Lecture. In general, Hart takes great pains to make the following simple point: one can accept democracy as the best form of government without accepting that the majority's decisions are beyond criticism. Advocates of democracy, according to Hart, are constantly in danger of confusing the above two points and advocating moral populism, the view that the majority's decisions are beyond criticism. Mill warned against this confusion, and there are "vestiges"[52] of this confusion in Devlin's Owen J. Roberts Memorial Lecture.

Hart maintains that few would dispute Devlin's contention that, if one is talking about positive morality, morality is a matter of popular vote and a question of fact. With respect to the question of what justifies the enforcement of positive morality, Devlin "seems content with his previous argument and his analogy with treason, criticized above."[53] As we have already seen, Hart's major criticism of Devlin is that Devlin provides no evidence for the view that lack of enforcement of popular morality will lead to the destruction of society. Devlin fails to answer Hart's challenge in the lectures Hart critically considers in *Law, Liberty, and Morality*.

The Enforcement of Morals

In 1965 Devlin's book *The Enforcement of Morals* appeared. This book contains the Maccabaean Lecture and Owen J. Roberts Memorial Lecture as well as lectures Devlin gave after the publication of Hart's *Law, Liberty, and Morality*. *The Enforcement of Morals* is useful, then, because it contains all of Devlin's attempts to combat Hart's arguments in *Law, Liberty, and Morality*.

Particularly revealing is a long footnote Devlin added to his original Maccabaean Lecture in order to combat one of Hart's criticisms. As we have seen, Hart accused Devlin of the Identity Fallacy. Devlin, he says, moved fallaciously from the truism that all society must have some morality to the absurdity that every society is identical with its morality. (The absurdity is shown by noting that, if society is identical with its morality, any change of morality will destroy society.)

Devlin argues in this remarkable footnote that Hart is mistaken about his position.[54] He does not maintain that *any* deviation from a society's shared morality threatens its existence but only that a deviation from society's shared morality is capable of threatening the existence of society and so is not beyond the law.

The trouble with this response, however, is that although it may have been what Devlin intended, it is much too weak a claim to support the legal punishment of homosexuality or any other infraction of positive morality. Given only the claim that homosexual behavior is *capable* of destroying society, nothing follows about whether homosexual behavior will destroy society or even whether homosexual behavior will probably destroy society. Yet Devlin's position surely was that homosexual behavior is a threat to society's existence, not just that it is capable of being a threat.

Devlin's Disgust Test is a test of the imminence of this threat. Although he cites no evidence that the Disgust Test is a reliable guide to when society is in danger of being destroyed, homosexual behavior, according to Devlin, passes the test. The footnote Devlin added to the Maccabaean Lecture fails to address the crucial issue. It might clear up a misunderstanding of Hart's, but it fails to answer Hart's major criticism. Granted that society has a right to protect itself, what is the evidence that private homosexual behavior is any threat to society? That it is *capable* of being a threat even Devlin admits does not justify its legal punishment.

In a 1964 address entitled "Morals and Contemporary Social Reality" reprinted in *The Enforcement of Morality* Devlin goes on the attack against Hart.[55] He counters Hart's statement that his views are hovering in the air above the *terra firma* of contemporary social reality by suggesting that Mill's doctrine and not his is out of touch with social reality, and he further maintains that the implications of Hart's theory for the law are by no means clear.

Mill's doctrine, according to Devlin, has made no "conquests on *terra firma*."[56] It has existed for over a century and no one has ever attempted to put it into practice. Indeed, Devlin claims that Mill's view would be rejected by the vast majority of the population. He points out that the Wolfenden Report's recommendation on private homosexual behavior was defeated in the House of Commons and has not gained public support.

What about Hart's charge that Devlin's view hovers above the *terra firma* of social reality? Devlin admits to it,[57] but one must suppose he is being ironical. After all, he claimed in the Maccabaean Lecture that the average man felt disgust, indignation, and intolerance toward homosexual behavior and even in the present address he uses the rejection of the House of Commons as a way of showing that Mill's view is out of touch with social reality and by implication that his view is not.

In assessing Devlin's response one should recall under what circumstances Hart accused Stephen's and Devlin's view of hovering in the air. Hart's point was that it was sociologically naive to assume, as Devlin does, that today there is a considerable degree of moral solidarity with regard to sexual morality. Even when people pay lip service to official sexual morality, they may not view offenders with hatred and resentment. (Hart admits that such moral solidarity may have existed in Stephen's time.)

The fact that the Wolfenden Report was defeated in the House of Commons and never received popular support does not justify the assumption that the average man would feel disgust, indignation, and intolerance about homosexual behavior. Indeed, Devlin cites no evidence that the vast majority of people would reject Mill's doctrine outside the fact that the House of Commons defeated the recommendations of the Wolfenden Report. However, it is well known that a legislature may defeat certain measures for various reasons that have nothing to do with public sentiment. In short, Devlin does little to combat Hart's original claim that he assumes much more moral solidarity than is justified by the evidence; yet in order to be justified in his argument this moral solidarity must exist.

What about Devlin's argument that Mill's harm principle has not been embraced by the law? One reply is that Mill's is a normative principle and that what the law in fact does is irrelevant to it. But this answer, as Devlin points out, is not exactly Hart's position. Hart agrees with the idea that if a principle conflicts with principles actually used in the law, this constitutes a *prima facie* objection against it.

Hart, as we have seen, does not believe that Devlin's principle of legal moralism has as much support from the actual principles used in the law as the latter supposes. He argues that some crimes specified by the law that Devlin claims can only be explained by the principle of legal moralism can be explained more easily by other principles, specifically legal paternalism and the public offense principle. It should be noted that in introducing these other principles Hart goes well beyond Mill. Devlin argues that since Hart rejects Mill's harm principle as the sole guide to legal interference, Hart "gains no advantage by citing Mill as an authority."[58] In fact, Hart's argument would have been clearer if Mill had been left out of it. According to Devlin, what exactly Hart's paternalism principle amounts to is quite unclear. Devlin asks: what exactly is the distinction between legal moralism (which Hart rejects) and legal paternalism (which Hart accepts)? Devlin suggests there are two things that Hart might mean by paternalism. First, Hart might be advocating physical paternalism, that the state has the right to protect people from physically harming themselves. Second, Hart might be advocating moral paternalism, that the state has a right to protect people from morally harming themselves.

Devlin argues that the distinction between physical and moral paternalism cannot be made in principle. He makes an analogy to the family. Fathers look after their children's physical welfare as well as their moral welfare. The state by analogy should look after both. "If, on the other hand, we are grown up enough to look after our own morals, why not after our own bodies?" In short, if society has "an interest which permits it to legislate in the one case, why not in the other?"[59]

Furthermore, the consideration Hart uses to justify physical paternalism could justify moral paternalism, he says. Hart argues that there has been "a general decline in the belief that people know their own interest best." Devlin comments that there can be no reason to believe they know their own moral good any better than their own physical good. Hart also maintains that

> choices may be made and consent given without adequate reflection or appreciation of the consequences; or in pursuit of merely transitory desires; or in various predicaments when judgement is likely to be clouded; or under inner psychological compulsion; or under pressure by others of a kind too subtle to be susceptible of proof in a law court.[60]

Devlin comments that "these words, it seems to me, might almost have been written with homosexuals in mind. It is moral weakness rather than physical that leads to predicaments when the judgment is likely to be clouded and is the cause of inner psychological compulsion."[61]

But if it is difficult to draw a line between moral and physical paternalism, it is, according to Devlin, impossible to draw a line between moral paternalism and legal moralism. For without recourse to public morality it would be impossible to determine what would be for someone's own good. But even if there was a distinction between moral paternalism and legal moralism, Devlin argues, it would not be relevant to the present discussion. In the present discussion, the issue is whether there is a realm of private morality that is not the law's business and paternalism must "make all morality the law's business."[62]

This critique of Hart's position does not work. First, the issue between Hart and Devlin is *not* whether there is a realm of private morality that is not the law's business. This is the issue between Mill and Devlin, but Hart rejects Mill's harm principle as the sole guide for legal intervention. Hart allows that in principle the state has the right *via* law to intervene in the *private* affairs of an individual who is harming himself or herself. He must allow this since (a) he allows that legal paternalism is an acceptable moral principle and (b) action that harms only the individual performing the action is by definition private. In the case of homosexual behavior, Hart apparently believes that there is no evidence that such behavior is reflexively harmful. Although there may be a tendency to understand the Hart-Devlin debate as a debate over whether there is a private realm of morality, this interpretation is wrong. As I argued above, the issue between Hart and Devlin seems to be whether certain behavior harms society by harming certain important institutions in society. They both admit either explicitly or implicitly that under some circumstances society has the right to outlaw certain behavior that harms these institutions; that is, they both seem to accept the institutional harm principle. They differ over whether private homosexual behavior brings about this institutional harm. As far as I can determine, Hart would admit that if it could be shown that private homosexual behavior did undermine certain important social institutions in our society, then society would have the right to intervene legally. This, of course, would not mean necessarily that society should intervene since the price of intervention might be too high.

Second, moral paternalism is distinguishable from moral legalism. Moral legalism is the right of the state to enforce positive morality, no matter how irrational, no matter how much it is based on prejudice and ignorance. Moral paternalism is the right of the state to intervene *via* law to prevent people from harming themselves morally. What harming themselves morally would be, would be dependent on principles of critical morality, not positive morality—not even of the positive morality of the man on the Clapham omnibus. Devlin may have forgotten this point in his above-mentioned comment on homosexuals.

Devlin seems to assume that homosexual behavior is based on a failure to appreciate the consequences of this action. The homosexual has a psychological compulsion and clouded judgment. In short, he believes that homosexual behavior is ill considered and irrational. Putting aside for the moment the question of whether there is any solid evidence that homosexual behavior is ill considered and irrational, this cannot be his rationale for legal intervention. Devlin's rationale is that homosexual behavior ought to be outlawed because it poses a grave danger to society. This would be Devlin's position even if homosexual behavior was not ill considered and irrational. On the other hand, if Hart wished to argue that private homosexual behavior should be prevented on paternalistic grounds, he might argue that it is ill considered and irrational. However, Hart does not seem to believe that in general homosexual behavior is ill considered and irrational.

Neither Devlin nor Hart cites any psychological evidence to support his views. Devlin cites no evidence that homosexual behavior is ill considered and irrational; Hart cites no evidence that it is not. Devlin, moreover, cites no evidence that homosexual behavior poses a grave threat to society.

Devlin points out that Hart's view goes beyond Mill's harm principle not only in advocating a paternalistic principle but in other ways. Hart advocates laws against cruelty to animals. But such laws would not be justified by the harm principle (or paternalism) because harm is there specified in terms of *human* harm. The harm principle might be modified to include all sentient beings and indeed, as Devlin points out, although animals are not included in Mill's well-known statement of the harm principle in *On Liberty*, Mill's words in *Utilitarianism* suggest some such idea as this.[63] But if the harm principle is modified in this way, Devlin argues, it is not clear what it could amount to since a duty toward animals "is not of the same kind as a duty towards other members of the same society."[64] Devlin, I believe, is correct on this point. Hart has not worked out the implications of a modified harm principle that would include harm to animals in such areas as food processing, leather goods manufacturing, and other areas of human life where animals are used.

Devlin also correctly notes that Hart introduces the principle of public offense. It is on this basis that Hart would outlaw bigamy since he argues that bigamy is a public act offensive to religious feelings. Devlin objects that marriage in a registry office is only in form a public act. No one with deep religious feelings is likely to attend and people who meet the couple will very probably not know that one of the parties is already married. Thus there would be really no public offense in bigamy.

In defense of Hart it could be said that since it is after all a matter of public record a bigamous marriage could become widely known and thus be a public affront to religious feelings. Perhaps this is all that is needed. In any case, the public offense principle may be as good an explanation of laws against bigamy as legal moralism. Where is the evidence that people today feel disgust, intolerance, and indignation toward a bigamist or even that bigamy would destroy our society? Or does having no bigamy *define* this society?

Devlin also points out that although Hart modifies Mill's harm principle and adds two other principles "we are still left with five crimes about which Professor Hart says nothing."[65] These are abortion, bestiality, incest, obscenity (for example, the sale of pornography), and offenses connected with prostitution (for example, brothel keeping). Devlin's point seems to be that it is unclear what Hart's position entails in regard to these.

Devlin is correct that in his writing up to that point Hart had not made clear his position on these five crimes. However, in his Southey Lecture entitled "The Abortion Law Reform: The English Experience," given at Melbourne University in 1970, Hart maintains that he would have voted for the English Abortion Act 1967 had he been a member of Parliament.[66] Although he admits that passage of the act caused some problems of overcrowding in hospitals, he argues that the advantages far outweigh these problems for the act has reduced the number of illegitimate children, the number of shotgun marriages, the number of deaths from illegal abortion, and the total number of illegal abortions. Furthermore, the act, according to Hart, has made it possible for women who do not wish to continue their pregnancy "to lay their case frankly before doctors and to discuss it without shame or without fear."[67]

In this lecture Hart does not attempt to analyze critically the various arguments and positions on the abortion issue, and one can only infer what his position is on the various difficult moral issues connected with this problem, for example, the moral status of the fetus. One supposes, for example, that he at least does not believe that a fetus is a full-fledged moral person.

Could we have predicted Hart's stand on abortion from what he said in *Law, Liberty, and Morality*? I do not think this would have been possible without knowing (a) his views on the moral status of a fetus and (b) his views on various social consequences of the passage of a pro-abortion law, for example, whether pro-abortion legislation would bring about fewer illegal abortions. But this is hardly a criticism. The implications of very general moral principles are not readily predictable unless they are supplemented by particular premises, both factual and moral.

What Hart's position would be on the four remaining issues mentioned by Devlin we do not know, but that he has not written on them and made his position clear hardly shows that the general principles he appeals to are faulty. After all, there are crimes that Devlin has not made his position clear on either. Does Devlin maintain that all acts now punishable by English and American criminal law should remain so? If not, which ones should be made illegal? That Devlin does not clearly answer these questions is hardly an objection against his general position.

Devlin also objects to Hart's separation of the issues of the gradation of punishment and the object of punishment. (Recall that Hart argued against Stephen's position thus: from the mere fact that the degree of punishment is in terms of moral wickedness it does not follow that the object of such punishment is to enforce moral wickedness.) Devlin thinks these are not independent questions but are just a convenient division of a single question: What justifies the sentence of punishment? He brings out his objection in the following way. Hart argues that the gradation of punishment can be justified on utilitarian grounds. For example, if legal punishment was not graded in terms of moral wickedness, then it might confuse people's judgment and bring the law into disrepute. But Devlin argues that these considerations apply with "equal force to the making of law." If laws against homosexuality were repealed

> moral judgements might be confused and law brought into disrepute because people would see moral wickedness going unpunished. That is one of the arguments against repeal. Against that there are arguments of the misery caused to individuals and so on. The answer may be a compromise. But Professor Hart will not compromise on this because he says homosexuality is within the realm into which the law has no claim to enter; he cannot therefore discuss terms of entry.[68]

Devlin's statement suggests that the differences between him and Hart are over basic moral principles and not merely over factual considerations. But he mistakenly interprets Hart as saying that private homosexual behavior should under no circumstances be interfered with. Hart has never claimed this. His point is that such outlawing seems unjustified on broadly conceived utilitarian grounds. In particular, there is little evidence that private homosexual behavior hurts other people (that is, it is not justified on the individual harm principle); there is little evidence that it hurts the homosexuals themselves (that is, it is not justified on the principle of legal paternalism); there is little evidence that it is a public affront to decency (that is, it is not justified by the public offense principle); and, more importantly to the Hart-Devlin debate, there is little evidence that it harms significant institutions of society (that is, it is not justified by the institutional harm principle).

In addition to misunderstanding Hart, Devlin seems to have shifted his position. He now seems to be arguing, not that homosexual behavior is dangerous to society and should be outlawed, but only that, if laws against private homosexual behavior were repealed, this might confuse people's moral judgment and this confusion would have to be weighed against other factors in order to decide whether homosexual behavior should be outlawed. It is not even clear that he is now advocating laws against homosexuality.

If Devlin's argument has shifted to one of utilitarian balancing and he is advocating laws against private homosexual behavior, it seems that Hart has the stronger utilitarian case. The misery caused by enforcement of laws against private homosexual behavior and the degrading practice of police snooping (all well-established facts) would have to be weighed against the alleged facts that repeal of the laws would confuse people's moral judgments and that because of this confusion the law would be brought into disrepute. Given these considerations, on balance most utilitarians would maintain that laws against private homosexual behavior should be repealed. On the other hand, if Devlin is not advocating such laws, there seems to be very little difference between his position and Hart's once the latter's position is correctly understood.

In any case, it is well to remember that Hart was using the distinction between the gradation of punishment and the object of punishment to refute an argument of Stephen's. Stephen's view, although not clearly stated, was certainly not utilitarian.

Hart's Last Shot

As far as the main participants are concerned the Devlin-Hart debate ended for all intents and purposes with the publication in 1967 of Hart's paper "Social Solidarity and the Enforcement of Morality."[69] Although Devlin's book *The Enforcement of Morals* had appeared and Hart had the opportunity to rebut Devlin's criticism of his position, he chose not to take this tack. Electing instead to consider in general terms what evidence would be needed to support Devlin's claim that the enforcement of morality is necessary to prevent the disintegration of society, he ignores Devlin's specific attempts to attack his position.

Hart's strategy here is a wise one, for Devlin's attack, as I have shown, is both largely irrelevant to the main issues and confused. Realizing this, Hart must have seen no point in correcting these elementary confusions. More importantly, as I have pointed out, the major issue separating Devlin and Hart is a factual one. This 1967 paper of Hart's is an attempt to make this point clear and to raise the discussion of it to a new level. Hart's paper, then, is not so much a last shot at Devlin as a last shot at putting the controversy into perspective. In so doing it makes new analytic distinctions while ranging over social scientific theories of social disintegration.

Hart points out, as he had done before, that sometimes Devlin seems to be merely stating a tautology. Devlin seems at times to define society in such a way that a change in the morality of society would necessitate a change in society. Hart maintains that such a claim is empty and that Devlin's position only becomes interesting if one interprets it as an empirical thesis. Hart calls this empirical thesis the disintegration thesis. Under the pressure of requests for empirical substantiation the disintegration thesis often collapses, however, into what he calls the conservative thesis. This thesis is the claim that "society has the right to enforce its morality by law because the majority have the right to follow their own moral convictions that their moral environment is a thing to be defended from change."[70] Hart only considers the disintegration thesis in this paper.

After pointing out relevant similarities between Devlin's views and those of Parsons and Durkheim, Hart undertakes the task of clarifying the disintegration thesis. One thing that advocates of the disintegration thesis could mean by the common morality that is essential to society and that is preserved by legal enforcement, he says, is that part of social morality that is essential to any society of human beings. In *The Concept of Law* he characterizes this part containing the restraints and prohibitions as the minimum content of natural law. But advocates of the disintegration thesis such as Devlin and Durkheim do not mean only this part of morality; they are also talking about moral rules that may differ from society to society.

The second thing that advocates of the disintegration theory could mean when they refer to the common morality that is essential to society, Hart says, is both the restraints and the prohibitions such as those relating to violence that are necessary to any society and what is essential for a particular society. There is in this view a central core of rules and principles that constitute its pervasive and characteristic style of life. For example, monogamy as a moral principle deeply pervades our culture: it is recognized as the sole form of legal marriage; it is at the heart of our conception of family life. The disappearance of monogamy would result in such vast changes in our society that we might well say that the character of this society had changed.

It is an empirical question whether any particular moral rule, for example, a rule outlawing private homosexual behavior, is so closely connected with the central core of morality of a society that its preservation is necessary in order to preserve that core. But, according to Hart, even on this view the question of whether the central core of morality is necessary to preserve society is *not* empirical since the preservation of society is identical with preserving the central core.

What needs to be done in order "to convert" this last-mentioned idea into an empirical disintegration thesis? According to Hart, "It must be the theory that the maintenance of the core elements in a particular society's moral life is in fact necessary to prevent disintegration, because the withering or malignant decay of the central morality is a disintegrating factor."[71] Further clarification, he adds, would be needed before an empirically testable hypothesis would be available. One would have to specify criteria for the central core of morality and criteria for disintegration. (Although Hart does not say so explicitly, these criteria must be logically independent of one another.)

Hart considers two types of evidence that would be relevant to evaluating the disintegration hypothesis once these criteria were specified: historical evidence, in which the units are societies and not individuals, and social psychological evidence. One would have to examine societies that have disintegrated and determine whether a malignant change in their common morality had taken place. Even if one found such a change, a causal connection would have to be shown between it and the disintegration. As Hart points out, there are difficulties in making macroscopic generalizations about society. One problem is that of generalizing from one type of society to another. If all our evidence was from "simple tribal societies or closely knit agrarian societies,"[72] we should not have much confidence in applying the results of our investigation to our modern society.

The relevant evidence from social psychology should be broken into two "subforms."[73] In the first the alternative to maintaining the common morality is uniform permissiveness in areas of life covered by common morality. On this alternative heterosexuality or homosexuality are matters of common personal tastes. In the second subform, the alternative to common morality may be moral pluralism in that there are different submoralities in relation to the same area of conduct.

Hart suggests picking criteria for disintegration in terms of a general increase in anti-social behavior that would infringe on minimal restraints and prohibitions that are necessary for social life: dishonesty, disrespect for property and human life.[74] Depending on what subform one was investigating, different psychological theories would connect the disintegration with the breakdown of social morality.

Thus, with respect to permissiveness the psychological theory to be tested would be that lack of discipline in one area of social life, for example, the sexual, would result in a general weakening of self-control. Thus permissiveness in sexual morality would result in increased violence and a general lapse of restraint. This idea, Hart suggests, may be behind Devlin's view that morality is a seamless web. The alternative theory is that permissiveness in one area of social life may make it easier for people to submit to restraints in another.

With regard to moral pluralism the theory to be tested is that quarrels over different submoralities destroy the minimal restraint necessary to society. The alternative theory would be that pluralism furthers mutual tolerance and is conducive to maintaining minimal restraint.

In conclusion, Hart suggests that until social scientists provide evidence to support the disintegration theory, supporters of the enforcement of morality such as Devlin would be well advised to "rest their case candidly on the conservative rather than on the disintegration thesis."[75]

Postscript to the Devlin-Hart Debate

Hart had the last word in his debate with Devlin. But by the time he did in a sense the controversy was moot for on May 11, 1965, Devlin co-signed a letter to the *Times*[76] arguing that the time had come to drop legal restrictions on private homosexual behavior. In it he explicitly endorsed the recommendations on homosexuality of the Wolfenden Report. Why did Devlin change his mind? As we have seen, as late as 1964 Devlin was attacking Hart and defending his stand on legal restrictions on homosexual behavior.

If we assume that Devlin's action was consistent with his past views, he must have come to believe in 1965 that homosexual behavior was no longer disgusting to the man in the Clapham omnibus. Does the *Times* letter cite evidence to support his belief that the average man's views have changed? The letter cites the endorsement of the Wolfenden Committee, recommendations of various church groups, the majority of national newspapers, and groups in the Labor and Conservative Parties. It also cites a "distinguished list of signatories" that wrote in the columns of the *Times* seven years before and maintained that the "existing laws clearly no longer represented either Christian or liberal opinion in this country."[77]

Two basic questions can be asked about this evidence. Is it evidence that the average man does not feel disgust toward homosexual activity? One might have supposed that, at best, it was evidence of the opinions of a very liberal and educated minority, the very sort of opinions that Devlin rejected as the moral basis for the law in "Democracy and Morality," and not the feelings of the man in the Clapham omnibus.

But supposing it is the right sort of evidence, why did it take Devlin so long to recognize it? Is this because the endorsement of the various groups he cites were a very recent occurrence? The distinguished list of signatories in the *Times* whose views the letter cites with approval had written *seven years* before. Further, Devlin's letter says that the national papers "consistently advocated"[78] reform. Presumably this means that the papers had advocated reform ever since 1958, when the Wolfenden Report appeared. It is unclear when the various church groups endorsed the Wolfenden Report, but one suspects their first endorsement came before 1964, when Devlin still opposed reform. The only recent endorsement actually cited by Devlin was that of the Liberal Party Council and various groups in the Liberal and Conservative Parties. It is difficult to believe that the endorsement of these groups could tip the scales of evidential support and indicate that the feelings of the average man had changed.

One is left with the lingering doubt that Devlin provided no good reason for his change of mind or at least no good reason that should not have persuaded him to change his mind much earlier. In 1967 the Wolfenden Report recommendation on homosexuality was finally implemented in the Sexual Offense Act. Ironically this was also the year the final shot was fired in the Hart-Devlin debate. Hart could well afford at this point to take the high road and decline to engage in detailed refutation of Devlin's arguments against him. Devlin had finally agreed with Hart that laws against homosexuality should be repealed and the Wolfenden Report recommendations were soon to become the law of England.

Conclusion

Although it seems clear that Hart had the better of Devlin in this debate, we still must ask what can be learned about Hart's philosophy from this encounter.

First, one sees Hart, the philosophical analyst, at work. He is constantly making distinctions in order to illuminate the issue and argue the point. As a result we see the discussion raised to a new level.

Second, we see Hart going well beyond Mill's liberalism and advocating two principles of critical morality, legal paternalism and public offense, in addition to Mill's harm principle. Mill would certainly have rejected legal paternalism and probably the public offense principle as well. On the other hand, Hart does not attempt to work out the details of these two additional principles.[79] Indeed, he leaves it quite unclear from his writing under what circumstances the state should interfere *via* law to protect people from themselves and under what conditions the state should interfere to prevent a public offense. Hart's position is presumably not that the state should always interfere in these circumstances. After all, people who live on Sugar Pops may be ruining their health and an atheist who hands out leaflets on a street corner on Easter Sunday in front of a Catholic church may be creating a public offense. But it is doubtful that Hart would advocate that the Sugar Pops eater and the atheist should be forced to stop.

Third, Hart is sensitive to the need for empirical evidence in evaluating certain issues in the philosophy of law in a way that many social philosophers are not. He is constantly pointing out the empirical assumptions Devlin is making without adequate foundation. On the other hand, he never explicitly uses historical or social scientific evidence in his own arguments. Sometimes hinting at the fact that such evidence is available, he himself never cites any. It is unclear why this is so but one supposes that he simply does not know the relevant evidence in a way that would permit him to cite it and refer to it explicitly. This is a pity since such knowledge would give his arguments a far greater weight than they have.

As we have seen, it was only after the debate was over that Hart seriously attempted to clarify the evidential status of the claim that separated Devlin's main position from his. But even at this point he did not cite empirical evidence to justify his position; rather, he was satisfied to present a clear and relatively sophisticated view of what evidence would be relevant.

Fourth, besides the three principles of critical morality already mentioned in the course of the debate, Hart indicates almost in passing other elements of his legal-social philosophy that he does not develop or integrate in a systematic way.

First, arguing that the mere fact that people have strong feelings about something is not enough to outlaw it, he advocates the use of critical intelligence in turning popular morality into criminal law.

Second, he questions whether society always has the right to protect itself and says that whether it does will depend on what sort of society it is, in particular on whether it is a moral society.

Third, he maintains that utilitarian arguments may be relevant to justifying gradation of punishment.

Fourth, following Mill, he maintains the possibility that the morality of society can be preserved by discussion, advice, and argument, not merely by legal enforcement.

Fifth, he stresses that an advocate of democracy need not maintain that the majority's decision is beyond criticism.

Finally, with Devlin, Hart believes that if a principle conflicts with the principles of criminal law there are *prima facie* grounds for rejecting it.

Many of these elements of Hart's philosophy seem to be based on factual assumptions that are never made explicit. For example, in his sixth point, Hart's acceptance of the idea that if a principle conflicts with the principles of criminal law there are *prima facie* grounds for rejecting it seems to assume that most systems of criminal law are on the whole just. If most systems were not just, it is difficult to see how conflict with the principles of some arbitrary system could create any *prima facie* claim. It is possible, of course, that by the principles of criminal law Hart was not referring to any arbitrary system but to the principles of criminal law embodied in English criminal law. If so, he seems to be assuming that most principles of the English criminal law are just. Otherwise it is difficult to see why, if some principles conflict with the principles of English criminal law, this would create any *prima facie* claim. But neither of these factual assumptions seems self-evident. The first is hardly obvious in light of the many unjust systems in the world; the second may well presume too sanguine a view of British criminal law.

In his fourth point the factual assumption is made that the morality of society is preserved in a certain way. Whether this assumption is true in general or only under some circumstances, for example, where there is a tradition of rational discussion, is quite unclear. Even his first point seems to be based on a factual assumption, namely that critical intelligence is more effective, more reliable, than strong feeling. Unlike John Dewey, however, who also appeals to the notion of critical intelligence, Hart introduces no historical or evolutionary evidence to support the claim.

In sum, Hart's philosophy, as manifested in his debate with Devlin, is strong in analysis but weak in systematic integration and empirical support.

Conclusion

WRITING IN A *Festschrift* in honor of Hart on his seventieth birthday, Hacker and Raz say:

> At mid-century political philosophy was said to be dead and legal philosophy appeared to be dying. The only fruits that could be obtained from that field of intellectual activity were the gleanings from ancestral sowings. A quarter of a century later a transformed landscape is revealed—legal philosophy flourishes as never before. The responsibility for this renaissance is H. L. A. Hart's. His work provides the foundations of contemporary legal philosophy in the English-speaking world and beyond. His teaching, in Oxford and elsewhere, has inspired many a young philosopher to turn to jurisprudence in the reasonable expectation of a good harvest. Herbert Hart has done for twentieth-century legal philosophy what Bentham did for eighteenth-century jurisprudence. He has integrated it into the mainstream of general philosophical thought.[1]

To this eloquent statement of Hart's significance we might add the observation that the range and depth of Hart's views and their subtlety and novelty is an achievement quite independent of their influence.

One suspects that Hart will be remembered primarily as a philosophical analyst of the law and a latter-day legal positivist, a philosopher whose work has its roots in Oxford-style ordinary language analyses and in the older tradition of Bentham and Austin. But, as the preceding chapters have shown, Hart is much more than this. He is also a liberal moral critic of law, a philosopher who uses his analytic training to illuminate moral issues and take to task conservative jurists.[2] Further, although Hart worked within a tradition, his contributions are novel and provocative. Surely no one could have predicted his analyses of legal system, legal cause, and legal definition from a study of those thinkers who influenced him.

In addition, even when Hart does take a stance that seems predictable in light of those who influenced him, there is often a new angle, a variation or twist that challenges our assumptions and prejudices. Hart is a legal positivist who holds a minimum natural law theory; he is a Millian liberal but with serious qualifications; he propounds a natural right theory but only conditionally; his theory of punishment is utilitarian in some respects and retributive in others. Their complexity and subtlety make any easy classification of Hart's theories difficult. His analysis of the concept of law has perhaps generated more critical responses than any analysis of legal concepts in the history of twentieth-century jurisprudence.

I will not venture to predict Hart's long-range influence as a legal philosopher, but his short-term influence is already clear. No doubt his historical importance in the long run will be contingent on the fate of analytic philosophy generally. Still, one may hope that the legal philosophers who follow Hart will learn not only from his positive contributions but also from his mistakes. In this book I have made many criticisms of Hart, some very specific and some very general. It would be inappropriate for me to review them here, but a few general comments are in order.

One basic problem with both Hart's analysis of legal concepts and his moral arguments is his insensitivity to the need for empirical information and his consequent failure to utilize empirical science. Even when he does see this need he usually makes no effort to obtain the relevant data. As is the case with many Oxford analysts Hart seems to think that one can have knowledge of the workings of ordinary legal language by sitting in one's armchair. Nor does he normally consider scientific evidence when empirical questions arise in his moral philosophy. For example, in his analysis of legal rights in his Inaugural Lecture Hart makes what seem to be empirical claims about the use of legal language without any empirical evidence to back them up. In his debate with Devlin on the enforcement of morality the differences between the two men seem to be based largely on empirical considerations. Throughout the debate Hart seems to be aware of this, but only at the end does he attempt to clarify the empirical issues involved and consider exactly what empirical evidence would be relevant.

No doubt Hart's background as a lawyer and an Oxford philosopher provided him with little training in empirical research and social scientific theory. Yet on rare occasions—notably in his discussion of the death penalty and in his paper "Social Solidarity and the Enforcement of Morality"—he was capable of appealing to these. Then we see Hart at his best.

Another problem with Hart's philosophy of law is his reliance on the internal point of view in understanding a legal system. He has been praised for using this hermeneutic approach but, as I have argued, in order to acquire a deep understanding it is often necessary to transcend the point of view of the legal actor.

Closely related to this second problem is Hart's tendency to base his analyses of legal concepts on the ordinary meaning of terms. Although in *The Concept of Law* he argued that when borderline cases are at issue theoretical and practical considerations should be taken into account in elucidating legal concepts, he does not entertain the possibility where borderline cases are not at issue theoretical and practical considerations should guide an elucidation.

Further, since Hart generally ignores the need for empirical research, he never approaches legal problems as programs for legal research. His analysis of legal formalism and rule skepticism as well as his views on the modern theory of causality could have been improved had he formulated these doctrines as such programs.

Still another basic problem with Hart's social philosophy is the lack of a systematic and integrated theory. Hart's Millian liberalism is qualified by the acceptance of paternalism and the public offense principle. However, he never works out the implications or the extent of these qualifications and how they are tied in with other aspects of his legal philosophy.

Finally, there are unreconciled tensions in Hart's legal philosophy. For example, his early advocacy of a conditional natural right theory and his skepticism about rights in his later writing are difficult to reconcile; his legal positivism and his advocacy of a minimum natural law theory seem *prima facie* inconsistent; his critique of Wootton and his own position on punishment and *mens rea* seem to be in conflict.

In 1983 Hart's *Essays in Jurisprudence and Philosophy* appeared.[3] This book consists of essays published from 1953 to 1981 together with a short introduction by Hart. In his introductory essay Hart admits that some of his early views were wrong or misleading. These up-to-date comments give us an excellent opportunity to see if in retrospect Hart himself has seen some of the basic problems with his philosophy and, if he has, how he attempts to deal with them.

In addition to the second thoughts set forth in *Essays in Jurisprudence and Philosophy*, the second edition of Hart and Honoré's *Causation in the Law* (1985) contains a long preface in which the authors attempt to answer some of the criticisms of their book.[4] Here again we have a chance to see if some of the problems that I have raised are acknowledged and, if so, how they have been treated.

Unfortunately, for the most part in neither of these works are the problems that are raised in this book acknowledged, let alone answered. In the introduction to *Essays in Jurisprudence and Philosophy* Hart still seems to appeal to linguistic intuition, not empirical science, to justify his view on legal language;[5] he still advocates the internal point of view and the hermeneutic method and rejects scientific methodology as a legitimate approach to understanding normative structure and rule-following behavior;[6] he does not seem to be aware of any problems in reconciling his legal positivism and his theory of the minimum content of natural law.[7] In the preface to the second edition of *Causation in the Law* Hart and Honoré are not concerned with the methodological basis of their claims about common sense causal notions; nor do they attempt to justify their particular common sense causal claims as either empirical hypotheses about ordinary usage or policies about causal attribution.[8]

However, there are indications, some clearer than others, that Hart may not be entirely unsympathetic to some of the criticisms raised in this book and, indeed, that he may even be moving in the directions I have suggested.

Hart now rejects his conditional natural rights theory although not perhaps because of the objections to it raised here. In Chapter 6 I argued that this theory has serious problems and that it is difficult to reconcile it with his later, rather skeptical, view about natural rights. Saying that he has decided not to include his essay "Are There Any Natural Rights?" in *Essays in Jurisprudence and Philosophy* since its main argument "seems to me to be mistaken and my errors not sufficiently illuminating to justify re-printing now,"[9] Hart seems to agree. Hart does not say why the main argument is mistaken. However, he does say that a theory of basic individual rights must rest on a specific conception of the human person. Thus, while continuing to be skeptical of recent theories of rights, he holds out some hope for a viable theory.

Hart may now be closer than he was to accepting the suggestion that I made in Chapter 4 that theoretical and practical considerations be used, not just in borderline cases, but on a much wider scale in the elucidation of legal concepts. Maintaining that a sophisticated and profound understanding of the working of language would not reconcile philosophical problems that arise from the "divergence between partly overlapping concepts reflecting a divergence of basic points of view or values or background theory, or which arise from conflict or incompleteness of legal rules,"[10] Hart holds that there might be this divergence even when there is perfect agreement about the application of a concept in clear cases. In order to solve philosophical problems in these cases one must first identify the conflicting points of view that led to the divergent concepts; then one must give reasoned arguments establishing the merits of the conflicting theories or divergent concepts or rules by showing how these could be made compatible by some suitable restriction in scope. This suggests that the elucidation of concepts may involve the introduction of theoretical and practical considerations in cases in which divergent background theories or values are the basis for the divergent concepts. Thus divergent concepts of law may result from underlying social or political theories or values. In order to elucidate these concepts one might have to criticize the underlying theory or values and make certain restrictions on the use of the concept that were justified in terms of the theoretical or practical considerations.

In my conclusion to Chapter 3 I suggested that it was possible to understand the modern theory of causality in a very general way, one quite different from the way advocates and critics of the theory usually understand it. I proposed that it be understood either as a methodological rule guiding empirical research that advocates looking for policy considerations as the basis of all legal causal judgments or as a normative rule that advocates that all legal causal judgments should be based directly or indirectly on policy considerations. In particular, I suggested that one might consider that the fact, if it is fact, that common sense causal notions play a dominant role in legal causality is based or should be based on policy considerations. Hart and Honoré in the second edition seem to admit that the use of common sense causal principles as a support and limit of legal responsibility rests on policy considerations. For example, they argue that basing legal responsibility on such notions preserves an individual's sense of himself or herself as a distinct person, which, they claim, is important for furthering the individual's sense of respect of self and others.[11] This suggests that Hart and Honoré might well find my reformulation of the modern theory congenial.

It is clear then that Hart's views continue to change and develop. We may venture to hope that they will develop even further along the lines recommended here and that Hart will offer further second thoughts and revisions of his philosophy in the coming years. If he does, they will certainly continue to inspire his admirers and challenge his critics as his views have done over three decades.

Notes and Index

Notes

Introduction

1. I rely here on Neil MacCormick's extensive biographical material. See Neil MacCormick, *H. L. A. Hart* (Stanford, Calif.: Stanford University Press, 1981), pp. 1–8.

2. See Marshall Cohen, "Herbert Lionel Adolphus Hart," in *The Encyclopedia of Philosophy*, ed. Paul Edwards (New York: Macmillan and Free Press, 1967), vol. 3, pp. 417–418; William Twining, "Academic Law and Legal Philosophy: The Significance of Herbert Hart," *Law Quarterly Review* 95 (1979): 557–580; Clifford L. Pannam, "Professor Hart and Analytic Jurisprudence," *Journal of Legal Education* 16 (1964): 379–404; Robert S. Summers, "The New Analytical Jurists," *New York University Law Review* 41 (1966): 861–896.

3. H. L. A. Hart, "Philosophy of Law and Jurisprudence in Britain (1945–1952)," *American Journal of Comparative Law* 2 (1953): 361.

4. Hart is referring to Glanville Williams' paper, "International Law and the Controversy Concerning the Word 'Law,'" *British Yearbook of International Law* 22 (1945): 146.

5. Hart, "Philosophy of Law and Jurisprudence in Britain (1945–1952)," p. 364.

6. William Twining, "Academic Law and Legal Philosophy," p. 576.

7. The classification of Hart as an ordinary language philosopher seems justified on at least two grounds. First, he thought of himself as being concerned with the analysis of ordinary language relevant to the law (see Hart, "Philosophy of Law and Legal Philosophy," p. 576). Second, commentators have stressed the strong influence of Oxford-style philosophizing on Hart (see, for example, Twining, "Academic Law and Legal Philosophy," and Cohen, "Herbert Lionel Adolphus Hart"), and this type of philosophizing was concerned, at least in large part, with the analysis of ordinary language. However, like many classifications, this one is misleading unless it is properly qualified. In Hart's work as a whole there is very little analysis that is entirely of ordinary language; moreover, he was influenced not only by J. L. Austin and other Oxford philosophers but by John Austin, the nineteenth-century jurist, and Hans Kelsen. Still, I believe that this classification when properly qualified illuminates more than it misleads and, therefore, I will continue to use it.

8. Strictly speaking I will consider here the analysis by Hart and A. M. Honoré, the joint authors of *Causation in the Law*. I believe I am justified in including this analysis, not because Hart was the dominant author in the book, but because the principal themes in it represent their shared views. Consequently, it is possible to say that Hart embraced those views and to hold him accountable for problems with them. Of course, Honoré can also be held accountable for them.

CHAPTER 1

1. Hints of some aspects of the views contained in *The Concept of Law* are to be found in Hart's earlier work. In 1955, his Inaugural Lecture, "Theory and Definition in Jurisprudence," was subjected to detailed criticism by Jonathan Cohen in an Aristotelian Society symposium. Hart attempted to answer these criticisms in the same symposium and, in the process of doing so, presented a sketch of an analysis of the concept of a legal system. See "Symposium: Theory and Definition in Jurisprudence," *Proceedings of the Aristotelian Society*, supp. 29 (1955): 213–264.

In criticizing Hart, Cohen claims that there are three criteria necessary for legal rules but not for other kinds of rules. Hart calls these three criteria "possibilities of argument," "sanction," and "universality of scope." Hart argues that although these criteria are important he is "not sure that in the case of concepts so complex as that of a legal system we can pick out any characteristics, save the most obvious and uninteresting ones, and say they are necessary." Hart goes on to argue (*ibid.*, pp. 251–252):

> Much of the tiresome logomachy over whether or not international law or primitive law is really law has sprung from the effort to find a considerable set of necessary criteria for the application of the expression "legal system." Whereas I think that all that can be found are a set of criteria of which a few are obviously necessary (e.g., there must be rules) but the rest form a sub-set of criteria of which everything called a legal system satisfies some but only *standard* or *normal* cases satisfy all.

Hart proceeds to list the main elements that are present in the standard case of a municipal legal system of an advanced modern society (*ibid.*, p. 252):

(1) Courts.
(2) Rules conferring jurisdiction on Courts and providing for the appointment and conditions of tenure of judicial office.
(3) Rules of procedure for Courts.
(4) Rules of Evidence for Courts.
(5) Substantive civil laws.
(6) Substantive criminal laws.
(7) A Legislature.
(8) Constitutional rules providing criteria valid for the system for the identification of rules of the system (sources of law).
(9) Sanctions.
(10) Possibility of Argument.
(11) Universality of Scope.

In a footnote (*ibid.*, p. 252n.9) Hart mentions that there are

> several additions to this list that could plausibly be made, e.g., it may be said that the criminal laws of a legal system must contain certain minimum vetoes against the use of personal violence and that either the criminal or civil laws or both must provide for a minimum form of property or possession in the sense of a right to exclude others from material objects at certain times for certain purposes.

Here we see Hart bringing in the idea of minimum content of natural law, to be discussed in Chapter 6, for the first time. He concludes by saying, "in the case of a concept so complex as a legal system we can do no more than identify the conditions present in a standard or paradigm case and consider under what circumstances the removal of any one of these conditions would render the whole pointless or absurd" (*ibid.*, p. 253).

In the context of Cohen's criticism of Hart and Hart's defense of his own position it is clear that the necessary criteria involved are *logically* necessary. Hart's counterexample of "men were more like angels than they are" makes it clear he attempts to refute Cohen's view that sanctions are necessary for a legal system by referring to men in some logically possible world. As we will see in Chapter 6 when Hart's natural law theory is considered, Hart believes that, although such men are logically possible, in our world at least it is a truism that men are not angels. Further, he believes that it is a natural (but not logical) necessity that there must be sanctions. It would seem then that, at least as far as sanctions are concerned, Hart could well agree with Cohen that the existence of sanctions is a necessary condition of "a legal system's existence" if "necessary" does not mean logical necessity but natural or factual necessity.

In the Hart-Fuller debate of 1958, Hart, in capsule form, brought up some of the criticisms of Austin's theory that he would develop at greater length three years later. He also hinted at one of his most significant positive theses; see H. L. A. Hart, "Positivism and the Separation of Law and Morals," *Harvard Law Review* 71 (1958): 593–629. In *The Concept of Law* (Oxford: Clarendon Press, 1961), Hart argues that in understanding a legal system a key concept is the concept of a secondary rule. In the Hart-Fuller debate he stresses that the "key to the science of jurisprudence" is not, as Austin claimed, the notion of a command but rather fundamentally accepted rules "specifying the essential lawmaking procedures" (Hart, "Positivism and the Separation of Law and Morals," p. 603). Here we see Hart introducing a notion that he uses three years later in *The Concept of Law*.

Hart also points out a more "radical defect" in Austin's command theory, namely that this theory fails to provide any account of laws that enable people to create "structures of rights and duties." Hart gives examples of rules enabling individuals to "make contracts, wills, and trusts, and generally to mould their legal relations with others" (*ibid.*, p. 604). Here Hart seems to be introducing another sense of what he will later call secondary rules.

2. Hart, *The Concept of Law*, p. 18. Hart is careful to distinguish the Austinian model that he criticized from Austin's actual views primarily found in *The Province of Jurisprudence Determined* (1832); see *The Concept of Law*, pp. 236–237. For recent attempts to defend an Austinian theory of law against the sort of criticisms raised by Hart see Robert Ladenson, "In Defense of a Hobbesian Conception of Law," *Philosophy and Public Affairs* 9 (1980): 134–159; Richard Foley, "Illegal Behavior," *Law and Philosophy* 1 (1982): 131–158; Russell Hardin, "Sanction and Obligation," *Monist* 68 (1985): 403–418; David Lyons, *Ethics and the Rule of Law* (Cambridge, Eng.: Cambridge University Press, 1984), pp. 43–48.

3. Hart and most of his commentators use masculine pronouns. When paraphrasing Hart and these commentators I will do so as well. When I speak for myself I will use expressions such as "he or she" or "him or her."

4. See Hans Kelsen, *General Theory of Law and State*, trans. Anders Wedberg (New York: Russell and Russell, 1961), and Martin P. Golding "Hans Kelsen," in *The Encyclopedia of Philosophy*, ed. Paul Edwards (New York: Macmillan and Free Press, 1967), vol. 4, pp. 328-329.

5. Hart, *The Concept of Law*, pp. 245-246, 35-41.

6. Hart offers further analysis and criticism of Kelsen in some of his later writings. See "Kelsen Visited" and "Kelsen's Doctrine of the Unity of Law," reprinted in H. L. A. Hart, *Essays in Jurisprudence and Philosophy* (Oxford: Clarendon Press, 1983).

7. Although Raz maintains that Hart's analysis does not apply to complex social rules, he holds that it provides a starting point for the analysis of other types of rules. See Joseph Raz, *The Concept of a Legal System* (Oxford: Clarendon Press, 1980), p. 149. However, if the criticism developed here is correct, even this modest goal for Hart's analysis seems mistaken.

8. In my treatment of Hart's theory of legal obligation I am indebted here and elsewhere in this chapter to Barry Hoffmaster, "Professor Hart on Legal Obligation," *Georgia Law Review* 11 (1977): 1303-1324.

9. What I mean by the distinction between descriptive and normative obligation can be further explained by invoking the distinction between positive and critical morality that Hart uses in *Law, Liberty, and Morality* (New York: Vintage Books, 1966), p. 20. Positive morality is simply the morality actually accepted and shared by a given social group whereas critical morality consists of general moral principles used in the criticism of positive morality as well as other institutions. As I understand Hart's account of obligation in terms of social rules, it is an account of the concept of obligation found in positive morality. In this sense it is purely descriptive. He does not attempt to give an account of normative obligation—that is, obligation found in critical morality—in terms of social rules. This same distinction between positive and critical morality is suggested in *The Concept of Law*, pp. 165, 178. My interpretation of Hart on this point should be contrasted with Lyons, *Ethics and the Rule of Law*, pp. 52-53, and Joseph Raz, *Practical Reason and Norms* (London: Hutchinson, 1975), pp. 50-58.

10. Richard Bernstein, "Professor Hart on Rules of Obligation," *Mind* 73 (1964): 563-566.

11. *Ibid.*, p. 564.

12. *Ibid.*

13. See Max Weber, *The Theory of Social and Economic Organization* (New York: Free Press, 1947).

14. Hart, *The Concept of Law*, p. 242.

15. Peter Winch, *The Idea of a Social Science* (London: Routledge and Kegan Paul, 1958). For a critique of the major theses of this book see Michael Martin, "Winch on Philosophy, Social Science, and Explanation," *Philosophical Forum* 23 (1966): 29-41.

16. Hart, *The Concept of Law*, pp. 86-89.

17. My analysis here should be compared with Neil MacCormick's discussion of Hart's hermeneutic method in *H. L. A. Hart* (Stanford, Calif.: Stanford University Press, 1981), pp. 33-40.

18. Failure to distinguish the as if evaluative internal point of view and the standard

evaluative internal point of view is perhaps the basis for Harris' misleading contention that Hart's internal point of view refers only to external behavior. See J. W. Harris, *Law and Legal Science* (Oxford: Clarendon Press, 1979), pp. 56–57.

19. Hart, *The Concept of Law*, p. 99.

20. I am indebted here to John D. Hodson in "Hart on the Internal Aspects of Rules," *Archiv für Rechts und Sozialphilosophie* 62 (1976): 381–399.

21. I have argued elsewhere for the necessity of theory in the social sciences that transcends the point of view of a social actor. See Michael Martin, *Social Science and Philosophical Analysis: Essays in Philosophy of Social Science* (Washington, D.C.: University Press of America, 1978), essays 6, 13, 17, and 23.

22. Donald Black, *The Behavior of Law* (New York: Academic Press, 1976).

23. *Ibid.*, p. 7.

24. *Ibid.*, p. 13.

25. Hart, *The Concept of Law*, p. vii.

26. *Ibid.*

27. J. L. Austin, "A Plea for Excuses," in Austin, *Philosophical Papers*, ed. J. O. Urmson and G. J. Warnock (Oxford: Clarendon Press, 1961), p. 133.

28. MacCormick, *H. L. A. Hart*, p. 36.

29. *Ibid.*, p. 37.

30. In fact, as I show in the Conclusion, in Hart's latest statement on the appropriate explanatory stance to take toward a legal system, he takes a very strong position, arguing that "the methodology of the empirical sciences is useless" in understanding rule-governed behavior and the only appropriate approach is the hermeneutic method. See Hart, *Essays in Jurisprudence and Philosophy*, p. 13.

31. Martin Krygier, "*The Concept of Law* and Social Theory," *Oxford Journal of Legal Studies* 2 (1982): 157.

32. Hart, *The Concept of Law*, p. 39.

33. Krygier, "*The Concept of Law* and Social Theory," p. 162.

34. *Ibid.*, p. 167.

35. Hart, *The Concept of Law*, pp. 78–79.

36. *Ibid.*, p. 92.

37. For further analysis of the concept of secondary rules see Raz, *The Concept of a Legal System*, and C. F. H. Tapper, "Powers and Secondary Rules of Change," in *Oxford Essays in Jurisprudence*, ed. A. W. B. Simpson (2nd ser.; Oxford: Clarendon Press, 1973).

38. Hart, *The Concept of Law*, p. 91.

39. *Ibid.*, p. 244.

40. *Ibid.*

41. For further criticisms of Hart's theory of differences between pre-legal and legal systems see Krygier, "*The Concept of Law* and Social Theory," pp. 171–178.

42. Hart, *The Concept of Law*, p. 100.

43. *Ibid.*, p. 101.

44. *Ibid.*, p. 103.

45. *Ibid.*, p. 104.

46. *Ibid.*, p. 105.

47. Raz, *The Concept of a Legal System*, p. 200, argues that there is no reason to suppose that there is only one rule of recognition in every legal system. He maintains that since a rule of recognition is directed to legal officials there may be different rules of recognition directed to different kinds of officials. However, it is unclear why one should suppose that there is more than one rule directed to different officials rather than one rule with several parts, each part directed to different officials. Clearly we have a problem of the individuation of rules of recognition, a problem that may have no easy solution. Although Raz discusses the problem of the individuation of laws in general terms in his book, I cannot see that he has provided a clear answer to the special problem of the individuation of rules of recognition. See also Raz, *Practical Reason and Norms*, pp. 146–148.

48. Hart, *The Concept of Law*, p. 113.

49. MacCormick, *H. L. A. Hart*, p. 109.

50. *Ibid.*, p. 119.

51. M. S. Blackman, "Hart's Idea of Obligation and His Concept of Law," *South African Law Journal* 94 (1977): 415–436.

52. Hart, *The Concept of Law*, p. 113.

53. H. L. A. Hart, "Definition and Theory in Jurisprudence," in Hart, *Essays in Jurisprudence and Philosophy*.

54. Rolf Sartorius, "Hart's Concept of Law," in *More Essays in Legal Philosophy*, ed. Robert S. Summers (Berkeley: University of California Press, 1971), p. 139.

55. See note 1 and Hart, "Positivism and the Separation of Law and Morals," p. 623. In his 1955 reply to Cohen, Hart states criteria that make up a set of *defining* criteria for a municipal legal system of an advanced modern society. He cites some of these criteria in 1958 in his *Harvard Law Review* paper when he argues that it is a "natural necessity" that a legal system have a certain minimum moral content. Hart's 1958 position is elaborated on in 1961 in *The Concept of Law*, where Hart again cites some of these criteria as constituting part of the minimum content of natural law. Since most of Hart's 1955 defining criteria clearly form the basis of his explication of a legal system in his later writing, without an explicit disavowal from Hart, one can assume that the minimum content of natural law remained part of that basis as well.

56. I am indebted in what follows to Note, "Hart, Austin, and the Concept of a Legal System: The Primacy of Sanctions," *Yale Law Journal* 84 (1975): 584–607. For further criticisms of Hart's attempt to distinguish morality from law see Kenneth A. Warner, "The Concept of Legal Obligation and the Separation of Law and Morality in H. L. A. Hart," *Juridical Review* 30 (1985): 69–84.

57. For example, Hart speaks of "an official monopoly of 'sanction'" (*The Concept of Law*, p. 91) and "centralized official 'sanctions'" (*The Concept of Law*, p. 95).

58. Sartorius, "Hart's Concept of Law," pp. 142–144.

59. See Michael Payne, "Hart's Concept of a Legal System," *William and Mary Law Review* 18 (1976): 287–319.

60. See note 1.

61. See note 1.

62. Cf. Raz, *Practical Reason and Norms*, pp. 158–159. Raz argues that a sanctionless legal system is logically possible but humanly impossible. As I will suggest in Chapter 6, it is an open question whether such a system is humanly possible.

CHAPTER 2

1. H. L. A. Hart, "Positivism and the Separation of Law and Morals," *Harvard Law Review* 71 (1958): 593–629, reprinted in Hart, *Essays in Jurisprudence and Philosophy* (Oxford: Clarendon Press, 1983), pp. 49–87.

2. *Ibid.*, pp. 628–629.

3. *Ibid.*, p. 629.

4. H. L. A. Hart, *The Concept of Law* (Oxford: Clarendon Press, 1961), chap. 7.

5. *Ibid.*, p. 124.

6. *Ibid.*, p. 131.

7. H. L. A. Hart, "Problems of Philosophy of Law," in *The Encyclopedia of Philosophy*, ed. Paul Edwards (New York: Macmillan and Free Press, 1967), vol. 6, pp. 264–276, reprinted in Hart, *Essays in Jurisprudence and Philosophy*, pp. 88–119.

8. *Ibid.*, p. 271.

9. *Ibid.*

10. *Ibid.*

11. *Ibid.*

12. H. L. A. Hart, "Law in the Perspective of Philosophy: 1776–1976," *New York University Law Review* 51 (1976): 551, reprinted in Hart, *Essays in Jurisprudence and Philosophy*, p. 157.

13. Rolf Sartorius, "Social Policy and Judicial Legislation," *American Philosophical Quarterly* 8 (1971): 160.

14. Ronald Dworkin, *Taking Rights Seriously* (Cambridge, Mass.: Harvard University Press, 1978), p. 33. Dworkin introduces the distinctions of weak and strong discretion, not to clarify Hart's earlier and later views on judicial interpretation, but to distinguish his own views from what he takes to be Hart's views. However, as I indicate, Hart was committed to the position of strong judicial discretion only in his early work.

15. See Joseph Horovitz, *Law and Logic: A Critical Account of Legal Argument* (New York: Springer-Verlag, 1972), p. 177.

16. *Ibid.*, p. 178.

17. Hart, *The Concept of Law*, pp. 124–125.

18. *Ibid.*, p. 125.

19. *Ibid.*, pp. 126–127.

20. *Ibid.*, p. 125.

21. *Ibid.*, p. 127.

22. *Ibid.*, pp. 127–128.

23. *Ibid.*, p. 132.

24. *Ibid.*, p. 126. My reinterpretation of legal formalism is indebted to Horovitz, *Law and Logic*.

25. Hart, *The Concept of Law*, p. 133. For a recent attempt to defend rule skepticism along different lines from the ones taken here see Andrew Altman, "Legal Realism, Critical Legal Studies, and Dworkin, "*Philosophy and Public Affairs* 15 (1986): 205–235.

26. See Horovitz, *Law and Logic*.

27. Hart, *The Concept of Law*, p. 137.

28. Dworkin, *Taking Rights Seriously*, pp. 81–130.

29. *Ibid.*, p. 23.

30. *Ibid.*, p. 107.

31. See Ronald Dworkin, "No Right Answer?," in *Law, Morality and Society: Essays in Honour of H. L. A. Hart*, ed. P. M. S. Hacker and J. Raz (Oxford: Clarendon Press, 1977), pp. 58–84. In this paper Dworkin qualifies his view to some extent, maintaining that on very rare occasions the arguments for plaintiff and defendant will be in perfect balance.

32. Dworkin, *Taking Rights Seriously*, pp. 39–45.

33. *Ibid.*, p. 40.

34. Hart, *The Concept of Law*, p. 92, quoted by Dworkin in *Taking Rights Seriously*, pp. 40–41.

35. Dworkin, *Taking Rights Seriously*, p. 98.

36. See Genaro R. Carrio, "Professor Dworkin's Views on Legal Positivism," *Indiana Law Journal* 55 (1979–1980): 234–239.

37. See, for example, David A. J. Richards, "Taking *Taking Rights Seriously* Seriously: Reflections on Dworkin and the American Revival of Natural Law," *New York University Law Review* 52 (1977): 1280–1292; E. Phillip Soper, "Legal Theory and the Obligation of a Judge: The Hart/Dworkin Dispute," *Michigan Law Review* 75 (1977): 473–518, reprinted with Dworkin's reply in *Ronald Dworkin and Contemporary Jurisprudence*, ed. Marshall Cohen (Totowa, N.J.: Rowman and Allanheld, 1986), pp. 3–27, 247–252.

38. Neil MacCormick, *H. L. A. Hart* (Stanford, Calif.: Stanford University Press, 1981), pp. 40–42.

39. Ronald Dworkin, review of Robert M. Cover, *Justice Accused: Anti-slavery and the Judicial Process, Times Literary Supplement*, Dec. 5, 1975, p. 1437. Others besides Hart have been skeptical of the one right answer thesis. See A. D. Woozley, "No Right Answer," *Philosophical Quarterly* 29 (1979): 25–34, reprinted with Dworkin's reply in Cohen, ed., *Ronald Dworkin and Contemporary Jurisprudence*, pp. 173–181, 275–278.

40. H. L. A. Hart, "Law in the Perspective of Philosophy: 1776–1976," p. 550, reprinted in Hart, *Essays in Jurisprudence and Philosophy*, p. 157.

41. *Ibid.*, n. 62.

42. See W. J. Waluchow, "Herculean Positivism," *Oxford Journal of Legal Studies* 5 (1985): 187–210.

43. Cf. Jules L. Coleman, "Negative and Positive Positivism," *Journal of Legal Studies* 11 (1982): 139–164, reprinted with Dworkin's reply in Cohen, ed., *Ronald Dworkin and Contemporary Jurisprudence*, pp. 28–48, 252–254; Charles Silver, "Negative Positivism and the Hard Facts of Life," *Monist* 68 (1985): 347–363; Joseph Raz, "Authority, Law and Morality," *Monist* 68 (1985): 295–324.

44. Cf. Robert S. Summers, "Professor MacCormick on H. L. A. Hart's Legal Theory," *American Journal of Comparative Law* 31 (1983): 483.

45. Indeed, Hart *may* hold such a view since his natural law theory with minimum content suggests that he may hold that some moral criteria are part of every rule of recognition; see Chapter 7. If this is Hart's position, there may be some difficulty in distinguishing Hart's positivism from some natural law theories that do not deny that some laws

could be evil. See David Lyons, "Moral Aspects of Legal Theory," *Midwest Studies in Philosophy* 7 (1982), reprinted in part with Dworkin's reply in Cohen, ed., *Ronald Dworkin and Contemporary Jurisprudence* in "Authority, Law and Morality," pp. 49–62. Raz argues that it is possible for there to be a necessary connection between morality and law and yet for the truth conditions of the rule of recognition not to contain any moral criteria. In particular, he argues that Hart holds (a) that there is a necessary relation between law and morality and yet (b) that the existence of a law can be determined by reference to social facts alone. I argue in Chapter 7 that Hart holds (a) but I am not convinced that he holds (b).

46. Hart, *The Concept of Law*, p. 92, quoted by Dworkin in *Taking Rights Seriously*, pp. 40–41. Whether Hart here is confusing the epistemic and semantic senses of a rule of recognition distinguished by Coleman, in "Negative and Positive Positivism," is not clear. In the semantic sense a rule of recognition specifies the conditions that a norm must satisfy to be a law; in the epistemic sense a rule of recognition is a standard that one can use to identify or discover a community's law. These may not be the same rules. A semantic rule SR of recognition may be: L is a law in system S IFF L is enacted by the legislature. An epistemic rule ER may be: if L is listed in the Official Monthly Record entitled "Laws on the Books," L is a law of S. Notice that ER may not be an infallible rule and may provide at best a probable indication of whether L is a law of S according to SR. Thus it is quite possible for one's knowledge of whether L is a law of S to be uncertain although one has perfect knowledge that SR is the rule of recognition in the semantic sense.

47. Sartorius, "Social Policy and Judicial Legislation," pp. 155–156.

48. Dworkin, *Taking Rights Seriously*, pp. 58–68.

49. This would only be a partial test since by itself it would not distinguish whether a judge viewed R from the standard evaluative point of view or from the as if evaluative point of view. In order to make this further distinction one would have to determine whether the hypothesis explained certain behaviors of the judge outside of judicial contexts.

50. H. L. A. Hart, "American Jurisprudence Through English Eyes: The Nightmare and the Noble Dream," *Georgia Law Review* 11 (1977): 986, reprinted in Hart, *Essays in Jurisprudence and Philosophy*, p. 141.

51. *Ibid.*, n. 42.

52. *Ibid.*, p. 986.

53. See Richards, "Taking *Taking Rights Seriously* Seriously," pp. 1306–1313; Kent Greenawalt, "Policy, Rights, and Judicial Decision," *Georgia Law Review* 11 (1977): 991–1172, reprinted in part with Dworkin's reply in Cohen, ed., *Ronald Dworkin and Contemporary Jurisprudence*, pp. 88–118, 263–268. See also Dworkin's reply to Richards and Greenawalt in *Taking Rights Seriously*, pp. 279–368.

54. See H. L. A. Hart, "Between Utility and Rights," *Columbia Law Review* 79 (1974): 828–846, reprinted in Hart, *Essays in Jurisprudence and Philosophy*, pp. 208–222, and reprinted with Dworkin's reply in Cohen, ed., *Ronald Dworkin and Contemporary Jurisprudence*, pp. 214–216, 282–291.

55. See Greenawalt, "Policy, Rights, and Judicial Decision," pp. 1004–1010, and Dworkin's replies in Cohen, ed., *Ronald Dworkin and Contemporary Jurisprudence*, pp. 263–268, and Dworkin, *Taking Rights Seriously*, pp. 291–368.

Chapter 3

1. H. L. A. Hart and A. M. Honoré, *Causation in the Law* (Oxford: Clarendon Press, 1959). This book was preceded by a three-part article by Hart and Honoré; see H. L. A. Hart and A. M. Honoré, "Causation in the Law," *Law Quarterly Review* 72 (1956): 58–90, 260–281, 398–417. They say in the preface to *Causation in the Law* (p. v.): "this book is however concerned with many aspects of the subject outside the scope of those articles [in the *Law Quarterly Review*] and diverges from them at certain points where further acquaintance with the complexities of the subject forced us to revise our views." In this chapter I will be concerned only with the more mature thought found in their book. Throughout this chapter I cite the first edition of *Causation in the Law*. As I make clear in the Conclusion to this book, the revisions in the second edition (1985) do not affect the major theses of this chapter.

2. H. L. A. Hart, *The Concept of Law* (Oxford: Clarendon Press, 1961), p. 125.

3. Hart and Honoré, *Causation in the Law*, p. 9.

4. *Ibid.*, p. 10.

5. *Ibid.*, p. 20.

6. *Ibid.*, p. 23.

7. *Ibid.*, p. 261.

8. *Ibid.*, p. 91.

9. *Ibid.*, pp. 84–85.

10. This idea was also used by J. L. Austin in "A Plea for Excuses," in Austin, *Philosophical Papers*, ed. J. O. Urmson and G. J. Warnock (Oxford: Clarendon Press, 1961), p. 150. This paper was Austin's presidential address to the Aristotelian Society in 1956. It is reasonable to suppose that Austin's idea influenced Hart and Honoré although they do not acknowledge a debt to Austin.

11. Hart and Honoré, *Causation in the Law*, p. 34.

12. Samuel Gorovitz, "Causal Judgments and Causal Explanations," *Journal of Philosophy* 62 (1965): 697–711.

13. Hart and Honoré, *Causation in the Law*, p. 11.

14. *Ibid.*, pp. 160–161.

15. *Ibid.*, p. 161.

16. *Ibid.*

17. *Ibid.*, p. 39.

18. *Ibid.*

19. *Ibid.*, pp. 48–52.

20. *Alexander v. The Town of New Castle*, 17 N.E. 200 (Ind. 1888).

21. *Cole v. German Savings and Loan Society*, 124 F. 113 (1903).

22. *Smith v. State*, 50 Ark. 545, 8 S.W. 941 (1888).

23. *People v. Elder*, 100 Mich. 515, 59 N.W. 237 (1894).

24. *Toledo and Ohio Central R. Co. v. Kibler and Co.*, 119 N.E. 733 (Ohio 1918).

25. *Carslogie S.S. Co. v. Royal Norwegian Government*, A.C. 292 (1952).

26. *Smith v. Kaye*, 20 T.L.R. 261 (1904).

27. Hart and Honoré, *Causation in the Law*, p. 176.

28. *Stansbie v. Troman*, 2 K.B. 48 (1948).

29. Hart and Honoré, *Causation in the Law*, p. 181.

30. *Ibid.*, p. 179.

31. *Ryan v. New York Central R. Co.*, 35 N.Y. 210, 91 Am. Dec. 9 (1886).

32. P. H. Nowell-Smith, "Critical Notice," *Mind* 70 (1961): 553–561.

33. *Ibid.*, p. 560.

34. *Ibid.*

35. *Ibid.*

36. *Ibid.*

37. *Ibid.*, p. 561.

38. Hart and Honoré, *Causation in the Law*, p. 151, n. 6.

39. *Ibid.*, p. 162.

40. *Ibid.*

41. *Ibid.*, p. 247.

42. Nowell-Smith, "Critical Notice," p. 561.

43. *Ibid.*

44. *Ibid.*

45. See Hart and Honoré, *Causation in the Law*, pp. 294–295.

46. *Ibid.*, p. 167.

47. Michael Martin, "Causal Importance and Objectivity," in Martin, *Social Science and Philosophical Analysis: Essays in Philosophy of Social Science* (Washington, D.C.: University Press of America, 1978), pp. 159–170.

48. M. P. Golding, "Causation in the Law," *Journal of Philosophy* 59 (1962): 90.

49. John H. Mansfield, "Hart and Honoré, *Causation in the Law*—A Comment," *Vanderbilt Law Review* 17 (1964): 490–492.

50. Feinberg attempts to assimilate Hart and Honoré's distinction to his own scheme. See Joel Feinberg, "Causing Voluntary Action—Rejoinders," in *Metaphysics and Explanation*, ed. W. H. Capitan and D. D. Merrill (Pittsburgh: University of Pittsburgh Press, 1966), pp. 58–59. Feinberg distinguishes the explanatory and non-explanatory standpoint. Hart and Honoré's distinction between the explanatory and the attributive context can be understood, according to Feinberg, as a distinction between the explanatory standpoint and one type of non-explanatory standpoint. But it is doubtful that Hart and Honoré's explanatory context is as liberal as Feinberg's explanatory standpoint. In particular, Feinberg does not show that in Hart and Honoré's scheme there is a confirmatory instance to H_2.

51. Hart and Honoré, *Causation in the Law*, p. 46.

52. For a critique of this view see Ernest Nagel, *The Structure of Science* (New York: Harcourt, Brace and World, 1961), pp. 480–485; Michael Martin, "Explanation in Social Science: Some Recent Work," in Martin, *Social Science and Philosophical Analysis*, pp. 195–215.

53. Hart and Honoré, *Causation in the Law*, p. 52.

54. *Ibid.*, p. 53.

55. J. L. Mackie, *The Cement of the Universe* (Oxford: Clarendon Press, 1980), chap. 5.

56. Feinberg, "Causing Voluntary Action," pp. 37–38.

57. *Ibid.*, pp. 31–32. According to Keith Lehrer in his comments to Feinberg's paper

("Comments," in *Metaphysics and Explanation*, ed. Capitan and Merrill, pp. 52–54), Feinberg's counterexamples do not work since human intervention negatives causal attribution, not causal explanation. But, as Feinberg argues in his rejoinder ("Causing Voluntary Action," p. 59), his counterexamples also work against attributive causal judgments. Further, as I have argued above, it looks like it is impossible to find a case in Hart and Honoré's scheme in which there are attributive causal judgments that are not explanatory.

CHAPTER 4

1. H. L. A. Hart, "The Ascription of Responsibility and Rights," in *Logic and Language*, ed. Antony Flew (1st and 2nd ser.; Garden City, N.Y.: Doubleday, 1965), pp. 151–173, first published in *Proceedings of the Aristotelian Society* 49 (1948–1949): 171–194. For a critique of Hart's view with a different emphasis than the one given below see G. P. Baker, "Defeasibility and Meaning," in *Law, Morality and Society: Essays in Honour of H. L. A. Hart*, ed. P. M. S. Hacker and Joseph Raz (Oxford: Clarendon Press, 1977), pp. 26–57.

2. Hart, "The Ascription of Responsibility and Rights," p. 151.

3. H. L. A. Hart, *Punishment and Responsibility: Essays in the Philosophy of Law* (Oxford: Clarendon Press, 1968), p. v. Hart cites two papers as examples of criticisms that are justified: P. T. Geach, "Ascriptivism," *Philosophical Review* 69 (1960): 221, and George Pitcher, "Hart on Action and Responsibility," *Philosophical Review* 69 (1960): 226. These two criticisms do not deal with Hart's account of legal definition and do not entail in any straightforward way that his theory of legal definition is in error.

4. Ludwig Wittgenstein, *Philosophical Investigations*, trans. G. E. M. Anscombe (Oxford: Basil Blackwell, 1953); Gilbert Ryle, *Dilemmas* (London, Eng.: Cambridge University Press, 1954). See also Gilbert Ryle's earlier "Systematically Misleading Expressions," *Aristotelian Society Proceedings* 32 (1931–1932): 139–170.

5. Hart cites J. L. Austin's "Other Minds," *Proceedings of the Aristotelian Society* supp. 20 (1946): 169–174. See Hart, "The Ascription of Responsibility and Rights," p. 165.

6. See, for example, J. O. Urmson, *Philosophical Analysis: Its Development Between the Two Wars* (Oxford: Clarendon Press, 1956); John Passmore, *A Hundred Years of Philosophy* (London: Gerald Duckworth, 1957), chaps. 15–18.

7. Hart, "The Ascription of Responsibility and Rights," p. 152.

8. *Ibid.*

9. *Ibid.*

10. *Ibid.*, p. 153.

11. *Ibid.*

12. *Ibid.*, p. 154.

13. *Ibid.*

14. *Ibid.*, p. 156.

15. *Ibid.*, p. 161.

16. *Ibid.*, p. 162.

17. *Ibid.*

18. *Ibid.*, p. 163.

19. *Ibid.*, pp. 159–160.
20. *Ibid.*, p. 158, n. 4.
21. *Ibid.*
22. *Ibid.*, pp. 161–162.
23. For this interpretation see Joseph Horovitz, *Law and Logic: A Critical Account of Legal Argument* (New York: Springer-Verlag, 1972), pp. 151–152.
24. *Ibid.*, pp. 154–155.
25. *Ibid.*
26. H. L. A. Hart, *Definition and Theory in Jurisprudence: An Inaugural Lecture* (lecture delivered before the University of Oxford on May 30, 1953; Oxford: Clarendon Press, 1953), reprinted in H. L. A. Hart, *Essays in Jurisprudence and Philosophy* (Oxford: Clarendon Press, 1983), pp. 21–48. See also Jonathan Cohen and H. L. A. Hart, "Symposium: Theory and Definition in Jurisprudence," *Proceedings of the Aristotelian Society* supp. 29 (1955): 213–264; Horovitz, *Law and Logic*, pp. 156–160; Edgar Bodenheimer, "Modern Analytic Jurisprudence and the Limits of Its Usefulness," *University of Pennsylvania Law Review* 104 (1956): 1080–1086; Carl A. Auerbach, "On Professor H. L. A. Hart's Definition and Theory in Jurisprudence," *Journal of Legal Education* 9 (1956): 39–51; Jose C. Laureta, "Linguistic Analysis and Law, Science and Policy: A Comparison of Method," *Philippine Law Journal* 39 (1964): 671–699; Comments, "Jurisprudence and the Nature of Language: Contrasting Views of Hart and Chomsky," *Washington Law Review* 42 (1967): 847–872; A. W. B. Simpson, "The Analysis of Legal Concepts," *Law Quarterly Review* 80 (1964): 535–558; P. M. S. Hacker, "Definition in Jurisprudence," *Philosophical Quarterly* 19 (1969): 343–347.
27. Hart, "Definition and Theory in Jurisprudence," in Hart, *Essays in Jurisprudence and Philosophy*, p. 23.
28. *Ibid.*
29. *Ibid.*, p. 25.
30. *Ibid.*, p. 21.
31. Wittgenstein, *Philosophical Investigations.*
32. J. L. Austin, "The Meaning of a Word," in Austin, *Philosophical Papers*, ed. J. O. Urmson and G. J. Warnock (Oxford: Clarendon Press, 1961), pp. 23–43.
33. On this point see A. M. Quinton, "Contemporary British Philosophy," in *A Critical History of Western Philosophy*, ed. D. J. O'Connor (New York: Free Press, 1964), p. 553. For a Chomskian critique of Hart's unsystematic approach to language see Comments, "Jurisprudence and the Nature of Language."
34. Hart, "Definition and Theory in Jurisprudence," in Hart, *Essays in Jurisprudence and Philosophy*, p. 23.
35. *Ibid.*, p. 26.
36. Bertrand Russell, *The Principles of Mathematics* (2nd ed.; London: G. Allen, 1937), chap. 3.
37. H. L. A. Hart, "Analytical Jurisprudence in Mid-twentieth Century: A Reply to Professor Bodenheimer," *University of Pennsylvania Law Review* 105 (1957): 961.
38. Hart, "Definition and Theory in Jurisprudence," in Hart, *Essays in Jurisprudence and Philosophy*, p. 27.
39. *Ibid.*, p. 35, n. 15.

40. Cohen and Hart, "Symposium," p. 251.

41. Hart, "Definition and Theory in Jurisprudence," in Hart, *Essays in Jurisprudence and Philosophy*, p. 27.

42. Cohen and Hart, "Symposium," p. 252.

43. Hart, "Definition and Theory in Jurisprudence," in Hart, *Essays in Jurisprudence and Philosophy*, p. 35.

44. For this interpretation see Horovitz, *Law and Logic*, pp. 156–160.

45. Hart, "Definition and Theory in Jurisprudence," in Hart, *Essays in Jurisprudence and Philosophy*, p. 35, n. 15.

46. H. L. A. Hart, "Bentham on Legal Rights," in *Rights*, ed. David Lyons (Belmont, Calif.: Wadsworth, 1979), p. 140.

47. Hart, "Definition and Theory in Jurisprudence," p. 36, n. 15.

48. Hart, "Bentham on Legal Rights," p. 145. Wellman has cited other counterexamples to Hart's choice theory that seem to be independent of typical constitutional rights. For example, a citizen's duty to serve on a jury and a judge's duty to issue a legally valid judgment are rights of the citizen and judge respectively in many legal systems, yet they are not based on free choice. According to Wellman, the unifying element in all cases of legal rights is not free choice but an adversarial context. See Carl Wellman, *A Theory of Rights* (Totowa, N.J.: Rowman and Allanheld, 1985), pp. 61–80.

49. See Hacker, "Definition in Jurisprudence."

50. Hart, "Definition and Theory in Jurisprudence," p. 28.

51. Cohen and Hart, "Symposium," pp. 213–238.

52. See Chapter 2.

53. See Benson Mates, "On the Verification of Statements About Ordinary Language," in *Ordinary Language*, ed. V. C. Chappell (Englewood Cliffs, N.J.: Prentice-Hall, 1964), pp. 64–74, for some ideas about how claims about ordinary language could be confirmed. However, as Fodor and Katz point out, Mates' conception of empirical investigation in linguistics is not completely tenable and more adequate methods are available. See Jerry A. Fodor and Jerrold J. Katz, "The Availability of What We Say," *Philosophical Review* 72 (1963): 71, n. 30.

54. See Brenda Danet, "Language in the Legal Process," *Law and Society Review* 14 (1980): 445–564.

55. See Herman Tennessen, "Ordinary Language *in Memoriam*," *Inquiry* 8 (1965): 234. See also J. L. Austin, "A Plea for Excuses," in Austin, *Philosophical Papers*.

56. See Gilbert Ryle, "Ordinary Language," and Stanley Cavell, "Must We Mean What We Say?," reprinted in Chappell, ed., *Ordinary Language*, pp. 24–40, 75–112.

57. Cavell, "Must We Mean What We Say?," pp. 78–79.

58. Fodor and Katz, "The Availability of What We Say," p. 60.

59. *Ibid.*, pp. 60–61.

60. Tennessen, "Ordinary Language *in Memoriam*."

61. See Comments, "Jurisprudence and the Nature of Language."

62. See Jerry A. Fodor and Jerrold J. Katz, "What's Wrong with the Philosophy of Language?," *Inquiry* 5 (1962): 197–237.

63. H. L. A. Hart, *The Concept of Law* (Oxford: Clarendon Press, 1961), chap. 1.

The critical response to this work has been too extensive to note here. However, almost all the studies have neglected the theory of definition contained therein.

64. *Ibid.*, p. 13.

65. *Ibid.*, p. 15.

66. *Ibid.*, p. 16.

67. *Ibid.*, p. 204.

68. *Ibid.*, pp. 204–205.

69. *Ibid.*, p. 209.

70. *Ibid.*

71. *Ibid.*, p. 16.

72. *Ibid.*, p. 17.

73. Richard Robinson, *Definition* (Oxford: Clarendon Press, 1954), p. 3.

74. Hart, *The Concept of Law*, p. 234.

75. Whether a definition of law can be extracted from his writing is an issue that I have considered in Chapter 1. For an attempt to extract a definition of law from *The Concept of Law* see Rolf Sartorius, "Hart's Concept of Law," in *More Essays in Legal Philosophy*, ed. Robert S. Summers (Berkeley: University of California Press, 1971), pp. 131–161.

76. Hart, *The Concept of Law*, p. 16.

77. The idea of giving a rational reconstruction of the concept of law à la Carnap or Hempel was even in 1961 foreign to Hart's thinking. See Rudolf Carnap, *Logical Foundations of Probability* (Chicago: University of Chicago Press, 1962), pp. 576–577.

78. Hart, *The Concept of Law*, p. 14.

79. Baker, "Defeasibility and Meaning."

80. Michael Martin, *Social Science and Philosophical Analysis: Essays in Philosophy of Social Science* (Washington, D.C.: University Press of America, 1978), prt. 4.

81. There may, of course, be difficulties in providing a reductive analysis of some of Hart's particular legal concepts. I only wish to argue that Hart provides no general reasons for ruling out a reductive analysis. Robert Ladenson, "In Defense of a Hobbesian Conception of Law," *Philosophy and Public Affairs* 9 (1980): 158–159, argues that because of a circularity in Hart's definitions of the rule of recognition a reductive analysis is impossible. For a discussion of the problem of circularity see Chapter 1.

82. For details on these changes see Quinton, "Contemporary British Philosophy."

Chapter 5

1. H. L. A. Hart and A. M. Honoré, *Causation in the Law* (Oxford: Clarendon Press, 1959), p. 362.

2. *Ibid.*, p. 363.

3. H. L. A. Hart, *Punishment and Responsibility: Essays in the Philosophy of Law* (Oxford: Clarendon Press, 1968), p. 233.

4. *Ibid.*

5. *Ibid.*, p. 3.

6. *Ibid.*, p. 231.

7. *Ibid.*, p. 4.

8. See Antony Flew, "The Justification of Punishment," *Philosophy* 24 (1954): 291.

9. Hart, *Punishment and Responsibility*, p. 4. On this point see Robert A. Samek, "Punishment: A Postscript to Two Prolegomena," *Philosophy* 41 (1966): 218–219.

10. Hart, *Punishment and Responsibility*, p. 5.

11. *Ibid.*, p. 6.

12. *Ibid.*, p. 9.

13. *Ibid.*, pp. 8–11. See Ted Honderich, *Punishment, The Supposed Justifications* (Harmondsworth, Middlesex, Eng.: Penguin Books, 1984), pp. 165–170, for a critique and amendment of Hart's account of the general aim of punishment.

14. Hart, *Punishment and Responsibility*, p. 10. Goldman argues that it is impossible for a theory of punishments that combines retributivism and utilitarianism to succeed. The utilitarian part of Hart's theory cannot exclude excessive punishments while the retributivist part cannot allow that benefits should outweigh the cost of punishments. See Alan H. Goldman, "Toward a New Theory of Punishment," *Law and Philosophy* 1 (1982): 57–76.

15. Richard Wasserstrom, "H. L. A. Hart and the Doctrines of *Mens Rea* and Criminal Responsibility," *University of Chicago Law Review* 35 (1967): 109–110.

16. Hart, *Punishment and Responsibility*, p. 12.

17. *Ibid.*

18. *Ibid.*, p. 28. For a critique of Hart's assumption of voluntary responsibility and an alternative view see John R. Silber, "Being and Doing: A Study of Status Responsibility and Voluntary Responsibility," *University of Chicago Law Review* 35 (1967): 47–91.

19. H. L. A. Hart, "The Ascription of Responsibility and Rights," in *Logic and Language*, ed. Antony Flew (1st and 2nd ser.; Garden City, N.Y.: Doubleday, 1951), p. 159.

20. Hart, *Punishment and Responsibility*, p. 18.

21. *Ibid.*, p. 19.

22. D. F. Thompson, "Retribution and the Distribution of Punishment," *Philosophical Quarterly* 16 (1966): 59–63.

23. Hart, *Punishment and Responsibility*, p. 21.

24. *Ibid.*, pp. 36–38.

25. Wasserstrom, "H. L. A. Hart and the Doctrines of *Mens Rea* and Criminal Responsibility," p. 95.

26. Hart, *Punishment and Responsibility*, p. 38.

27. I say "seems" because it is not completely clear if Hart believes these rationales are meant to justify this contention or are separate utilitarian rationales. Wasserstrom, "H. L. A. Hart and the Doctrines of *Mens Rea* and Criminal Responsibility," p. 99, seems to suppose they are answers to the question why it is unjust to punish in the absence of a voluntary action. But Daniel Lyons, in "Is Hart's Rationale for Legal Excuses Workable?," *Dialogue* 8 (1969): 496–502, assumes that these rationales are separate utilitarian considerations.

28. Hart, *Punishment and Responsibility*, p. 47.

29. Cf. David Lyons, "On Sanctioning Excuses," *Journal of Philosophy* 66 (1969): 646–651.

30. See Lyons, "Is Hart's Rationale for Legal Excuses Workable?," p. 501. In addition, as Honderich argues, there are other gains in a system of excuses not mentioned by Hart. See Honderich, *Punishment*, p. 167.

31. Cf. Laurence D. Houlgate, "Excuses and the Criminal Law," *Southern Journal of Philosophy* 13 (1975): 187–195; Fred R. Berger, "Excuses and the Law," *Theoria* 31 (1965): 9–19.

32. See Hart, *Punishment and Responsibility*, pp. 113–135.

33. *Ibid.*, p. 134.

34. Cf. Wasserstrom, "H. L. A. Hart and the Doctrines of *Mens Rea* and Criminal Responsibility," pp. 102–104.

35. Hart, *Punishment and Responsibility*, pp. 178–180, 195–209.

36. *Ibid.*, p. 205.

37. *Ibid.*, p. 206.

38. *Ibid.*, p. 208.

39. *Ibid.*, p. 204.

40. *Ibid.*, p. 24.

41. *Ibid.*, p. 25.

42. *Ibid.*, p. 162.

43. *Ibid.*, p. 25.

44. *Ibid.*, p. 171. Hart does not explore in any systematic way the possibility of solving the problems of utilitarianism as a theory of punishment, not by introducing retributive elements into the theory, but by introducing a principle of equality as a principle of distributive justice. See Honderich, *Punishment, The Supposed Justifications*, p. 240, and Ted Honderich, "The Question of Well-being and the Principle of Equality," *Mind* 90 (1981): 481–504 for a more systematic treatment of this possibility.

45. Hart, *Punishment and Responsibility*, p. 237.

46. *Ibid.*, p. 79.

47. *Ibid.*, p. 72.

48. *Ibid.*

49. *Ibid.*, p. 83.

50. *Ibid.*

51. *Ibid.*

52. *Ibid.*, p. 84.

53. *Ibid.*, p. 85.

54. *Ibid.*

55. *Ibid.*

56. *Ibid.*, pp. 251–252.

57. See Hugo Adam Bedau, ed., *The Death Penalty in America* (3rd ed.: Oxford: Oxford University Press, 1982), pp. 93–185.

58. *Ibid.*, p. 97.

59. Hart, *Punishment and Responsibility*, p. 86.

60. *Ibid.*

61. *Ibid.*, p. 87.

62. *Ibid.*, p. 88.

63. W. J. Bowers and G. L. Pierce, "Deterrence or Brutalization: What Is the Effect of Executions?," *Crime and Delinquency* 26 (1980): 481, quoted in Bedau, ed., *The Death Penalty in America*, p. 99.

64. Hart, *Punishment and Responsibility*, p. 89.

65. *Ibid.*

66. *Ibid.*

67. Bedau, ed., *The Death Penalty in America*, pp. 65–92.

68. Hart, *Punishment and Responsibility*, p. 25. Hart does not consider constitutional-type arguments for or against the death penalty. See Raoul Berger, *Death Penalties* (Cambridge, Mass.: Harvard University Press, 1982), for a recent argument for the constitutionality of the death penalty.

69. Bedau, ed., *The Death Penalty in America*, pp. 74–75.

70. *Ibid.*, pt. 5.

Chapter 6

1. To name but two well-known philosophical critics of Hart who do not critically evaluate Hart's theory of natural law, Dworkin does not seem to concern himself with it and Sartorius, although he brings it into his discussion, raises no criticisms against it. See Ronald Dworkin, *Taking Rights Seriously* (Cambridge, Mass.: Harvard University Press, 1978), and Rolf Sartorius, "Hart's Concept of Law," in *More Essays in Legal Philosophy*, ed. Robert S. Summers (Berkeley: University of California Press, 1971), pp. 131–161. Even Finnis in his long study of natural law has no extended discussion of Hart's major argument. See John Finnis, *Natural Law and Natural Rights* (Oxford: Clarendon Press, 1980).

2. See Neil MacCormick, *H. L. A. Hart* (Stanford, Calif.: Stanford University Press, 1981), p. 150. However, as I argue in Chapter 8, it is unlikely that Hart bases this principle in his debate with Devlin on his natural right theory.

3. H. L. A. Hart, *Law, Liberty, and Morality* (New York: Vintage Books, 1966), p. 20.

4. MacCormick, *H. L. A. Hart*.

5. See Richard Wollheim, "Natural Law," in *The Encyclopedia of Philosophy*, ed. Paul Edwards (New York: Macmillan and Free Press, 1967), vol. 5, pp. 450–454. Finnis, in *Natural Law and Natural Rights*, pp. 364–365, argues that the natural law tradition did not maintain simply, as it has often been asserted, that evil rules were not law. The traditional position was rather that an evil rule could not be a law in a central sense of "law."

6. Hart's theory is presented in the most developed form in *The Concept of Law* (Oxford: Clarendon Press, 1961), pp. 189–195.

7. St. Thomas Aquinas, *Summa Theologica*, quest. 90, art. 2.

8. *Ibid.*, quest. 94, art. 2.

9. *Ibid.*

10. Hart, *The Concept of Law*, p. 195.

11. Aquinas, *Summa*, quest. 94, art. 4.

12. *Ibid.*, quest. 95, art. 2. How Aquinas should be interpreted here is not completely clear. David Lyons, *Ethics and the Rule of Law* (Cambridge, Eng.: Cambridge University Press, 1984), p. 8, interprets him to be saying that unjust positive laws are perversions of the ideal of law, which is given by reason and natural law. One might also understand him to mean that unjust positive laws are not laws in some central meaning of "law." If so, his view would be close to Hart's.

13. Stanley I. Benn, "Rights," in Edwards, ed., *The Encyclopedia of Philosophy*, vol. 7, pp. 195–199.

14. See A. I. Melden, *Human Rights* (Belmont, Calif.: Wadsworth, 1970), pp. 135–149.

15. H. L. A. Hart, "Are There Any Natural Rights?," in *Rights*, ed. David Lyons (Belmont, Calif.: Wadsworth, 1979), pp. 14–25, first published in *Philosophical Review* 64 (1955): 175–191.

16. *Ibid.*, p. 14.

17. *Ibid.*

18. *Ibid.*, p. 15.

19. Stanley I. Benn, "Rights."

20. Joel Feinberg, *Social Philosophy* (Englewood Cliffs, N.J.: Prentice-Hall, 1973), p. 95.

21. Hart, *The Concept of Law*, p. 188.

22. *Ibid.*, p. 189.

23. *Ibid.*, pp. 189–190.

24. *Ibid.*, p. 195.

25. *Ibid.*, p. 189.

26. It might be objected that by stating Hart's thesis in the formal way I do the normative import of the informal version of the argument is lost. In the formal version, (2), a descriptive statement, is supposed to be entailed by (R) and (K_1) and (N). But in the informal version, (1) is supposed to be a conclusive reason why (2) should be the case. However, the normative import of Hart's claim is not lost in the formal explication since what rational people will do given certain knowledge that they have, if they are not prevented, has a normative implication.

27. Hart, *The Concept of Law*, p. 192.

28. Hart, "Are There Any Natural Rights?," p. 16.

29. *Ibid.*, p. 17.

30. *Ibid.*, pp. 17–18.

31. One special right that Hart believes is involved in situations of mutual forbearance in political contexts has been developed by John Rawls in *A Theory of Justice* (Cambridge, Mass.: Harvard University Press, 1971) into his principle of fairness. Hart, in "Are There Any Natural Rights?," p. 21, puts the basis of this special right in this way: "when a number of persons conduct any joint enterprise according to rules and thus restrict their liberty, those who have submitted to these restrictions when required have a right to a similar submission from those who have benefited by their submission." This Hart-Rawls principle of fairness has been criticized by Robert Nozick in *Anarchy, State, and Utopia* (New York: Basic Books, 1974), p. 93. For a revision of the principle of fairness in order to meet Nozick's criticisms see Richard J. Arneson, "The Principle of Fairness and the Free-Rider Problems," *Ethics* 92 (1981–1982): 616–633.

32. Hart, "Are There Any Natural Rights?," p. 23.

33. *Ibid.*, p. 15.

34. See N. G. E. Harris, "Hart on Natural Rights," *British Journal of Political Science* 2 (1972): 125–127.

35. Hart, "Are There Any Natural Rights?," pp. 24–25.

36. *Ibid.*, p. 24.

37. Maurice Cranston, "Liberalism," *The Encyclopedia of Philosophy*, ed. Paul Edwards, vol. 4, pp. 458–460.

38. Cf. David Lyons, "Introduction," in Lyons, ed., *Rights*, p. 5; Hillel Steiner, "Nozick on Hart on the Right to Enforce," *Analysis* 41 (Jan., 1981): 50.

39. Hart, "Are There Any Natural Rights?," p. 16, n. 6.

40. H. L. A. Hart, "Bentham on Legal Rights," in Lyons, ed., *Rights*, p. 145. For a detailed critique of Hart's theory of legal rights see Carl Wellman, *A Theory of Rights* (Totowa, N.J.: Rowman and Allanheld, 1985), pp. 61–80.

41. See Eric Mack, "Hart on Natural and Contractual Rights," *Philosophical Studies* 29 (1976): 283–285; Hillel Steiner, "Mack on Hart on Natural Rights: A Comment," *Philosophical Studies* 32 (1977): 321–322; Eric Mack, "A Comment on Steiner on Presupposed Rights," *Philosophical Studies* 33 (1978): 423–424.

42. William Frankena, "Natural and Inalienable Rights," *Philosophical Review* 64 (1955): 219.

43. In Hart's discussions of morality in *The Concept of Law*, *Punishment and Responsibility*, and *Law, Liberty, and Morality* moral rights seem to play no important role.

44. H. L. A. Hart, "Between Utility and Rights," *Columbia Law Review* 79 (1974): 828.

45. H. L. A. Hart, "Utilitarianism and Natural Rights," in Hart, *Essays in Jurisprudence and Philosophy* (Oxford: Clarendon Press, 1983), p. 196. For an attempt to meet Hart's challenge and to develop an adequate theory of rights see David A. J. Richards, "Rights and Autonomy," *Ethics* 92 (1981–1982): 3–20.

46. See Hart, "Between Utility and Rights."

47. Hart, "Utilitarianism and Natural Rights," p. 187.

48. *Ibid.*, p. 186.

49. H. L. A. Hart, "Law in the Perspective of Philosophy: 1776–1976," *New York University Law Review* 51 (1976): 545.

50. Hart does not refer to this paper in *The Concept of Law*, *Punishment and Responsibility*, *Law, Liberty, and Morality*, or in "Between Utility and Rights," "Utilitarianism and Natural Rights," or "Law in the Perspective of Philosophy."

51. See Hart, *Essays in Jurisprudence and Philosophy*, p. 17.

52. See H. L. A. Hart, "Death and Utility," *New York Review of Books*, May 15, 1980, 25–32; Hart, "Utilitarianism and Natural Rights."

53. See Hart, "Between Utility and Rights."

54. See Hart, *Essays in Jurisprudence and Philosophy*, p. 17.

55. William Frankena, *Ethics* (Englewood Cliffs, N.J.: Prentice-Hall, 1963), p. 35.

Chapter 7

1. See John Finnis, *Natural Law and Natural Rights* (Oxford: Clarendon Press, 1980), pp. 450–453, and David Lyons, *Ethics and the Rule of Law* (Cambridge, Eng.: Cambridge University Press, 1984), chap. 3.

2. H. L. A. Hart, "Positivism and the Separation of Laws and Morals," *Harvard Law Review* 71 (1958): 617.

3. Lon L. Fuller, "Positivism and Fidelity to Law—A Reply to Professor Hart," *Harvard Law Review* 71 (1958): 657.

4. *Ibid.*, p. 659.

5. Hart, "Positivism and the Separation of Law and Morals," pp. 593–629.

6. Fuller, "Positivism and Fidelity to Law," pp. 630–672.

7. H. L. A. Hart, *The Concept of Law* (Oxford: Oxford University Press, 1961). See especially pp. 195–207.

8. Lon L. Fuller, *The Morality of Law* (New Haven, Conn.: Yale University Press, 1964).

9. H. L. A. Hart, "Review of *The Morality of Law* by Lon Fuller," *Harvard Law Review* 78 (1965): 1281–1296.

10. Lon L. Fuller, *The Morality of Law* (rev. ed.; New Haven, Conn.: Yale University Press, 1969), chap. 5.

11. See, for example, Ronald M. Dworkin, "The Elusive Morality of Law," *Villanova Law Review* 10 (1965): 631–639; Marshall Cohen, "Law, Morality and Purpose," *Villanova Law Review* 10 (1965): 640–654; George Nakhnikian, "Professor Fuller on Legal Rules and Purpose," *Wayne Law Review* 2 (1956): 190–203; Christine Pierce, "Mabe on Fuller," *Southern Journal of Philosophy* 13 (1975): 5111–5113; Alan R. Mabe, "Fuller and the Internal Morality of Law," *Southern Journal of Philosophy* 13 (1975): 515–521; William T. Blackstone, "The Relationship of Law and Morality," *Georgia Law Review* 11 (1977): 1359–1391; David A. J. Richards, "Rules, Policies, and Neutral Principles: The Search for Legitimacy in Common Law and Constitutional Adjudication," *Georgia Law Review* 11 (1977): 1069–1114; George Breckenridge, "Legal Positivism and the Natural Law: The Controversy Between Professor Hart and Professor Fuller," *Vanderbilt Law Review* 18 (1965): 945–964; Lyons, *Ethics and the Rule of Law*, pp. 74–78.

12. Hart, "Positivism and the Separation of Law and Morals," p. 594.

13. *Ibid.*, p. 595.

14. *Ibid.*, p. 597.

15. *Ibid.*

16. *Ibid.*

17. *Ibid.*, p. 599.

18. *Ibid.*, p. 606.

19. *Ibid.*, p. 612.

20. *Ibid.*, pp. 617–618.

21. *Ibid.*, p. 618.

22. *Ibid.*, p. 627.

23. *Ibid.*

24. *Ibid.*

25. As we saw in Chapter 2, Hart seems to have changed his mind on this point in his later work.

26. Fuller, "Positivism and Fidelity to Law," p. 633.

27. *Ibid.*, p. 635.

28. *Ibid.*
29. *Ibid.*, p. 636.
30. *Ibid.*
31. *Ibid.*, p. 640.
32. See Fuller, *The Morality of Law*, chap. 2.
33. See Fuller, "Positivism and Fidelity to Law," p. 646.
34. *Ibid.*, p. 650.
35. *Ibid.*, p. 656.
36. *Ibid.*, p. 663.
37. *Ibid.*, p. 669.
38. Hart, *The Concept of Law*, pp. 254–255, 202. Hart here refers to "one critic of positivism."
39. See Hart, *The Concept of Law*, p. 206. David Lyons, in his review of MacCormick's *H. L. A. Hart* in *Philosophical Review* 93 (1984): 114–115, uses this passage to argue that Hart regards the law as *always* meriting respect. But this interpretation is not borne out by the text. Indeed, Hart puts his point weakly and negatively, saying "the certification of something as legally valid is not conclusive of the question of obedience." It is significant, I believe, that Lyons does not cite any other passages in Hart where his interpretation is confirmed. MacCormick's interpretation of Hart on this point is also in error. See Neil MacCormick, *H. L. A. Hart* (Stanford, Calif.: Stanford University Press, 1981), p. 160.
40. Reprinted in Carl Cohen, *Communism, Fascism, and Democracy* (2nd ed.; New York: Random House, 1972), pp. 375–376.
41. Hart, *The Concept of Law*, p. 202.
42. *Ibid.*, pp. 254–255.
43. Fuller, *The Morality of Law*, rev. ed., p. 154; Hart says this in *The Concept of Law*, p. 202.
44. Fuller, *The Morality of Law*.
45. *Ibid.*, p. 155.
46. *Ibid.*, p. 162.
47. Hart, "Review of *The Morality of Law* by Lon Fuller," p. 1287.
48. For example, see Hart's use of the imaginary king, Rex, in the early chapters of *The Concept of Law*.
49. Hart, "Review of *The Morality of Law* by Lon Fuller," p. 1287.
50. *Ibid.*
51. *Ibid.*
52. *Ibid.*, p. 1288.
53. *Ibid.*, p. 1286.
54. Fuller, *The Morality of Law*, rev. ed., pp. 223–224.
55. Lon L. Fuller, "A Reply to Professors Cohen and Dworkin," *Villanova Law Review* 10 (1965): 655–666.
56. *Ibid.*, p. 664.
57. *Ibid.*
58. *Ibid.* This quote is found in Fuller, *The Morality of Law*, rev. ed., p. 154.
59. Fuller, "A Reply to Professors Cohen and Dworkin," p. 664.

60. For a similar overall appraisal of the situation see Blackstone, "The Relationship of Law and Morality," p. 1377. On the other hand, Breckenridge, "Legal Positivism and the Natural Law," p. 945, argues that the differences between Hart and Fuller seem "irreconcilable." For an attempt to argue that natural law theory and legal positivism are complementary theories see David O. Brink, "Legal Positivism and Natural Law Reconsidered," *Monist* 68 (1985): 364–387. Brink's reconciliation between legal positivism (LP) and natural law (NL) is based on a distinction between theories of legal validity and theories of adjudication. Brink shows that it is possible to hold that morality is irrelevant to questions of legal validity (LP1) but relevant to how judges should adjudicate the law (NL2). Whatever the general importance of this distinction, it is unclear that it is useful in helping to reconcile, or even to understand, the Hart-Fuller debate. For example, it is certainly not obvious that Hart was defending LP1 while Fuller was defending NL2.

61. Cf. Lyons' discussion of the Minimal Separation Thesis, that is, the thesis that the law is morally fallible, and Finnis' interpretation of Fuller. See David Lyons, "Moral Aspects of Legal Theory," *Midwest Studies in Philosophy* 7 (1982): reprinted in *Ronald Dworkin and Contemporary Jurisprudence*, ed. Marshall Cohen (Totowa, N.J.: Rowman and Allanheld, 1986), and Finnis, *Natural Law and Natural Rights*, pp. 26, 360, 364–365.

62. Cf. Richards, "Rules, Policies, and Neutral Principles," p. 1075.

63. See Hart, "Review of *The Morality of Law* by Lon Fuller," p. 1288.

64. Thus Hart does not seem to embrace what might be called the Strong Separation Thesis, that is, the thesis that there is no conceptual connection between law and morality. Cf. Lyons, "Moral Aspects of Legal Theory," and Jules L. Coleman, "Negative and Positive Positivism," in Cohen, ed., *Ronald Dworkin and Contemporary Jurisprudence*, pp. 28–48. Raz maintains that it is possible to hold that there is a necessary connection between law and morality but deny that the truth conditions of the rule of recognition contain moral principles. In particular, he maintains that Hart holds (a) that there is a necessary connection between law and morality and (b) the Incorporation Thesis, that is, all law is either source-based (in the sense that it can be identified by social facts alone) or entailed by source-based law. It is unclear to me if Raz is correct in attributing the Incorporation Thesis to Hart. See Joseph Raz, "Authority, Law and Morality," *Monist* 68 (1985): 295–324.

65. See Hart, *The Concept of Law*, p. 202. I do not believe that Hart's statement here is merely a rhetorical device (cf. Mabe, "Fuller and the Internal Morality of Law," pp. 516–517). Hart in *The Concept of Law*, p. 202, argues for a necessary connection between minimum forms of justice and law; he does the same thing in "Positivism and the Separation of Law and Morals," pp. 622–624.

66. Hart, *The Concept of Law*, p. 202. For a criticism of Hart's thesis that the germ of justice is found in the application of a general rule of law see Lyons, *Ethics and the Rule of Law*, pp. 78–87.

67. Hart, *The Concept of Law*, p. 205.

68. *Ibid.*

69. Dworkin, "The Elusive Morality of Law," p. 633. See also Lyons, *Ethics and the Rule of Law*, pp. 74–78.

70. Dworkin, "The Elusive Morality of Law," p. 633.

CHAPTER 8

1. John Stuart Mill, *On Liberty* (London: Parker, 1859).

2. James Fitzjames Stephen, *Libert, Equality and Fraternity* (London: Smith Elgard & Co., 1874).

3. Committee on Homosexual Offences and Prostitution, Report, Cmd. 247 (1957).

4. Patrick Devlin, *The Enforcement of Morals* (Maccabaean Lecture in Jurisprudence of the British Academy, 1959; Oxford: Oxford University Press, 1959).

5. H. L. A. Hart, "Immorality and Treason," *The Listener*, July 30, 1959, pp. 162–163, reprinted in Richard A. Wasserstrom, ed., *Morality and the Law* (Belmont, Calif.: Wadsworth, 1971), pp. 49–54.

6. H. L. A. Hart, *Law, Liberty, and Morality* (New York: Vintage Books, 1966; originally published, Stanford, Calif.: Stanford University Press, 1963). In this chapter I will use the Vintage edition.

7. Patrick Devlin, *The Enforcement of Morality* (Oxford: Oxford University Press, 1965).

8. *The Times* (London), May 11, 1965.

9. H. L. A. Hart, "Social Solidarity and the Enforcement of Morality," *University of Chicago Law Review* 35 (1967): 1–13.

10. See, for example, Yves Caron, "The Legal Enforcement of Morals and the So-Called Hart-Devlin Controversy," *McGill Law Journal* 15 (1965): 9–47; F. S. McNeilly, "Immorality and the Law," *Proceedings of the Aristotelian Society* NS 66 (1966): 167–182; J. C. Dybikowski, "Lord Devlin's Morality and Its Enforcement," *Proceedings of the Aristotelian Society* NS 75 (1974–1975): 89–109; Noel B. Reynolds, "The Enforcement of Morals and the Rule of Law," *Georgia Law Review* 11 (1977): 1325–1358; Jeffrie G. Murphy, "Another Look at Legal Moralism," *Ethics* 77 (1966–1967): 50–56; Ronald Dworkin, *Taking Rights Seriously* (Cambridge, Mass.: Harvard University Press, 1978), pp. 241–258; Ferdinand Schoeman, "The Enforcement of Matters of Custom and Taste," *Philosophical Studies* 30 (1976): 341–346.

11. Kenneth Monoque, "Conservatism," in *The Encyclopedia of Philosophy*, ed. Paul Edwards (New York: Macmillan and Free Press, 1967), vol. 2, pp. 195–198.

12. *Ibid.*

13. Devlin, *The Enforcement of Morality*, p. 4.

14. *Ibid.*, p. 6.

15. *Ibid.*, pp. 6–7.

16. It has been argued by Dybikowski, "Lord Devlin's Morality and Its Enforcement," that Devlin's view of morality is subjective and that his idea of immorality as such prevents us from considering harm and injury as reasons for judging that an action is immoral. Whether this interpretation is correct I cannot consider here, but in any case it must be stressed that Devlin's major thesis is that homosexuality is a threat to society; it is immoral and harmful.

17. Devlin, *The Enforcement of Morals*, p. 15.

18. *Ibid.*, p. 22.

19. *Ibid.*, p. 17.

20. Hart, "Immorality and Treason," p. 51.

21. Maurice Cranston, "Liberalism," in Edwards, ed., *The Encyclopedia of Philosophy*, vol. 4, pp. 458–461.

22. Hart, "Immorality and Treason," p. 54.

23. *Ibid.*, p. 51.

24. *Ibid.*, p. 53.

25. *Ibid.*

26. *Ibid.*

27. Caron, in "The Legal Enforcement of Morals and the So-Called Hart-Devlin Controversy," p. 21, argues that Devlin and Hart "do not even speak the same language" and suggests that the Hart-Devlin debate is a matter of words. But if my argument is correct, the controversy is real enough and indeed is primarily a factual dispute.

28. McNeilly, in "Immorality and the Law," introduces a distinction between a restricted sense and an unrestricted sense of "harm." In the restricted sense some particular action, for example, a particular homosexual act, is harmful if it brings about harm; in the unrestricted sense a particular action may not be harmful but a widespread practice, for example, a widespread homosexuality, may be harmful. McNeilly admits that he can find no convincing evidence for the unrestricted harm of homosexual practice. However, he says that it would not be "entirely unreasonable" for someone to think that there was a *prima facie* case for regarding homosexual practice as possibly harmful in the unrestricted sense and to conclude that prohibiting the practice was the safest policy in the absence of sufficiently strong evidence to decide the issue. Unfortunately McNeilly does not cite any evidence that would support the *prima facie* case he maintains.

29. Patrick Devlin, "Democracy and Morality," in Devlin, *The Enforcement of Morals*, pp. 86–101. This was first published in the *University of Pennsylvania Law Review* 110 (1962): 635–649 under the title "Law, Democracy, and Morality."

30. *Ibid.*, p. 90.

31. *Ibid.*, p. 95.

32. *Ibid.*, p. 94.

33. Hart, *Law, Liberty, and Morality*, p. 19.

34. *Ibid.*, p. 20.

35. See Neil MacCormick, *H. L. A. Hart* (Stanford, Calif.: Stanford University Press, 1981), p. 150.

36. See Joel Feinberg, *Social Philosophy* (Englewood Cliffs, N.J.: Prentice-Hall, 1973), p. 25.

37. Eugene Rostow, "The Enforcement of Morals," *Cambridge Law Journal* 1958–1960 (1960): 174–198.

38. Hart, *Law, Liberty, and Morality*, p. 38.

39. *Ibid.*, p. 51.

40. *Ibid.*, p. 60.

41. *Ibid.*, p. 63.

42. *Ibid.*, p. 66.

43. *Ibid.*

44. *Ibid.*, p. 67.

45. *Ibid.*, p. 68.

46. *Ibid.*, p. 69.

47. *Ibid.*, p. 70.
48. *Ibid.*, p. 72.
49. *Ibid.*, p. 74.
50. *Ibid.*, p. 75.
51. *Ibid.*, p. 77.
52. *Ibid.*, p. 79, n. 22.
53. *Ibid.*, p. 80, n. 22.
54. Devlin, *The Enforcement of Morality*, p. 13, n. 1. Cf. Dworkin's analysis of this footnote in Dworkin, *Taking Rights Seriously*. pp. 240–258.
55. Devlin, *The Enforcement of Morality*, pp. 124–139.
56. *Ibid.*, p. 126.
57. *Ibid.*, p. 125.
58. *Ibid.*, p. 133.
59. *Ibid.*, pp. 135–136.
60. Hart, *Law, Liberty, and Morality*, p. 33.
61. Devlin, *The Enforcement of Morals*, p. 136.
62. *Ibid.*, p. 137.
63. *Ibid.*
64. *Ibid.*
65. *Ibid.*, p. 138.
66. H. L. A. Hart, "Abortion Law Reform: The English Experience," *Melbourne Law Review* 8 (1972): 388–411.
67. *Ibid.*, p. 411.
68. Devlin, *The Enforcement of Morality*, p. 131.
69. Hart, "Social Solidarity and the Enforcement of Morality," pp. 1–13.
70. *Ibid.*, p. 2.
71. *Ibid.*, p. 11.
72. *Ibid.*
73. *Ibid.*, p. 12.
74. Now it has been argued by Reynolds, in "The Enforcement of Morals and the Rule of Law," p. 1335, that Hart's criticism of Devlin in this paper and in his earlier paper is based on a misunderstanding. Hart, Reynolds argues, has refused to recognize that Devlin is not ultimately committed to claiming that disintegration results from moral change. Devlin's position, according to Reynolds, is that, because societies believe that social disintegration would follow moral disintegration, they are justified in using legal measures to suppress immorality. Now whether this is in fact Devlin's position is unclear. Reynolds cites little evidence to support this interpretation and he admits that Devlin's writing lacks clarity. In any case, this position seems untenable. Hart could surely point out that a society's belief that something is so, if it is irrational and unsupported, provides no justification for legal suppression. Schoeman, in "The Enforcement of Matters of Custom and Taste," suggests a theory of social viability in which certain social practices or conventions provide standards that contribute to a sense of social identity through social sharing. Thus, attacking these practices or conventions may seriously weaken the social institutions on which that particular society is based. He argues that the evidence suggested by Hart in "Social Solidarity and the Enforcement of Morality," that is, evidence that malignant

change in common morality leads to anti-social behavior such as dishonesty, violence, and disrespect for property, would make this theory less implausible. Schoeman cites studies as relevant evidence indicating that 90 percent of the adult population have committed crimes for which they could be imprisoned although he admits that such evidence may indicate correlations, not causal connections. However, even if causality is established, the crucial question for the Hart-Devlin debate is whether we can trace the cause to homosexuality; Schoeman provides no evidence for this.

75. Hart, "Social Solidarity and the Enforcement of Morality," p. 13.

76. *The Times* (London), May 11, 1965.

77. *Ibid.*

78. *Ibid.*

79. Christine Pierce in "Hart on Paternalism," *Analysis* 35 (1974–1975): 205–207, argues that it is unclear which of four possible positions Hart is espousing: (1a) harming others, even if they consent, is legally culpable; (1b) consenting to being harmed is legally culpable; (2a) causing others to suffer, even if they consent, is legally culpable; (2b) consenting to being made to suffer is legally culpable. Thus, she argues that Hart provides no coherent theory of legal paternalism.

Conclusion

1. *Law, Morality and Society: Essays in Honour of H. L. A. Hart*, ed. P. M. S. Hacker and Joseph Raz (Oxford: Clarendon Press, 1977), p. v.

2. See Marshall Cohen, "Herbert Lionel Adolphus Hart," in *The Encyclopedia of Philosophy*, ed. Paul Edwards (New York: Macmillan and Free Press, 1967), vol. 3, pp. 417–418.

3. H. L. A. Hart, *Essays in Jurisprudence and Philosophy* (Oxford: Clarendon Press, 1983).

4. H. L. A. Hart and Tony Honoré, *Causation in the Law* (2nd ed.; Oxford: Clarendon Press, 1985), pp. xxxiii–lxxxi.

5. Although Hart maintains that the insights of linguistic philosophy are of "permanent value" and the study of the law "has been advanced" by them, he now sees defects in his "deployment" of these insights. In particular, he points out that in his Inaugural Lecture he confused the relative constant meaning or sense of a sentence fixed by the conventions of language and the varying force or way in which it is put forward by the writer or speaker on different occasions. He now believes that it is wrong to say that statements of legal rights are conclusions drawn from legal rules, "for such sentences have the same meaning on different occasions of use whether or not the speaker or writer puts them forward as inferences he has drawn." Hart's repudiation of his earlier view is well taken but his reasons reveal his failure to grasp the empirical aspects of his claim and his continued reliance on intuitive linguistics rather than theory and evidence. In Chapter 4 I argued that Hart's view that sentences of the form "X has a legal right" are conclusions drawn from legal rules is either false or unjustified since empirical evidence is needed to establish his claim on the most plausible interpretation of it. Hart now appeals to the sense or meaning of sentences of the form "X has a legal right," something not at issue in the Inaugural

Lecture. It is significant that in invoking his distinction between meaning or sense and force he appeals, not to the findings of linguistic science, but to a linguistic intuition that now seems obvious to him as did his conflicting intuition of 1953. In fact Hart ends up giving his 1953 view a most implausible interpretation for he seems to think that his earlier view is refuted if one can find cases in which a sentence of the form "X has a legal right" is not a conclusion of law. This, however, assumes that he was saying that in every case a sentence of the form "X has a legal right" is a conclusion of law. But if he is interpreted, as he should be, as suggesting that the characteristic use of sentences of this form are as conclusions of law, typical counterexamples do no damage. Thus in this case, at least, Hart has not completely grasped the lesson to be drawn from his mistake. See Hart, *Essays in Jurisprudence and Philosophy*, pp. 4–5.

6. *Ibid.*, pp. 13–14.

7. Curiously enough, never mentioning that he holds a minimum natural law view, Hart criticizes John Finnis' view in *Natural Law and Natural Rights* (Oxford: Clarendon Press, 1980) on natural law. He ends up saying, "The contrary positivist stress on the elucidation of the concept of law, without reference to the moral values which it may be used to promote, seems to me to offer better guarantees of clear thought" (*ibid.*, p. 12). However, Hart has not elucidated the concept of law with complete moral neutrality. Given his use of minimum content natural law in his elucidation of the concept of law (and in the definition of a legal system that can be extracted from his writing) as well as his acceptance of certain ideals of procedural justice as being a necessary part of a legal system, one might well ask: Would not clear thought be better served without reference to these moral considerations in the elucidation of the concept of law and in the definition of a legal system? Hart fails to realize that his comments on Finnis can be applied to his own theory.

8. Hart and Honoré admit that, although they have not changed in any significant way the philosophical analysis of causality that they gave in their original work, their theory was controversial and generated a large critical response. However, since an adequate response to such criticism would "require a book on its own," in their preface they only consider "points of criticism which, if well founded, would clearly call for a revision of what we have said in the first edition about particular cases" (Hart and Honoré, *Causation in the Law*, p. xxxvii).

9. Hart, *Essays in Jurisprudence and Philosophy*, p. 17.

10. *Ibid.*, p. 6.

11. Hart and Honoré, *Causation in the Law*, pp. lxxx–lxxxi.

Index